CONFIDENTIAL COMPUTING

CONFIDENTIAL COMPUTING

Principles and Technology

JIEWEN YAO

ELSEVIER

机械工业出版社
CHINA MACHINE PRESS

Elsevier
Radarweg 29, PO Box 211, 1000 AE Amsterdam, Netherlands
125 London Wall, London EC2Y 5AS, United Kingdom
50 Hampshire Street, 5th Floor, Cambridge, MA 02139, United States

ISBN: 978-0-443-54067-7

For information on all Elsevier publications visit our website at https://www.elsevier.com/books-and-journals

Publisher: Matthew Deans
Acquisitions Editor: Glyn Jones
Editorial Project Manager: Akansha Rathi
Production Project Manager: M. Balakrishnan
Cover Designer: Raman Kumar

Typeset by TNQ Tech

Dedicated to my wife, Wenjun Zeng,
for her continuous encouragement and unconditional support!

Contents

About the author

Jiewen Yao is a Principal Engineer at Intel Corporation, primarily focusing on the security architecture of hardware, firmware, and system software. He specializes in areas such as secure boot, trusted computing, and confidential computing. Currently, he serves in positions in industry standard working groups, including the Distributed Management Task Force (DMTF), the Trusted Computing Group (TCG), the Unified Extensible Firmware Interface (UEFI) organization, and the RISC-V organization. He participates in and leads the development and promotion of relevant specifications, and has received the TCG Key Contributor Award and the DMTF Star Award. He also serves as a maintainer in open source communities such as EDKII, SPDM, CoCo, and CCC, leading the development and maintenance of the security-related software projects, including EDKII, libspdm, td-shim, and spdm-rs. He holds about 50 patents.

Foreword 1

Confidentiality and integrity are the cornerstone properties of information technology security. The use of cryptography in conjunction with more traditional access controls and other isolation mechanisms is now widespread, well understood, and accepted when protecting data at rest or in motion. For example, we use encrypted filesystems or self-encrypting storage devices when we save or backup data on our computers and computing devices, and we look for a lock symbol in our web browser address bar when we conduct business online because it signifies the use of Transport Layer Security (TLS), a secure communication protocol that relies heavily on cryptography.

As we as individuals and businesses rely more and more on computing environments that we may not directly control, there is heightened interest in the use of cryptography to protect data that is actively in use. Here too, cryptographic technologies have great promise and potentially huge implications for the outsourcing of private computation to environments such as those we see with various cloud computing models. For example, Fully Homomorphic Encryption (FHE) supports arbitrary computation on ciphertexts, or encrypted data. There have been significant advances in FHE since it was theorized in the late 1970s, followed by the publication of the first plausible construction of FHE in 2009. Unfortunately, implementations of FHE and other promising cryptographic technologies such as Secure Multi-Party Computation may have a long way to go before they are practical for generic computation in common computing environments.

Trusted Execution Environments (TEEs) are hardware-based computing environments that combine cryptographic isolation of code and data in memory, along with more traditional isolation techniques, to provide strong confidentiality and integrity assurances that are practical today for generic computation in all computing environments. Intel Software Guard Extensions (SGX) and Trust Domain Technology (TDX), as well as AMD Secure Encrypted Virtualization (SEV), and Arm Confidential Computing Architecture (CCA) are examples of such TEEs. The author of *Confidential Computing – Principles and Technologies* examines these and other technologies to better understand the assurances these technologies provide, the capabilities they enable today, and the opportunities and challenges remaining as we seek stronger security assurances for our most common computing environments.

This practical and emerging secure computing paradigm that TEEs enable is called ***Confidential Computing***, and it is important to understand not just how these technologies work and the important security properties they support, but also why these technologies will be critical to the continued growth of computing as an efficient utility, supported by a global-scale and largely shared computing infrastructure that is quickly spreading from large distributed datacenters to localized "edge" environments with the availability of ever faster connectivity. Confidential Computing drastically reduces the Trusted Computing Base (TCB), those elements of the traditional hardware and system software stack that must be relied upon for the security of a specific application or workload and its data. Whereas for the past fifty or more years we have relied upon a purely hierarchical TCB that includes the underlying computing hardware, the now billions of lines of code that make up the operating system and other system software, the computing infrastructure management software, and the myriad other applications and workloads on any particular system, with TEE-supported Confidential Computing, the TCB consists of the target application or workload plus select elements of the underlying hardware and firmware. A much more significantly tractable TCB with a commensurate order of magnitude reduction in risk from vulnerabilities and attacks, resulting in much greater confidentiality, privacy, and integrity of the computing environment as well as the application or workload, all of which is measurable and verifiable from any place and at any time via remote attestation.

I encourage you to join the growing number of computer scientists, engineers, and information technology professionals that are advancing Confidential Computing. There is no better way to get started than by studying the contents of *Confidential Computing – Principles and Technologies*.

Ron Perez
Former Intel Fellow and Chief Security Architect

Foreword 2

If we were to pick a trending word for 2023, "fraud" would certainly be near the top of the list. The world still has as many bandits as before; they just no longer dare to rob houses with open violence and have instead increased their technical sophistication—for example, by using scams to trick victims into transferring money from their bank cards. Actually, every bank has its own comprehensive "risk control system" that uses big data computation methods to determine whether a transfer might be initiated by a victim in a "confused" state. If a transfer is deemed risky, it is immediately intercepted.

Here's the problem: different financial institutions have different data. For the same transfer from account A to account B, computation using Alipay's data might flag it as fraud that should not be approved. However, "XX Bank," lacking this data, might see no risk and approve the transfer. Consequently, scammers learn to exploit this—they make victims try transferring through different channels until they find a bank that happens to lack the necessary risk control data and doesn't block the transaction, leading to a successful scam. What's the best way to deal with these "persistent" scammers? Naturally, it's to combine the data from Alipay and banks A, B, C, and D for joint computation. This way, everyone effectively shares the strongest armor.

But the real world is often full of constraints. Restricted by data security regulations and corporate interests, financial institutions cannot share their raw data with others. Yet, they still want to benefit from the "risk control capability" derived from computing on this combined data—a real dilemma.

This brings us to the subject of this book—*Confidential Computing*! Confidential computing can securely protect data while it's in use, achieving the effect where data is usable but not visible. Applying confidential computing technology to the joint risk control and antifraud scenario allows various banks to compute on combined data while ensuring the security of their own raw data.

Of course, secure joint computation of data is just one application of confidential computing. It can also be used in numerous scenarios like big data analytics, model protection, input privacy protection for large models, confidential databases, blockchain privacy protection, and cloud computing data security.

Confidential computing is one of the crucial supporting technologies for secure and efficient data element transfer. Compared to other technologies, it offers advantages such as strong performance, good versatility, and low R&D costs. Academician Dengguo Feng pointed out at the 2023 CNCC Confidential Computing Forum that confidential computing is currently the most practical technology for secure data-in-use. It can be said that confidential computing is a burgeoning new technology and industrial ecosystem with broad prospects. Precisely because it is in the ascendant, there currently exist various implementation methods, programming models, threat models, and attestation models for confidential computing, which lack a unified framework for understanding and learning. Technicians wanting to enter this field are often faced with a plethora of confusing terms, complex academic papers, and technical documents from different hardware vendors, finding no easy entry point and facing a steep learning curve. The field desperately needs a book that comprehensively and systematically explains the technical principles and working mechanisms of confidential computing. Actually, I've long wanted to write such a book myself, but have been unable to do so due to mundane affairs.

In this sense, Jiewen's monograph on confidential computing arrives at a perfect time, truly filling this gap. This book starts with basic concepts like the differences between confidential computing and other data security technologies. It then constructs a unified narrative framework consisting of security models, lifecycles, attestation models, attacks and countermeasures, etc., explaining the general design principles and usage methods of Trusted Execution Environments (TEEs) from a common perspective. It then maps these principles and frameworks to concrete implementations using various specific TEE examples. This allows readers to grasp both the general principles at an abstract level and understand the specific considerations and trade-offs made by different vendors in actual TEE implementations. Remarkably, the book not only uses this framework to explain CPU TEEs but also extends it to device TEEs (or TEE I/O), helping people understand and use accelerator TEEs, thus expanding confidential computing capabilities from general-purpose computing to intelligent accelerated computing. The significance of this in the current era of large models is undeniable.

Finally, as a practitioner in the field of confidential computing, I sincerely recommend this book to readers. I believe that whether you wish to learn and understand confidential computing technology or aim to design confidential computing software and hardware systems, you will find valuable insights in this book.

Shoumeng Yan
Head of Trusted Security Computing Department,
Ant Group Director, Computing Systems Lab,
Ant Technology Research Institute

Foreword 3

It gives me great pleasure to introduce this book, *Confidential Computing—Principles and Technologies*. The author, Jiewen Yao, has long been recognized as a leader in the firmware security domain for his deep understanding of platform firmware (UEFI). He has been an active contributor to the open source community for firmware, management standards (DMTF), and Trusted Computing (TCG), which are key building blocks of Trusted Execution Environments. It is Jiewen's deep technical expertise, paired with his ability to strategically and passionately contribute to open source software and standards, that helps move the community forward and makes him an ideal author of this technical book.

I have had the honor of working directly with Jiewen for many years, as I worked on developing architectures for exploit prevention and Trusted Execution Environments at Intel Corp., where I built the first hardware virtualization-based system for operating system run-time integrity, followed by developing the hardware security architecture for VM-based Confidential Computing on the 64-bit x86 architecture. Along this journey, Jiewen has been a close partner in identifying technical gaps, developing open source software, and leading standards for the building blocks needed for confidential computing. He has been a key champion for confidential computing in the UEFI project, and has contributed many extensions, such as guest firmware for confidential virtual machines, container-based deployment models, standards for TEE-IO, SPDM, and platform and device attestation standards, to name a few. In every stage of development, Jiewen has led through open source code and deep implementation experience.

What further sets this book apart is its balance between theoretical insights and practical examples—it provides the technical background while imparting concepts in a practical manner, with insights into architecture and design choices, thus guiding the reader and enabling them to understand the lifecycle of software and hardware deployed for Confidential Computing. It describes the history and evolution of the security requirements, the hardware/software design and implementation trade-offs, and the security lifecycle. Jiewen considers different architectures from x86 to ARM and RISC-V while identifying common threads that are being tackled as projects within the Confidential Computing

Consortium. As we enter an era where privacy-sensitive data analysis, machine learning, and artificial intelligence are infused into all digital industries—the need for data-in-use protection within and across organizations with large-scale federated and multiparty computation requirements is increasing exponentially—this technical manual provides a roadmap to navigate the inflection point that Confidential Computing represents.

Whether you're a novice eager to explore the fundamentals of Confidential Computing or an experienced practitioner seeking to deepen your knowledge, this book will be a key technical reference. I am glad to have the opportunity to write this foreword for this comprehensive technical reference for the Confidential Computing community. In conclusion, *Confidential Computing—Principles and Technologies* is a must-read for anyone interested in understanding the technical "why, what, and hows" of Confidential Computing. Through clear explanations, practical examples, and practitioner insights, I am confident this book will empower leaders, architects, and developers to build and evolve powerful Confidential Computing capabilities.

Ravi Sahita
Ex-Principal Security Architect (Rivos Inc.)
Ex-Vice Chair of the Security Horizontal Committee
(RISC-V International)
Ex-Chair of Trusted/Confidential Computing SIG
Ex-Chair of Confidential VM TG
Ex-Senior Principal Security Architect (Intel Corp.), 1999–2021

Preface

Two millionaires want to compare who has more money, but they are each cautious and do not want to reveal the exact amount of their wealth. How can this be achieved? This is the Millionaires' Problem proposed by Turing Award winner Andrew Chi-Chih Yao in 1982. Let us look at a simplified version of the solution. Assume the two millionaires' wealth is between 1 and 10. The process can be carried out as follows:

1. Millionaire A obtains 10 identical boxes, labels them 1 to 10 on the outside, and places two colored balls inside each box. A white ball represents that the wealth value corresponding to the label is less than or equal to A's wealth, and a gray ball represents that the wealth value corresponding to the label is greater than A's wealth. A then locks the boxes and gives them to Millionaire B.
2. Millionaire B cannot open the boxes. Based on the labels on the 10 boxes, B selects the box corresponding to B's own wealth value, destroys the other nine boxes, removes the label from the single selected box, and returns this unlabeled box to Millionaire A.
3. Millionaire A and Millionaire B open the selected box together. If it contains a gray ball, Millionaire B has more wealth; if it contains a white ball, Millionaire A has more wealth. Because Millionaire B could not open the boxes, B does not know A's wealth value. Because Millionaire B destroyed the other boxes and tore off the label from the selected box, A does not know B's wealth. They obtain the comparison result without revealing their own wealth amounts. Fig. 1 shows an example where Millionaire A's wealth is 4 and Millionaire B's wealth is 7; the gray ball indicates that Millionaire B has more wealth.

The Millionaires' Problem only reflects one aspect of privacy needs. More than 40 years later, with the application of big data and artificial intelligence, the demand for privacy protection has increased significantly. Concepts such as Privacy Preserving Data Mining and Privacy Preserving Machine Learning have become increasingly well-known. China's Data Security Law, the US's American Data Privacy and Protection Act, and the European Union's General Data Protection Regulation all explicitly

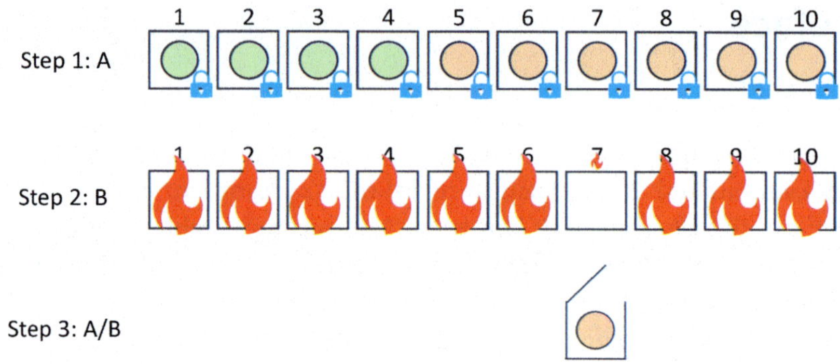

Figure 1 Simplified version of the millionaires' problem.

stipulate requirements regarding data privacy. The white paper "Privacy-Preserving Computing Techniques Handbook" by the UN Big Data Global Working Group summarizes five major technical directions: Secure Multiparty Computation, Homomorphic Encryption, Differential Privacy, Zero Knowledge Proof, and Trusted Execution Environment (TEE). Among these, only TEE represents an innovation in computer hardware architecture, whereas the other four are cryptography-related technologies.

As a major branch of privacy computing, confidential computing based on TEE possesses unique characteristics. It provides an isolated environment that directly protects data during dynamic operation. As long as data reside inside the TEE, any program outside the TEE cannot perceive information about those data. Compared with cryptographic solutions, it offers features such as strong versatility and high performance. In 2024, Academician Dengguo Feng published "Six Aspects Cybersecurity Science and Technology Should Focus On," one of which states: "Technologies like zero trust, confidential computing, privacy computing, and resiliency will continue to flourish." Major CPU manufacturers or alliances such as Intel, AMD, ARM, and RISC-V are all deploying TEE for confidential computing. Furthermore, GPU device manufacturers such as NVIDIA are also supporting and launching related products. Cloud service providers such as Microsoft, Google, Ant Group, and ByteDance have also initiated research and development related to TEE confidential computing. Amidst this wave, engineers need a deep understanding of TEE hardware design and working principles to use TEE better, select appropriate confidential computing software application frameworks, and protect private data and applications.

Main content of this book

Many companies have launched their own confidential computing solutions, posing considerable challenges for users. This book summarizes the common design principles of various mainstream TEE hardware types. By introducing their commonalities, it helps readers understand the working principles of TEE hardware, enabling users to define TEE usage scenarios through some abstract commonalities. The book introduces TEE design principles and usage methods from the perspectives of security model, life cycle, attestation model, attack methods, and protection strategies, helping readers understand the security attributes and implementation essentials of confidential computing. Simultaneously, using industry-common x86, ARM, and RISC-V architectures as examples of TEE implementations, it analyzes the implementation methods of hardware TEE and their similarities and differences, aiding readers in deeply understanding the pros and cons of different implementations, hoping to provide insights for future TEE hardware and software designers.

Target audience

The target audience for this book is programmers with a strong interest in confidential computing who wish to understand its underlying working principles. Junior programmers can learn the principles of confidential computing through this book, enabling them to understand not just how but also why when using various confidential computing software. Experienced programmers can understand the similarities, differences, pros, and cons of different confidential computing implementations, allowing them to make informed choices when selecting and designing confidential computing solutions. Researchers can understand the development and current state of confidential computing, contemplate new application scenarios and unsolved problems, and contribute to the advancement of confidential computing and privacy computing. Confidential computing TEE is a new concept and architecture, and the industry is in its initial stages. It is hoped that readers can understand the software and hardware design concepts of TEE through this book, and perhaps design and implement their own TEE hardware or software in the future.

Content organization and structure

This book is divided into three parts. The first part includes Chapters 1 and 2, aiming to introduce the basics of privacy computing and confidential computing. Chapter 1 briefly introduces the goals of privacy computing and technologies such as Secure Multiparty Computation, Homomorphic Encryption, Differential Privacy, and Zero Knowledge Proof, as well as applications of privacy computing including Federated Learning. Chapter 2, based on the definition provided by the Confidential Computing Consortium, introduces the concept of confidential computing, the classification of hardware TEE solutions, and software implementation methods.

The second part includes Chapters 3–8, aiming to introduce various aspects of TEE comprehensively. Chapter 3 introduces the confidential computing security model, helping readers understand the security attributes required for confidential computing, considering which threats to defend against or which not to consider. Chapter 4 introduces the TEE life cycle, including TEE memory layout, TEE boot process, and teardown, providing examples. Because attestation is a fundamental security requirement of confidential computing, Chapter 5 introduces the TEE attestation model, including the TEE trusted boot process, evidence generation and transmission, evidence verification and attestation result conveyance, as well as two advanced topics, providing TEE attestation examples. Chapter 6 introduces optional TEE features, including sealing, nesting, virtual Trusted Platform Module (vTPM), live migration, and runtime update. Chapter 7 introduces confidential computing software development, including various modules of confidential virtual machines, software support for secure enclaves, TEE remote attestation related software, TEE secure communication methods, and methods for ensuring data security within TEE. Chapter 8 introduces TEE attacks and protections, covering risk points such as TEE software implementation, cryptographic applications inside TEE, side channels and fault injection, and discusses protection against simple physical attacks, as well as attacks and protections specific to TEE.

To improve efficiency, workloads during computation (such as artificial intelligence workloads) may be offloaded to device accelerators. Considering such use cases, TEE needs to extend from the host side to the device side. The third part will introduce various aspects of TEE-IO, including Chapters 9–14. Chapter 9 introduces the TEE-IO security model and threat model, including security requirements on the device side and host side, providing examples. Chapter 10 introduces the Trusted Execution Environment - Input/Output (TEE-IO) life cycle, including system and device initialization, establishing a secure management channel with the device, establishing a secure data channel with the device, device configuration locking, trusted device attestation, key update for secure sessions, termination of device connection and device removal, as well as error handling for TEE-IO devices, including error triggering, reporting, and recovery, providing relevant examples. Attestation is more complex in TEE-IO. Chapter 11 introduces the TEE-IO attestation model, including TVM (Trusted Virtual Machine (VM)) attestation to the device and third-party attestation of a TVM bound to a device, covering evidence generation and transmission, and bidirectional attestation between device and host, providing relevant examples. Chapter 12 introduces special TEE-IO features, including resiliency of TEE-IO devices, runtime update of devices, peer-to-peer transmission between Peripheral Component Interconnect Express (PCIe) devices, and the use of Compute Express Link (CXL) devices in confidential computing. Chapter 13 introduces TEE-IO software development, including device support for confidential VMs, device attestation, and secure device communication. Chapter 14 introduces TEE-IO attacks and protections, with risk points including the host side of TEE-IO, the device connection, and the device side. Besides general software security, side channels, and fault injection, DMA and Memory-Mapped Input/Output (MMIO) security are key considerations.

The industry has begun deploying the TEE part of confidential computing, whereas TEE-IO represents the future development direction. Junior programmers can focus primarily on Parts One and Two of this book, whereas senior programmers or architects need to focus on Part Three to prepare for future research and development work in confidential computing.

Confidential computing involves an extremely wide range of technologies. Horizontally, it involves technologies and knowledge in areas such as threat modeling, trusted computing, resiliency, cryptography, side channels, and software/hardware security attacks and defenses. Vertically, it involves software and hardware stacks including SOC hardware, device buses, firmware, virtual machines, operating systems, and system applications. For engineers seeking a comprehensive understanding of confidential computing, this book provides a map helping readers understand which areas of knowledge require study. Owing to space limitations, this book cannot describe all aspects in detail, focusing only on parts closely related to confidential computing. However, for a security solution, comprehensiveness is a necessary choice; otherwise, there is a risk that "a small leak will sink a great ship." Therefore, frankly speaking, studying this book alone is insufficient. The resources accompanying this book include lists of books and literature for extended reading. Readers who wish to master confidential computing technology in depth can study further; readers can download these from the publisher's website.

Acknowledgments

The author began participating in Extensible Firmware Interface (EFI) firmware projects in 2003, engaging with computer security from both software and hardware perspectives, and started participating in the architecture, design, and development of Intel TDX confidential computing in 2017, witnessing the project's initiation, development, maturity, and deployment. The completion of this book benefited from intellectual exchanges with other excellent engineers, discussions with standardization organizations such as DMTF, PCI-SIG, RISC-V, TCG, and UEFI, and contributions from open-source communities such as CCC, CoCo, EDK II, Linux, and SPDM. Special thanks to the following colleagues and mentors (listed alphabetically by company and surname): Jiang Liu, Jia Zhang from Alibaba Group; Abner Chang, Tom Lendacky, Michael Roth from AMD; Vincent von Boken, Dave Harriman, Chris Li from Ampere; Shoumeng Yan from Ant Group, Samer El-Haj-Mahmoud from ARM; Amy Nelson from Dell; Erdem Aktas from Google; Jeff Hilland from HPE; Arie Aharon, Joseph Cihula, Eddie Dong, Mark Doran, Jiaqi Gao, Anas Hlayhel, Simon Johnson, Hormuzd Khosravi, Susie Li, Wei Liu, Ken Lu, Xiaoyu Lu, Krystian Matusiewicz, Dan Middleton, Alberto Munoz, Jun Nakajima, Ronald Perez, Makaram Raghunandan, Elena Reshetova, Xiaoyu Ruan, Vincent Scarlata, Ned Smith, Junli Sun, Dan Williams, Hao Wu, Haidong Xia, Min Xu, Longlong Yang, Andy Zhao, Peter Zhu, Vincent Zimmer from Intel; Jon Lange from Microsoft; Steven Bellock, Joe Pennisi, Tim Prinz from NVIDIA; Paolo Bonzini, Laszlo Ersek, Gerd Hoffmann, David Gilbert from RedHat; Samuel Ortiz, Ravi Sahita, Vedyvas Shanbhogue from Rivos (now Meta); and Wenhui Zhang from ByteDance.

Finally, I would like to thank Shoumeng Yan, Shuang Liu, Jin Zhang, Bojun Zhu, etc. from Ant Group, Wenhao Wang from the Institute of Information Engineering, Chinese Academy of Sciences, Professor Fengwei Zhang and students Lijian Huang, Jiatong Chen, Yujun Liang from Southern University of Science and Technology for reading this book and providing valuable feedback. I also thank Professor Huang Bo from East China Normal University for facilitating this book, the editors at China Machine Press for their work in publishing the Chinese version, and the editors at Elsevier for publishing the English version.

Confidential computing technology evolves rapidly. By the time this book is published, new requirements and use cases may continue to emerge, and the views presented by the author may become outdated or inappropriate. Comments and corrections from experts and readers are welcome.

CHAPTER 1

Introduction to privacy computing

This chapter mainly introduces privacy computing. Confidential computing is a method within privacy computing.

1.1 Goals of privacy computing

According to the white paper "UN Handbook on Privacy-Preserving Computation Techniques" published by the UN Global Working Group on Big Data, the statistical analysis process can be broken down into three parts: input party (source data), computing party (statistical analysis), and result party (statistical results), as shown in Fig. 1.1. The corresponding goals of privacy computing are divided into the following three categories:

- **Input privacy**: The computing party cannot access or infer the input data provided by the input party, nor can it access intermediate data or intermediate results during the computation process. It is important to note that even if the computing party cannot directly access the data,

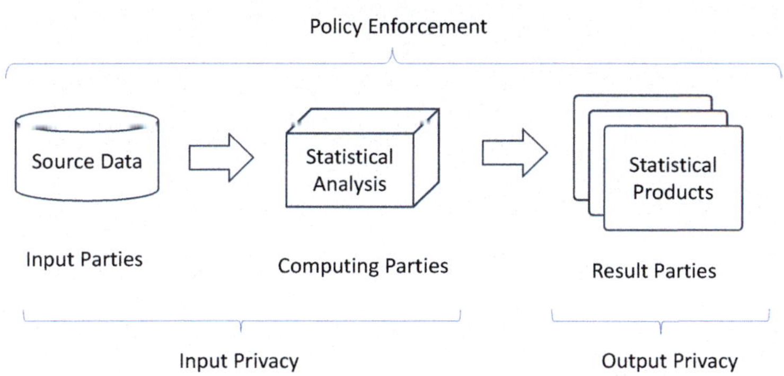

Figure 1.1 Goals of privacy computing. *(Reference: UN Handbook on Privacy-Preserving Computation Techniques.)*

Confidential Computing
ISBN 978-0-443-54067-7
https://doi.org/10.1016/B978-0-443-54067-7.00003-6

they might still infer input data through side-channel attacks, which is also a consideration for input privacy.

- **Output privacy**: Beyond what the input party permits, the published results must not contain any identifiable input data. Output privacy addresses the issue of measuring and controlling information leakage from computation results.
- **Policy enforcement**: Policies control which sensitive data the input party provides to the computing party and which data results the output party can output.

1.2 Privacy computing techniques

Currently, commonly used privacy computing techniques in the industry include homomorphic encryption (HE), secure multiparty computation (MPC), zero-knowledge proof (ZKP), differential privacy (DP), and trusted execution environment (TEE).

Fig. 1.2 illustrates the relationship between privacy computing techniques and privacy computing goals.

1.2.1 Homomorphic encryption

After the famous Rivest, Shamir, Adleman (RSA) algorithm was invented by the "RSA trio," Rivest, Adleman, and Dertouzos published an article

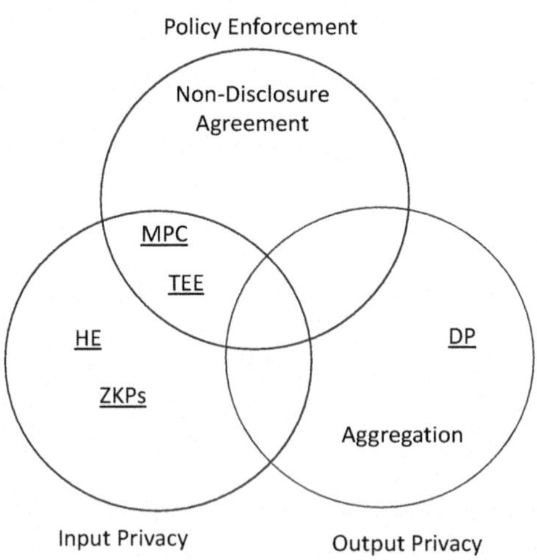

Figure 1.2 Relationship between privacy computing techniques and privacy computing goals. *(Reference: UN Handbook on Privacy-Preserving Computation Techniques.)*

titled "On data banks and privacy homomorphisms" in 1978, first elaborating on the concept of homomorphic encryption. Homomorphic encryption allows computations to be performed directly on ciphertext data, generating an encrypted result which, when decrypted, matches the result of operations performed on the plaintext. This characteristic is called homomorphism.

RSA and the subsequent ElGamal algorithm could only achieve partially homomorphic encryption (PHE) for multiplication, meaning only multiplication operations could exhibit homomorphism. In 1999, Paillier published the paper "Public-key cryptosystems based on composite degree residuosity classes," proposing a practical additive partially homomorphic algorithm (also known as the Paillier algorithm), addressing this gap.

A breakthrough in homomorphic encryption came in 2009. Gentry, in "Fully homomorphic encryption using ideal lattices," first implemented a fully homomorphic encryption (FHE) algorithm based on ideal lattices. Currently, homomorphic encryption continues to evolve, with algorithms such as: the BV algorithm proposed by Brakerski and Vinod Vaikuntanathan in their 2011 paper "Efficient fully homomorphic encryption from (standard) LWE"; the BGV algorithm proposed by Brakerski, Gentry, and Vaikuntanathan in their 2012 paper "(Leveled) fully homomorphic encryption without bootstrapping"; the Bra algorithm proposed by Brakerski in his 2012 paper "Fully homomorphic encryption without modulus switching from classical GapSVP"; the BFV algorithm proposed by Fan and Vercauteren in their 2012 paper "Somewhat practical fully homomorphic encryption"; the GSW algorithm proposed by Gentry, Sahai, and Waters in their 2013 paper "Homomorphic encryption from learning with errors: conceptually-simpler, asymptotically-faster, attribute-based"; and the CKKS algorithm proposed by Cheon, Kim, Kim, and Song in their 2017 paper "Homomorphic encryption for arithmetic of approximate numbers." However, these algorithms still need to address computational overhead and performance issues.

Homomorphic encryption protects data privacy by performing computations directly on encrypted data. As shown in Fig. 1.3, a homomorphic encryption algorithm typically includes the following functional modules:

- **HE.KeyGen**(): Key generation, generates ephemeral HE keys based on parameters.
- **HE.Encrypt**(): Encryption, uses HE keys to encrypt plaintext input data, generating encrypted input data.
- **HE.Evaluate**(): Evaluation, performs operations on the encrypted input data, generating encrypted output data.

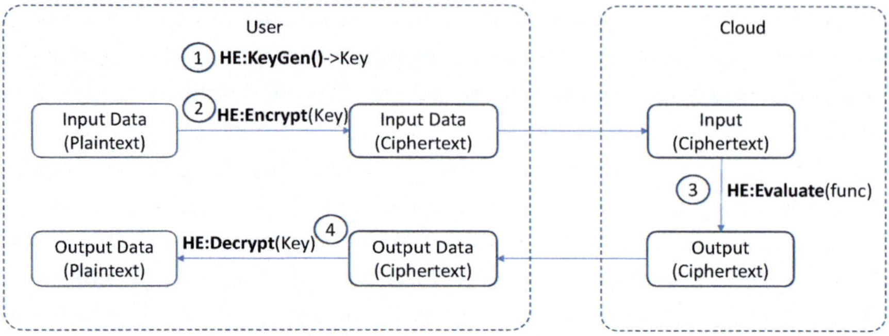

Figure 1.3 Functional modules of homomorphic encryption algorithms.

- **HE.Decrypt**(): Decryption, uses HE keys to decrypt the encrypted output data, generating plaintext output data.

Homomorphic encryption is particularly well-suited for cloud computing application scenarios. Users who wish to leverage cloud computing power but do not want to expose their private data can upload encrypted sensitive data to the cloud for computation, obtain the result, and then decrypt it locally after downloading.

Currently, the security of homomorphic encryption is ensured by its underlying cryptographic primitive: the learning with errors (LWE) problem. As long as the LWE problem remains unbroken, homomorphic encryption is considered secure.

Homomorphic encryption is a cryptographic primitive, not a protocol. When used alone, it cannot fully provide input privacy functionality. If computation requires input from multiple parties, homomorphic encryption cannot guarantee that each input is only visible to the key owner. Additionally, homomorphic encryption typically provides indistinguishability (IND), meaning an adversary cannot gain information about the plaintext, but it does not provide nonmalleability (NM), meaning an adversary might be able to modify the ciphertext.

The "UN Handbook on Privacy-Preserving Computation Techniques" white paper points out that constructing secure protocols based on homomorphic encryption requires cryptographic expertise, and most secure protocols based on homomorphic encryption are only secure against semihonest adversaries.

1.2.2 Secure multiparty computation

Turing Award winner Andrew Chi-Chih Yao proposed the "Millionaires' Problem" in his 1982 paper "Protocols for secure computations," initiating research on privacy-preserving secure multiparty computation. Currently, secure multiparty computation includes methods such as oblivious transfer (OT), garbled circuit (GC), and secret sharing (SS).

1.2.2.1 Oblivious transfer

Rabin introduced the concept of oblivious transfer in his 1981 article "How to exchange secrets with oblivious transfer." Suppose two parties each have their own secret and wish to exchange them without a trusted third party, but with a requirement: the owner of the secret should not know whether the other party actually received the secret. For example, Alice wants to send a secret to Bob, but when she sends it, Bob can only probabilistically receive it, preventing Alice from knowing for sure whether Bob actually obtained the secret.

Later, Evan, Goldreich, and Lempel, in their 1985 article "A randomized protocol for signing contract," proposed what is considered true oblivious transfer, known as 1-out-of-2 OT. In this scenario, Alice sends two secrets (m_0, m_1) in the communication. Bob chooses to receive one of them, but Alice does not know which one Bob chose, and Bob, having chosen one, cannot learn the other secret. This process is shown in Fig. 1.4. Brassard, Crepeau, and Robert, in their 1986 article "Information theoretic reductions among disclosure problems," extended 1-out-of-2 OT to 1-out-of-N OT, meaning Alice sends N secrets at once, allowing Bob to choose one. This was later extended to K-out-of-N OT.

1.2.2.2 Garbled circuit

The concept of garbled circuits was proposed by Andrew Chi-Chih Yao in his 1986 paper "How to generate and exchange secrets." This method achieves the following: Alice and Bob wish to compute a result based on their combined inputs. Both know their own input and the final result, but neither wants the other to learn their specific input. Fig. 1.5 shows a simple example of a garbled circuit and its workflow.

Assume their computation is represented by a circuit. Take the truth table for an AND operation as an example. Alice's input can be 0 or 1, represented by keys Key_{A0} and Key_{A1}; Bob's input can be 0 or 1,

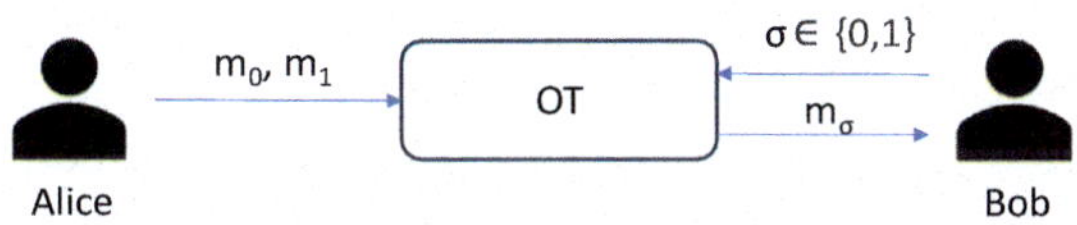

Figure 1.4 1-out-of-2 oblivious transfer.

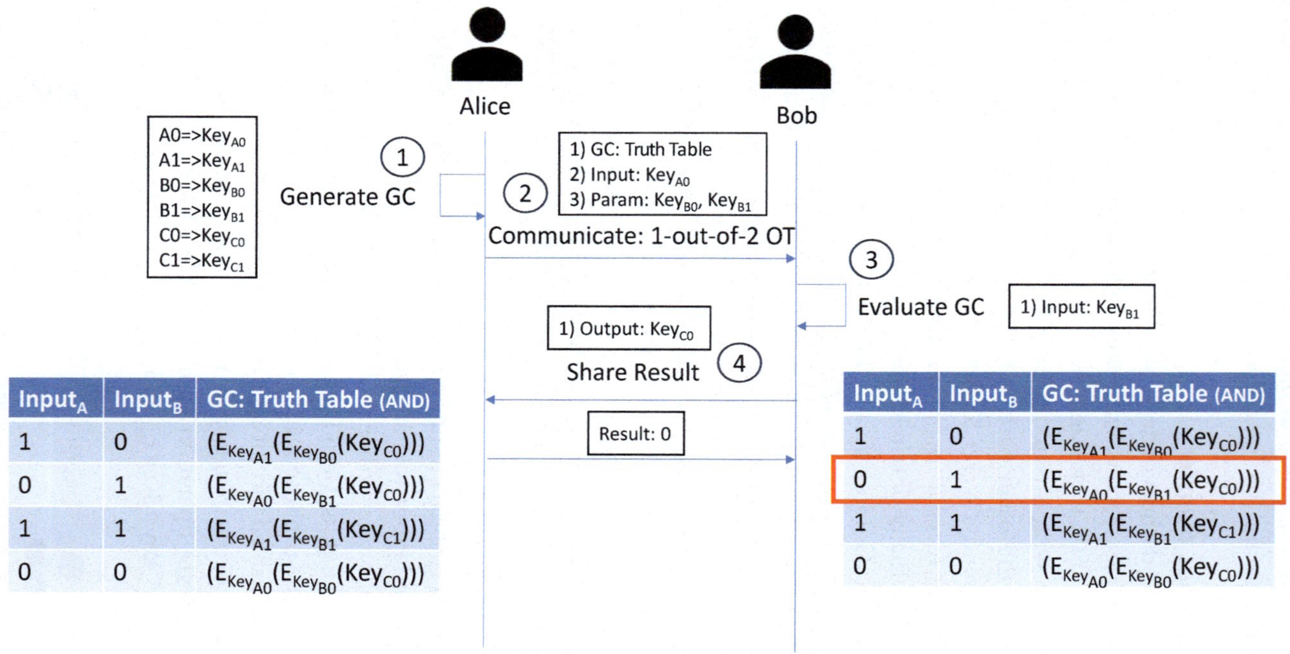

Figure 1.5 Garbled circuit and its workflow.

represented by keys Key_{B0} and Key_{B1}; the output can be 0 or 1, represented by keys Key_{C0} and Key_{C1}. Alice generates the truth table, encrypts the output results using the corresponding input keys, and shuffles the order. This process of encryption and shuffling is the core working principle of garbled circuits.

The workflow of a garbled circuit is as follows:

1. **Garbled circuit generation**: Alice generates the garbled circuit truth table.
2. **Communication**: Alice sends the truth table, Alice's own input key (e.g., Key_{A0}), and both of Bob's keys (Key_{B0} and Key_{B1}) to Bob. This communication uses 1-out-of-2 oblivious transfer, so Bob can only choose one of the keys without learning the other. Simultaneously, Alice does not learn which key Bob actually chose.
3. **Garbled circuit evaluation**: Bob selects his input key (e.g., Key_{B1}), attempts to decrypt each row of the garbled truth table. Only the row corresponding to the correct combination of inputs will decrypt successfully, yielding the output key (e.g., Key_{C0}).
4. **Result sharing**: Bob sends the resulting output key to Alice. Alice looks up the corresponding plaintext value (0 or 1) and tells Bob the result.

Bob does not know what Alice's input key Key_{A0} represents; he only combines it with his own input key Key_{B1} to try decrypting the rows. The only row that decrypts successfully yields the result key Key_{C0}. Alice only sees the final result key Key_{C0}, but she does not know which row of the truth table Bob successfully decrypted, and thus does not know which key Bob used. This satisfies the condition of not revealing input information.

Note: Yao's garbled circuit protocol is secure against semihonest participants, but not against malicious ones.

Goldreich, Micali, and Wigderson, in their 1987 paper "How to play ANY mental game," extended Yao's garbled circuits into the GMW protocol, generalizing it from two parties to multiple parties and from Boolean circuits to arithmetic circuits, and providing security against some malicious participants. The BMR protocol, proposed by Beaver, Micali, and Rogaway in their 1990 paper "The round complexity of secure protocols," uses a distributed method for the garbled circuit generation process. This prevents any single party from obtaining the secret information of the garbled circuit alone and makes the communication complexity of the generation process independent of the depth of the circuit being computed.

1.2.2.3 Secret sharing

Shamir's "How to share a secret" and Blakley's "Safeguarding cryptographic keys," both published in 1979, proposed multiparty secret-sharing schemes. The core idea of a (K, N) threshold scheme is to protect a secret S using N shares (subkeys). Possessing any K of these shares allows reconstruction of the original secret, but having fewer than K shares reveals no information about it. Fig. 1.6 illustrates a secret-sharing scheme based on a (3, 5) threshold scheme. Here, a secret is protected by five shares, and collecting any three of them allows recovery of the secret.

Shamir's method uses a simple mathematical principle: given a polynomial $f(x) = a_{k-1}x^{k-1} + \ldots + a_2x^2 + a_1x + a_0$, knowing any k distinct points $(x, f(x))$ on its graph is sufficient to uniquely determine the polynomial, while knowing fewer than k points leaves it undetermined. For a secret S and a (K, N) threshold, one randomly generates $K - 1$ parameters for $a_{k-1}, \ldots, a_2, a_1$, sets the secret S as a_0, thus obtaining a polynomial $f(x)$ of degree $K - 1$. Then, N distinct nonzero x values are randomly generated and substituted into the polynomial to get N corresponding $f(x)$ values. Finally, these N pairs $(x, f(x))$ are distributed as shares to N users. Any K users together can use their K shares to set up a system of K equations and solve for the K coefficients, where the coefficient a_0 is the secret S.

Blakley, on the other hand, employed a different geometric approach. Imagine the secret is a point in three-dimensional space. Five planes intersecting at this point could serve as shares. Collecting any three of these planes would be sufficient to determine the unique point of intersection (the secret). Generalizing this from three dimensions to a K-dimensional space yields Blakley's algorithm: the secret is treated as a point in a K-dimensional space, and N hyperplanes passing through this point are

Figure 1.6 Secret sharing based on a (3, 5) threshold scheme.

distributed as shares to participants. Any K of these hyperplanes intersect exactly at that point, allowing reconstruction of the secret.

In many cases, a (N, N) threshold scheme is used, meaning possession of all N shares is necessary and sufficient to reconstruct the secret. MPC can leverage the homomorphic properties of certain secret-sharing schemes, allowing computations (like addition or multiplication) to be performed on the shares themselves. Combining the results of these operations on shares yields the correct result of the operation on the original secrets. Fig. 1.7 shows an example of addition using secret sharing. The steps are:

1. **Input party secret splitting**: Alice splits secret A into shares S_{A1} and S_{A2}. Bob splits secret B into shares S_{B1} and S_{B2}.
2. **Share distribution**: Alice sends S_{A1} to computing party 1 and S_{A2} to computing party 2. Bob sends S_{B1} to computing party 1 and S_{B2} to computing party 2.
3. **Computation by computing parties**: Computing party 1 calculates $CP_1 = S_{A1} + S_{B1}$. Computing party 2 calculates $CP_2 = S_{A2} + S_{B2}$. At this point, neither computing party can learn the original secrets A or B.
4. **Result transmission**: Each computing party sends its result to the output party.
5. **Result reconstruction by output party**: The output party calculates $CP_1 + CP_2$, which equals Secret A + Secret B. Thus, the result party learns the sum of the secrets without ever knowing the individual original secrets A and B.

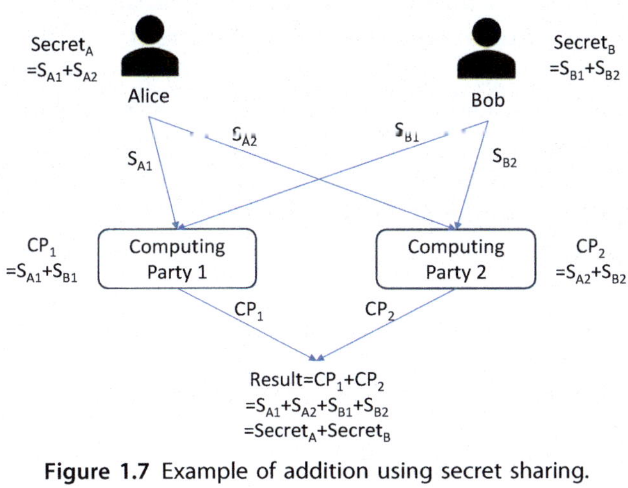

Figure 1.7 Example of addition using secret sharing.

The BGW protocol, presented by Ben-Or, Goldwasser, and Wigderson in their 1988 paper "Completeness theorems for non-cryptographic fault-tolerant distributed computation," is based on Shamir's secret-sharing scheme. Chaum, Crepeau, and Damgard also proposed a similar protocol, CCD, in their 1988 paper "Multiparty unconditionally secure protocols."

1.2.2.4 Security model

The threat model for secure multiparty computation introduces a special type of adversary: the insider. We need to consider the following characteristics:

- **Honesty**: Honesty is typically categorized into three types: semihonest, covert, and malicious. In the semihonest (also called honest-but-curious) model, compromised participants follow the protocol correctly but may try to learn additional information from the messages they receive. In the covert model, an adversary may deviate from the protocol to cheat, but does not want to be caught. In the malicious model, an adversary may arbitrarily deviate from the protocol to compromise security, without concern for being detected.
- **Mobility**: Mobility refers to whether the set of compromised parties can change over time. Static adversary: The set of corrupted parties is fixed at the beginning of the protocol. Adaptive (or mobile) adversary: The adversary can choose to corrupt parties during the protocol execution, potentially based on information gathered so far. For example, starting with participants A and B as adversaries, after some computation, the adversary might also compromise participant C.
- **Portion of compromised parties**: This relates to the number of parties the adversary controls. Honest majority: The majority of participants are honest. Dishonest majority: The majority of participants may be corrupted.

Different secure multiparty computation protocols offer different properties, relating to the following aspects:

- **Input privacy**: Participants do not reveal their private inputs to other participants.
- **Correctness**: All honest participants receive the correct output of the computed function.
- **Fairness**: Either all parties receive the output, or no party does. A malicious party should not be able to obtain the output while preventing honest parties from getting it.

- **Guaranteed output delivery**: Honest parties are guaranteed to receive the output regardless of the actions of malicious parties.

An excellent reference book on secure multiparty computation is "A Pragmatic Introduction to Secure Multi-Party Computation" by Evans, Kolesnikov, and Rosulek, which includes introductions to the GMW protocol, BMR protocol, BGW protocol, and CCD protocol.

1.2.3 Zero-knowledge proof

Goldwasser, Micali, and Rackoff introduced the concept of zero-knowledge proofs in their 1985 paper "The knowledge complexity of interactive proof-systems." This allows a prover to convince a verifier of the truth of a statement without revealing any additional information beyond the validity of the statement itself.

We can illustrate this concept using the cave problem mentioned in the 1989 article "How to explain zero-knowledge protocols to your children" by Quisquater et al. As shown in Fig. 1.8, there is a secret door between points C and D inside a cave. The prover claims to know the password for the secret door but does not want to reveal the password to the verifier. How can the prover convince the verifier? The verifier can repeat the following steps:

1. The verifier stands at point A. The prover goes to point B (inside the cave).
2. The prover randomly chooses to go to either point C or point D, but the verifier cannot see which path the prover took.
3. The verifier then goes to point B and calls out, asking the prover to come out from either the left or the right passage (the verifier randomly chooses left or right).
4. The prover must now emerge from the specified passage.

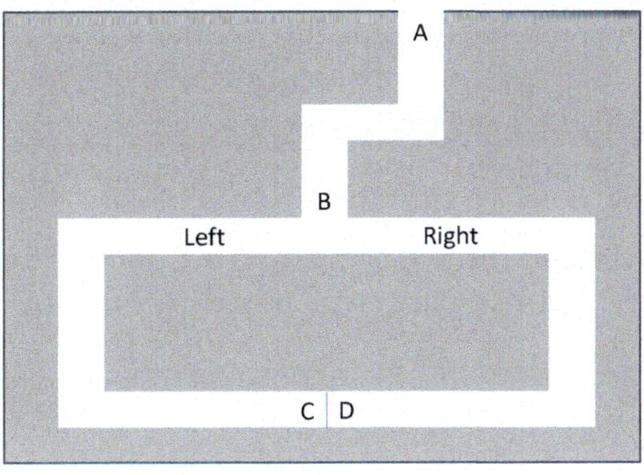

Figure 1.8 The cave problem for zero-knowledge proof.

If the prover truly knows the password for the secret door, they can always emerge from the requested passage (by using the door if necessary). If the prover does not know the password, they can only emerge from the requested passage by chance, with a probability of 1/2 for each round (by having guessed correctly which path the verifier would ask for). By repeating this process many times, the probability of the prover successfully guessing correctly every time becomes extremely small. If the prover succeeds in a sufficiently large number of rounds, the verifier gains confidence that the prover likely knows the password, without ever learning the password itself.

Zero-knowledge proofs can be interactive or noninteractive. Cryptographic digital signatures can be seen as a type of noninteractive zero-knowledge proof, for example, in the identification protocol mentioned by Schnorr in his 1991 paper "Efficient signature generation by smart cards."

Classic methods in zero-knowledge proofs include Zero-Knowledge Succinct Non-interactive Argument of Knowledge (zk-SNARKs), formally developed from works like Groth's 2010 paper "Short pairing-based non-interactive zero-knowledge arguments" and the formalization by Bitansky, Canetti, Chiesa, and Tromer in their 2012 paper "From extractable collision resistance to succinct non-interactive arguments of knowledge, and back again." Another important development is Zero-Knowledge Scalable Transparent Arguments of Knowledge (zk-STARKs), proposed by Ben-Sasson, Bentov, Horesh, and Riabzev in their 2018 paper "Scalable, transparent, and post-quantum secure computational integrity," which offers transparency and is believed to be secure against quantum attacks.

Zero-knowledge proofs must satisfy the following properties:

- **Completeness**: If the statement is true and both the prover and verifier follow the protocol honestly, the verifier will be convinced (accept the proof).
- **Soundness**: If the statement is false, no cheating prover can convince an honest verifier that it is true (except with some negligible probability).
- **Zero-knowledge**: If the statement is true, the verifier learns nothing other than the fact that the statement is true. No other secret information is revealed.

The security of zero-knowledge proofs relies on different hard mathematical problems. For example, succinct noninteractive arguments often rely on nonfalsifiable assumptions. If an adversary can break this assumption, the verification could be compromised, becoming a potential bottleneck for the system's overall security.

1.2.4 Differential privacy

Dwork, Kenthapadi, McSherry, Mironov, and Naor introduced the concept of differential privacy in their 2006 paper "Our data, ourselves: privacy via distributed noise generation." In privacy-preserving statistical databases, differential privacy works by injecting random noise into the query results to perturb the true answer. Unlike other privacy computing techniques, differential privacy focuses on protecting the output of computations.

We can use a simple example based on the method from Warner's 1965 paper "Randomized response: A survey technique for eliminating evasive answer bias." Suppose we want to estimate the percentage of students who have cheated on an exam in a school of 300 students. If we simply ask each student, "Have you ever cheated on an exam?," students who have cheated might not answer honestly due to the sensitivity of the question. How can we solve this?

A differential privacy-based solution is illustrated in Fig. 1.9. Before asking each student the question, you give them a coin and instruct them to flip it twice before answering, without telling you the outcomes. The rule is: If the first flip is Heads, answer truthfully (Yes if cheated, No

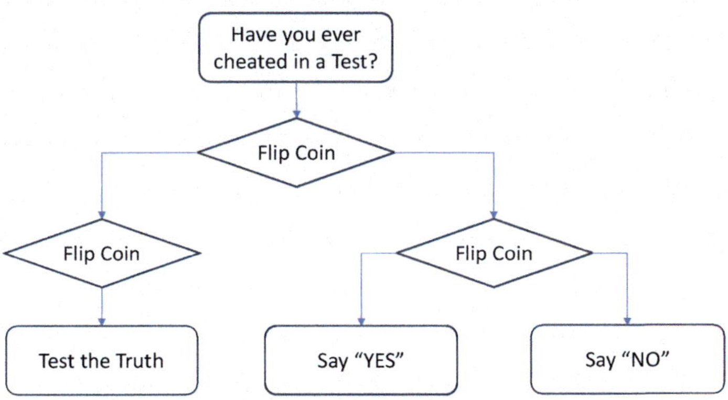

Figure 1.9 Example of a differential privacy scheme.

otherwise), regardless of the second flip. If the first flip is Tails, then look at the second flip: If the second flip is Heads, always answer "Yes" (regardless of actual truth). If the second flip is Tails, always answer "No" (regardless of actual truth). Because the coin flips introduce randomness, you cannot determine any individual student's true status. As the number of students increases, the randomness from the coin flips averages out. Suppose the true cheating rate is *c*. The expected proportion of "Yes" answers obtained through this method will be $c/2 + 1/4$. Therefore, we can work backwards from the observed proportion of "Yes" answers to estimate the true cheating rate *c*.

This is a simple illustration of differential privacy. The introduction of the coin flips anonymizes each individual response, providing each respondent with plausible deniability, yet we can still statistically infer the true aggregate result.

The principles behind differential privacy are versatility and robustness. Based on when the privacy algorithm is applied, differential privacy operates in two main modes:

- **Local mode**: Differential privacy is applied directly to the data by each individual before they are collected and aggregated.
- **Curator mode**: A trusted curator collects the raw data from individuals and then applies a differential privacy algorithm (adds noise) before publishing the output results.

Differential privacy aims to ensure that the inclusion or exclusion of a single record in the database has a negligible effect on the final output of a query. Due to the introduction of probabilistic noise, whether a specific record is present or not (delta-X), the probability distribution of the query result (delta-Ɛ) is very similar, as shown in Fig. 1.10. Consequently, an adversary cannot gain significant information about that specific record by

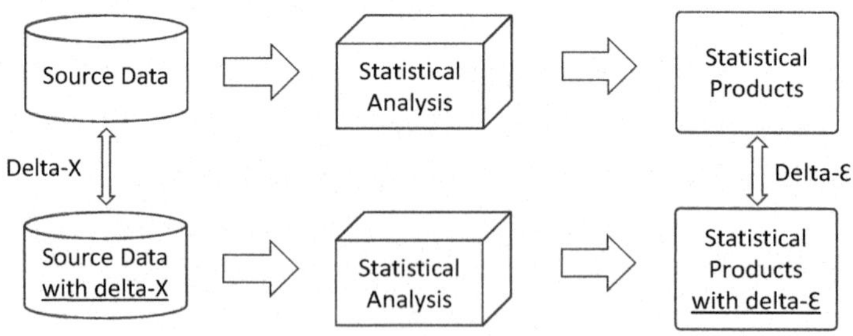

Figure 1.10 Differential privacy output.

comparing query results obtained from databases that differ only by that record, even if the adversary has auxiliary information (side knowledge). This property is known as statistical indistinguishability. For more information, please refer to Nissim et al., "Differential Privacy: A Primer for a Non-technical Audience."

1.3 Applications of privacy computing

In addition to the four categories mentioned above, privacy computing also includes confidential computing based on trusted execution environments, which will be detailed in the next chapter.

Currently, besides secure multiparty computation and trusted execution environments, one of the most prominent applications of privacy computing is federated learning (FL). This is primarily used for training and prediction in artificial intelligence models and is also known as federated machine learning (FML). Federated learning was proposed by McMahan et al. in their 2017 paper "Communication-efficient learning of deep networks from decentralized data." The main idea is to train data locally on mobile or edge devices and build a shared model by aggregating the computed updates (like gradients) from these local devices, without the raw data ever leaving the devices. Federated learning adopts a decentralized approach. To comply with privacy protection regulations, machine learning applications need to use data in a distributed manner: they cannot directly exchange raw data, nor should any party be able to infer private data from another party. This is the problem federated learning aims to solve in the artificial intelligence (AI) field. In 2020, the IEEE published IEEE 3652.1—"IEEE Guide for Architectural Framework and Application of Federated Machine Learning," standardizing the federated machine learning process. Private data from data owners in different locations are used to train local submodels. These submodel updates are then aggregated by a coordinator to form and refine a global federated model.

Table 1.1 compares secure multiparty computation, trusted execution environments, and federated learning within privacy computing. For introductory books on privacy computing, refer to "Privacy Computing" by Chen Kai and Yang Qiang, or "Privacy Computing in Simple Terms" by Li Weirong.

TEE is not contradictory to other privacy computing techniques. Secure multiparty computation, homomorphic encryption, zero-knowledge proofs,

Table 1.1 Comparison of secure multiparty computation, trusted execution environments, and federated learning.

Technology	Performance	Generality	Security	Trusted party	Overall description	Technical maturity
Secure MPC	Medium/low	High	High	Not required	High generality, high computation and communication overhead, high security, long research history, well-tested, performance continuously improving	High
TEE	High	High	Medium/high	Required (hardware vendor)	High generality, strong performance, complex development/deployment, requires trust in hardware manufacturer	Rapidly growing
Federated learning	Medium	Medium	Medium	Can be either	Integrates MPC, DP, HE methods; mainly used for AI model training and prediction	Rapidly growing

differential privacy, and even federated learning can be deployed within a TEE. Even if one technology has a potential vulnerability, another can still protect data privacy—a classic example of defense in depth.

CHAPTER 2

Introduction to confidential computing

Chapter 1 introduced privacy computing, of which confidential computing is one method. In this chapter, foundational concepts of confidential computing are introduced. It should be noted that this book primarily references the definitions provided by the Confidential Computing Consortium (CCC).

2.1 The concept of confidential computing

According to the definition in the white paper "Common Terminology for Confidential Computing" by the CCC, confidential computing refers to "the protection of data in use by performing computation in a hardware-based, attested Trusted Execution Environment." Let's explain this definition. As shown in Fig. 2.1, data are generally categorized into three states: data at rest, data in transit, and data in use. First, the primary focus of confidential computing is data in use. Data in transit can be protected by network security protocols such as TLS, IPsec, MACsec. Data at rest can be protected by secure storage mechanisms such as disk encryption, file encryption, and database access controls. Second, confidential computing is hardware-based, requiring special hardware support because standard, general-purpose hardware cannot provide sufficient protection during execution, where code and data exist in plaintext. This hardware basis is derived from the CCC definition, but it does not imply that only hardware can achieve computation confidentiality. Cryptographic methods introduced in Chapter 1, such as homomorphic encryption and secure multiparty computation, can also provide confidentiality, although cryptographic operations may introduce performance overhead. A high-privilege software module, like a hypervisor, could theoretically provide a software-based confidential environment, but such

Confidential Computing
ISBN 978-0-443-54067-7
https://doi.org/10.1016/B978-0-443-54067-7.00021-8

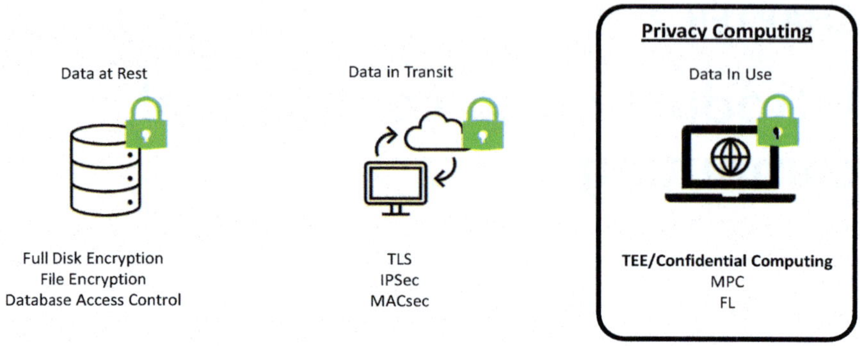

Figure 2.1 Data states.

pure software solutions cannot defend against hardware physical attacks. The security and threat models of confidential computing are described in Chapter 3. Finally, confidential computing requires a trusted execution environment (TEE), and crucially, this TEE must be attested.

For confidential computing, a TEE primarily needs to provide three types of security properties:

- **Data confidentiality**: Unauthorized entities cannot read data inside the TEE during runtime.
- **Data integrity**: Unauthorized entities cannot add, delete, or tamper with data inside the TEE during runtime.
- **Code integrity**: Unauthorized entities cannot add, delete, or tamper with the code inside the TEE during runtime.

Different TEEs may offer additional properties:

- **Code confidentiality**: Unauthorized entities cannot read the code inside the TEE during runtime. For instance, if a user is concerned about the intellectual property of their code and does not want anyone to see it, even in binary form, then the TEE needs this property. If the code being executed is already open source, this property may not be necessary.
- **Authenticated launch**: Some TEEs can verify the initial boot code at launch time, for example, through signature verification. Unknown boot code would be rejected by the TEE. However, authenticated launch requires predeployment of authentication policies. Taking signature verification as an example, the public key of the signing entity needs to be deployed. Who deploys it? How is the deployed public key trusted? If a public key expires or a private key is compromised, how is the deployment updated? Additionally, signature verification needs to

consider security version numbers (SVNs) to prevent rollback attacks, where an attacker could launch a signed but known-vulnerable version of code. Due to the complexity of policy deployment, this feature is not strictly necessary for all confidential computing use cases.

- **Programmability**: Some TEEs contain fixed code for specific functions, while general-purpose TEEs allow external users to load arbitrary code. The specific requirements depend on the use case.
- **Attestability**: A TEE must provide evidence of its code and data origin and its current operational state. This evidence is typically represented by measurements (hashes) of the code and data. A local or remote verifier can validate this evidence to determine if the TEE is trustworthy. Since evidence needs to be transmitted over potentially insecure channels, TEE hardware usually provides cryptographic mechanisms, such as digital signatures or message authentication codes, to ensure the integrity of the evidence.
- **Recoverability**: Some TEEs can provide recovery mechanisms. For example, during an authenticated launch, if a module fails signature verification, it might automatically load a known good module, update, and relaunch. Paraphrasing NIST SP 800-193 (Platform Firmware Resiliency Guidelines), such resilient TEEs typically define various root of trust (RoT) components, including root of trust for detection (RTD), root of trust for update (RTU), and root of trust for recovery (RTRec).

Attestability is a particularly crucial property. It is a fundamental requirement of trusted computing as promoted by the Trusted Computing Group (TCG), enabling a verifier to confirm that the program running on a system is indeed the expected one. If a TEE cannot provide attestability, it cannot be considered a TEE for confidential computing. Without attestability, a user of confidential computing cannot know the true origin of the code and data inside the TEE; unknown code could lead to data leakage, negating confidentiality. Trusted computing and TEE attestation models are discussed in detail in Chapter 5.

Note: *We generally say a TEE provides a* ***trusted*** *environment, but this does not mean it is a* ***secure*** *environment. Attestability provides proof of the origin of code and data, establishing trust in them. However, attestability does not prove that the code is free of security vulnerabilities, such as buffer overflows or side-channel weaknesses. Confidential computing only guarantees that the integrity of the code is not maliciously compromised during runtime and provides proof to a verifier. The security of the code itself remains the responsibility of its provider.*

At the 2023 OC3 conference, in his keynote "Welcome Keynote and Introduction to Confidential Computing," Schuster outlined the problems confidential computing aims to solve, workload security requirements, and the attributes of TEEs. These TEE attributes include:

- **Isolation**: A TEE must be isolated from non-TEE environments and also from other TEEs.
- **Runtime memory encryption**: A TEE must provide runtime encryption for its memory to protect against offline physical attacks on memory (e.g., cold boot attacks, bus snooping).
- **Remote attestation**: A TEE must provide remote attestation capability to prove to a third party that the environment has been established in a trustworthy manner.

Isolation is likely uncontroversial, and the importance of attestation has been discussed. Let's focus on runtime memory encryption. This is a newer requirement introduced by confidential computing. Currently, some industry TEEs provide execution environment isolation but not runtime memory encryption, such as ARM TrustZone. Strictly speaking, ARM TrustZone is not considered a confidential computing technology by the CCC definition, which is why ARMv9 introduced the Confidential Compute Architecture (CCA). However, projects like the Open Enclave SDK still support ARM TrustZone. The RISC-V-based KeyStone scheme provides isolation but treats runtime memory encryption as optional, which could be handled by runtime software or a separate memory encryption engine (MEE). Users must choose solutions based on their specific project requirements.

Academician Dengguo Feng, in his report "From Trusted Computing to Confidential Computing" at the 2021 China Computer Congress, compared trusted computing and confidential computing, as summarized in Table 2.1.

The fundamental difference between trusted computing and confidential computing lies in the security problems they aim to solve. Trusted computing emerged in the early 2000s (TCG founded in 2003) and focused on establishing platform trustworthiness, relying on a hardware trusted platform module (TPM). Manufacturers or users could decide which software was allowed to run on a local machine; trusted computing did not specifically focus on data privacy. Confidential computing emerged around the late 2010s/early 2020s (CCC founded in 2019) to define and accelerate its adoption. Its core purpose is to solve the problem of data security in use, protecting data from disclosure, complementing

Table 2.1 Comparison between trusted computing and confidential computing.

Item	Trusted computing	Confidential computing
Hardware foundation	Root of trust, TPM/TCM security chip	Hardware TEE, central processing unit (CPU) security support
Technical architecture	Holistic security solution covering hardware, software, network; trust anchor is hardware root of trust	Holistic security solution; trust anchor is the CPU security features
Core focus	Based on underlying hardware trust, focuses on code attestation and trust mechanisms; emphasizes static TEEs (fixed number, created at boot)	Based on TEE system isolation, focuses on data protection; emphasizes dynamic TEEs (created/destroyed on-demand, can be migrated)
Data security	Relatively weak data protection, mainly limited to keys and critical data	Protects confidentiality and integrity of large amounts of data (including algorithms and code)
Cloud/Edge/End applications	Focuses on securing endpoints and edge devices; broader application in personal computers (PCs), Internet of Things (IoT), mobile, cloud platforms	Requires higher hardware/software performance; applied in cloud environments, focuses on securing cloud-side data
Privacy	Less related to privacy computing; direct anonymous attestation (enhanced privacy) is a privacy computing method	A technical approach to realizing privacy computing; provides support for MPC, HE, federated learning within privacy computing

protections for data in transit and at rest. Furthermore, confidential computing provides data privacy protection, addressing growing modern privacy needs.

2.2 Classification of hardware TEE solutions in confidential computing

According to the CCC's definitions, existing hardware TEE solutions can be broadly classified into the following categories:

- **Secure enclave**: Leveraging CPU hardware features, a user can create an enclave as a TEE. An enclave in confidential computing refers to a completely isolated execution environment. Code and data executed within the enclave are protected and isolated from anything outside the enclave or within other enclaves. Typically, enclaves operate at the application level, as shown in Fig. 2.2. For example, enclaves created using Intel Software Guard Extensions (SGX) are called SGX Enclaves.
- **Confidential virtual machine (CVM)**: A user can create a full virtual machine as a TEE, as illustrated in Fig. 2.3. Examples include Intel Trust Domain Extensions (TDX), AMD Secure Encrypted Virtualization (SEV), the Realm Management Extension (RME) of ARM Confidential Compute Architecture (CCA), and RISC-V Confidential VM Extension (CoVE). The primary advantage of this approach is maximum compatibility for existing applications; only modifications to the operating system (guest OS) are typically needed to enable confidential computing support for applications running inside the VM.
- **Confidential accelerator**: In many use cases, applications rely on hardware accelerators, such as graphics processing units (GPUs) for

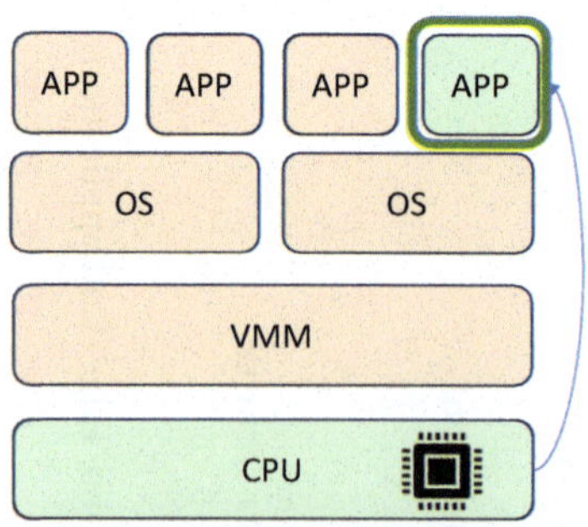

Figure 2.2 Secure enclave.

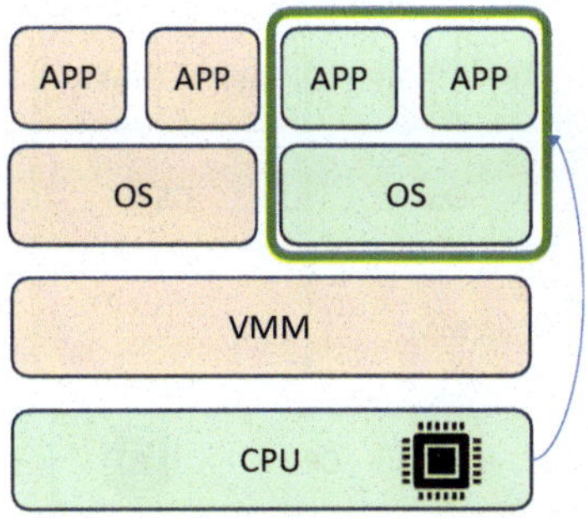

Figure 2.3 Confidential virtual machine.

artificial intelligence (AI) computation. If the host-side TEE requires such hardware acceleration, the device side needs to provide confidential accelerator functionality, as shown in Fig. 2.4. For example, NVIDIA's Hopper H100 provides a confidential computing solution based on confidential devices.

Finally, there is also the category of **isolated TEE**. Examples include ARM TrustZone, RISC-V KeyStone, RISC-V MultiZone, and RISC-V Penglai TEE. Fig. 2.5 provides a schematic diagram of an isolated TEE. In a broader sense, certain secure processors or security chips could also be considered isolated TEEs, such as Apple's T2 security chip, Google's Titan M2, Amazon's Nitro security chip, and the TCG-defined TPM. However, such security chips typically run only vendor-specific programs and are not fully open for end-user code, so they are not discussed in detail in this book.

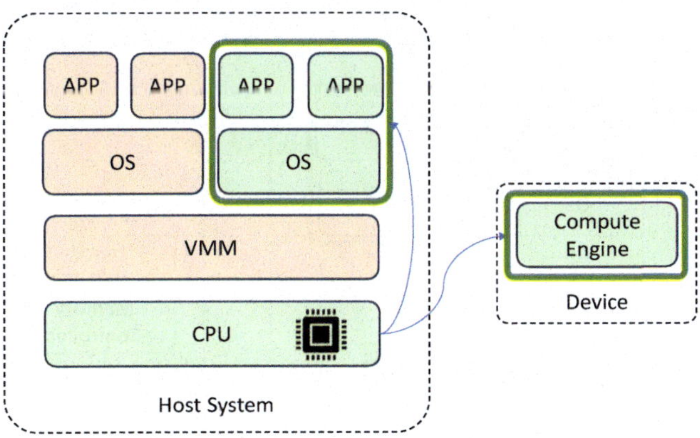

Figure 2.4 Confidential accelerator.

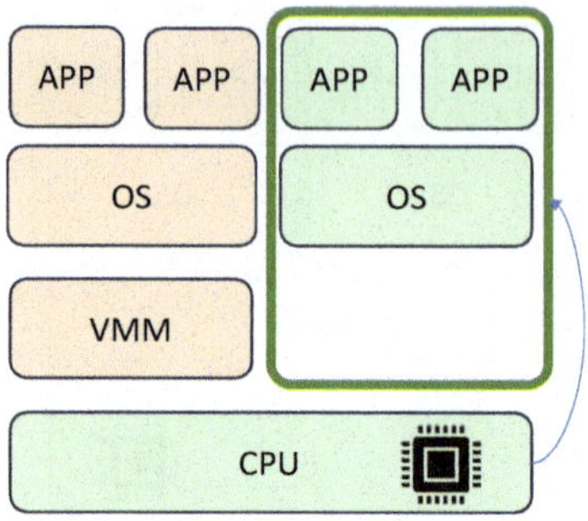

Figure 2.5 Isolated TEE.

There is an implicit assumption here: either the platform's CPU system-on-chip (SoC) integrates the memory controller (MC), or the connection between the CPU SoC and the MC is trusted and not subject to attack. This allows the MC to perform memory encryption without needing to trust the Dynamic Random Access Memory (DRAM) itself. However, if the MC is external to the SoC and the connection is untrusted, a mechanism is needed to make the MC trustworthy, as depicted in Fig. 2.6.

Secure enclave and confidential virtual machine solutions are discussed in Part 2, and confidential accelerator solutions in Part 3.

2.3 Software implementations of confidential computing

The CCC's "Common Terminology for Confidential Computing" white paper introduces the concept of a software packaging model, which

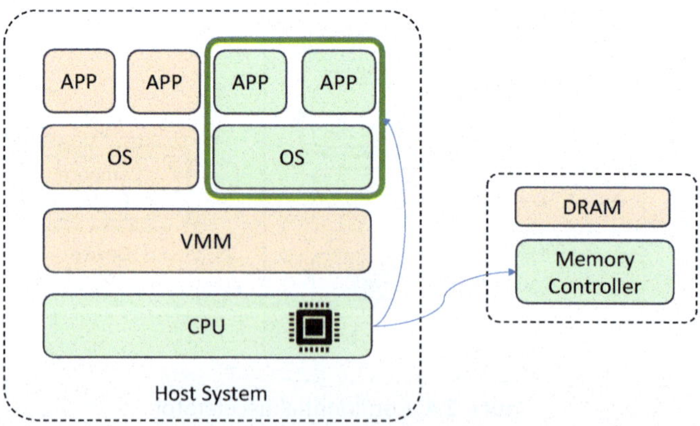

Figure 2.6 TEE with an external memory controller (MC).

describes the form in which software runs within a TEE. The main categories are:

- **Confidential library**: A software library (e.g., an enclave) executes within the TEE. This TEE-resident library provides services to applications running outside the TEE.
- **Confidential process**: A process (e.g., a trusted application) executes within the TEE.
- **Confidential container**: A container image conforming to the Open Container Initiative (OCI) standard executes within the TEE.
- **Confidential virtual machine**: A full virtual machine executes within the TEE.

Regardless of the type, the goal of the TEE is to protect specific portions of code and data executing within the host environment, isolating them from non-TEE code/data and from code/data in other TEEs. This software can be provided by hardware vendors or by third-party software vendors such as OS vendors (OSVs) or cloud service providers (CSPs).

It's important to note that the software packaging model does not have to strictly correspond to a specific hardware TEE classification. For example, software packaged as a confidential VM could potentially run on a hardware TEE designed for CVMs, but it might also run on a secure enclave type of TEE with appropriate virtualization support.

Current projects registered with the CCC include the following. Occlum and Gramine: use a library OS approach to help developers package existing applications into SGX confidential libraries. Enarx: provides a WebAssembly-based runtime TEE, allowing developers to deploy applications written in various languages like Rust, C/C++, C#, Go, Java, Python. Enarx supports SGX (confidential library) and AMD SEV (confidential VM). Open enclave SDK: helps build TEE-agnostic applications, supporting SGX (confidential library) and TrustZone (confidential process).

2.4 Applications of confidential computing

With the rapid advancement of AI, security and privacy concerns have become paramount. Confidential computing can provide confidentiality and integrity protection for machine learning workloads. The paper "Machine learning with confidential computing: a systematization of knowledge" by Mo et al. [65] provides a systematic overview of machine learning assisted by confidential computing. Server-side centralized machine learning offers training as a service (TaaS) and inference as a service (IaaS). Using TEEs can protect the privacy of the data being processed and the intellectual property of the models. Client-side distributed machine learning involves on-device inference (ODI) and on-device personalization (ODP). These client devices can also act as participants in federated learning, contributing to a global model. Using TEEs on the client side can protect the intellectual property of the deployed models.

Introducing confidential computing can potentially lead to AI performance loss due to the additional encryption and isolation overhead. A paper presented at IEEE Cloud 2024, "Securing AI inference in the cloud: is CPU-GPU confidential computing ready?" by IBM researchers, studied the performance of AI inference using Intel TDX systems and NVIDIA H100 GPUs. Since a full TEE-IO hardware encryption architecture was not yet employed, communication between the CPU and GPU relied on software encryption, which became a performance bottleneck. The study showed that using pipelined processing could mitigate this I/O bottleneck, allowing inference performance for large language models (LLMs) in a CPU-GPU TEE setup to approach that of nonconfidential computing scenarios.

CHAPTER 3

Confidential computing models

In Chapter 2, we introduced the foundational concepts of confidential computing. In this chapter, we will delve into the general models of confidential computing.

3.1 Confidential computing security model

Simply put, confidential computing protects data in use. The Confidential Computing Consortium, in its white paper "A Technical Analysis of Confidential Computing," provides a more stringent definition of the goal: confidential computing aims to "minimize the ability of the system platform owner/administrator/attacker to access data and code inside a TEE, making attacking a running program economically or logically infeasible." This statement is somewhat nuanced. The key point in the first half is that apart from the TEE user, **no other system platform personnel should possess the capability to access data and code within the trusted execution environment (TEE) during runtime**. This differs from our past experience; before confidential computing, system platform administrators (e.g., root users) often held supreme privileges, capable of modifying user permissions, accessing user data, etc. The second half clarifies the limitations, emphasizing that attacks should be economically or logically infeasible. We know that absolute security does not exist. In cryptography, according to Shannon, only the one-time pad is theoretically perfectly secure; existing cryptographic systems are based on computational security. This implies that: (1) If an attacker possesses unlimited resources (time or computing power), they might break confidential computing protections; but if the resources required to break the scheme outweigh the potential gain, the existing scheme remains secure. (2) An attacker might have a very small probability of success, but if that probability is negligible, there is no cause for concern.

Confidential Computing
ISBN 978-0-443-54067-7
https://doi.org/10.1016/B978-0-443-54067-7.00006-1

In terms of usability and cost, compared to other methods, TEEs significantly enhance the ability to protect data in use, allowing software designers/implementers/operators dealing with sensitive data to focus on other aspects of the system.

Although confidential computing itself focuses solely on data security during use, for a complete system solution, data security both at rest and in transit is equally important. For example, we need to consider the following:

- Local or remote attestation of the TEE: the user needs to ensure the TEE was correctly launched by the administrator.
- Transmission of workload and data to/from the TEE: the user needs to ensure workload and data are securely transmitted to the TEE, with confidentiality and integrity intact.
- Storage of TEE-related data in non-TEE nonvolatile storage (NVS): the user needs to ensure the confidentiality and integrity of these TEE-related data, and also protect against replay attacks.
- Migration of workload and data between TEEs: the user needs to define security policies specifying which TEEs can be migrated to and from.

3.1.1 General architecture model of confidential computing

Fig. 3.1 shows a general architecture model for TEE-based confidential computing. Dark green boxes are used to represent the TEE trusted computing base (TCB), light green boxes for the TEEs themselves, and red boxes for untrusted modules.

First, the system's central processing unit (CPU) and memory controller (MC) must be trusted, as they form the foundation for computation and

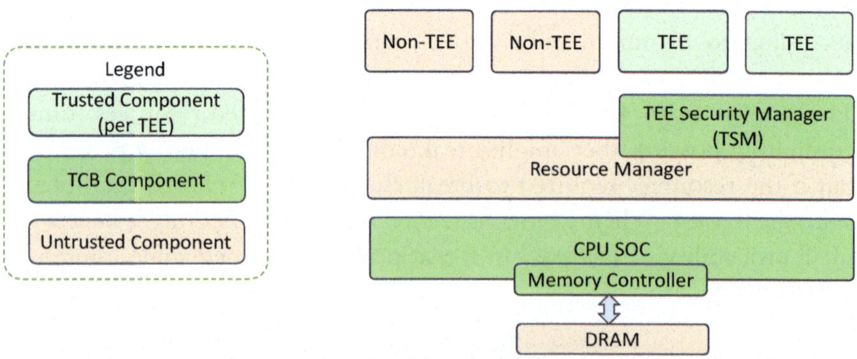

Figure 3.1 General architecture model for TEE-based confidential computing.

must be part of the TEE TCB. Dynamic Random Access Memory (DRAM) can be untrusted because the MC can include a memory Encryption Engine (MEE) and store encrypted content in DRAM. Gueron's 2016 paper "A memory encryption engine suitable for general purpose processors" introduced the design and security model of a general-purpose MEE. The security goals of an MEE are:

- Confidentiality of data stored in DRAM.
- Integrity of data stored in DRAM, with protection against replay attacks, ensuring that data read from DRAM are the most recently written data.

Note: *According to the MEE design and security model described above, MEE does not need to be designed as oblivious RAM (ORAM). The concept of ORAM was introduced by Goldreich and Ostrovsky in their 1996 paper "Software protection and simulation on oblivious RAMs." ORAM is a computational model where, for any two inputs that run for the same amount of time, the sequences of memory accesses are identical, thereby protecting software. MEE allows an attacker to observe DRAM modifications, cache line access addresses, etc.*

The MEE needs to satisfy the following security properties:

- MEE keys must be generated uniformly and randomly during the boot phase and must never leave the chip.
- MEE encryption keys and authentication keys must be separate, corresponding to confidentiality and integrity respectively.
- MEE integrity verification must follow a "drop-and-lock" strategy. During a read operation, the MEE calculates a Message Authentication Code (MAC) and compares it with the expected value from the integrity tree. If consistent, it proceeds. However, if the MEE detects any inconsistency, it must immediately signal a failure, abort the current transaction, and lock the MC, causing subsequent transactions to also fail. The MC is then in a halted state and can only be restored by a reboot.

Second, there can be one or more TEEs, depending on the system architecture implementation. If multiple TEEs exist, they must be isolated from each other. The security of one TEE should not depend on other TEEs, as an attacker might launch a malicious TEE as a coconspirator.

Third, to facilitate the management of multiple TEEs, the system may have a TEE security manager (TSM). The TSM can be part of the CPU SoC hardware extension, or it can be one or more independently running software modules. The TSM is responsible for managing all TEEs and their metadata, such as TEE context. The TSM is also part of the TEE-TCB. The TSM must be isolated from all other modules, including the TEEs themselves.

Finally, all other modules in the system are considered untrusted, including the resource manager and other non-TEE parts managed by it. Here, if the TEE is a user-mode secure enclave, the resource manager is the operating system, and non-TEEs are other applications. If the TEE is a confidential Virtual Machine (VM), the resource manager is the virtual machine manager (VMM), and non-TEEs are ordinary VMs.

The software and hardware modules in this architecture are classified into three categories: TEE-TCB, TEE, and untrusted modules. Their relationships are shown in Fig. 3.2.

- Trust relationships: trust relationships between various system TEE-TCB components are determined by the system architecture. A TEE can trust all TEE-TCB components, but multiple TEEs cannot trust each other.
- Protection relationships: TEE-TCB must protect itself from attacks by any TEE or untrusted module. TEE-TCB must protect each TEE and its TEE metadata from attacks by other TEEs and untrusted modules. A TEE must protect itself from attacks by other TEEs and untrusted modules. If a TEE has authenticated launch capability, the TEE-TCB is responsible for performing authentication at boot time.
- Attestation relationship: The TEE-TCB, acting as the root of trust for measurement (RTM), must support establishing a measurement chain of trust (CoT) for the TEE. To facilitate fine-grained measurements, the TEE-TCB may support TEE runtime measurements. The TEE-TCB, acting as the root of trust for storage (RTS), must provide protected measurement storage space for the TEE. The TEE's measurements can be part of the TEE's metadata. The TEE-TCB, acting as the root of trust for reporting (RTR), must support reporting the

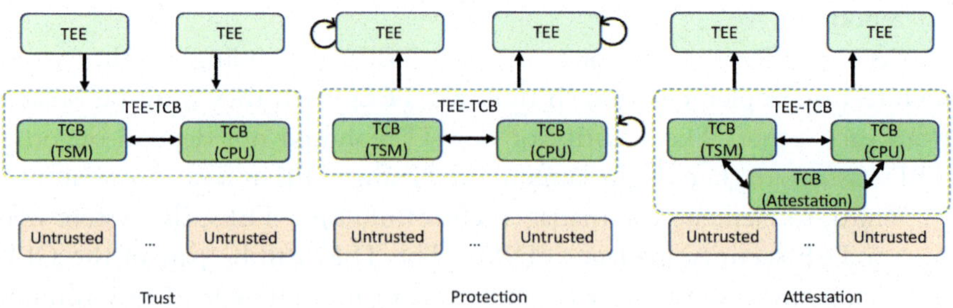

Figure 3.2 Relationships between TEE-TCB, TEEs, and untrusted modules.

measurements of all TEE-TCB modules and each individual TEE as evidence. To assist with remote attestation, the TEE-TCB may include one or more attestation-TCB modules as part of the RTR.

Let's further discuss the roles and responsibilities of some important modules in this architecture.

- Resource manager: The resource manager is the administrator of TEEs, responsible for managing and coordinating all TEEs, including TEE startup and shutdown, CPU and memory configuration, scheduling, and execution. The resource manager needs to inform the TSM about the TSM's configuration.
- TSM: the TSM is the enforcer of TEE security policies, responsible for protecting TEE resources from attacks by other modules and locking the resource manager's configuration of the TEE.
- TEE: there is a decision-maker inside the TEE that makes decisions based on policies. For example, the decision-maker needs to decide whether to accept the resource manager's configuration for the TEE.

3.1.2 TEE permissions in confidential computing

Availability is generally not a concern for confidential computing, because the system's resource manager is responsible for managing all system resources, and the TEE is only one part of it. Although it cannot access the TEE, the resource manager has the authority to start or shut down the TEE. Therefore, **the availability of the TEE does not need to be considered.**

However, from the perspective of the entire platform, we do need to consider the availability of the system, that is, the availability of the resource manager. Similar to the traditional threat model for nonconfidential computing, in this scenario the attacker could be a TEE, and the system resource manager needs to protect itself. Here are the relationships from the resource manager's perspective:

- **Trust relationships**: We consider the resource manager can trust the TEE-TCB, because the TEE-TCB typically holds high privileges and is part of the platform's TCB, such as the CPU SoC. However, the resource manager cannot trust any TEE.
- **Protection relationships**: The resource manager needs to protect itself from being attacked by TEEs. The resource manager does not need to protect the TEE-TCB or other TEEs, because in the confidential computing model, the resource manager is untrusted.

- **Attestation relationships**: The resource manager does not need attestation capabilities because it is untrusted.

We now specifically discuss availability to illustrate the permission issues related to confidential computing TEEs. Broadly speaking, any independent trusted execution environment can be called a TEE. A TEE can have the highest system privileges, affecting system usability, or it can have minimal privileges, protecting only a small portion of a user-mode application. For example, Intel introduced System Management Mode (SMM) as early as the 386SL processor, as shown in Fig. 3.3. However, SMM has the highest system priority, even surpassing the VMM. Using SMM as a general-purpose TEE would not be appropriate. Similarly, ARM's TrustZone, introduced in ARMv6KZ, is a security technology that creates a Secure World TEE, as shown in Fig. 3.4. Here, the Monitor-mode

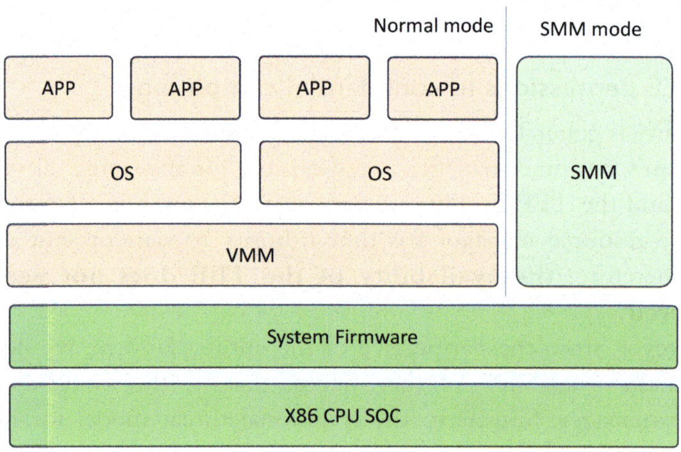

Figure 3.3 System management mode (SMM).

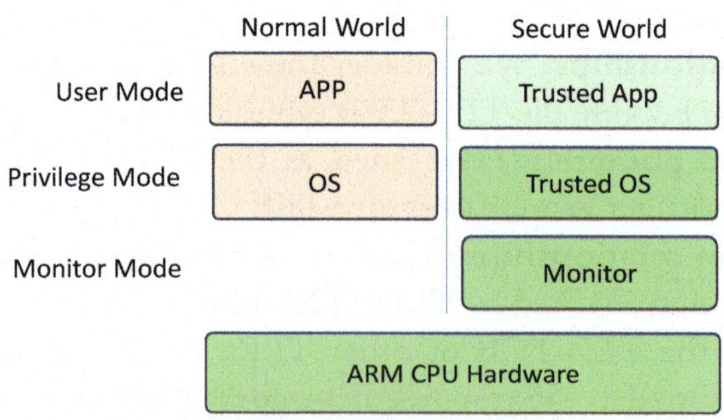

Figure 3.4 ARM TrustZone.

TrustZone monitor software possesses the highest privilege. This means if such a TEE were used as a confidential computing TEE, it would grant privileges far beyond what the execution environment actually needs, violating the least privilege principle of computer security protection proposed by Saltzer and Schroeder in their 1975 paper "The protection of information in computer systems." Smith's 2012 article "A contemporary look at Saltzer and Schroeder's 1975 design principles" revisited these design principles, reaffirming the continued importance of least privilege. Therefore, this is not the optimal choice for a confidential computing TEE.

Note: *This is not to say the designs of SMM or TrustZone are useless. There were valid reasons for such designs at the time. SMM's powerful privileges allowed for system patching and resolving compatibility issues. TrustZone placed the highest privilege monitor in the secure world to boot the system and used monitor mode to isolate the nonsecure world, resulting in a simple design. At that time, the industry did not have the requirements of confidential computing. Now, with different security needs for confidential computing TEEs, the introduction of new hardware designs is unsurprising.*

3.1.3 The scope of TEE-TCB

The Trusted Computing Base (TCB) is not a new concept. Lampson, Abadi, Burrows, and Wobber, in their 1992 paper "Authentication in distributed systems: theory and practice," defined TCB as "the small part of the computer system's software and hardware that we distinguish as responsible for security, such that the malfunctioning of other parts does not affect security." The US Department of Defense (DoD) publication DOD 5200.28 "Trusted Computer System Evaluation Criteria" (the Orange Book) in 1983 defined the role and responsibilities of the TCB under various security levels. The National Institute of Standards and Technology (NIST) defines TCB as "the totality of protection mechanisms within a computer system, including hardware, firmware, and software, the combination of which is responsible for enforcing a security policy." The importance of the TCB for system security is evident; the TCB protects system security under the premise of protecting its own security. Therefore, system designers often invest significant effort in designing and implementing the TCB. To reduce overhead and potential risks, it is widely accepted that the TCB should be as small as possible. Tanenbaum, the designer of MINIX, in his debate with Linus Torvalds, prioritized operating system reliability, suggesting we could "move most of the operating system's functionality into a series of user processes, each driving a user process for its function, and then provide a set of system services. This wouldn't reduce the number of bugs in the code, but it would greatly diminish the harm caused by each potential bug, **reducing the size of the trusted base**."

In the early stages of system design, the operating system played the role of the TCB to some extent. It was responsible for isolating and protecting each user process, acting as the TCB for each. With the advent of virtualization technology, the dependencies for user process security became more complex, involving from the bottom up:

- System-on-chip (SoC): CPU, memory manager, including system hardware patches like CPU microcode. Provided by the chip manufacturer.
- Platform peripheral: memory modules (DRAM). Provided by memory device manufacturers.
- System firmware: BIOS or UEFI firmware. Provided by the original equipment manufacturer (OEM).
- VMM: e.g., Linux KVM, Windows Hyper-V. Provided by the VMM vendor.
- Operating system (OS): e.g., Linux, Windows. Provided by the OS vendor.

To address the trust issue, the TCG proposed the Trusted Platform Module (TPM) and trusted boot specifications, such as the trusted boot based on the static root of trust for measurement (SRTM) described in the Platform Firmware Profile (PFP), as shown in Fig. 3.5a. China also released

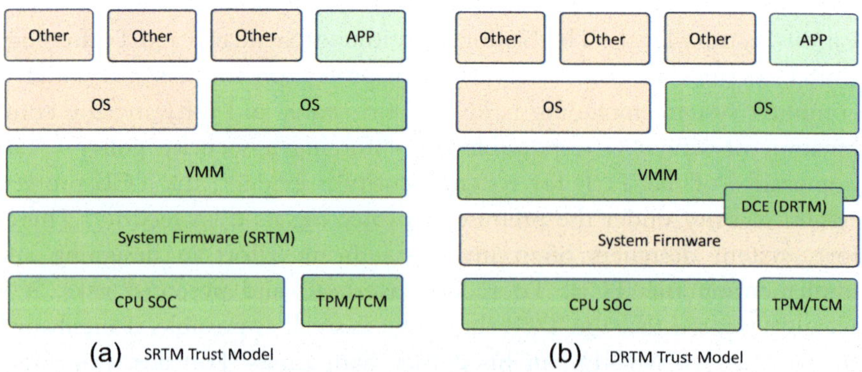

Figure 3.5 Trust models of SRTM and DRTM.

the Trusted Cryptography Module (TCM), similar to TPM, supporting SRTM-based boot. SRTM is a mature technology; existing systems on the market (like Linux and Windows) support SRTM-based trusted boot. However, to ensure a user-mode application is trustworthy, a verifier needs to check the measurements of all system components, including hardware patches, system firmware, VMM, OS, etc. Since different components come from different vendors, establishing the CoT is very complex. Moreover, the TCB composed of these components is very large; a problem in any one of these components compromises security. System firmware poses one of the biggest threats. Because the SMM code in system firmware has the highest privilege, once a security vulnerability exists in the system firmware, it necessitates reflashing and reinstalling the system.

Subsequently, the TCG proposed trusted boot based on the dynamic root of trust for measurement (DRTM), as shown in Fig. 3.5b. With the help of the hardware vendor's DRTM configuration environment (DCE), a dynamic launched measured environment (DLME) can be created at any time, establishing a dynamic RTM without needing to trust the system firmware. This design excludes the OEM system firmware from the TCB, eliminating the security risks it introduces. Currently, Intel's Trusted Execution Technology (TXT) and AMD's Secure Virtual Machine (SVM) are hardware implementations supporting DRTM technology. Microsoft's System Guard Secure Launch and SMM protection in Windows 11 Secure Core PCs utilize DRTM-based trusted boot. Compared to SRTM, DRTM is an improvement. However, DRTM implementations still include the entire VMM in the TCB as part of the trust chain. For confidential computing TEEs, the TCB is still not minimal enough. Furthermore, in cloud environments, the VMM is typically provided by the cloud service provider (CSP). The tenant of a VM may only want to use the CPU compute power offered by the CSP, but not trust the CSP or expose their data to them. DRTM cannot satisfy these requirements.

Therefore, in the security model of confidential computing TEEs, we directly exclude the VMM (system resource manager) from the TCB, minimizing its size to the greatest extent. Ideally, only the hardware, firmware, and software modules provided by the chip manufacturer constitute the TEE's TCB. Then, the TEE user only needs to trust the chip manufacturer, greatly reducing the risk of problems within the TCB components. It is generally accepted that the SoC and TSM in the general confidential computing trust model belong to the TEE-TCB, and the

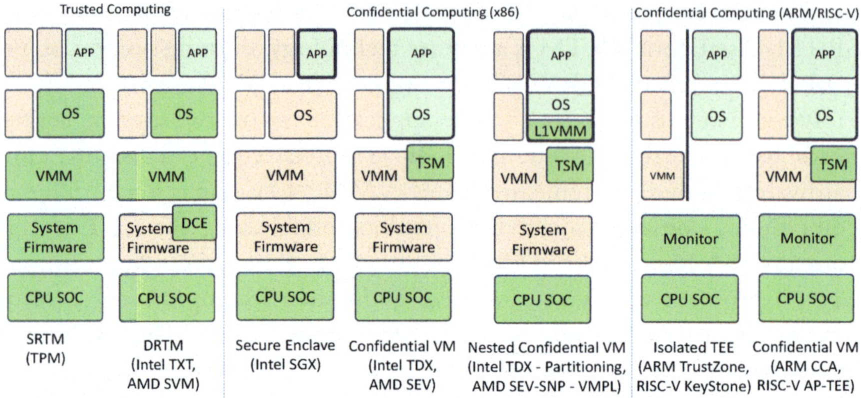

Figure 3.6 Trusted computing and various confidential computing TEE architectures.

TEE-TCB may include more modules; the specific design depends on the TEE hardware implementation.

Fig. 3.6 summarizes trusted computing and various confidential computing TEE architectures. On the left is the previously introduced trusted computing architecture, including both SRTM- and DRTM-based types. The middle part shows ×86-based confidential computing solutions, including secure enclaves and confidential VMs. The characteristic of these solutions is the exclusion of complex system firmware and VMM from the TCB. Note that this includes a subclass—nested confidential VMs—which refers to launching a lightweight L1 VMM inside a confidential VM to support unmodified OSs. For example, Intel TDX's TD Partitioning and AMD SEV's VM Privilege Level (VMPL) can be considered nested schemes. An interesting phenomenon is that ×86 confidential computing TCB initially in the SGX solution excluded all privileged components (like the OS), but it was found that this required modifying existing system applications. Therefore, new TCB modules were gradually added to support existing systems and maintain compatibility. It can be seen that the difficulty in system design lies not only in security but also in the support of the entire ecosystem. To make a product usable, architects sometimes have to make trade-offs between security and usability. The right part shows confidential computing solutions based on ARM and RISC-V architectures, including the earlier proposed isolated TEE environments and the current confidential VM solutions. Unlike ×86 architectures, ARM and RISC-V systems typically have a highest-privilege monitor used to switch between different worlds, including the VMM, and provide services. This monitor has always been part of the system's TEE-TCB.

3.1.4 The concept of root of trust (RoT)

When discussing TCB, we mentioned the RoT. Let's discuss this concept in detail here, as it will be used later. According to NIST's definition, an RoT is "a set of highly reliable hardware, firmware, and software components that perform specific, critical security functions. Because RoTs are inherently trusted, they must be secure by design. RoTs provide a solid foundation for building security and trust." RoTs reside within the TCB, but not all modules inside the TCB are necessarily RoTs, as RoTs can extend the scope of trust by establishing a CoT.

Generally, RoTs can be viewed from two dimensions:

- **Location of RoT**: e.g., Platform RoT (P-RoT) responsible for platform boot, Silicon RoT responsible for CPU SoC internal boot, Active Component RoT (AC-RoT) responsible for device boot, etc.
- **Function of RoT**: e.g., RTM, RTS, and RTR in trusted boot; root of trust for detection (RTD), root of trust for update (RTU), and root of trust for recovery (RTRec) in secure boot and platform firmware resiliency.

Confidential computing TEE-TCB is typically responsible for trusted boot by the Silicon RoT, incorporating RTM, RTS, and RTR to assist the remote attestation of the TEE. If the TEE-TCB firmware and software provide upgrade and recovery functions, the TEE-TCB will introduce RTD, RTU, and RTRec. We introduce the design of these RoTs in later content.

If the system needs to support confidential device accelerators, the system also requires an active component root of trust to be responsible for the startup of confidential devices and to provide remote attestation for the devices. We introduce this in Part 3.

3.2 Threat model for confidential computing

The introduction in this section still references the general threat model provided in the Confidential Computing Consortium's white paper "A Technical Analysis of Confidential Computing." It is important to note that specific confidential computing implementations from different vendors and generations may have different threat models.

3.2.1 Threats in scope

The primary goal of confidential computing is to ensure the confidentiality and integrity of the TEE. The main types of threats that confidential computing needs to consider are:

- **Software attacks**: The software here can be any software or firmware on the system platform. For example: VMM, OS, any non-TEE programs, other TEE programs, system firmware (also called BIOS), untrusted device firmware (such as NIC firmware, disk firmware, GPU firmware, keyboard firmware). The TEE needs to defend against direct access attacks from such software.
- **Protocol attacks**: The protocol here refers to the security protocols used when the TEE exchanges data with other (non-TEE) entities. Cryptographic schemes are typically needed to protect these protocols. For example, the TEE interacts with a third-party verifier for remote attestation, or the TEE uses an authenticated key exchange protocol to securely import workloads and data.
- **Cryptographic attacks**: TEEs typically need to incorporate cryptographic schemes to protect data. It is important to note that cryptography is constantly evolving. On one hand, cryptographic algorithms advance. With the advent of the quantum computing era, current algorithms like RSA, DH, and ECC will be replaced by new post-quantum cryptography (PQC) algorithms. NIST has announced a series of PQC algorithms, such as Module Lattice-based Key-Encapsulation Mechanism (ML-KEM), Module Lattice-based Digital Signature Algorithm (ML-DSA), Stateless Hash-based Digital Signature Algorithm (SLH-DSA), and two stateful hash-based signature algorithms. On the other hand, key lengths will change. In the quantum computing era, 128-bit AES must be upgraded to 256-bit AES, and 256-bit SHA algorithms must be upgraded to 384-bit SHA. The NSA's Commercial National Security Algorithm Suite (CNSA) 2.0 specifies a timeline for migrating from traditional cryptography to PQC: migration work is expected to begin around 2025, with PQC deployment completed by 2030–33. The design of TEE firmware needs to consider cryptographic agility to prepare for future upgrades.
- **Simple physical attacks**: Although attacks targeting the CPU chip itself are typically considered out of scope, confidential computing needs to consider attacks against other physical peripherals. This includes cold DRAM extraction, bus monitoring, cache monitoring, and device hot-plugging (e.g., PCIe devices, USB devices).

- **Basic upstream supply-chain attacks**: While attacks targeting the TEE component supply chain are generally out of scope, simple, global attacks also need consideration, such as an attacker adding a debug port to the system.

Here, because simple physical attacks include offline DRAM reading, runtime memory encryption becomes a necessary condition. Relying solely on TEE isolation cannot protect against offline DRAM reading.

Additionally, the Confidential Computing Consortium's threat model specifically points out some gray areas, such as integrity checking, rollback attacks, and various software/hardware-based replay attacks. Completely defending against these threats would require significant hardware design changes. Therefore, the CCC allows vendors to consider these based on their use cases.

Note: *In* Chapter 2, *it was mentioned that the CCC proposed that security attributes for TEEs include integrity, but here it is stated that integrity is a gray area. Why is this? Integrity encompasses many aspects, including integrity protection against software attacks and hardware attacks, logical integrity (LI) protection and cryptographic integrity (CI) protection, replay attack protection across TEEs, and replay attack protection within the same TEE. Therefore, the CCC loosened the requirements, allowing vendors to decide which protection measures to adopt.*

We know there is no 100% reliable security in the world. Security considerations in design ultimately come down to **risk control**. For example, for end-users, usability like system performance must be considered; for commercial product design, return on investment is a factor. If design complexity increases solely for security enhancement, leading to higher costs and lower performance, such a product is unlikely to succeed. Therefore, the final products on the market are typically "good enough," but not necessarily the absolute best.

We introduce examples of TEE implementations from various CPU vendors in Section 3.3. For instance, Intel's TDX offers both CI and LI modes. AMD's SEV initially only provided memory encryption protection; the second generation, SEV-ES, added CPU state protection; the third generation, SEV-SNP, added integrity protection. ARM's RME architecture initially did not prevent leakage across Realm boundaries; later, Realm-specific independent key functionality was introduced, and RME does not require providing physical replay attack protection. RISC-V's CoVE does not mandate TVM-specific independent key encryption, nor does it mandate protection against hardware-based integrity attacks. These are all considerations made for system performance.

3.2.2 Threats out of scope

Confidential computing typically does not consider the following types of threats:

- **Complex physical attacks**: e.g., chip scraping or electron microscope probing.
- **Upstream hardware supply chain attacks**: e.g., injecting hardware Trojans during chip fabrication.
- **Availability attacks/denial of service (DoS) attacks**: Generally, a TEE is not the system's overall manager. The manager for a secure enclave is the OS, and for a confidential VM, it's the VMM. The TEE must communicate with the outside world through the untrusted OS or VMM, which can ignore the TEE's communication requests. Therefore, general-purpose TEEs cannot prevent availability/DoS attacks.

3.2.3 Side-channel attacks and mitigations

Although TEE hardware provides data confidentiality protection for confidential computing, vulnerabilities in TEE software design can still expose confidential data. Besides common buffer overflows, side-channel attacks like Spectre and Meltdown have garnered the most attention in recent years. The original intent of confidential computing TEE design was to solve data security problems during runtime. For example, a user could deploy keys within a TEE without worrying about key leakage during use; a user could run proprietary code within a TEE without worrying about the private code being stolen by other processes. For these two scenarios, side-channel attacks can target two aspects:

- **Recovering arbitrary memory information within the TEE**: This is a general side-channel attack unrelated to cryptography, completely breaking TEE confidentiality.
- **Recovering cryptographic keys within the TEE**: This involves side-channel attacks targeting key operations, including recovering symmetric keys or private keys in asymmetric systems. It is closely related to various cryptographic algorithms. Common attack methods include cache side channels, timing side channels, power side channels, and fault injection (e.g., voltage or electromagnetic attacks).

  We detail various general side-channel attacks in Chapter 8.

3.3 Threat models of confidential computing TEE examples

Now let's examine the threat models of several typical confidential computing TEE examples.

3.3.1 Intel SGX threat model

SGX (Software Guard Extensions) was Intel's earliest proposed confidential computing solution. A user can split an application into trusted and untrusted parts. The trusted part executes within an SGX user-mode (Ring-3) enclave, leveraging SGX to protect its confidentiality and integrity, as shown in Fig. 3.7. An enclave constitutes a confidential computing TEE. Each enclave is isolated from non-enclave code and other enclaves. Intel SGX does not have a software TSM; the TSM functionality is handled by CPU microcode. SGX implements isolation of code and data within the enclave and uses an MEE to ensure the confidentiality, integrity, and freshness of memory data. However, Intel SGX hardware itself does not inherently defend against side-channel attacks.

Intel began disseminating information about SGX around 2013, publishing papers including "Innovative instructions and software model for isolated execution" and "Innovative technology for CPU based attestation and sealing." Costan et al. studied SGX and published papers in 2016 ("Intel SGX Explained") and 2017 ("Secure processors part I: background, taxonomy for secure enclaves and intel SGX architecture" and "Secure processors part II: Intel SGX security analysis and MIT Sanctum architecture"), detailing Intel SGX's design, implementation, and security features. Below is a summary of some threats considered by Intel SGX.

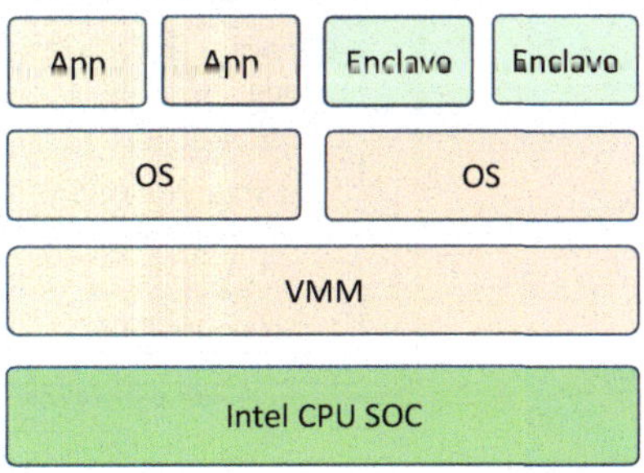

Figure 3.7 Intel SGX architecture.

- **Physical attacks**: SGX assumes DRAM and the DRAM bus to be untrusted. Therefore, SGX uses an MEE to protect memory data. However, **SGX does not consider side-channel power analysis attacks.**
- **Privileged software attacks**: SGX considers all system software untrusted, including VMM, OS, BIOS, etc. First, SGX implementation uses a special enclave page cache (EPC) to store enclave control structures (SGX enclave control structure—SECS), code, data, and thread control structures (TCSs). The EPC resides in protected memory, inaccessible to other software. Second, enclaves need to interact with other software (nonenclave or other enclaves). SGX CPU microcode saves the execution state upon enclave exit and reloads it upon enclave entry. When a hardware interrupt triggers an asynchronous enclave exit (AEX), the enclave's register state is saved to the enclave-specific state save area (SSA), inaccessible to other system software, as shown in Fig. 3.8.
- **Memory mapping attacks**: SGX uses an independent enclave page cache map (EPCM) to store EPC page table information and their types within the enclave's virtual address space. During CPU address translation, addresses not permitted for enclave access are directly blocked by the EPCM before reaching the page table TLB. SGX allows system software to evict EPC pages to DRAM, while SGX uses cryptographic

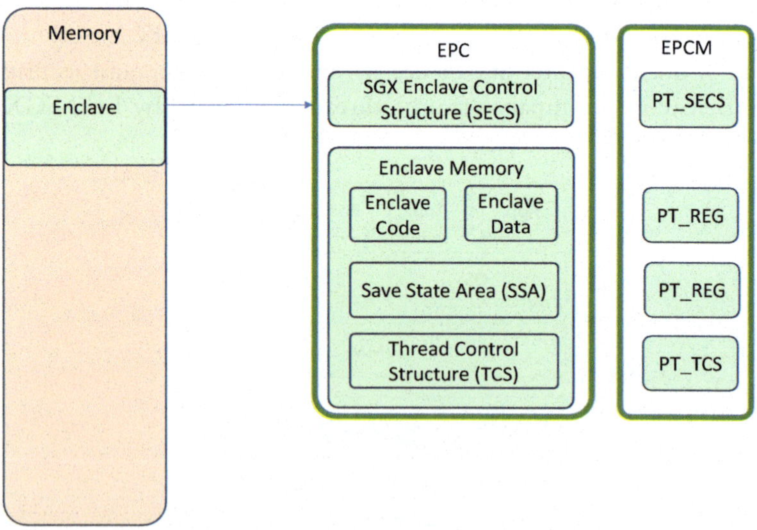

Figure 3.8 Intel SGX enclave components.

methods to protect the data of the evicted EPC page and its associated EPCM metadata.

- **Software attacks from peripherals**: SGX only trusts components inside the CPU SoC, including the MC. SGX does not trust any peripherals, such as the external PCI express bus or DRAM. SGX ensures the security of EPC contents via the MEE, including defense against rowhammer attacks.
- **Cache timing attacks**: SGX hardware does not inherently mitigate cache timing side-channel attacks. An untrusted OS could control the mapping of enclave memory to specific cache regions, facilitating side-channel attacks.
- **Software attacks on private microarchitectural state**: Research indicates SGX hardware does not protect microarchitectural information, such as the enclave's branch execution history.
- **Other software side-channel attacks**: A user's enclave typically relies on a quoting enclave (QE) to provide an SGX quote for remote attestation. The SGX quote requires the QE to sign it with a private key. Since SGX hardware does not provide side-channel attack protection, following cryptographic side-channel best practices means enclave developers need to write code with no data-dependent memory accesses when handling keys.

Additionally, Georgia Tech has published learning materials on the SGX101 website. Currently, a series of side-channel attacks targeting SGX enclaves have emerged in the industry. For example, Weichbrodt et al. [100] proposed AsyncShock, exploiting multithreading synchronization bugs within enclaves. Götzfried et al. [101] explained cache attacks on Intel SGX. Lee et al. [102] proposed branch shadowing attacks. Van Bulck et al. [104] presented Foreshadow, extracting keys from SGX enclaves using transient out-of-order execution. Chen et al. [105] demonstrated SgxPectre, a Spectre variant on SGX. Murdock et al. [106] introduced Plundervolt, a software-based fault injection attack. Puddu et al. [107] proposed Frontal Attack, leaking control-flow via the CPU frontend. Wang Peng et al. [108] and Fei et al. [109] provided surveys on SGX security vulnerabilities and countermeasures. These are considerations for SGX enclave software designers. Readers can refer to Intel's series of best practices for mitigating side-channel attacks, such as "Managed runtime speculative execution side channel mitigations," "Security best practices for side channel resistance," and "Guidelines for mitigating timing side channels against cryptographic implementations."

3.3.2 Intel TDX threat model

Secure enclaves allow loading user-mode applications into the enclave, but this introduces limitations: to use the enclave, users must rewrite and refactor code to fit the enclave model. Confidential VMs, on the other hand, conveniently run unmodified code. In a confidential VM solution, only the operating system (Windows or Linux) within the VM needs modification, allowing easy execution of existing applications.

TDX (Trust Domain Extensions) is Intel's VM-based confidential computing solution. Intel's confidential VM is called a trust domain (TD), which is the confidential computing TEE VM (TVM). Each TD is isolated from the VMM, non-TDs (ordinary VMs), and other TDs. TDX relies on the Multi-Key Total Memory Encryption (MK-TME) engine for memory encryption and adds additional modes for integrity. Each TD has its own key.

Securely managing a VM is more complex than managing an enclave, especially managing TD runtime state and context switching between TD and VMM. Therefore, Intel introduced a software module called the Intel TDX Module to assist the VMM in management. This serves as the software TSM for confidential computing. Simply put, the VMM handles the nonsecure parts, while the Intel TDX Module handles security-related aspects. For each TD, the Intel TDX Module is part of the TCB, acting as an extension of the hardware CPU. The main functions of the Intel TDX Module include managing the state of each TD and managing the switching between TDs and the VMM. The architecture of Intel TDX is shown in Fig. 3.9.

The TDX white paper details TDX security features (as shown in Fig. 3.10).

- **Memory confidentiality and integrity**: TDX relies on the TME-MK engine to provide TD-specific keys for encryption and integrity

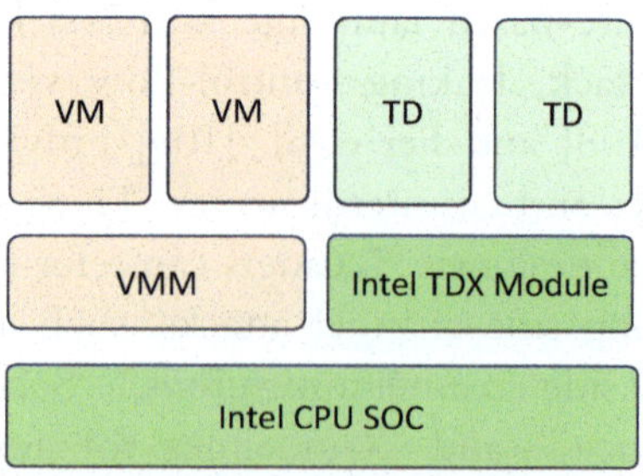

Figure 3.9 Intel TDX architecture.

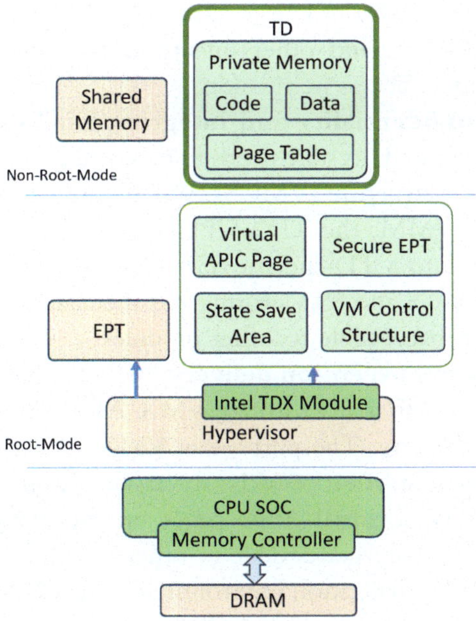

Figure 3.10 Intel TDX components and access control.

checking. TDX uses a host key identifier (HKID) to tell the MEE which encryption key to use. Each TD is assigned a private HKID at launch for encrypting its private memory, while shared memory is encrypted using a shared HKID. TDX memory integrity offers two modes: first, CI, where memory integrity is ensured by message authentication codes and TD owner bits, defending against software tampering attacks and some hardware damage attacks like row hammer; second, LI, where memory integrity is only ensured by TD owner bits, only defending against software accessing TD ciphertext but not against hardware attacks.

- **Address translation integrity**: A TD can access two types of memory: private memory, accessible only by the TD itself, encrypted with a specific ephemeral memory encryption key assigned to the TD to ensure confidentiality and integrity; and shared memory, which is not additionally protected by the TDX trusted module and is also accessible by the VMM. Typically, in the presence of a VMM, a VM's physical page tables are managed by the VMM through extended page tables (EPT), also called shared EPT. When TDX is enabled, the physical page tables for TD private memory are managed by another set of secure-EPTs (S-EPT). The location of S-EPTs is managed by the Intel TDX Module, and other unauthorized software (VMM, VM, TD) has no direct access permission.

- **CPU state confidentiality and integrity**: Similar to ordinary VMs, when a TD is created, its state needs to be saved in a TD-specific virtual machine control structure (VMCS). When context switching between a TD and the VMM, the TD's CPU registers are saved by the Intel TDX Module into a TD-specific SSA. The Intel TDX Module manages all TD VMCS and SSA, storing this metadata in encrypted memory, making it inaccessible to other modules.
- **Secure interrupt/exception delivery**: In TDX, interrupts and exceptions are delivered to a TD through VMX-APIC virtualization and virtual interrupt delivery. The purpose of VMX-APIC virtualization is to reduce software emulation of APIC for easier management and reduced overhead. In TDX, virtual APIC pages are also managed by the Intel TDX Module and are inaccessible to other unauthorized modules.

In a non-TDX virtualization environment, the VMM can manage the mapping from guest physical address (GPA) to host physical address (HPA) by setting up EPTs. In a TDX environment, a similar mapping from TD GPA to HPA is needed. However, the VMM cannot arbitrarily modify this mapping, so TDX introduces two page table components: shared EPT and secure EPT, as shown in Fig. 3.11.

In the TD environment, all guest virtual address (GVA) to GPA mappings are handled through ordinary page tables managed via the CR3 register. However, the page tables in the TD environment have a SHARED bit indicating whether the page is TD private memory or shared memory. Subsequently, when the CPU translates GPA to HPA, it uses the SHARED bit to decide whether to use the shared EPT or the secure EPT for address translation. If a TD page is shared, the SHARED bit is 1, and the CPU uses the shared EPT. If a TD page is private the SHARED bit is 0, and the CPU uses the secure EPT. The shared EPT resides in VMM

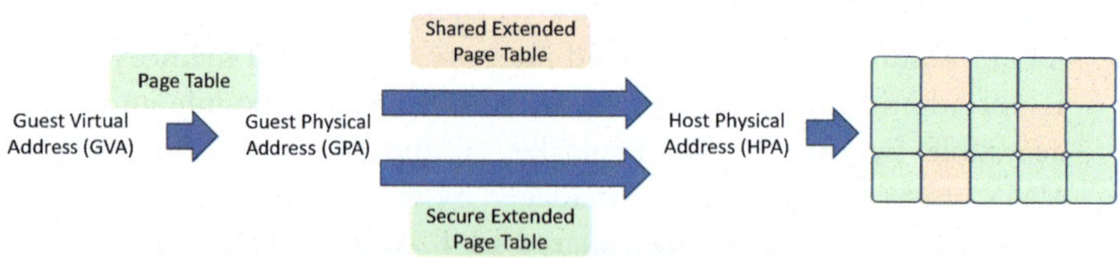

Figure 3.11 Intel TDX memory management.

memory and is directly managed by the VMM. However, the secure EPT needs to be located in private memory managed by the TDX Module and encrypted with the TD's ephemeral key. The VMM cannot directly modify the secure EPT and can only send commands to the TDX Module to build and manage it.

At the final stage of address translation, the CPU sets the HKID in the HPA, telling the MEE which encryption key to use. The TDX architecture divides the HKID space into shared HKID and private HKID. TD shared memory is encrypted using the shared HKID, while TD private memory uses the TD-specific private HKID.

For Memory-Mapped Input/Output (MMIO) address spaces of ordinary devices, the TD must explicitly set the SHARED bit to identify them, allowing device passthrough mode. In this case, the device is considered untrusted, and the TD must verify device data before use.

Intel TDX hardware primarily considers two main types of threats:

- **System software attacks**: System software includes internal attackers with system administrator privileges, as well as privileged software like the VMM, ordinary VMs, other TDs, and BIOS (including system management mode). These entities could launch attacks by running potentially malicious software modules. For example, an attacker might attempt to directly access TD private memory, inject into private memory, execute private memory, modify CPU state, use direct memory access (DMA) engines, exploit EPT page tables, remap memory, trigger memory alias access, or inject virtual interrupts to obtain confidential information from the TD.
- **Physical attacks**: As mentioned earlier, TDX considers simple physical attacks like DRAM bus snooping and cold boot attacks. The memory encryption provided by TME-MK, especially with the private HKID per TD, is designed to protect against such attacks. However, TDX, like SGX, may not fully protect against all complex physical attacks or advanced side-channel attacks that require physical proximity and sophisticated equipment.

In addition, Google's Aktas et al. published an audit report on Intel TDX in 2023, titled "Intel Trust Domain Extensions (TDX) security review" [116]. IBM's Cheng et al. also published a research report on Intel TDX in 2023, titled "Intel TDX demystified: a top-down approach" [117].

Like SGX, TDX cannot fully prevent side-channel attacks. Users of TDs need to adopt software security best practices to ensure the security of TDs. To this end, Intel published reports on TDX security practices, namely "Trust domain security guidance for developers" [118] and "Intel trust domain extension guest kernel hardening documentation" [119], as well as a report on side-channel attack mitigation for TME-MK, "MKTME side channel impact on Intel TDX" [120].

The Intel TDX family also includes Intel TDX Connect, which is used to support trusted confidential devices. We will describe this in detail in Part III.

3.3.3 AMD SEV-SNP threat model

AMD's Secure Encrypted Virtualization (SEV) technology has evolved. The latest generation, SEV-SNP (Secure Nested Paging), provides integrity protection in addition to confidentiality. In an SEV-SNP system, each SNP VM acts as a confidential computing TEE. The management of SNP VMs is handled by the AMD Secure Processor (AMD-SP), a hardware module that serves as the hardware TSM. Both the AMD-SP and the AMD CPU SoC are part of the SEV-SNP TCB, as illustrated in Fig. 3.12.

SEV-SNP's private memory management strategy differs from TDX. Instead of using isolated secure nested page tables, it adds a reverse map table (RMP) alongside the nested page tables (NPTs), as shown in Fig. 3.13.

In an SNP-VM environment, all GVA to GPA mappings are handled through ordinary page tables managed by the CR3 register. The page tables have a C (enCryption) bit to indicate whether a page is encrypted private memory or nonencrypted shared memory. After GPA is translated to system physical address (SPA) using NPTs (nCR3), the CPU checks the

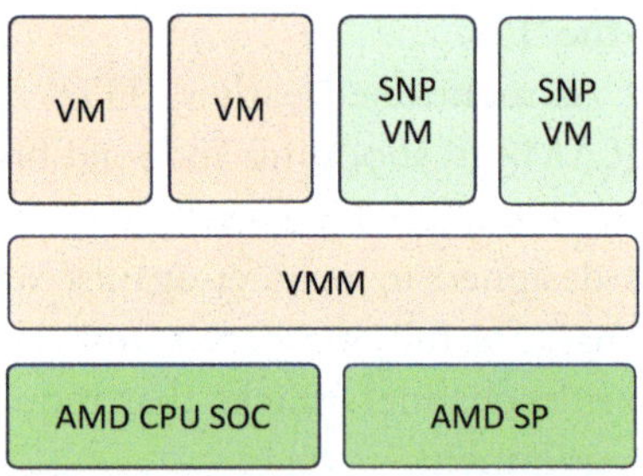

Figure 3.12 AMD SEV-SNP architecture.

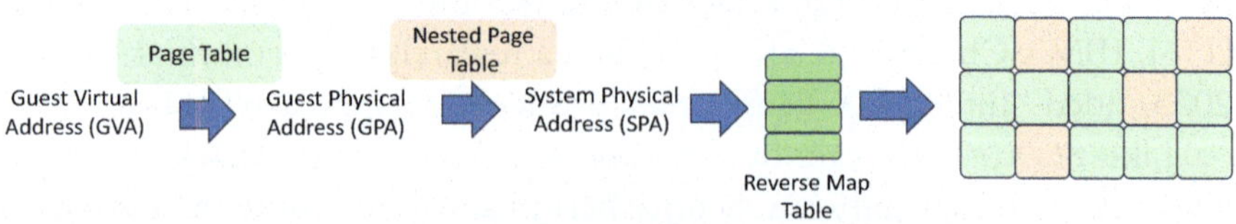

Figure 3.13 AMD SEV-SNP memory management.

RMP. The RMP table records the owner (VMM, AMD-SP, or a specific SNP-VM) of all used 4KiB pages. Memory access is only allowed after passing the RMP permission checks. Similarly, the RMP itself needs protection; the VMM cannot directly modify the RMP table and can only modify it through special commands.

Like TDX, for MMIO address spaces of ordinary devices, the SNP-VM must clear the C bit to indicate shared memory, supporting pass-through mode for untrusted devices.

The SEV-SNP white paper "AMD SEV-SNP: strengthening VM isolation with integrity protection and more" outlines the threat model.

- **Confidentiality**: As the name implies, memory within an SNP VM is encrypted. VM register state is protected. DMA protection prevents access from untrusted devices to SNP VM memory. At launch, each SNP VM gets an address space identifier (ASID) used to tell the MC which VM encryption key (VEK) to use for encrypting VM memory.
- **Integrity**: SEV-SNP introduces the RMP to support memory integrity checking. This helps defend against memory corruption attacks (writing arbitrary garbage data), memory replay attacks (writing back old data), remapping attacks (swapping pages mapped to the VM), and alias access attacks (two VMs mapping to the same DRAM page).
- **Availability**: SEV-SNP can guarantee availability for the VMM, but it does not guarantee availability for the SNP VM itself.
- **Physical access attacks**: SEV-SNP can defend against offline DRAM attacks (e.g., cold boot). However, SEV-SNP does not consider online DRAM integrity attacks, such as directly manipulating the DDR bus while the VM is running.
- **Other**: SEV-SNP can partially defend against interrupt/exception injection attacks, partially defend against indirect branch predictor poisoning attacks, and partially defend against debug attacks (e.g., modifying breakpoints during debugging). SEV-SNP cannot fully prevent side-channel attacks.

The industry has also researched AMD SEV security. For example, Du et al. (2017) in "Secure encrypted virtualization is unsecure" proposed potential attacks exploiting SEV's lack of integrity checking. Morbitzer et al. [126] in "SEVered: subverting AMD's virtual machine encryption" proposed SEVered, an attack using a malicious VMM to obtain TEE contents. Buhren et al. [127] in "Insecure until proven updated: analyzing AMD SEV's remote attestation" discussed SEV remote attestation issues due to CPU key leakage; in 2021 [128] they proposed using glitches for fault injection to make the ASP execute malicious code and decrypt VM memory. Li et al. [129] in "Exploiting unprotected I/O operations in AMD's secure encrypted virtualization" showed attacks using unprotected I/O against SEV; in 2021, they demonstrated TLB poisoning attacks [130], CrossLine attacks [131], and side-channel attacks on SEV-SNP called CipherLeaks [132,133].

Google's Cohen et al. published an audit report in 2022: [134].

For side-channel attacks, AMD has also published mitigation guidelines: [135].

The AMD SEV family includes SEV-TIO, supporting trusted confidential devices. We describe this in Part 3.

3.3.4 ARM RME threat model

ARMv8 and earlier systems supporting ARM TrustZone could create a secure world isolated from the normal world to act as a TEE. However, this secure world could only be created statically, limiting TEE scalability. More controversially, the secure world's privilege level was considered too high, exceeding what a typical TEE needs, and thus it is not considered a general-purpose solution for confidential computing.

ARMv9 introduced the VM-based Confidential Compute Architecture (CCA), a major new feature. ARM CCA adds the concept of a realm world. The system uses the Realm Management Extension (RME) to create Realm VMs within the realm world. Each Realm VM is a confidential computing TEE. The TSM role is fulfilled by the Realm Management Monitor (RMM), which manages Realm VMs. A monitor at Exception Level 3 (EL3) handles switching between the three different worlds (normal, secure, realm). The architecture of ARM CCA is shown in Fig. 3.14.

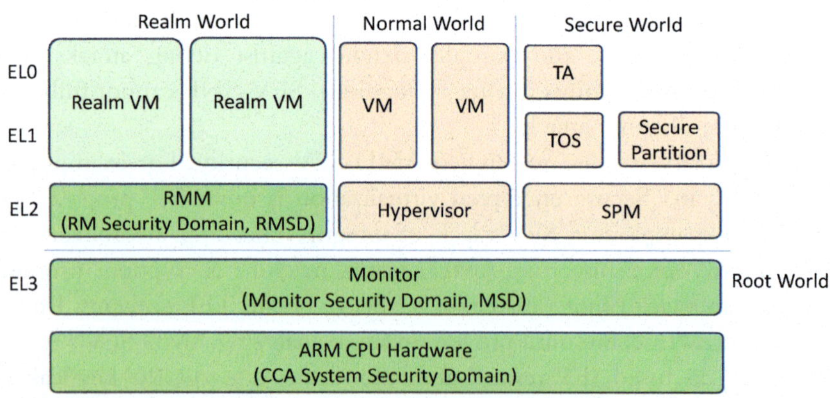

Figure 3.14 ARM CCA architecture.

ARM DEN-0129 "Arm Realm Management Extension (RME) System Architecture" describes RME security features. ARM DEN-0096 "ARM CCA Security Model" details the ARM CCA security model. Because the EL3 monitor responsible for switching between worlds still runs in ARM systems, the composition and security design of CCA are more complex.

The CCA security domains are:

- **CCA system security domain (CCA SSD)**: Trusted hardware and firmware, part of the system TCB, trusted by other domains (MSD and RMSD).
- **Monitor security domain (MSD)**: Includes all firmware running in the root world, responsible for secure switching between different worlds. It ensures that other worlds (secure, normal) cannot affect the realm world. The MSD is part of the realm world's TCB and is trusted by the RMSD.
- **Realm management security domain (RMSD)**: Includes all firmware running in the realm world, responsible for isolating and protecting each Realm VM. The RMSD is part of each Realm VM's TCB, acting as the TSM, and is trusted by the Realm VMs.

Since the ARM CCA architecture retains the "secure world" concept, the security of the secure world remains unchanged, meaning the realm world cannot affect the secure world. This is guaranteed by the CCA system security domain and the MSD.

ARM CCA considers the following memory-related threat models. Additionally, CCA lists minimum security requirements as a baseline for implementing confidential computing.

- **Direct memory access**: Unauthorized software entities directly accessing realm data. The ARM CCA isolation mechanisms can defend against this.
- **Probing**: Attackers using physical methods to directly access realm data in memory. The ARM CCA memory encryption mechanisms can defend against this.
- **Replay**: Attackers using physical methods to replay previously captured old memory contents. The ARM CCA baseline does not provide replay attack protection. If a system employs memory integrity protection with temporal freshness, it can defend against replay attacks, but this impacts system performance and increases memory overhead.
- **Leakage**: Attackers obtaining realm contents through misconfiguration of the CCA platform. The ARM CCA baseline primarily prevents

leakage across world boundaries, but **it does not prevent leakage across realm boundaries.** If the system employs realm-specific independent key encryption, it can prevent leakage across realm boundaries, but this may impact cache performance.

- **Software-based side-channel attacks**: e.g., timing side-channel attacks, row hammer attacks. The ARM CCA baseline does not include software side-channel protection.

Secure memory management for an ARM CCA Realm involves multiple components, as shown in Fig. 3.15. First, within a realm, Stage 1 page tables can be set up for virtual address (VA) to intermediate physical address (IPA) mapping. Second, the VMM requests IPA to physical address (PA) mapping from the RMM. The RMM establishes Stage 2 page tables, also called realm translation tables (RTTs), describing the realm's address space information. A realm's IPA space can be divided into protected and unprotected parts, corresponding to confidential memory and shared memory, respectively. Finally, the root world monitor sets up granule protection tables (GPTs) based on the physical address space (PAS). PA access to system physical memory is only allowed after passing GPT checks. Each world has its own PAS, e.g., root PAS, realm PAS, secure PAS, and nonsecure PAS. The GPT describes access control policies for different worlds to different PASs. For example, the realm world and root world can access the realm PAS, but other worlds cannot access the realm PAS.

The ARM CCA RME architecture introduces the Memory Encryption Context (MEC) extension. Without MEC, there is only one encryption key derived based on the PAS in each world. Although the realm world, secure world, and root world use different encryption keys, every realm uses the same encryption key, and isolation between realms is handled by the RMM. When MEC exists, a realm world can have multiple encryption keys derived based on the MEC identifier (MECID). This allows the RMM and each realm to have their own encryption keys, satisfying the requirements of defense in depth.

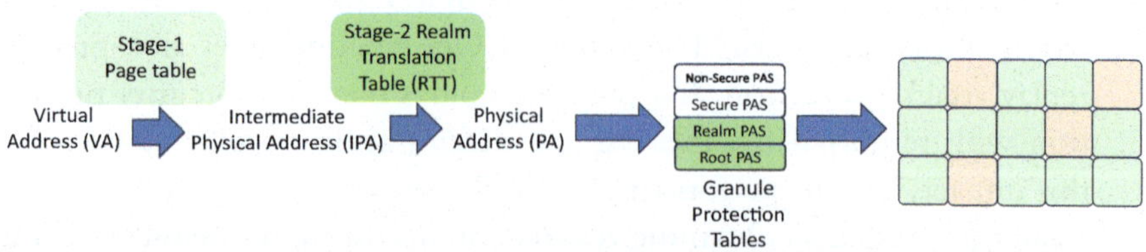

Figure 3.15 ARM CCA realm secure memory management.

The ARM Security Center has published a series of white papers including "Speculative processor vulnerability latest updates" to help ARM developers understand and mitigate side-channel attacks such as Spectre/Meltdown and their variants.

The ARM CCA RME architecture includes RME device assignment (RME-DA) to support trusted confidential devices. We describe this in Part 3.

3.3.5 RISC-V CoVE threat model

The RISC-V AP-TEE task group drafted a specification in 2023 for a confidential VM solution based on the RISC-V architecture, called CoVE. RISC-V's CoVE scheme is similar to ARM CCA RME, with the difference that RISC-V does not have a concept of a "secure world." Confidential VM Extension (CoVE) refers to the confidential computing TEE as a TEE VM (TVM) or domain. It directly calls the module that protects and isolates TVMs the TSM or domain security manager (DoSM). A monitor in machine mode (M-mode), also called the root security manager (RSM), is responsible for switching between the TEE world and the non-TEE world. The architecture of RISC-V CoVE is shown in Fig. 3.16.

The CoVE specification and security model, "RISC-V Platform Security Model," very clearly defines the threat model and security requirements. Security requirements are divided into mandatory requirements and implementation-dependent requirements. Below is a brief summary of the mandatory requirements.

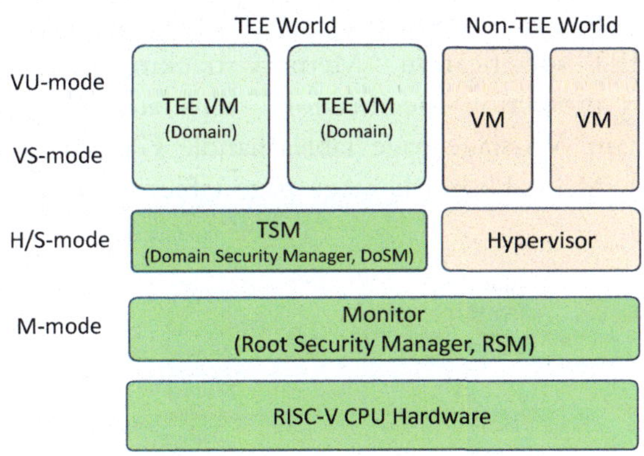

Figure 3.16 RISC-V CoVE architecture.

- **CPU state protection**: Prevents untrusted code from accessing or modifying CPU state.
- **Memory confidentiality**: Memory access must be isolated, and memory should be encrypted. However, **CoVE does not mandate TVM-specific independent key encryption.**
- **Memory integrity**: Must defend against software-based attacks, including code execution. However, **CoVE does not mandate defense against hardware-based attacks, including row hammer.**
- **I/O protection**: Untrusted devices cannot access the TEE.
- **Secure interrupt request (IRQ)**: Must prevent IRQ injection that violates interrupt priority or masking.
- **Secure timestamp**: Must ensure a consistent timestamp source for the TEE.
- **Performance analysis**: Must both ensure the TEE obtains correct performance monitoring unit (PMU) information and prevent confidential information leakage via the PMU.
- **Debug**: Debug ports must be disabled in production devices.
- **Availability**: Must prevent TVMs from launching DoS attacks against the system. However, DoS attacks by the VMM against TVMs are out of scope.
- **Side channels**: CoVE mandates providing protected address mappings and microarchitectural side-channel protection, such as for branch prediction, to defend against attacks like Spectre/Meltdown. It must also provide mechanisms to prevent single-step/zero-step attacks and interrupt/exception injection. However, **CoVE does not mandate defense against CPU architecture cache side channels and timing side channels.**

CoVE confidential computing memory security management is defined by the SmMPT specification "Memory tracking table for supervisor domain access protection specification," illustrated in Fig. 3.17. First, within a domain, VS-stage page tables handle GVA to GPA mappings. Second, the TSM establishes G-stage page tables responsible for GPA to

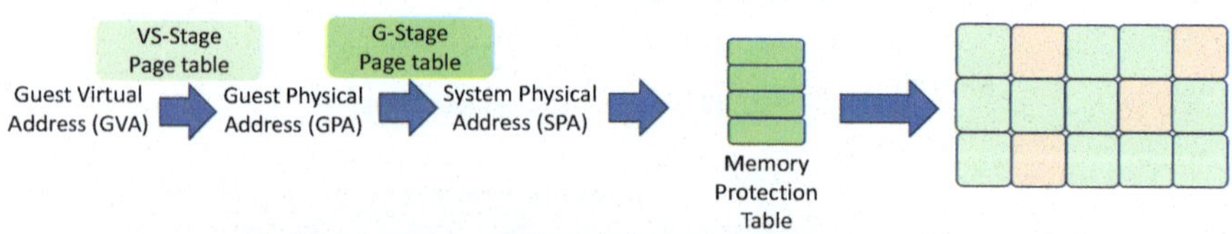

Figure 3.17 RISC-V CoVE memory security management.

system physical address (SPA) mapping. Finally, a key functional component in CoVE is the memory protection table (MPT). Each RISC-V hardware thread (HART) has an MPT checker extension, working alongside the existing page-table-based memory management unit (MMU) and physical memory protection (PMP) mechanisms. Machine mode software uses the MPT (or the memory tracking table—MTT) to create an isolated environment, including CPU state and memory isolation. Another role of the MPT is to specify physical memory attributes. The TSM can designate memory as confidential (C) or nonconfidential (NC).

Another important functional module in CoVE is the Supervisor Domain Physical Address Metadata Selector (Svpams). When MPT access is allowed, privileged mode software uses Svpams to more precisely control memory access policies. Additionally, metadata specified by Svpams can be used together with other identifiers like supervisor domain ID (SDID), virtual machine ID (VMID), and address space ID (ASID) to specify a cryptographic context, thereby providing memory protection functions.

The RISC-V microarchitectural side-channels (uarch-side-channels) task group has drafted the "Transient Execution: Implementer's Security Guide" to help RISC-V developers understand and mitigate software side-channel attacks.

The RISC-V CoVE family also includes CoVE-IO to support trusted confidential devices. We describe this in Part 3.

CHAPTER 4

Trusted execution environment (TEE) lifecycle

In Chapter 3, we introduced the security model of a TEE. A TEE system consists of components such as the TEE-TCB, multiple independent TEEs, and an untrusted system resource manager. In this chapter, we first introduce the memory layout of a TEE, then discuss the lifecycle of a TEE, including its launch and teardown. Finally, we present several examples.

4.1 TEE memory layout

Fig. 4.1 shows a generic memory layout for a confidential computing TEE system. In the figure, the dark green sections represent TEE-TCB memory, the light green sections represent TEE private memory, and the dark red box sections represent system privileged memory.

From a confidential computing perspective, the access control for these four types of memory is as follows:

- TEE-TCB memory: This is the memory where the TEE-TCB resides. Other modules cannot access it; only the TEE-TCB itself can access it. If the system has multiple TEE-TCB components, this memory can be further subdivided. For example, if the root of trust (RoT) within the Trusted Computing Base (TCB) provides private key signing services or Message Authentication Code (MAC) services for other TCB mod ules, then for security, other TCB modules should not be able to tamper with the code in the RoT or directly access its private keys or MAC keys.
- TEE private memory: This is the memory dedicated to each individual TEE. Other TEEs or non-TEE modules, including the resource manager, cannot access it. TEE private memory typically includes the TEE's code and private data. The initial content of TEE private memory is usually loaded by the resource manager, while the TEE-TCB performs

Confidential Computing
ISBN 978-0-443-54067-7
https://doi.org/10.1016/B978-0-443-54067-7.00018-8

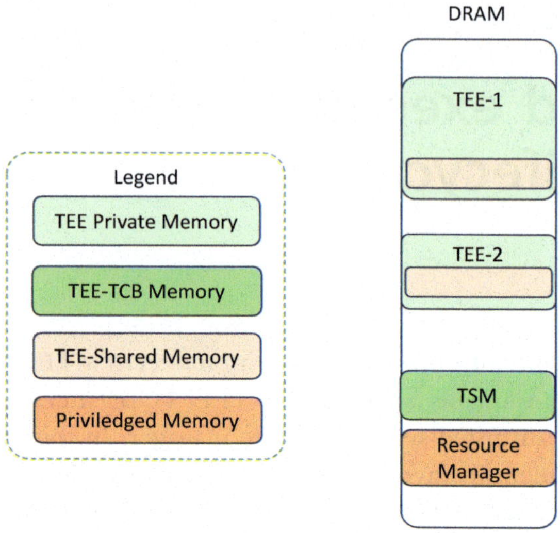

Figure 4.1 Generic memory layout of a confidential computing TEE system.

measurements on it, recording them in dedicated TEE measurement registers. These measurements are used for TEE remote attestation.

- TEE shared memory: This is memory shared between the TEE and other modules, such as other TEEs, non-TEE modules, or the resource manager. Shared memory is typically used to exchange information with the outside world. It is important to note that the content of shared memory is untrusted and must be verified before use. A common TEE practice is to copy data from TEE shared memory into private memory for verification before using it.
- System privileged memory: This is the memory where the resource manager resides. For confidential computing, this part is also considered untrusted. However, for the overall system, the TEE and other ordinary nonprivileged applications could potentially disrupt the operational state of the system privileged level. Therefore, the resource manager needs to designate privileged memory and ensure it is protected from tampering by TEEs, thereby maintaining system availability. Although TEE users trust the TEE, from the perspective of system privileged software, the system privileged software does not trust the TEE.

The above model represents only a generic memory layout. Different TEE hardware implementations may have more memory types to support finer-grained access control. For example, the monitor module in ARM's monitor mode or RISC-V's machine mode belongs to the platform/system-level TCB and has higher privileges than the TEE Security Manager (TSM). Although both the monitor and the TSM are part of the TEE-TCB, the monitor can access the TSM, while the TSM cannot access the monitor.

The two types, TEE private memory and TEE shared memory, can be switched between by setting the TEE memory attributes from within the TEE code. The following security factors need to be considered during switching: (1) Before switching from TEE private memory to TEE shared memory, confidential data in the private memory must be cleared to prevent leakage to non-TEE modules. (2) Before switching from TEE shared memory to TEE private memory, the shared memory must be zeroed to prevent data injection caused by erroneous reads by the TEE.

When creating a TEE, the system's resource manager needs to set up the TEE's initial private memory to allow the TEE to start running. Subsequently, the TEE's private memory can also be dynamically added by the resource manager. Dynamically added TEE private memory has two states:

- Unaccepted memory (TEE): Unusable memory. This is TEE private memory that has been added by the resource manager and notified to the TEE, but the TEE has not yet decided to use it. The TEE cannot directly access this region; any read, write, or execute attempt will trigger an exception.
- Accepted memory (TEE): Usable memory. The TEE needs to explicitly notify the TSM that it intends to use this newly added memory. This action is called acceptance. The TSM will zero and lock this memory, assigning it to the TEE, transitioning it to accepted memory. After this, the TEE can access this private memory (Fig. 4.2).

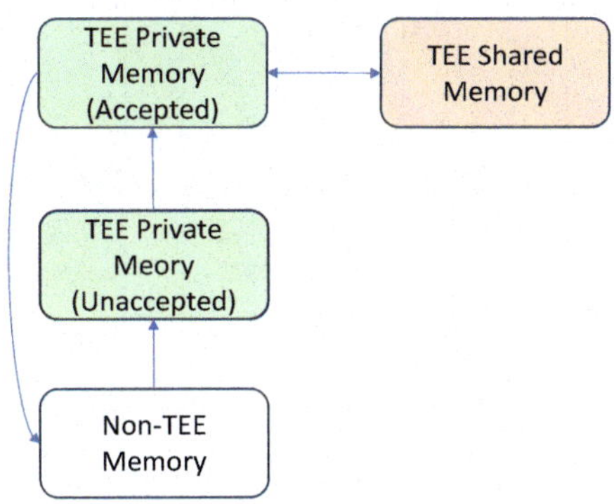

Figure 4.2 TEE memory states and transitions.

4.2 TEE launch and teardown

Fig. 4.3 illustrates a generic launch and loading process for TEE-based confidential computing. In the figure, solid arrows represent data loading, dashed arrows represent code calls, and dotted dashed arrows represent extending data into measurement registers (MRs) using the common cryptographically secure extend algorithm found in trusted computing. The MR extend algorithm is similar to TPM2's TPM2_PCR_Extend(). The pseudocode is as follows:

```
extend_mr(mr_index, data) // Extend data into measurement register
{
    data_hash = hash(data); // hash() is a cryptographic hash function
    mr_hash = read_mr(mr_index); // Read current MR value from register
    new_mr_hash = hash(mr_hash || data_hash); // "||" denotes concatenation
    write_mr(mr_index, new_mr_hash); // Write new MR value back to register
    // write_mr() is never exposed externally
}
```

***Note** that MRs can be freely read (Read). From a security perspective, direct write (Write) to MRs is prohibited. Modifications to MRs can only be done via the*

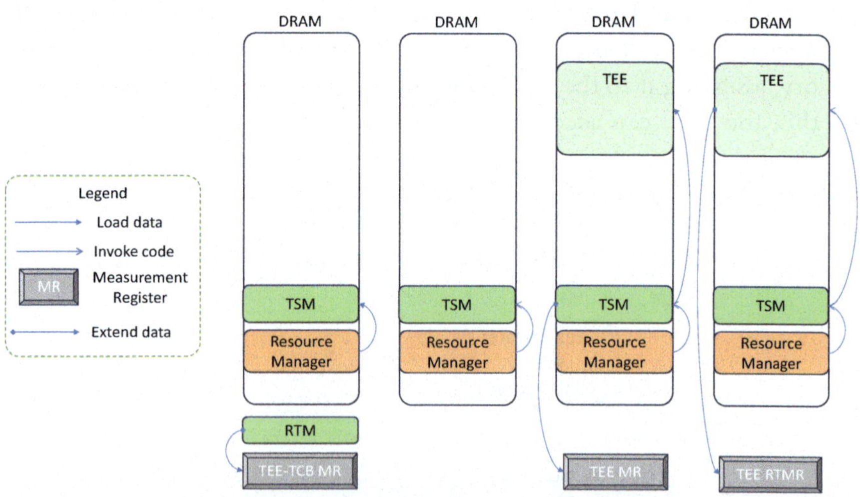

Figure 4.3 Launch and loading of a confidential computing TEE system.

extend operation. This ensures that all previous extend actions are reflected in the measurement value through the hash algorithm. Because there is no direct write operation, any component can only add new measurement values but cannot modify existing ones. In other words, an attacker can add new measurement values, potentially making the system untrusted—this is a typical denial-of-service attack, which is generally out of scope. However, an attacker cannot modify existing measurement values to make an untrusted system appear trusted, which is guaranteed by the properties of the hash algorithm.

Typically, the TEE system launch steps are as follows:

1. The system's resource manager loads the TSM into protected TEE-TCB memory. To ensure integrity, the central processing unit (CPU) system on chip (SoC)'s root of trust for detection (RTD) needs to verify the TSM, for example, by checking a digital signature, to ensure the TSM's source is trustworthy. Simultaneously, to support remote attestation, the CPU SoC's root of trust for measurement (RTM) extends the TSM's information into the TEE-TCB measurement registers (part of the root of trust for storage—RTS). This step can have variations. For example, the TSM might be a firmware module that doesn't require software loading. The TSM software could also be loaded by other modules like system firmware. The TSM needs to provide two types of interfaces: one for the Virtual Machine Manager (VMM), the TEE management interface (TMI), for managing TEEs; and another for the TEEs, the TEE service interface (TSI). The TSM and its interfaces are shown in Fig. 4.4.
2. The resource manager calls initialization functions in the TSM TMI to help the TSM complete its initialization. Typically, before calling, the resource manager needs to allocate system resources for the TSM and report the allocation information to the TSM.
3. The resource manager calls load functions in the TSM TMI to have the TSM load the target TEE into TEE private memory. Besides the TEE's code and data, this process also involves establishing the TEE's metadata

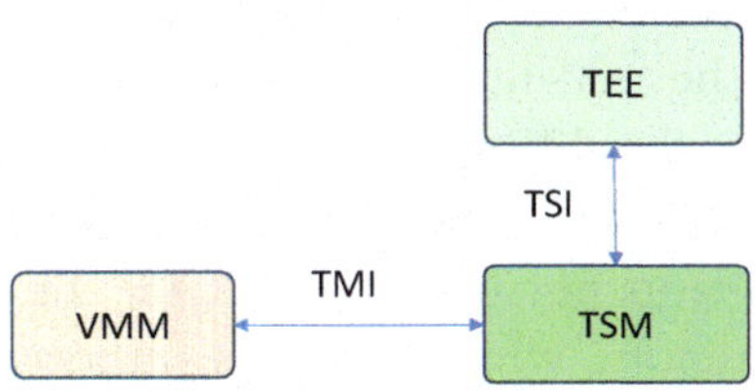

Figure 4.4 TSM and its provided interfaces.

in private memory, used to record various necessary information about the TEE, such as physical address space, TEE secure level 1 page tables, TEE register state, etc. If the TEE supports authenticated launch, the TSM needs to verify the TEE's source, typically using digital signature verification. Again, to support remote attestation, the TSM, acting as the RTM for the TEE, needs to extend the loaded TEE information into the TEE's measurement registers. We strictly distinguish between TEE-TCB MRs and TEE MRs, because the TEE-TCB serves the entire system, while there can be many TEEs, each with its own TEE MRs.

4. The resource manager calls TEE functions within the TSM, causing the TSM to invoke the TEE's entry function and launch the target TEE. The TEE can then load additional data or code. Similarly, the TEE, acting as its own chain of trust for measurement (CTM), can further call the TSM's TSI runtime extend functions to extend new TEE data or code into the TEE's runtime measurement registers (RTMRs). RTMRs complement the initial MRs by recording data input to the TEE during runtime. The TEE's MRs and RTMRs collectively represent the TEE's identity information. Additionally, the TEE can call the TSM's TSI to generate a TEE attestation report. Subsequently, the resource manager can add more memory to the TEE, and the TEE needs to accept this memory. The TEE can also switch between private and shared memory, using shared memory to communicate with the outside world.

Note *that MR here is a generic abstract concept. An actual TEE-TCB may not necessarily have such a register or a set of registers, but the TEE-TCB needs a mechanism to store various information about the TEE-TCB and TEEs. This mechanism can be designed by each TEE hardware designer. We describe this in more detail in Chapter 5.*

Trusted boot and secure boot are two fundamental modes for system startup. Fig. 4.5 illustrates the difference between trusted boot and secure boot in the TEE launch process.

The steps for trusted boot are as follows (see Fig. 4.5b):

1. Steps (1)–(6): In the odd-numbered steps, each module measures the next module into the MRs, establishing the chain of trust. In the even-numbered steps, the module loads and executes the next module.
2. Step (7): After all launches are complete, the TEE owner can obtain a TEE attestation report, which includes information from the TEE-

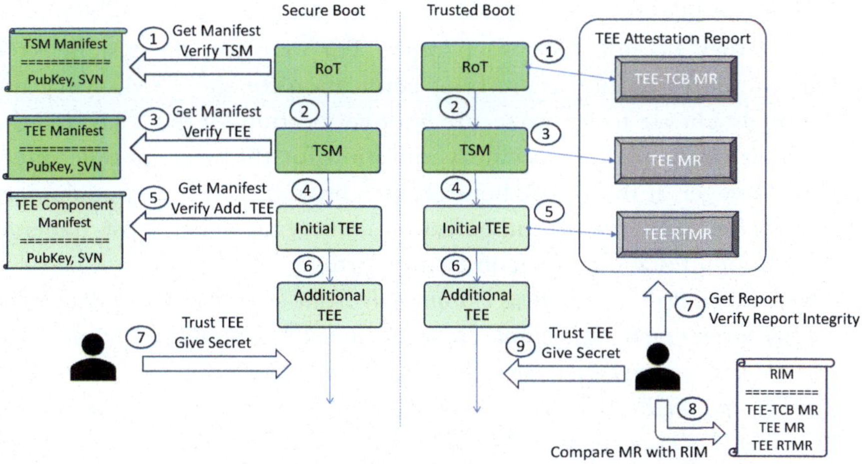

Figure 4.5 Comparison of trusted boot and secure boot.

TCB MRs, TEE MRs, and TEE RTMRs. The TEE owner needs to verify the integrity of the report, e.g., via digital signature or MAC.

3. Step (8): The TEE owner compares the MRs in the report with a known reference integrity manifest (RIM).
4. Step (9): If the conditions are satisfied, the TEE owner can trust the launched TEE and transmit confidential information to the TEE over a secure channel, such as Transport Layer Security (TLS) over the network or the platform's security protocol and data model (SPDM) protocol.

Steps (7)–(9) here are a very simple example; we will discuss them in more detail in the "General model of the attestation process" section in Chapter 5 [covering steps similar to (7)–(9)]).

The steps for secure boot are as follows (see Fig. 4.5a):

1. Steps (1)–(6): In the odd-numbered steps, each module verifies whether the next module meets predefined requirements. In the even-numbered steps, it loads and executes the next module. The relevant requirements can be written into a boot manifest file and deployed to the system. For example, this could include the public key file for digital signatures, module security version number (SVN), etc.
2. Step (7): Because the boot manifest enforces mandatory requirements, a TEE that does not meet the conditions will definitely not be launched. If a TEE is launched, it must meet the conditions, allowing the user to transmit confidential information directly to the launched TEE.

Each module in secure boot can have its own independent boot manifest; they do not affect each other. For example, the system RoT might choose to enable secure boot verification for the TSM, while the TSM might choose to ignore secure boot verification for the TEE, and the TEE itself might perform secure verification for the next module internally. However, if the secure boot chain is broken (i.e., one module does not perform secure boot authentication), the final TEE must undergo trusted boot attestation to become trustworthy.

Note*: Consider the limitations of using only secure boot. Everything depends on the TEE owner's prior deployment. However, in practice, it is difficult for the TEE owner to deploy everything, especially the various modules of the TEE-TCB. Generally, the TEE-TCB needs to be deployed by its owner, who informs the TEE owner. For example, the CPU SoC vendor informs the TEE owner about the latest SVN. The question then returns: How can the TEE owner be sure that the current environment's TEE-TCB has the latest SVN? Evidently, even with secure boot, we still need trusted boot to provide system information.*

As discussed in Chapter 2, in confidential computing, trusted boot is essential. It provides remote attestation to the TEE owner, allowing them to believe that the launched TEE environment has not been tampered with. Secure boot (also called authenticated launch) is optional, depending on the TEE's functionality. Often, secure boot and trusted boot are used in combination. Fig. 4.6 shows a scenario where both secure boot and trusted boot are enabled.

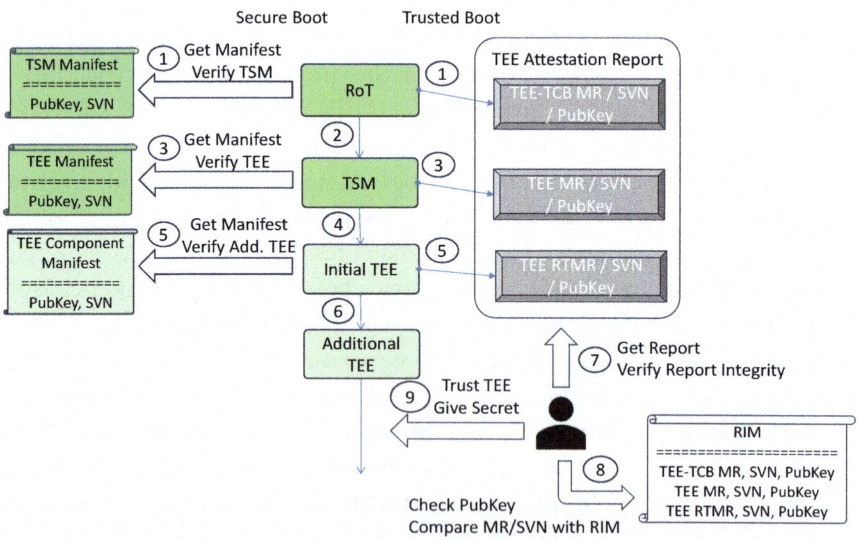

Figure 4.6 Enabling both secure boot and trusted boot.

1. Steps (1)–(6): Each module verifies that the next module meets predefined requirements, measures information about the next module (including the verification key and SVN, etc.) into the MRs to establish the chain of trust, and then loads and executes the next module. Here, measuring the public key and SVN has the advantage that the verifier does not need to rely on potentially frequently changing specific measurement values of each module. They only need to know the module's origin based on the public key and determine its security level based on the SVN value, greatly simplifying the verification process.
2. Step (7): After all launches are complete, the TEE owner can obtain a TEE attestation report. The report includes information from TEE-TCB MRs, TEE MRs, TEE RTMRs, the secure boot manifest, and the actual public keys and SVNs of the running modules. The TEE owner needs to verify the integrity of the report, e.g., via digital signature or MAC.
3. Step (8): The TEE owner compares the MRs, public keys, SVNs, etc., in the report with a known RIM. According to policy, MRs and public keys may need to match exactly, while for SVN, a "greater than or equal to" policy can be used (i.e., the SVN in the report must be $\geq$ the reference SVN).
4. Step (9): If the conditions are satisfied, the TEE owner can trust the launched TEE and transmit confidential information to the TEE over a secure channel, such as TLS or the platform's SPDM protocol.

Note: *Let's discuss the order of the three actions in steps (1)–(6): verification, measurement, and execution. First,* ***verification must occur before execution****. Secure boot acts like a security guard verifying identity; only after verifying identity can entry be allowed, otherwise a malicious actor entering poses a security risk. Second,* ***measurement must occur before execution****. Trusted boot acts like a security guard registering identity; only those with registered identity can enter, otherwise a malicious actor could freely forge registration records, a term known as forge measurement. Based on our earlier discussion about the properties of measurement registers, an attacker can only create new measurement values, not modify existing ones.*

Finally, regarding the ***order of verification and measurement****, the safest method is a three-step process: first measure the request for action, then verify the information, and finally measure the result of the action. Using the security guard analogy, the strictest approach is to first register "person with identity X requests entry at time T," then perform identity verification, and finally record "person with identity X is about to enter the system." The advantage is that once the action* *request is measured, it is recorded and cannot be erased, facilitating subsequent auditing. Otherwise, if problems occur during the information verification phase (e. g., a buffer overflow in the verification code allows an attacker to gain highest system privileges), the attacker could forge registration records. However, from another perspective, verifying information first is not absolutely insecure. From the TEE owner's perspective, they must trust an unbroken chain of trust. That is, for the TEE owner to trust the final TEE, they must trust* ***every previous module****. If one module has a known vulnerability, the chain of trust from that module onward is broken, and subsequent results become untrustworthy. The difference between measuring and not measuring the action request lies in whether auditors can identify the attacker if only the verification module is vulnerable, while the measurement module is not. However, if both verification and measurement modules are vulnerable, measuring makes no difference. Using the guard analogy, if we know one security guard has been compromised by a malicious actor, all their records are untrustworthy. If there are two guards, one responsible for recording and one for verifying, even if the verifier is compromised, we can still use the records to see who was let in.*

Some isolated TEEs do not support dynamic teardown; once launched, they persist until system shutdown or reboot. Secure enclaves and confidential VMs can support multiple modules running concurrently, with dynamic launch and dynamic teardown.

TEE teardown is relatively simple. When a TEE completes its task, it can voluntarily exit. According to the security model, the resource manager can also choose to tear down a TEE at any time, especially if it detects an anomaly or a hung state. When tearing down a TEE, the resource manager needs to notify the TSM to clean up the TEE's context and release resources. This allows the TSM to better launch other TEEs. Tearing down a TEE results in the loss of TEE MR-related content, but as long as the TSM exists, TEE-TCB MR-related content persists.

4.3 Confidential computing TEE example lifecycles

Now let's look at the lifecycles of several typical TEE examples.

4.3.1 Intel SGX lifecycle

Intel SGX is Intel's earliest confidential computing technology, aiming to protect individual applications using a very small runtime environment, immune to the OS, VMM, and other modules. This runtime environment is the secure enclave, simply called enclave. The creation and protection of an enclave rely only on the CPU SoC and its corresponding microcode, with no other special software TCB. The OS acts as the resource manager responsible for loading and running enclaves. (The documents "Overview of Intel SGX part 1 SGX internals" and "Overview of Intel SGX part 2 SGX internals" by Quarkslab, which discuss the internal logic and external calls of SGX, are worth referencing.)

The enclave launch process is shown in Fig. 4.7.

1. The application requiring the enclave provides the code, data, and execution environment information to the OS's SGX driver. The SGX driver then calls the ECREATE instruction to create the initial environment for the enclave instance, the SGX enclave control structure (SECS).
2. The SGX driver loads the enclave program's code pages, data pages, and thread control structures (TCSs) into enclave memory. The EADD instruction is responsible for loading and measures the loaded address, updating it into MRENCLAVE. The EEXTEND instruction is responsible for measuring the loaded content and updating it into MRENCLAVE. Finally, the EINIT instruction ends the loading phase and computes the final MRENCLAVE value, which becomes part of the enclave's identity.
3. The application requiring the enclave uses the EENTER instruction to enter enclave mode and perform a series of initialization operations.
4. SGX2 supports adding additional pages to the enclave using the EAUG instruction.

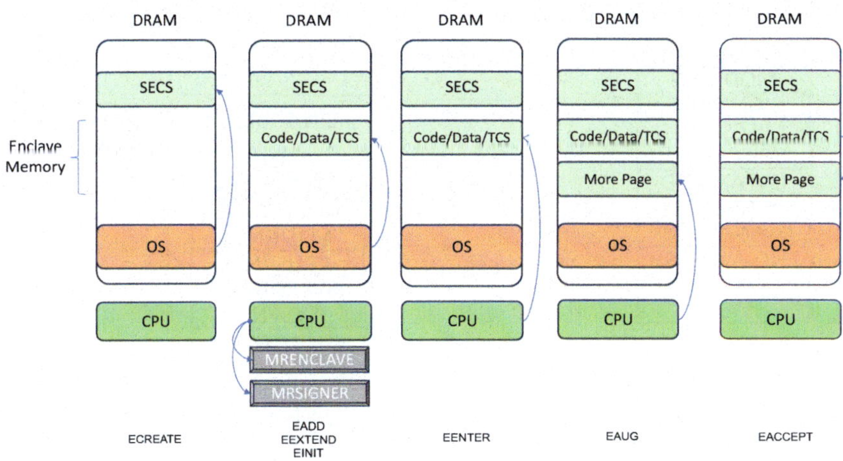

Figure 4.7 Enclave launch process.

5. Inside the enclave, the EACCEPT instruction must be used to accept the added page before the enclave can use it normally.

EINIT also has the task of performing launch-time authentication. Fig. 4.8 shows the data structures related to SGX authenticated launch.

- Enclave signature structure (SIGSTRUCT): Each enclave must have a SIGSTRUCT signed by the developer. It contains the enclave signer's public key (MODULUS), SVN, enclave attributes, the expected enclave measurement value (MRENCLAVE), and its own digital signature. After the enclave successfully launches, the hash of the signer's public key (MODULUS) is loaded into the MRSIGNER register, becoming part of the enclave's identity along with other information. This is used in the enclave REPORT for remote attestation.
- IA32_SGXLEPUBKEYHASH model specific register (MSR): Records the hash of the public key of the enclave signer permitted to launch.
- EINIT token: A parameter when calling EINIT. If a launch enclave (LE) possesses the EINITTOKEN key, it can generate an EINIT token to control the launch of other enclaves. The EINIT token contains a valid bit, expected enclave attributes, expected MRENCLAVE, expected MRSIGNER, and its own message authentication code (MAC).

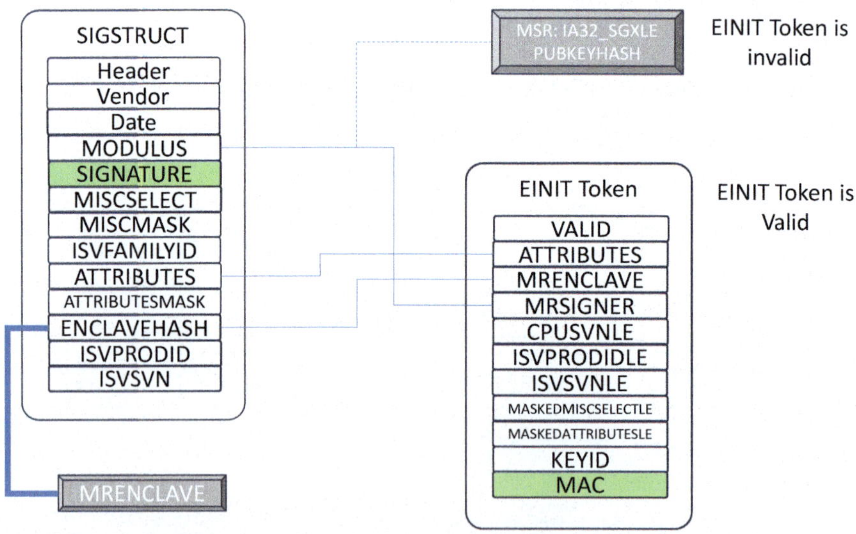

Figure 4.8 Data structures for SGX authenticated launch.

During launch, EINIT performs the following checks sequentially. Only if all checks pass does EINIT return successfully.

1. Verify the digital signature in the enclave signature structure is correct.
2. Verify that the enclave measurement value in the enclave signature structure matches the calculated actual MRENCLAVE.
3. If the EINIT token is invalid, verify that the hash of the public key in the enclave signature structure matches the IA32_SGXLEPUBKEY-HASH MSR.
4. If the EINIT token is valid, verify the EINIT token MAC value is correct.
5. Verify that the enclave attributes, enclave measurement value, and enclave signer's public key hash in the enclave signature structure match the expected enclave attributes, expected MRENCLAVE, and expected MRSIGNER in the EINIT token.

In the first generation of SGX, the IA32_SGXLEPUBKEYHASH MSR was read-only, and only one Intel-signed LE could be launched by hardware; other enclaves had to be launched by this LE. In later SGX generations, this MSR became writable in flexible launch control (FLC) mode. This means the module launching enclaves in the OS can write the hash of the desired enclave signer's public key (MRSIGNER) into the IA32_SGXLEPUBKEYHASH MSR to complete deployment. Theoretically, any enclave could be an LE, simplifying the launch process.

4.3.2 Intel TDX lifecycle

The launch process for an Intel TDX confidential computing TEE is similar to the generic launch process. The TEE-TCB for TDX consists of the SoC, the authenticated code module (ACM), and the TDX-Module. The TDX-Module is the TSM for TDX; a TD (trust domain) is the TEE, and its loading is managed by the TDX-Module. The TDX-Module itself is loaded into SEAM memory by a module called the SEAM loader, which is an ACM defined by Intel's trusted execution technology (TXT).

SEAM stands for security arbitration mode, and is a CPU architecture extension Intel made for TDX. Code executed in SEAM mode must reside in SEAM memory, specified by the SEAM range register (SEAMRR). Only ACMs (here, the SEAM loader) and internal SEAM modules (i.e., the TDX-Module) can access SEAM memory. Other modules like the VMM, OS, and even system management mode (SMM) and SGX enclaves cannot access SEAM memory. It is important to note that although only the SEAM loader (specifically NP-SEAMLDR) actually participates in the TDX launch process, all ACMs have extremely high privileges to access SEAM memory. Therefore, all ACMs are included in the TEE-TCB.

The TEE launch process for TDX is detailed in the SEAM loader specification and the TDX-Module specification. The entire process can be divided into two parts. The first part is the launch of the TSM itself, including the SEAM loader and the TDX-Module. This part only needs to be launched once and remains effective. The second part is the TEE launch, i.e., the launch of a TD. The system can create multiple TDs, and the launch process for each TD is similar. We focus on security-related content.

The TSM startup process is shown in Fig. 4.9.

1. VMM loads the nonpersistent SEAM loader (NP-SEAMLDR): This NP-SEAMLDR is a standard ACM, signed with Intel's private key. The VMM needs to copy the NP-SEAMLDR into memory that meets Intel TXT requirements.
2. VMM runs the NP-SEAMLDR: The VMM calls the GETSEC [ENTERACCS] instruction to start the NP-SEAMLDR. Because ACMs have very high system privileges, the CPU microcode verifies

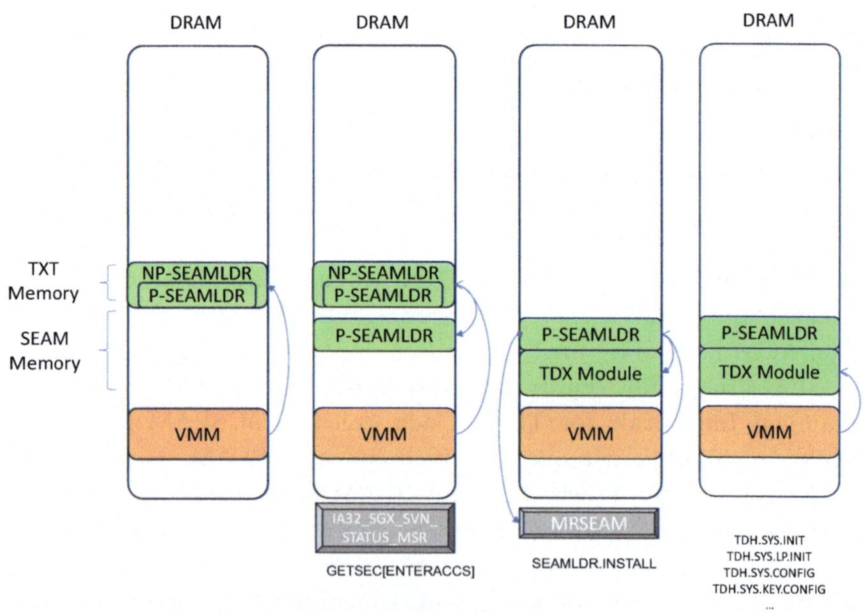

Figure 4.9 TSM launch process.

the digital signature of the NP-SEAMLDR ACM during execution to ensure its source is trustworthy. The function of the NP-SEAMLDR is to load its persistent SEAM loader (P-SEAMLDR) into SEAM memory, supporting subsequent loading of the TDX-Module. The SVN information of the NP-SEAMLDR ACM is reported in bits 63:56 of the IA32_SE_SVN_STATUS MSR. The ACM can be loaded multiple times for updates; the SVN of a newly launched ACM module must be greater than or equal to the existing SVN to prevent rollback attacks.

3. VMM invokes P-SEAMLDR to load the TDX-Module: The VMM can use the P-SEAMLDR-provided interface SEAMCALL [SEAMLDR.INFO] to obtain information about P-SEAMLDR and the TDX-Module. It then uses the SEAMCALL[SEAMLDR.INSTALL] instruction to load the TDX-Module. The TDX-Module comes with a digital signature structure called SEAM_SIGSTRUCT, verified by the CPU microcode to ensure integrity. The TDX-Module can be loaded multiple times for updates. In this case, P-SEAMLDR needs to check the SEAM security version number (SEAMSVN) field in SEAM_SIGSTRUCT, ensuring the new module's SEAMSVN is greater than or equal to the existing SEAMSVN. SEAM_SIGSTRUCT also includes the measurement value of the TDX-Module (MRSEAM). P-SEAMLDR needs to verify its correctness and then save it in TEE_TCB_INFO as part of the TDX-Module's identity information.
4. VMM runs the TDX-Module: Once the TDX-Module is loaded, it provides a series of TD host (TDH) interfaces to the VMM and a series of TD guest (TDG) interfaces to TDs. The VMM can call a series of TDH initialization functions for the TDX-Module, such as TDH.SYS.INIT, TDH.SYS.LP.INIT, TDH.SYS.CONFIG, and TDH.SYS.KEY.CONFIG. Because confidential computing requires memory encryption, the VMM needs to call TDH.SYS.KEY.CONFIG to configure a global ephemeral hardware AES-XTS tweak key. The TDX-Module uses this global key to manage its own data.

The TEE (TD) launch process is shown in Fig. 4.10.

1. VMM calls TDX-Module to create TD metadata structures: This involves interfaces like TDH.MNG.CREAT, TDH.MNG.KEY.CONFIG, TDH.MNG.ADDCX, and TDH.MNG.INIT. Notably, TDH.MNG.KEY.CONFIG configures a TD-unique ephemeral hardware AES-XTS tweak key, used to encrypt memory data associated with this TD.

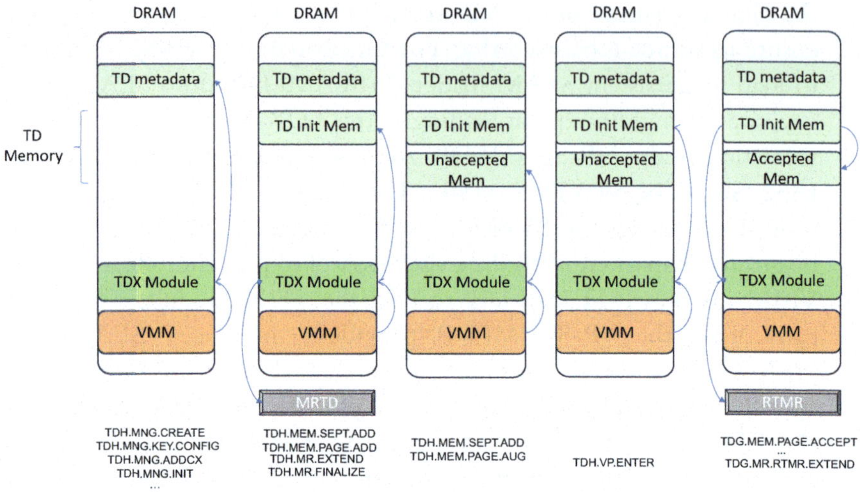

Figure 4.10 TEE (TD) launch process.

2. VMM calls TDX-Module to load initialized TD data and TD executable code: This involves interfaces like TDH.MEM.SEPT.ADD, TDH.MEM.PAGE.ADD, TDH.MR.EXTEND, and TDH.MR.FINALIZE. TDH.MEM.SEPT.ADD creates the secure EPT (S-EPT) for the TD. TDH.MEM.PAGE.ADD copies memory into the TD's private page space and measures the GPA of the TD private page into the TD measurement register (MRTD). TDH.MR.EXTEND measures the content of TD private pages into MRTD. Note that besides the content of TD private pages, the GPA of the pages is also measured into MRTD, thus ensuring the order of page loading. Typically, the initialized TD data are a boot firmware within the TD, which could be 8MiB, 16MiB, etc. After all initial modules are measured, the VMM calls TDH.MR.FINALIZE to generate the final MRTD. MRTD is part of the TD report and serves as the TD's identity at launch.
3. VMM can call TDX-Module to add uninitialized TD pages: This involves interfaces like TDH.MEM.SEPT.ADD and TDH.MEM.PAGE.AUG. The TDX-Module does not measure these pages, significantly saving TD creation time. These memories are called unaccepted memory and cannot be directly accessed by the TD. For example, the entire system memory space (e.g., 4GiB, 64GiB) might be established this way.

4. VMM calls TDX-Module to launch the TD: The VMM uses TDH. VP.ENTER to make the TDX-module schedule the CPU to enter the TD's start address and begin executing the TD's program. The TD's start address is typically provided by the TDX virtual firmware (TDVF). The VMM can input some boot parameters to the TD, informing it about memory size, location, etc.
5. If the TD needs to access unaccepted memory: The TD needs to call TDG.MEM.PAGE.ACCEPT to accept these VMM-added but unmeasured memory pages. The TDX-Module will zero the memory, changing its state to accepted memory, allowing the TD to access it. For security, the TD extends some dynamic information (such as memory information input by the VMM) into RTMRs using TDG.MR. RTMR.EXTEND. RTMRs are also part of the TD report, serving as the TD's runtime identity. Separating RTMRs from MRTD helps verifiers distinguish between the TD's static boot data and its dynamic input data.

Unlike SGX, TDX does not support TEE authenticated launch. Only the ACM and TDX-Module have Intel digital signatures; user TDs do not require digital signatures. Anyone can create their own TD. Precisely because TDX lacks authenticated launch, TDs do not have the concept of SVN; only ACMs and the TDX-Module have SVN.

4.3.3 AMD SEV-SNP lifecycle

For AMD SNP (SEV-SNP), the TEE-TCB includes the AMD SoC and the AMD secure processor (AMD-SP). The biggest difference from TDX is the TSM. TDX's TSM is a software module (TDX-Module), whereas SEV's TSM is hardware (AMD-SP), a separate processor independent of the AMD ×86 SoC. It provides a series of software interfaces known as the SEV-SNP firmware interface. The AMD-SP assists the VMM in managing TEEs, i.e., SNP VMs.

Since the AMD-SP is a hardware module on the motherboard, its launch process is relatively simple. After system power-on, the VMM only needs to call the SNP_INIT or SNP_INIT_EX firmware interface to initialize the SNP-related modules within the AMD-SP. The VMM needs the AMD-SP's assistance to launch an SNP VM. This launch process is illustrated in Fig. 4.11.

1. The VMM allocates memory and uses RMPUPDATE to create various types of memory defined by SEV-SNP, including firmware

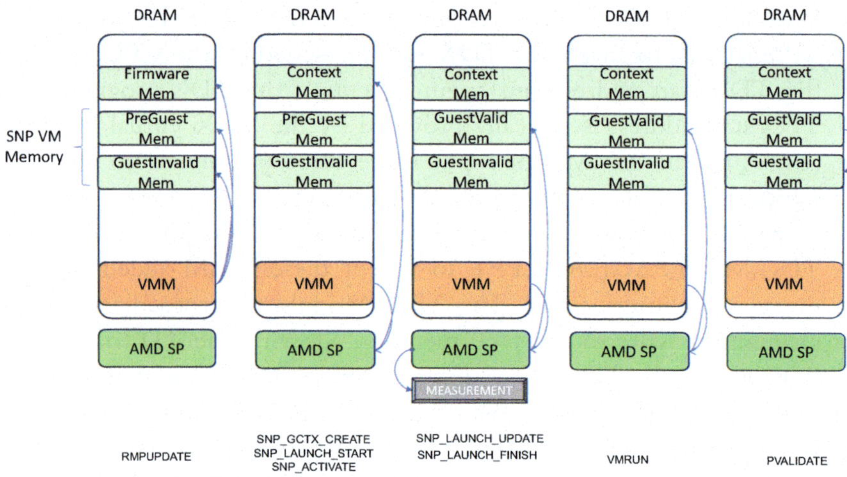

Figure 4.11 SEV-SNP launch: SNP VM loading.

memory, preguest memory, and guest invalid memory. RMP stands for reverse map table, a new mechanism introduced in SEV-SNP to track the owner (VMM, VM, or AMD-SP) of each page. With RMP, the CPU checks ownership before accessing any page, ensuring only the page owner can perform write operations. Here, firmware memory is exclusively for the AMD-SP; preguest memory and guest invalid memory are for SNP VM use.

2. The VMM calls AMD-SP interfaces to create the SNP VM context. For example, SNP_GCTX_CREATE, SNP_LAUNCH_START, and SNP_ACTIVATE. SNP_GCTX_CREATE converts AMD-SP-managed firmware memory into VM context memory, used to record the VM's runtime information. SNP_ACTIVATE binds the VM's ASID (address space identifier), which tells the memory controller which VM encryption key (VEK) to use for encrypting the VM's memory.
3. The VMM calls AMD-SP interfaces to create the SNP VM boot firmware memory and launch the VM, such as SNP_LAUNCH_UPDATE and SNP_LAUNCH_FINISH. SNP_LAUNCH_UPDATE converts the VM's preguest memory into guest valid memory. The content of the guest valid memory is measured into the SNP VM's boot measurement value. SNP_LAUNCH_FINISH generates the final boot measurement value. This boot measurement value will be reflected in the guest attestation report signed by the AMD-SP firmware, serving as

the SNP VM's identity at launch. The SNP VM's boot measurement value is analogous to TDX's MRTD.

4. The VMM uses VMRUN to start the SNP VM. Execution jumps to the SNP VM's start address.
5. During runtime, the SNP VM will encounter guest invalid memory. To use this memory, the SNP VM uses the PVALIDATE instruction to convert guest invalid memory into guest valid memory. This step is similar to TDX's TDG.MEM.PAGE.ACCEPT. SEV-SNP does not provide runtime measurement registers analogous to TDX's RTMRs.

SEV-SNP supports optional authenticated launch. Fig. 4.12 shows the data structures related to SEV-SNP authenticated launch.

- ID block (IDBlock): An optional parameter for SNP_LAUNCH_FINISH. The ID block describes the SNP VM's information, including the launch digest (LD), FAMILY_ID, IMAGE_ID, VERSION, GUEST_SVN, and the Guest POLICY structure. This information becomes part of the guest's identity and is provided in the attestation report for remote attestation.
- ID authentication information: Also an optional parameter for SNP_LAUNCH_FINISH. It provides authentication information related to the ID block, used to verify the ID block's integrity. It contains the signature of the ID block, the ID block signing key (ID_KEY), the signature of the ID_KEY (ID_KEY_SIG), and the authoritative signing key (AUTHOR_KEY) used to sign the ID_KEY.

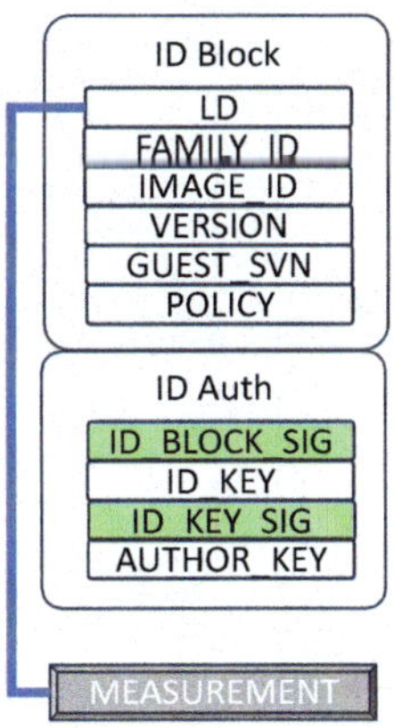

Figure 4.12 Data structures for SEV-SNP authenticated launch.

The digests of the ID_KEY and AUTHOR_KEY also become part of the guest's identity in the attestation report.

SEV-SNP authenticated launch requires the following checks. The launch proceeds only if all checks pass.

1. If an authoritative signing key (AUTHOR_KEY) is present, verify the digital signature of the ID block signing key (ID_KEY).
2. If an ID block is present, verify the digital signature of the ID block using the ID block signing key (ID_KEY).
3. If an ID block is present, verify that the LD in the ID block matches the computed boot measurement value.

4.3.4 ARM RME lifecycle

ARMv9 introduced RME to support ARM CCA. The TEE-TCB in CCA includes the ARM SoC hardware, the monitor running in EL3 root world, and the RMM (realm management monitor) running in realm world EL2. The TSM can be considered the RMM, and the TEE is the realm VM running in the realm world, including the OS at EL1 and applications at EL0.

According to ARM CCA architecture documents DEN0126, DEN0127, and DEN0128, the loading process for a realm VM is illustrated in Fig. 4.13.

1. The host allocates memory and loads the RMM. The RMM provides the realm management interface (RMI) to the host VMM and the realm service interface (RSI) to realms.

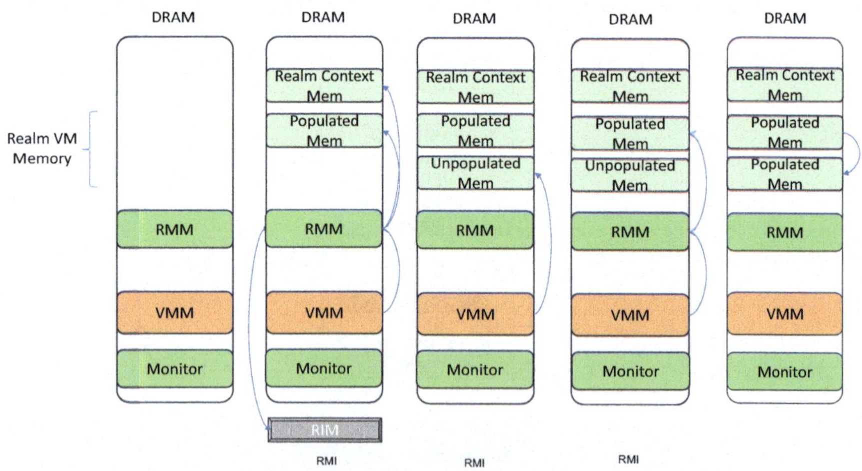

Figure 4.13 ARM CCA launch: Realm VM loading.

2. The host creates a realm instance. The host notifies the RMM via RMI calls, providing realm data, realm address translation tables, realm descriptor, and realm execution contexts. Realm data need to be mapped into the realm's address space. The realm translation tables (RTTs) describe the characteristics of the realm's address space. The realm descriptor (RD) stores the realm's characteristics. The realm execution contexts (RECs) store the VCPU states for the realm. The RMM copies the initialized content into realm PAS memory and maps it into the realm's IPA space. This memory is now populated memory for the realm. The RMM measures the loaded realm memory and register states as initial content into the realm initial measurement (RIM), which is stored as part of the realm descriptor. The realm descriptor serves as proof of the realm's identity at launch, with the RIM analogous to TDX's MRTD or SEV's boot measurement value.
3. The host can add additional unpopulated memory for the realm to use later.
4. The host uses RMI interfaces to start and run the realm.
5. The realm can convert unpopulated memory to populated memory and begin using it.

4.3.5 RISC-V CoVE lifecycle

The RISC-V organization has drafted the CoVE (confidential VM extension) specification, a VM-based confidential computing solution. CoVE categorizes the TEE-TCB into three parts: (1) platform hardware TCB, including the hardware RoT in the CPU SoC, CPU, memory controller subsystem, etc.; (2) platform software TCB, including M-mode firmware and the TSM driver; and (3) TSM (referred to directly as TSM in CoVE), loaded by the TSM driver. The TEE is named TVM (TEE VM).

According to the CoVE specification, the TSM loading process is shown in Fig. 4.14.

1. The CoVE architecture defines RTM, RTS, and RTR for TCB modules. During platform initialization, the RTM needs to measure various modules, such as RoT firmware, SoC subsystem firmware, and all M-mode firmware.
2. The platform loads the TSM driver (part of M-mode firmware). The TSM driver provides ECALL services for the VMM and TSM, facilitating switching between the VMM and TSM. The RTM needs to measure the TSM driver within the M-mode firmware.

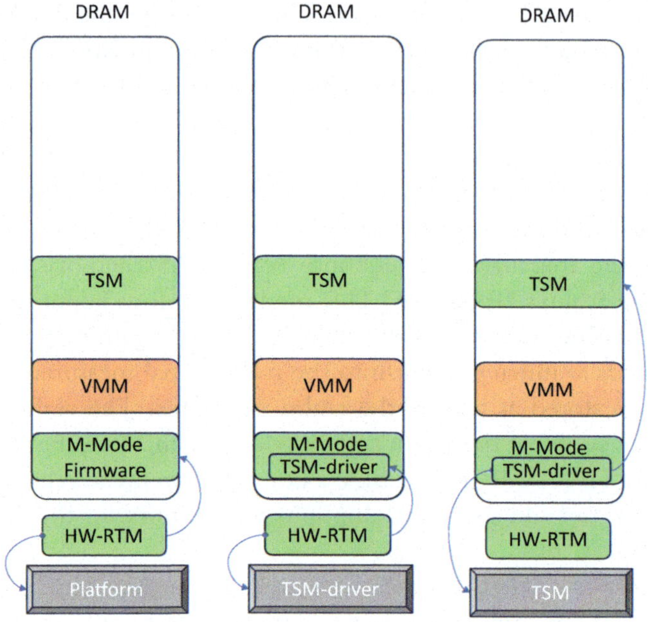

Figure 4.14 RISC-V CoVE launch: TSM loading.

3. The TSM driver is responsible for loading the TSM module. During loading, the TSM driver needs to measure the TSM so that the TSM's identity can be reflected in the attestation report provided by the RTR. The TSM driver may optionally authenticate the TSM, e.g., via digital signature. If the TSM completes authentication, the RTM may also record the TSM's SVN. The TSM provides TEE-host ABI (TH-ABI) to the VMM and TEE-guest ABI (TG-ABI) to TVMs.

The TVM launch process, assisted by the TSM, is shown in Fig. 4.15.

1. The VMM calls the TSM's TH-ABI to create a TVM instance, e.g., sbi_covh_create_tvm. The TSM creates the TVM's context information.
2. The VMM calls the TSM's TH-ABI to add pages to the TVM, such as sbi_covh_add_tvm_page_table_pages, sbi_covh_add_tvm_measured_-pages, and sbi_covh_add_finalize_tvm. Notably, sbi_covh_add_tvm_-measured_pages adds initialized data and measures them into the TVM's initial measurement registers. sbi_covh_add_finalized_tvm finalizes the measurement, producing the TVM's final initial measurement value.

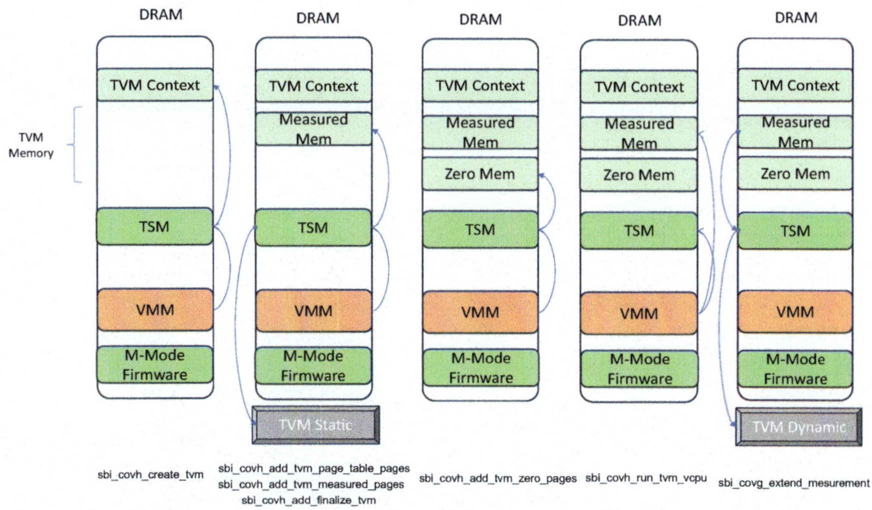

Figure 4.15 RISC-V CoVE launch: TVM loading diagram.

3. The VMM can call the TSM's TH-ABI to add unmeasured pages to the TVM, such as sbi_covh_add_tvm_zero_pages. This instructs the TSM to add zero-initialized pages to the TVM.
4. The VMM calls the TSM service sbi_covh_run_tvm_vcpu to start and run the TVM.
5. After the TVM starts, it can call the TSM's TG-ABI sbi_covg_extend_measurement to measure information about runtime modules. This is similar to TDX's TDG.MR.RTMR.EXTEND interface. Finally, the TVM's attestation report will include both initial measurement information and runtime measurement information.

CHAPTER 5

TEE attestation model

In Chapter 4, we introduced the trusted execution environment (TEE) life cycle, particularly how a chain of trust needs to be established during the launch process to provide a TEE attestation report. Only after the TEE attestation report is verified will the TEE owner trust the TEE and transmit secrets to it for further processing. In this chapter, we will detail the TEE attestation model.

5.1 Application of attestation in everyday life

For a person, attestation is about proving, through reliable materials and information, that "you" are who you claim to be and possess the "attributes" you claim.

For example, after a baby is born, the hospital provides a birth certificate. The local public security bureau, based on the birth certificate and other materials such as the parents' ID cards, issues an ID card as proof of identity for the baby. When a third party requires verification of the child's identity, the ID card can be presented. Because the third party trusts the public security bureau, they will trust the child's identity. This is a simple attestation process.

However, an ID card is valid only domestically. If traveling abroad, one needs to apply for a passport from the exit-entry administration bureau using the ID card. The reason is that foreign immigration authorities do not trust the domestic public security bureau; they trust only the exit-entry administration of the citizen's home country. Here, the public security bureau is no longer the root of trust; the root of trust becomes the national exit-entry administration. In this attestation process, the citizen must present a passport to prove their identity.

In addition to a passport, a visa is often required for entry. The visa acquisition process involves the applicant submitting relevant materials, including their passport, to the consular visa section of the destination

Confidential Computing
ISBN 978-0-443-54067-7
https://doi.org/10.1016/B978-0-443-54067-7.00005-X

country, explaining the purpose of travel (e.g., study, business, tourism). After investigating the applicant, the visa section of the destination country issues a visa as proof for entry. Upon entry, immigration officials trust the visa issued by the visa section and thus permit entry.

IETF RFC 9334, "Remote Attestation Procedures Architecture," uses the **Passport Model** to describe this situation, as shown in Fig. 5.1.

1. The **attester** presents **evidence** to the **verifier.**
2. The **verifier** verifies the **evidence** and returns an **attestation result** to the **attester.**
3. The **attester** presents the **attestation result** to the **relying party.**

An important concept here is the **Trusted Authority**. This is an entity that the relying party trusts, and therefore the relying party trusts the attestation result. Note that there can be many authorities, and a relying party may choose to trust only some of them, not all. Only an authority trusted by the relying party can be called a trusted authority for that relying party.

In the previous ID card example, the newborn is the **attester**, the birth certificate is **evidence**, and the public security bureau is the **verifier**. After verifying the evidence (birth certificate), the public security bureau issues the ID card as the **attestation result**. The newborn can then present this attestation result (the ID card) to a third party (the **relying party**) to prove identity. In the passport example, the citizen is the **attester**, the **evidence** is the ID card, the exit-entry administration is the **verifier** responsible for verification, and it issues the passport as the **attestation result**. The citizen can present the passport to a **relying party** (immigration officials) to prove identity. Finally, in the visa example, the citizen is the attester, the evidence becomes the passport, the destination country's visa center is the verifier, which issues the visa as the attestation result. The citizen can present the visa to the relying party (immigration inspectors) for inspection.

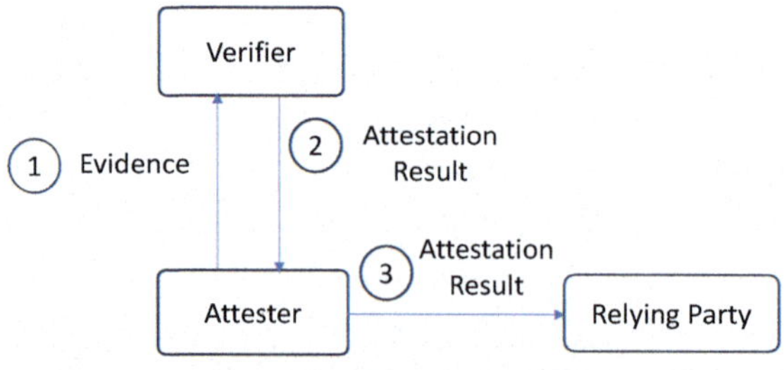

Figure 5.1 Passport model.

The public security bureau, the citizen's national exit-entry administration, and the destination country's visa center are all authorities. The public security bureau is a trusted authority domestically, but for the immigration inspector, only the national exit-entry administration and the destination country's visa center are trusted authorities. Therefore, upon entry, immigration inspectors check only the passport and visa, not the domestic ID card, because they need to confirm that the attestation result was issued by a trusted authority.

The Passport Model is not the only attestation model. Consider another example. A university graduate is hired by a company. After joining, they submit various materials to the human resources (HR) department, including their university name, transcripts, awards, and so on. The HR department contacts the university to confirm the authenticity and validity of the materials provided. Finally, the university responds stating whether the information is true or not.

IETF RFC 9334 uses the **Background-Check Model** to describe this situation, as shown in Fig. 5.2.

1. The **attester** presents **evidence** to the **relying party.**
2. The **relying party** sends the **evidence** to the **verifier.**
3. The **verifier** verifies the **evidence** and returns the **attestation result** to the **relying party.**

In this example, the graduate is the **attester**. The submitted materials serve as **evidence** provided to the **relying party** (the HR department). The HR department provides the evidence to the **verifier** (the university) for verification. Finally, the university provides a response (confirmation or denial) as the **attestation result**. Because the company trusts the university as an authority, if the university confirms the information is true, the company can trust the attester.

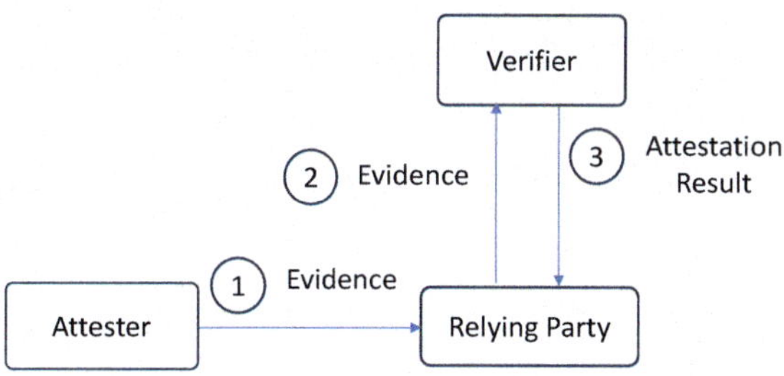

Figure 5.2 Background-check model.

5.2 General model of the attestation process

The Passport Model and Background-Check Model introduced in the previous section are two typical examples in remote attestation. IETF RFC 9334 provides a conceptual data flow model, as shown in Fig. 5.3. The lower part of the figure involves the concepts of **Attester**, **Evidence**, **Verifier**, **Attestation Result**, and **Relying Party**, which have been introduced earlier. Now let us look at the concepts in the upper part of the figure, which are all related to verification.

In the previous example, the HR department provided evidence to the university for verification. How does the university actually perform the verification? One possibility is that the university staff contacts the specific college to check student lists, transcripts, award records, and so on to see if the student's claims are true, and then decides on the outcome. Here, the university is the **Endorser**, providing **endorsements** possibly in the form of documents with the university seal (e.g., diploma). The college is the **Reference Value Provider**, providing student lists, transcripts, award records, and such, which are called **Reference Values**. Note that evidence and reference values may not always correspond one-to-one. For example, a student might provide only records of awards received but not specific grades, which might be acceptable. However, if the student provides only a name without a student ID, it might be impossible to confirm their identity, which would be unacceptable. This depends on the **Appraisal Policy for Evidence**, which needs to be defined by the **Verifier Owner** and provided to the **verifier**. After the HR department receives the **attestation result** from the university, the basis for deciding

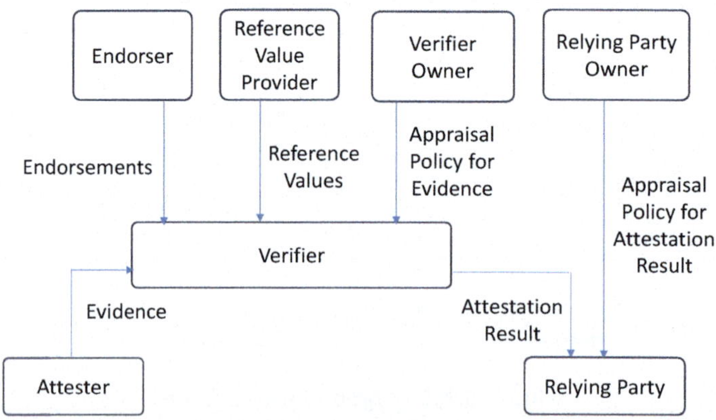

Figure 5.3 Conceptual data flow for remote attestation (source: RFC 9334).

whether to trust this result is the **Appraisal Policy for Attestation Result**. For example, the attestation result must be a result obtained after the HR department submitted the verification request, not an old, previously obtained result. This is because a student's degree could be revoked later owing to academic misconduct, so an earlier result cannot be relied upon. Such a policy needs to be uniformly defined and provided by the headquarters as the **Relying Party Owner**.

The attestation concept for TEEs is similar to these cases. The TEE acts as the **attester**, submitting a TEE Attestation Report as **evidence**. A **verifier** validates this evidence and provides a result to the **relying party** for the final decision (pass or fail). The relying party provides only secrets (e.g., keys) to the TEE for decrypting data and performing computations after successful verification.

Note: *It is important to point out that attestation can guarantee* only *the integrity of the TEE's program code and initial data. Once the TEE engages in unpredictable data exchanges and handles interrupts with the outside world, attestation cannot guarantee that the TEE's state at every moment is operating exactly as intended, especially as global variables, program stacks, and heaps are constantly changing. Swami, in a 2017 Black Hat talk titled "Intel SGX Remote Attestation is not Sufficient," gave an example requiring two generals to authorize launching a nuclear missile. In the example, an attacker could exploit SGX's Asynchronous Enclave Exit (AEX) mechanism to potentially launch the missile even with only one general present. As long as computer programs are written by humans, they may have security vulnerabilities that TEEs cannot prevent, and attestation cannot guarantee the state of a program at an arbitrary moment. Attestation is necessary but not sufficient.*

The following three subsections will discuss Evidence Conveyance, Verification, and Attestation Result Conveyance. Among these, the generation and conveyance of evidence are most closely related to hardware TEE design, whereas verification and result conveyance are more related to the software ecosystem.

5.2.1 Evidence generation and conveyance

Essentially, evidence generation and conveyance is the process of establishing and conveying a chain of trust. The most classic example is the Trusted Computing Group (TCG)-defined trusted boot using a Trusted Platform Module (TPM). We will first introduce the TCG-defined trusted boot and then transition to TEE trusted boot.

Note: *We introduce TCG trusted boot first for two reasons: First, it is a widely accepted industry standard, and TEE design architectures often reuse concepts from it. Second, a trend in TEE confidential computing software solutions is to use a virtual TPM for remote attestation to maintain compatibility with existing systems and software. Therefore, understanding TCG trusted boot and attestation is helpful for mastering TEE attestation. For basic principles of TPM 2.0, readers can refer to relevant literature, such as* A Practical Guide to TPM 2.0: Using the Trusted Platform Module in the New Age of Security, *by Will Arthur and David Challener.*

5.2.1.1 TCG trusted boot

The TPM specification introduces three essential Root of Trust modules in trusted boot, all indispensable:

- **Root of trust for measurement (RTM)**: Responsible for providing integrity-related information (e.g., measurements) to the RTS. Typically, the RTM is the first module to execute instructions after system platform startup, such as the BIOS boot block or an Authenticated Code Module used by Intel Boot Guard technology. Because the TPM is a passive device, it is generally not considered the RTM.
- **Root of trust for storage (RTS)**: Responsible for providing trusted storage. The TPM itself provides isolation, preventing other modules from directly accessing its internal memory. Therefore, the TPM is considered to provide RTS capability.
- **Root of trust for reporting (RTR)**: Responsible for reporting the contents of the RTS. To ensure the integrity of the report, the RTR's report typically includes a digital signature. The TPM also provides RTR capability.

The static trusted boot process based on a TPM is illustrated in Fig. 5.4.

1. Steps ① to ⑧: Starting from the RTM, through system firmware, Operating System (OS) loader, OS kernel, applications, and so on, each module first (odd-numbered steps) calculates the hash of the next module and then uses the TPM extend algorithm to measure this hash into a TPM Platform Configuration Register (PCR). Subsequently (even-numbered steps), it executes the next module. The values in these PCRs represent the final measurements of the platform boot modules and can be considered evidence of the platform boot.
2. Step ⑨: A user can use the TPM2_Quote command to perform remote attestation of the platform.

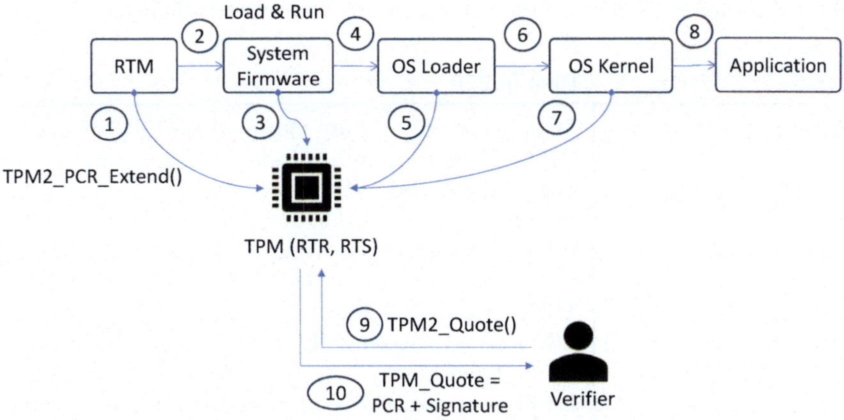

Figure 5.4 Static trusted boot process based on TPM. *PCR*, Platform Configuration Register; *RTM*, Root of Trust for Measurement.

3. Step ⑩: The TPM returns the TPM_Quote, which contains the PCR information and a signature over it, serving as the report for the platform boot. Through this method, evidence is securely conveyed to the user.
   In a TPM, the PCR Extend algorithm is:

$$\text{PCR[index]}_{\text{new}} = \text{Hash}_{\text{alg}}(\text{PCR[index]}_{\text{old}} \mid\mid \text{DataHash})$$

where "||" denotes concatenation.

TCG defines that a TPM can have 24 PCRs, each storing different types of data, as shown in Table 5.1.

In Table 5.1, the content for PCR [0-7] is defined by TCG, while PCR [8-15] content is OS-defined. Microsoft, in the paper "Protect key with TPM method of the win32_Encryptable volume class," detailed the usage for BitLocker. The Linux User space API group also defines PCR usage in Linux systems in the "Linux TPM PCR Registry."

From these steps, a single TPM PCR may contain measurements of multiple modules. Because of the nature of the extend algorithm, it is impossible to know the exact measurement of each individual module from the PCR value alone. How can we know which specific module was launched? The TCG Platform Firmware Profile (PFP) specification mandates that the platform must also provide an event log. This log contains a series of events, each recording the module measurement value at the time the extend algorithm was called. By examining the event log,

Table 5.1 Data types stored in platform configuration registers (PCRs).

Type	PCR index	Data in PCR
Static	0	Static Root of Trust for Measurement (SRTM), BIOS, platform firmware code, including built-in option Read-Only Memory (ROMs)
Static	1	Platform firmware configuration
Static	2	Unified Extensible Firmware Interface (UEFI) driver code, including option ROMs from add-on cards
Static	3	UEFI driver configuration
Static	4	UEFI boot manager code, boot attempts, including UEFI applications
Static	5	UEFI boot manager code configuration, disk GUID Partition Table (GPT)
Static	6	Platform vendor specific
Static	7	Secure boot policy, secure boot authority
Static	8–15	OS defined
Static	16	Debug
Dynamic	17	Dynamic Root of Trust for Measurement (DRTM) Configuration environment (DCE) details
Dynamic	18	DCE authority (PCR 17 and 18 can be swapped)
Dynamic	19	Dynamically launched measured environment (DLME) authority
Dynamic	20–22	DLME defined
Static	23	Supporting application

one can determine the measurement value of any module. Fig. 5.5 shows the relationship between PCR values and the event log.

The event log itself does not require special protection because the integrity of measurements within the log can be verified by replaying the events to regenerate the PCR values. The subsequent pseudocode

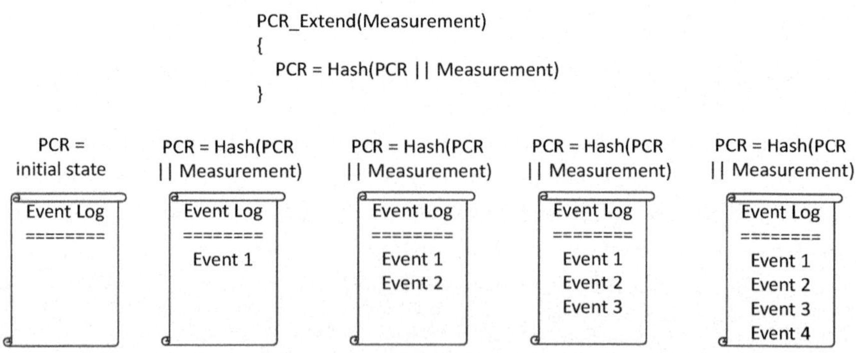

Figure 5.5 Platform Configuration Register (PCR) and event log.

illustrates this. The replay_event_log( ) function takes an event log as input and uses software to replay the events, calculating the expected PCR values (pcr_value). The verify_event_log( ) function determines whether the provided event log is consistent with the actual TPM PCR.

```
replay_event_log(event_log) {

    pcr_value = 0;

    event_entry = first_event_log_entry;

    while (event_entry is valid) {

        // The following steps simulate PCR calculation

        pcr_value = hash(pcr_value || event_entry.digest);

        event_entry = next_event_log_entry;

    }

    return pcr_value;

}


verify_event_log(event_log) {

    pcr_value = replay_event_log(event_log);

    if (pcr_value == read_tpm2_pcr()) {

        return true;

    } else {

        return false;

    }

}
```

Besides measurement hashes, event logs can store plaintext data, providing additional information such as the actual configuration data or module version information being measured.

5.2.1.2 Device Identifier Composition Engine trusted boot

We will introduce trusted boot based on the Device Identifier Composition Engine (DICE) in detail in Chapter 11.

5.2.1.3 Trusted execution environment evidence generation and conveyance

The generation of TEE evidence was introduced when discussing the TEE launch process in Chapter 4. The TEE trusted boot part is similar to the TPM static trusted boot. Fig. 5.6 illustrates the trusted boot process for a confidential Virtual Machine (VM) TEE. However, TEE solutions do not necessarily require a system TPM. The functions of RTR and RTS are implemented by other TEE-Trusted Computing Base (TCB) modules, such as the CPU System on Chip (Soc). Similar to TPM PCRs, the RTS of the TEE-TCB typically provides Measurement Registers (MRs), allowing one module to measure the content of the next module. The RTR provides an interface for attestation, generating a cryptographically protected TEE report.

1. Steps ① to ⑧: Starting from the RTM, through virtual firmware, OS loader, OS kernel, applications, and such, each module first (odd-numbered steps) calculates the hash of the next module and then uses the MR extend algorithm to measure this hash into the TEE-TCB's MR. Subsequently (even-numbered steps), it executes the next module. The values in these MRs represent the final measurements of the TEE-TCB and TEE boot modules and can be considered evidence of the TEE boot.
2. Step ⑨: A user can use the Get_TEE_Quote command to perform remote attestation of the TEE.

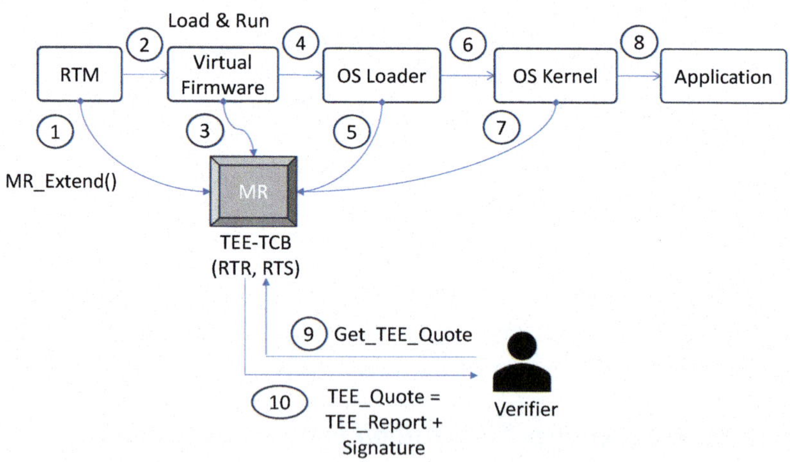

Figure 5.6 Trusted boot of a confidential VM trusted execution environment (TEE). *MR*, Measurement Register; *RTM*, Root of Trust for Measurement; *RTR*, Root of Trust for Reporting; *RTS*, Root of Trust for Storage; *TEE*, trusted execution environment.

3. Step ⑩: The TEE-TCB returns the TEE_Quote, which contains the TEE_Report and its signature, serving as the quoted evidence for the TEE boot. Through this method, evidence is securely conveyed to the user.

TEE environment MRs can be categorized into three types based on different measurement requirements, storing different data types, as shown in Table 5.2.

Not every TEE hardware provides all three types. For example, some systems lack TEE Runtime MRs. In such cases, runtime modules need to ensure their integrity through other means, such as digital signature verification or data encryption, to maintain the chain of trust. According to trusted boot rules, a non-RTM module cannot measure itself. Therefore, even within the TEE-TCB, an upper-level TEE-TCB module must measure the next-level TEE-TCB module.

Through this series of operations, we extend the root of trust into a chain, called the Chain of Trust. Correspondingly, we have a Chain of Trust for Measurement, a Chain of Trust for Storage, and a Chain of Trust for Reporting.

5.2.1.3.1 Types of trusted execution environment evidence

TEE evidence can be stored in different ways.

- MRs: Provide an extend operation allowing the TEE to append evidence. Advantages: Small size, simple computation. Disadvantages: Limited number of MRs, limited information recorded, cannot individually record specific content. MRs are analogous to TPM PCRs.
- Event Logs: Record the content of each extend operation. They correspond to MRs and perfectly compensate for their shortcomings. For example, event logs have no size limit and can record any information. The integrity of the TEE's event log is guaranteed by the MRs, similar to TCG event logs. Disadvantage: The event log is provided by the TEE itself, and the TEE-TCB typically does not provide it.
- Dedicated TEE Read-Only Registers: The TEE-TCB can have some read-only registers for the TEE. These registers are writable only by the TEE-TCB and read-only for the TEE. They can store simple additional information, such as Security Version Number (SVN) and hash of secure boot public key.

The types of evidence a TEE can store include:

Table 5.2 Data types stored in Measurement Registers (MRs).

Type	Subject of measurement	Data in MR
Trusted execution environment (TEE)-TCB MR	System Root of Trust for Measurement (RTM), upper-level TEE-TCB modules	Code and data of TEE-TCB, such as RTM in Fig. 5.6
TEE boot MR	TEE Security Manager (TSM) in TEE-TCB	Code and data of TEE at boot time, such as virtual firmware in Fig. 5.6
TEE runtime MR	TEE itself	Code and data loaded by TEE during runtime, such as OS loader and OS kernel in Fig. 5.6

- Module Code Information: Typically stored as hashes in MRs. This includes code loaded at boot time and runtime code loaded later. Different code should be placed in different MRs to avoid confusion.
- Module Configuration Information: Can be stored in MRs and event logs. Simple configurations can also be placed directly in the report. Similarly, configurations include those set at boot time and those passed in during runtime. Different configurations should also be placed in different MRs.
- Module Version Number: Can be stored in MRs and event logs.
- Module SVN: Can be stored in MRs and event logs, or directly in the report.
- Secure Boot Policy/Manifest: Refers to the predeployed secure boot manifest. Can generally be stored in MRs and event logs. If the manifest consists of a single item, it can also be placed directly in the report. The boot policy could be a signing public key, hash of a public key, module hash, module SVN, and so forth.
- Secure Boot Authority: Refers to the specific policy from the secure boot manifest used to verify the next module during the actual boot process. If there are multiple lower-level modules, each may have its own authority. Can generally be stored in MRs and event logs. If the secure boot manifest has only one item, it is the sole authority and can be omitted.

- Debug Functionality: The TEE-TCB needs to report whether the TEE supports debugging, because confidentiality and integrity may not be protected during debugging. TEE owners must treat this with caution. Additionally, there are some less common types of evidence:
- Secure Boot Revocation/Forbidden Policies: Generally, if the secure boot policy can be updated, a separate forbidden policy might not be needed; one simply removes the forbidden part from the policy. A special case arises if the deployed policy can only be added to, not deleted. Then a separate forbidden policy is needed to disallow certain known-unsafe modules explicitly. If a forbidden policy exists, it is typically stored alongside the secure boot policy.
- Instance-Specific Information: The final verifier needs to compare the obtained evidence with reference values. Generally, reference value manifests are generic, valid for a class of devices; therefore, evidence is usually class-specific. In some cases, devices can report unique information that can be used to locate or identify the specific device, which we call instance-specific information. Examples include serial numbers, asset tags, device certificates, and so on. This type of information is typically stored separately and not placed in the same MR as other evidence.
- Dynamically Generated Information: Some information changes with every boot, or even with every request for evidence. This includes measurement information such as voltage, temperature, or fan speed; or random information such as cryptographic nonces. This type of information is also typically stored separately and not placed in the same MR as other evidence.

Note: *Let us specifically discuss class-specific, instance-specific, and dynamically generated information. When TCG began defining trusted boot and TPM PCR usage, only class-specific information was intended to be measured, and this principle remains. Instance-specific and dynamically generated information are not placed in PCRs. However, the industry has requirements for conveying instance-specific and dynamically generated information. To address this, TCG, in the PFP 1.06, defined two new dedicated TPM Nonvolatile (NV) Indexes to store instance-specific and dynamically generated information separately. Similar to the TPM2_Quote command for PCRs, the TPM2_NV_Certify command can be used to obtain the data from these NV indexes along with a digital signature.*

Therefore, TEE evidence can include instance-specific and dynamically generated information, but during design, these three different types of information must be kept separate and not mixed. If they are to be measured into specific MRs, it is best to use different MRs for each type.

Because the TEE is launched by the TEE-TCB, the TEE's report must include information about the TEE-TCB components (beyond the root of trust itself) to provide a complete chain of trust. The types of evidence for TEE-TCB are similar to those described earlier. The RoT must provide separate MRs for the TEE-TCB, distinct from the TEE's MRs.

There is no unified standard for TEE evidence format; each TEE hardware vendor defines its own format.

5.2.1.3.2 Security elements in trusted execution environment evidence conveyance

Once the TEE has gathered all evidence, it needs to convey it to the verifier. This conveyance may occur over untrusted channels, so various factors must be considered.

- Integrity: The TEE report must not be tampered with by anyone. This is typically achieved through cryptography, with digital signatures being the most common method. Using public-key cryptography, the TEE's RTR signs the report with its private key, and the verifier validates it with the corresponding public key. Message Authentication Codes (MACs) are another method using symmetric cryptography. The RTR generates an MAC for the TEE report using an MAC key, and the verifier validates it with the same key. Generally, MAC keys are secret and should not be disclosed to third parties. One approach is for the TEE's RTR to expose an interface to validate the TEE report's MAC, allowing the verifier to send the obtained report and MAC to the RTR for integrity verification.
- Freshness: The TEE report needs to be fresh, much like a digital certificate should have a validity period. If the system's RTR has access to a trusted time source, it could timestamp the TEE report. However, most systems lack this capability. The current solution is for the verifier to provide a onetime nonce as a challenge for the TEE attestation. The RTR must include this nonce when generating the digital signature or MAC for the TEE report. Finally, the verifier, while checking the signature or MAC, also checks if the nonce in the TEE report matches the challenge. This proves the report was generated in response to that specific challenge. This challenge-response mode based on nonces is the most common pattern in remote attestation.

- Atomicity: Atomicity of a TEE report means that the report should be conveyed as a single, cohesive unit representing the system state at a particular point in time, not as separate pieces. This is especially important for systems supporting runtime updates. Without atomicity, a verifier might end up knowing the state of module A at time T1, module B at time T2, and module C at time T3, but cannot determine if the entire system was secure at any single moment (e.g., at T3, modules A and B might have been updated). If the entire TEE report is too large to transmit at once, the RTR can rely on transport-layer fragmentation, and the verifier can reassemble the fragments before validation.
- Completeness: Completeness of a TEE report means that the report must contain information about all modules within the chain of trust, as well as security-relevant configuration information. All necessary information must be conveyed to the verifier; missing any part is unacceptable. In practice, achieving completeness is difficult because system designers must decide what needs to be measured and what does not. For example, a system might omit measuring some debugging information during boot, leading to an incomplete report. Conversely, indiscriminately measuring everything would result in reports that are too large and complex, making verification or referencing difficult.

Generally, TEE reports do not need to consider confidentiality. Sensitive data such as user passwords or encryption keys should not be reported. If TEE code involves intellectual property, it can be protected by measuring its hash. In special cases where confidentiality is required, a secure channel (e.g., Transport Layer Security (TLS) over the network or Security Protocol and Data Model (SPDM) can be established between the RTR and the verifier for encrypted communication. The RTR would verify the verifier's identity before sending the TEE report encrypted over the secure channel.

5.2.1.3.3 Examples of trusted execution environment local and remote attestation

Fig. 5.7 illustrates a remote attestation flow for a TEE based on digital signatures (Mode A). Implementation details may vary across hardware TEEs, but the concepts are similar. We use the term remote because the verifier and the RTR can be on different machines, with potentially untrusted entities relaying messages in between:

① The verifier randomly generates a Nonce.
② The verifier sends a Get_TEE_Quote request to the TEE.
③ The TEE forwards the request to the RTR.

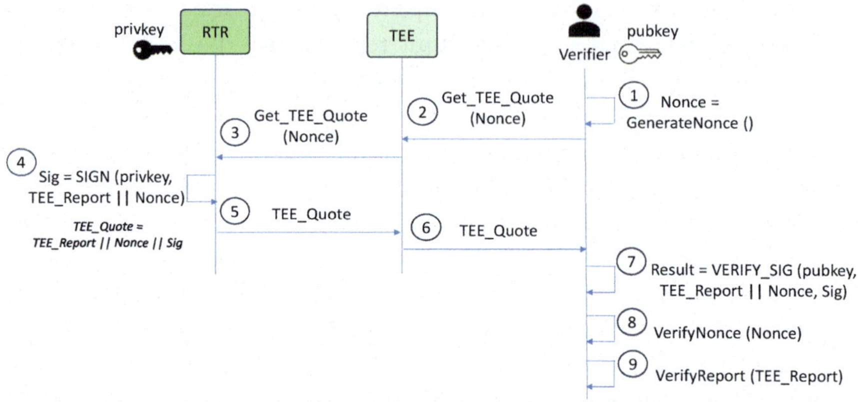

Figure 5.7 Trusted execution environment (TEE) attestation flow: remote attestation based on digital signature (Mode A).

④ The RTR concatenates the TEE_Report and the Nonce, then signs them using its private key (privkey). The final TEE_Quote includes the TEE_Report, Nonce, and Sig (digital signature).
⑤ The RTR returns the signed TEE_Quote to the TEE.
⑥ The TEE returns the signed TEE_Quote to the verifier.
⑦ The verifier first verifies the digital signature using the public key (pubkey) to ensure the integrity of the TEE_Quote.
⑧ The verifier verifies the Nonce to ensure the freshness of the TEE_Quote.
⑨ The verifier validates the content of the TEE_Report, including measurement values, SVN, secure boot policy, and so on.

Fig. 5.8 illustrates a local attestation flow for a TEE based on an MAC (Mode B.1). Implementation details may vary, but concepts are similar. It is termed local because it relies on the verifier also being a TEE, allowing for a trusted secure channel with the RTR, typically achievable only on the same machine.

① The verifier randomly generates a Nonce.
② The verifier generates its own MR information.
③ The verifier sends a Get_TEE_ReportMac request to the TEE, including the Nonce and its own MR.
④ The TEE forwards the request to the RTR.
⑤ The RTR derives an MAC key (mackey) specific to this verifier based on its own Root Key and the verifier's MR based on a KDF (Key Derivation Function).

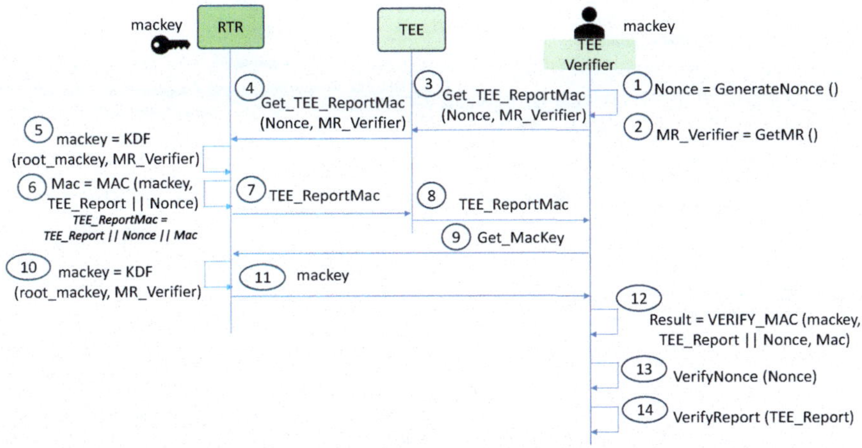

Figure 5.8 Trusted execution environment (TEE) attestation flow: Local attestation based on Message Authentication Code (MAC) (Mode B.1). *MR*, Measurement Register.

⑥ The RTR concatenates the TEE_Report and the Nonce, then generates an MAC using the derived MAC key.
⑦ The RTR returns the TEE_ReportMac (which includes the report, nonce, and MAC) to the TEE.
⑧ The TEE returns the TEE_ReportMac to the verifier.
⑨ To verify the MAC, the verifier first needs to generate the MAC key. The verifier sends a request to the RTR to obtain the MAC key.
⑩ Upon receiving the request, the RTR looks up the requester's MR (based on the request context) and generates the MAC key.
⑪ The RTR returns the MAC key to the verifier. This step requires a secure channel between the RTR and the TEE verifier.
⑫ The verifier verifies the MAC using the obtained key, ensuring the integrity of the TEE_ReportMac.
⑬ The verifier verifies the Nonce to ensure freshness.
⑭ The verifier validates the content of the TEE_Report, including measurements, SVN, secure boot policy, and so forth.

Note: *The key point here is that the MAC key is bound to the verifier's MR. This ensures that even though the verifier obtains the MAC key, it can verify only MACs generated for its own reports, not generate arbitrary MACs. Also, when requesting the MAC key, the verifier does not need to input its MR again; the RTR looks it up from its cache, ensuring the requester gets only its own key.*

Fig. 5.9 shows another local attestation flow based on MAC (Mode B.2). This is a variant of Mode B.1 that simplifies the process for the TEE verifier by not requiring it to obtain the MAC key.

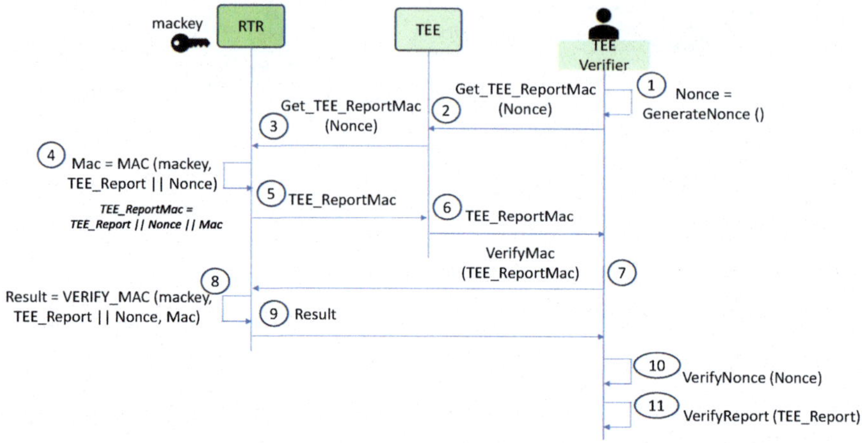

Figure 5.9 Trusted execution environment (TEE) attestation flow: Local attestation based on Message Authentication Code (MAC) (Mode B.2). *MR*, Measurement Register.

① The verifier randomly generates a Nonce.
② The verifier sends a Get_TEE_ReportMac request to the TEE.
③ The TEE forwards the request to the RTR.
④ The RTR concatenates the TEE_Report and the Nonce, then generates an MAC using its MAC key. The TEE_ReportMac includes the TEE_Report, Nonce, and MAC.
⑤ The RTR returns the TEE_ReportMac to the TEE.
⑥ The TEE returns the TEE_ReportMac to the verifier.
⑦ The verifier sends a request to the RTR to verify the MAC, ensuring the integrity of the TEE_ReportMac.
⑧ The RTR verifies the TEE_ReportMac using its MAC key.
⑨ The RTR returns the verification result to the verifier. This step requires a secure channel between the RTR and the TEE verifier.
⑩ The verifier verifies the Nonce to ensure freshness.
⑪ The verifier validates the content of the TEE_Report, including measurements, SVN, secure boot policy, and so forth.

If a TEE hardware supports only MAC functionality and not digital signatures, how can it achieve remote attestation? Fig. 5.10 illustrates a method that uses a special TEE Quoting Service to convert the MAC used for local attestation into a digital signature suitable for remote attestation (Mode C). Steps related to Fig. 5.10 are outlined next, omitting the details of the local attestation part (which could follow Mode B.1 or B.2):

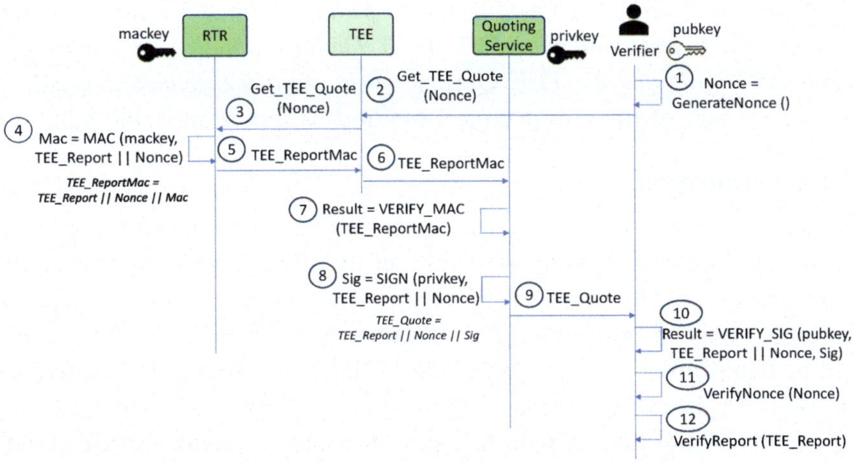

Figure 5.10 Trusted execution environment (TEE) attestation flow: remote attestation based on quoting service (Mode C). *MAC*, Message Authentication Code.

① The verifier randomly generates a Nonce.

② The verifier sends a Get_TEE_Quote request to the TEE.

③ The TEE sends a Get_TEE_ReportMac request to the RTR (as in local attestation).

④ The RTR generates the TEE_ReportMac (Report, Nonce, MAC) using its MAC key.

⑤ The RTR returns the TEE_ReportMac to the TEE.

⑥ The TEE returns the TEE_ReportMac to the TEE Quoting Service.

⑦ The TEE Quoting Service verifies the integrity of the TEE_ReportMac. Depending on the RTR's capabilities, the Quoting Service can either obtain the MAC key (Mode B.1) or directly get the verification result (Mode B.2).

⑧ If the MAC verification succeeds, the TEE Quoting Service concatenates the TEE_Report and the Nonce, then signs them with its private key. The final TEE_Quote includes the TEE_Report, Nonce, and Sig (digital signature).

⑨ The TEE Quoting Service returns the signed TEE_Quote to the verifier via the TEE.

⑩ The verifier verifies the digital signature using the public key, ensuring the integrity of the TEE_Quote.

⑪ The verifier verifies the Nonce to ensure freshness.

⑫ The verifier validates the content of the TEE_Report.

***Note**: Here, the TEE Quoting Service participates in the remote attestation flow and thus becomes part of the TEE-TCB. During verification, the verifier must additionally verify that the TEE Quoting Service meets the required standards.*

A summary of these four typical methods is shown in Table 5.3.

5.2.2 Verification

Verification is the process in which the verifier, after receiving a set of evidence from the attester, produces an attestation result by consulting other resources. The input to the verification process is evidence, and the output is an attestation result. The exact method is not strictly defined and can be determined by each verifier. IETF RFC 9334 provides a reference architecture. In its conceptual data flow model (Fig. 5.3), it suggests that the verifier should consult three types of resources: endorsements, reference values, and appraisal policies, each with a different focus.

- **Endorsements**: After receiving evidence, the verifier must first confirm that its integrity has not been compromised. Endorsements are the mechanisms we mentioned earlier, such as digital signatures and MACs, providing security guarantees. The verifier not only needs to verify the integrity of this evidence but also needs to validate the RTR itself (e.g., the RTR's public key) to ensure the evidence genuinely originated from a trusted RTR.
- **Reference Values**: After receiving evidence, the verifier needs to compare it against known good values. These known good values are called reference values.
- **Appraisal Policy**: In the early days, we often assumed the verifier's comparison policy was simply "are they the same?" This works for measurement values. As evidence content becomes more diverse, sameness is not the only option. For example, for SVN, the policy could be greater than or equal to a certain value. For a voltage measurement, the policy could be within a specific range. Therefore, the policy owner needs to provide clear and specific definitions.

5.2.2.1 Verification in TCG trusted boot

Broadly speaking, in TCG trusted boot, the RTM measures the modules involved in the boot process into the TPM's PCRs as evidence of the platform boot. The conveyance process involves the verifier obtaining the TPM Quote containing the PCRs from the TPM hardware. The verification process generally consists of two parts:

- Verifying Endorsements: This means the verifier needs to confirm that the TPM itself is a trusted TPM. Typically, each TPM comes from the

Table 5-3 Four trusted execution environment (TEE) attestation methods.

Mode	Application	Cryptographic primitive	TEE-TCB	Involved examples
A	Remote attestation	Digital signature	Root of Trust for reporting (RTR)	Trusted Platform Module (TPM), AMD Secure Encrypted Virtualization Secure Nested Paging (SEV-SNP) attestation
B.1	Local attestation	Message authentication code (MAC)	RTR	Software Guard Extensions (SGX) local attestation
B.2	Local attestation	MAC	RTR	Trust Domain Extensions (TDX) local attestation
C	Remote attestation	MAC + digital signature	RTR and quoting service	SGX and TDX remote attestation

factory with a unique EK and an EK Certificate. The TPM's EK Certificate is issued by the manufacturer's Certificate Authority (CA). Fig. 5.11 shows the TPM certificate chain. If the verifier chooses to trust the TPM manufacturer, it means trusting the manufacturer's

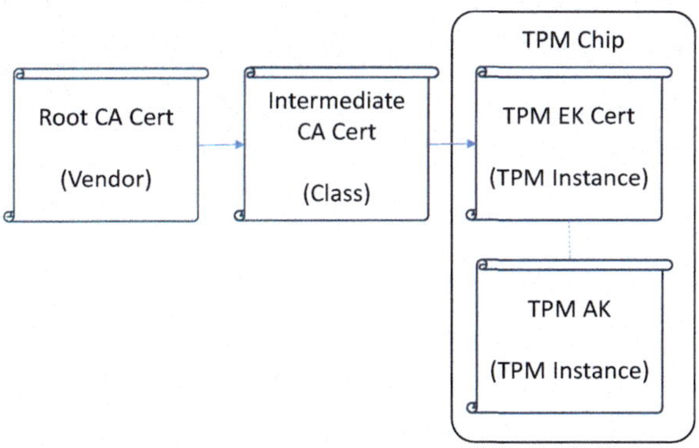

Figure 5.11 TPM certificate chain. *AK*, Attestation Key, *CA*, Certificate Authority; *EK*, Endorsement Key.

Root CA Cert (the endorser). Consequently, it will trust the TPM's EK Certificate and thus trust the TPM hardware itself.

- Verifying Reference Values: This means the verifier needs to check if the PCR values in the TPM match the expected values. Typically, the motherboard manufacturer provides a set of reference PCR values for the platform after a known good boot. If the verifier trusts the motherboard manufacturer, it can compare the reference PCR values with the actual PCR values obtained.

Note: *We are omitting the step of verifying the digital signature of the TPM Quote here, not because it's unnecessary, but because integrity is a fundamental cryptographic requirement for secure transmission. We are also omitting freshness checks, as they are also essential security requirements for transmission and not directly related to trust in the manufacturer.*

Verifying the TPM endorsement and the signature on the TPM_Quote is a complex process. The root cause is that the TPM's EK is generally used only for identification, not signing. The key used to sign the TPM_Quote is the TPM's Attestation Key (AK). So the verifier needs to have the EK and AK but also to confirm that the AK it has is indeed bound to the same TPM hardware as the EK. The tpm2-software community (tpm2-software.github.io) provides a TPM Remote Attestation Best Known Method. Fig. 5.12 shows a simplified flow illustrating how a TPM Quote is obtained and verified.

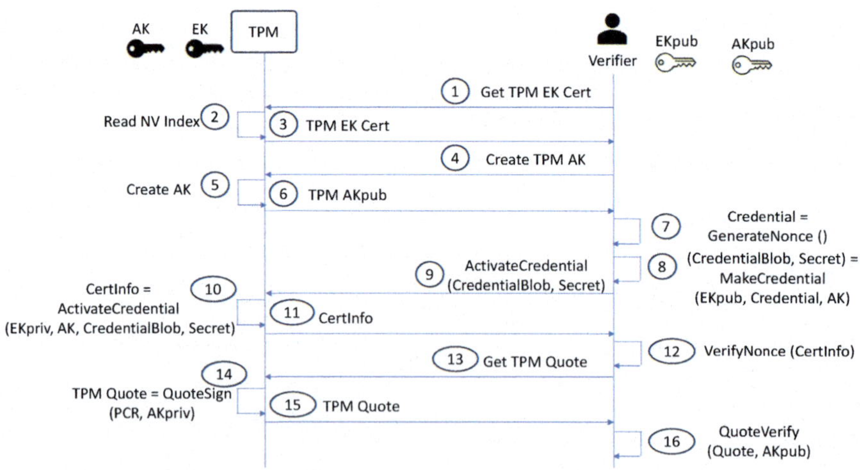

Figure 5.12 Flow for obtaining and verifying a TPM quote. *AK*, Attestation Key; *EK*, Endorsement Key; *PCR*, Platform Configuration Register.

① The verifier requests the TPM's EK certificate.
② The TPM reads the NV Index containing the EK certificate.
③ The TPM returns the EK certificate.
④ The verifier requests the generation of a new TPM AK.
⑤ The TPM invokes a local command to generate a new AK public/private key pair.
⑥ The TPM returns the AK public part.
⑦ The verifier begins the process to verify that the AK and EK belong to the same TPM hardware. The verifier first generates a random number as a challenge value called the Credential.
⑧ The verifier uses the logic defined by TPM2_MakeCredential, using the EK public key, the AK name, and the Credential value to generate a CredentialBlob and a Secret. The main principle is to encrypt with the EK public key and bind to the AK. Pseudocode is:

```
MakeCredential(EKpub, Credential, AK) {
    Seed = GenRandom();
    Secret = AsymEncrypt(Seed, EKpub);
    HmacKey = KDF(Seed);
    SymKey = KDF(Seed || AK.name);
    CredentialBlob.Data = SymEncrypt(Credential, SymKey);
    CredentialBlob.Mac = HMAC(CredentialBlob.Data, HmacKey);
    return (CredentialBlob, Secret);
}
```

⑨ The verifier sends the CredentialBlob and Secret to the TPM, requesting an ActivateCredential operation.
⑩ The TPM invokes its local ActivateCredential command, using the EK private key and the bound AK to decrypt and retrieve the CertInfo (which should be the original Credential). Pseudocode is:

```
ActivateCredential(AK, EKpriv, CredentialBlob, Secret) {
    Seed = AsymDecrypt(Secret, EKpriv);
    HmacKey = KDF(Seed);
    SymKey = KDF(Seed || AK.name);
    Mac = HMAC(CredentialBlob.Data, HmacKey);
    if (CredentialBlob.Mac != Mac) { return ERROR; }
    CertInfo = SymDecrypt(CredentialBlob.Data, SymKey);
    return CertInfo;
}
```

⑪ The TPM returns the CertInfo to the verifier.

⑫ The verifier compares the CertInfo with the original challenge Credential. If they match, it proves that the TPM indeed possesses both the EK (used for identity) and the bound AK (used for signing). Steps ⑦ through ⑫ are a specific design in TPM. TEE attestation flows can adopt different designs, but the principle of separating identity keys and signing keys is valuable.

⑬ The verifier requests a TPM Quote.

⑭ The TPM signs the PCR values using the AK to generate the Quote.

⑮ The TPM returns the TPM Quote.

⑯ The verifier verifies the signature on the TPM Quote using the AK public key, confirming its integrity.

Regarding the verification of platform reference values, the TCG Platform Firmware Integrity Measurement specification outlines a comparison method based on the event log, as shown in Fig. 5.13.

① The verifier obtains the TPM Quote, verifies its integrity, and extracts the PCR value(s).

② The verifier obtains the event log representing the platform state.

③ The verifier replays the event log to regenerate the expected PCR value and compares it with the PCR value from the Quote. If they match, it indicates that the event digests in the log have not been tampered with.

④ The verifier obtains a Reference Integrity Manifest (RIM), which contains the expected event log information (reference values).

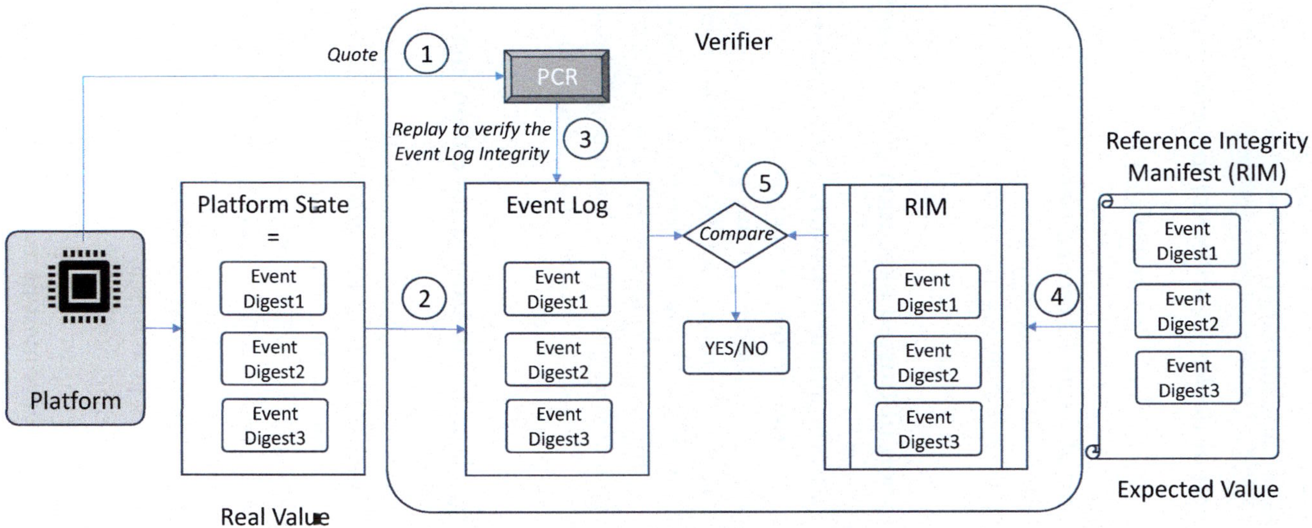

Figure 5.13 TCG verification based on event log.

⑤ The verifier compares the platform state (from the event log) with the reference values in the RIM. If they match, the boot is considered trusted; otherwise, it is untrusted.

5.2.2.2 Verification of device identifier composition engine evidence

We will introduce verification of DICE-based evidence in Chapter 11.

5.2.2.3 Verification of trusted execution environment evidence

Verification of TEE evidence also requires considering both endorsement verification and reference value verification, applying specific appraisal policies.

5.2.2.3.1 Verification of trusted execution environment endorsements

Generally, the hardware manufacturer acts as the endorser for a TEE, because the root of trust resides in the hardware. However, specific methods may vary. For hardware supporting public-key cryptography, the manufacturer can issue a certificate for the hardware signed by its CA during manufacturing. If the key in this certificate supports signing, it can be used directly for remote attestation, as shown in Fig. 5.7. For hardware supporting only symmetric cryptography, it can only support MAC-based local attestation (Figs. 5.8 and 5.9) and transformed remote attestation using a quoting service (Fig. 5.10).

5.2.2.3.2 Security elements in trusted execution environment evidence verification

The TEE provider typically supplies reference values for the measurement registers. If the verifier trusts the TEE provider, it can compare the obtained MR values against these reference values. Comparing only the TEE's MRs is insufficient; the verifier must also compare the TEE-TCB's reference values to confirm that the environment loading the TEE is also trustworthy. This can be considered from two aspects:

- **Completeness of TEE-TCB set verification**: A system may have multiple different TEE-TCB modules, such as the CPU SoC hardware, CPU microcode, TEE Security Manager, and, in earlier examples, the TEE Quoting Service. Apart from the root of trust in special cases, all these TEE-TCB modules must be verified; none can be omitted.

- **Completeness of TEE boot chain verification**: A TEE itself may have different loading modules. A module is trustworthy only if all modules loaded before it are also trustworthy. From the example in Fig. 5.6, to verify that the OS kernel is trustworthy, one cannot just look at the OS kernel's MR value; one must also check that the virtual firmware and OS loader loaded before it are as expected. This is crucial because a malicious virtual firmware could forge false measurement values for subsequently loaded OS modules, deceiving the verifier.

5.2.2.3.3 Examples of trusted execution environment reference value provisioning

TEE reference values are typically provided by the TEE provider. Two main methods exist:

- **Signed reference values**: This is the most common approach. The TEE provider endorses the reference values by signing them. If the verifier trusts the TEE provider, it trusts the signed reference values. This simple method presents a challenge to the TEE provider: the reference value list needs timely updates and maintenance. For closed-source software, signed reference values seem the only viable option.
- **Rebuildable open source code**: If the TEE is an open-source project, the verifier can directly rebuild the TEE and run tools to calculate the reference values. If the open-source project and tools undergo strict code review to ensure correctness, the calculated reference values can be trusted.

The industry has defined some reference value specifications. TCG uses ISO/IEC 19770-2:2015 Part 2 defining Software Identification Tags (SWID), NISTIR 8060 "Guidelines for the Creation of Interoperable SWID Tags," IETF RFC 9393 defining Concise Software Identification Tags (CoSWID), and IETF draft specifications for Concise Reference Integrity Manifest (CoRIM). SWID is based on XML format; CoSWID is a concise version based on CBOR, better suited for embedded environments. SWID and CoSWID focus on software inventories. To describe hardware inventories, IETF started defining Concise Module Identifier, which led to the introduction of CoRIM.

TCG's Reference Integrity Manifest Information Model and PC Client RIM specifications use SWID or CoSWID.

5.2.2.3.4 Examples of TEE evidence appraisal policies

We have listed various types of TEE evidence storage and evidence types. Appraisal policies are also diverse as long as they adhere to the security elements defined earlier. Some common policies are:

- Exact Match for All MRs: Requires all measurement values (code measurements, configuration measurements, secure boot measurements, etc.) to be identical. This is arguably the strongest security policy.
- Partial Match for Code-Related MRs: Requires code measurement values to be identical, but configurations may differ. For example, the TEE's code must be identical, but the Virtual Machine Manager (VMM) could allocate either 4 GiB or 8 GiB of memory to the TEE at launch, both of which are acceptable.
- Partial Match for Secure Boot-Related MRs: Requires the module's SVN and secure boot public key to match the reference values. For instance, some TEE code might differ, but the SVN of that code must be identical, indicating the same security level.

Note: *SVN must be used in conjunction with secure boot. Using SVN alone is meaningless because an attacker can arbitrarily forge an SVN. Without secure boot and measurement checks, such forgery cannot be detected. In practice, a combination of code MRs and secure boot MR + SVN is the most common strategy.*

- Partial Match for Certain Modules in the Event Log: The verifier may be interested only in specific modules, ignoring others. However, one must ensure the completeness of the TEE-TCB boot chain and the TEE boot chain. That is, all modules in the TEE-TCB and all previously loaded modules within the TEE must be verified. Verification of any module can use the code measurement method mentioned earlier, or the SVN plus secure boot public key method.

The industry is adopting languages such as Rego, defined by the Open Policy Agent, to describe these policies.

5.2.3 Conveyance of attestation results

The conveyance of attestation results involves the verifier and the relying party. This part is less directly related to the TEE itself but is crucial for the overall remote attestation architecture. These factors need consideration during attestation result conveyance:

- **Integrity**: The attestation result must not be tampered with by an attacker. The most common method is using the verifier's digital signature. If the relying party trusts the verifier's public key, it can trust the signed attestation result issued by the verifier.

- **Freshness**: The attestation result also needs freshness; otherwise, an attacker could replay a previous result to the relying party. Freshness can be ensured by a nonce. The relying party includes a nonce in its verification request, and the verifier includes a signature over this nonce in the returned result.
- **Correlation**: The attestation result must be correlated with the evidence; otherwise, an attacker could tamper with the evidence provided by the relying party to the verifier. The attestation result needs to include data related to the evidence, such as the evidence itself or a hash of the evidence, for the relying party to verify.

Regarding implementation, one can refer to IETF draft specifications such as Entity Attestation Token (EAT) based on JSON Web Token format (RFC 7951) and EAT Attestation Result.

5.3 Other topics

Finally, let us introduce some other topics related to attestation.

5.3.1 Nonmeasurement schemes for runtime environments

In the TCG TPM trusted boot specifications, the focus is on measuring system firmware and establishing a chain of trust from the boot module to the OS. However, they do not specify how to measure various applications within the OS, nor do they cover measuring kernel drivers, likely owing to the high complexity of measuring an OS. Users can freely open and close applications without a fixed order; users can also plug in new cards and load new drivers. Even if user actions were measured, how would one verify them? Only in high-assurance systems where user behavior is restricted and programs loaded by the OS are fixed can runtime measurement be used. For ordinary commercial machines, a simpler approach is to combine secure boot methods with signature verification.

The same applies to TEEs. If the TEE's runtime environment is closed, measuring all modules is feasible. If the TEE's runtime environment is open to users, measuring all runtime programs is impractical. Enabling secure boot for programs within the OS and measuring the secure boot policy is a simple and effective method. Fig. 5.14 illustrates the process of digital signature verification for TEE runtime components.

1. Steps ① to ⑥: Starting from the RTM, through virtual firmware, OS loader, OS kernel, and on to applications, each module first (odd steps) measures the next module into the TEE-TCB's MRs using the extend

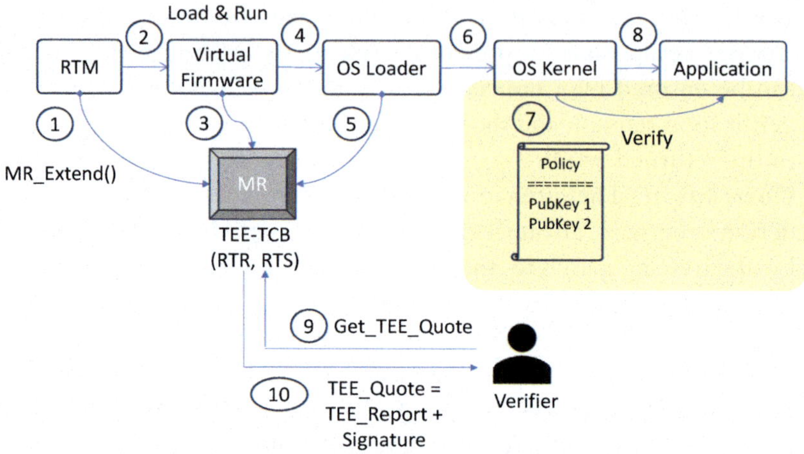

Figure 5.14 Trusted execution environment (TEE) runtime digital signature verification. *MR*, Measurement Register; *RTM*, Root of Trust for Measurement; *RTR*, Root of Trust for Reporting; *RTS*, Root of Trust for Storage.

operation. Then (even steps), it executes the next module. These MR values are the final measurements of the TEE-TCB and TEE boot modules, serving as evidence for the TEE boot.

2. Step ⑦: This step changes from measurement to verification. The OS kernel verifies whether it can launch the application based on its secure boot policy. To enable final verification, this secure boot policy must have been measured into an MR before this verification step.
3. Step ⑧: If verification succeeds, the application is loaded.
4. Step ⑨: This part remains the same. The verifier can use the Get_-TEE_Quote command for remote attestation of the TEE.
5. Step ⑩: After obtaining the TEE_Quote, the verifier validates it. At this point, the verifier needs to examine the secure boot policy (which was measured), not the specific measurement value of the application itself.

Secure boot requires a boot policy. What if the TEE provider does not want to maintain a boot policy, or the current environment does not support secure boot? Another approach is to use an ancient cryptographic solution: encryption and decryption. Fig. 5.15 shows the steps for TEE runtime encryption/decryption verification.

1. Steps ① to ⑥: These steps remain the same as before.
2. Step ⑦: This step changes from measurement to application decryption. The OS kernel needs to request a decryption key from a Key

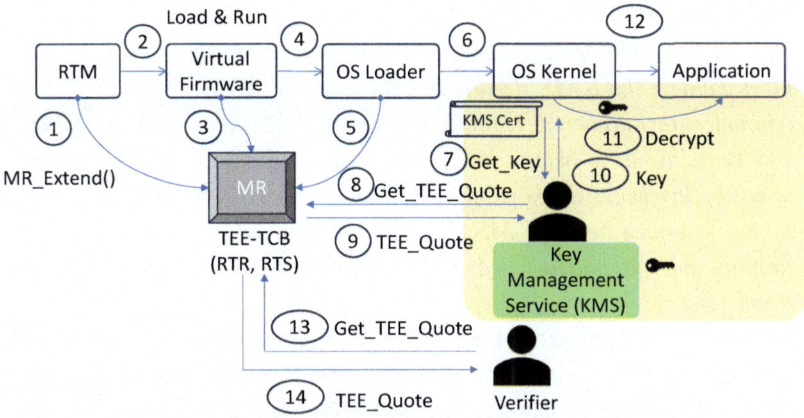

Figure 5.15 Trusted execution environment (TEE) runtime encryption/decryption verification. *MR*, Measurement Register; *RTM*, Root of Trust for Measurement; *RTR*, Root of Trust for Reporting; *RTS*, Root of Trust for Storage.

Management Service (KMS). Because the key is confidential, the OS kernel must establish an authenticated secure channel with the KMS, such as TLS over the network. The OS kernel must deploy the KMS's certificate to confirm it is communicating with the genuine KMS. Furthermore, for final verification, this KMS certificate must have been measured into an MR before this step.

3. Step ⑧: The KMS also needs to authenticate the TEE with which it is communicating. A common practice is to use remote attestation to identify the TEE. So, the KMS sends an attestation request.
4. Step ⑨: The KMS receives the TEE's Quote and verifies it, confirming this is the expected TEE.
5. Step ⑩: If verification succeeds, the KMS delivers the key to the TEE.
6. Step ⑪: The OS kernel decrypts the application. At this point, the OS kernel should also verify the integrity of the decrypted application.
7. Step ⑫: If decryption and verification succeed, the application is loaded.
8. Step ⑬: This part remains the same. The verifier can use the Get_-TEE_Quote command for remote attestation.
9. Step ⑭: After obtaining the TEE_Quote, the verifier validates it. Now, the verifier needs to examine the KMS certificate deployed by the OS kernel (which was measured), not the measurement of the application itself.

Note: *Several points need emphasis:*

1. *Because the KMS manages keys, it becomes part of the TEE-TCB. The verifier must validate the KMS's certificate and trust the KMS.*
2. *Mutual authentication is required between the OS kernel and the KMS. The OS kernel needs to obtain the key from a trusted KMS, and the KMS needs to ensure it releases the key only to a known and verified TEE. The authentication performed by the KMS here is not traditional public-key-based authentication, but attestation-based authentication. We will describe this in more detail later.*
3. *Symmetric key systems offer algorithms that simultaneously ensure confidentiality and integrity (authenticated encryption). It is advisable to use such algorithms rather than composing a separate encryption algorithm and an integrity algorithm, to avoid potential errors.*

At the same time, we must recognize that this method, lacking measurement, cannot securely trace the history of all programs run by a TEE. Even if the OS kernel maintains a list of launched applications in software, this software list lacks the hardware MR's append-only property. If the OS kernel has a vulnerability, an attacker could potentially overwrite this list.

5.3.2 Secure communication protocols based on remote attestation

In TEE-based confidential computing architectures, TEEs often need to communicate with each other. Because communication must traverse the untrusted VMM, a secure connection needs to be established between TEEs, for example, using a known authenticated key exchange protocol.

TLS is a classic protocol for network security and thus an option for secure communication between TEEs. Normal TLS authentication can be based on certificates or preshared keys (PSKs). However, both are difficult to use directly for TEE authentication. Using ordinary X.509 certificates would require the TEE to possess the associated private key. Using ordinary PSK would require the PSK to be predeployed in the TEE. This presents a chicken-and-egg problem in general-purpose TEE solutions: the TEE needs to be attested first before securely deploying a private key or PSK.

Addressing the specific needs of TEEs, in "Integrating Intel SGX remote attestation with transport layer security," Knauth et al. proposed the concept of Remote Attestation TLS (RA-TLS). The left side of Fig. 5.16 shows the RA-TLS flow, which follows the same steps as certificate-based TLS. The only difference lies in certificate generation and

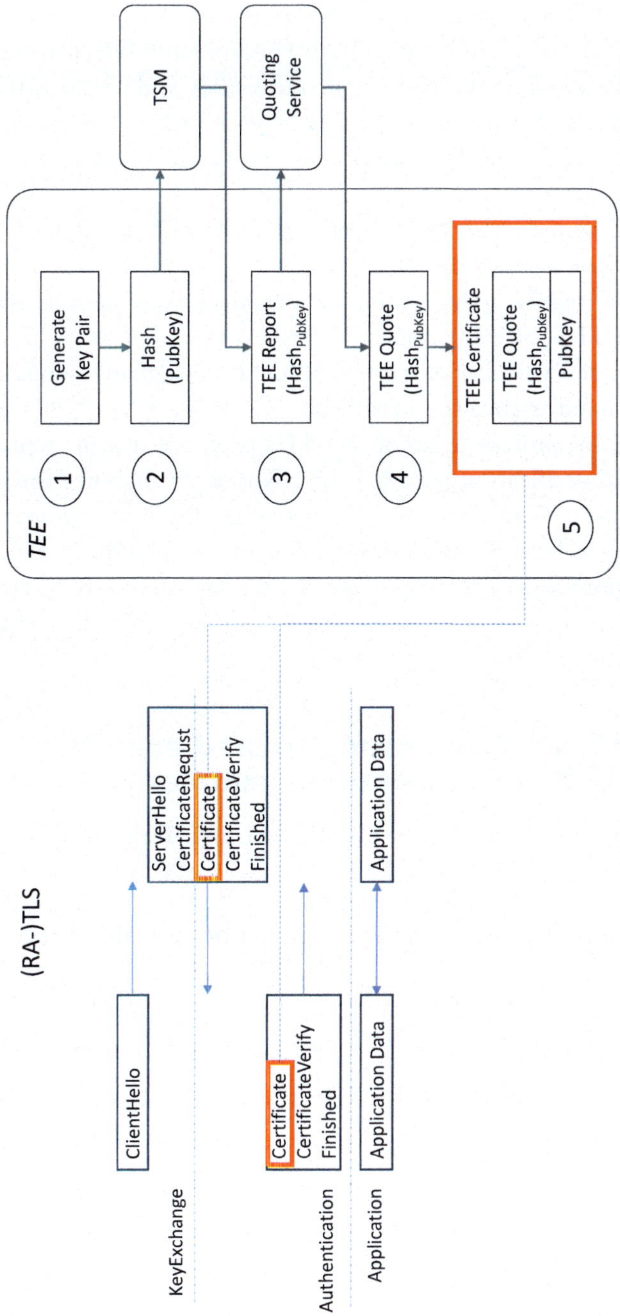

Figure 5.16 Dynamic generation flow for Remote Attestation TLS (RA-TLS) certificate. *TEE*, trusted execution environment.

verification. The right side of Fig. 5.16 shows the dynamic generation flow for an RA-TLS certificate, with these steps:

① The TEE dynamically generates an ephemeral public/private key pair.

② The TEE calculates the hash of the public key and uses it as REPORT-DATA, passing it to the TSM to obtain a TEE Report.

③ The TEE sends the TEE Report to a Quoting Service to generate a TEE Quote.

④ The TEE includes the TEE Quote as part of an Object Identifier (OID) in an X.509 certificate.

⑤ The TEE registers the generated certificate (containing the Quote) with the TLS software stack.

Similarly, the verification part of RA-TLS essentially verifies the TEE Quote contained within the certificate.

RA-TLS maximizes reuse of the TLS protocol design, replacing only the certificate verification part. It is therefore a good choice for inter-TEE communication. The CCC's interoperable-RA-TLS project aims to define X.509 certificate extensions based on TCG DICE. Furthermore, IETF has proposed attestation-based extensions for TLS and DTLS, detailed in "Using attestation in transport layer security (TLS) and datagram transport layer security."

5.4 Confidential computing trusted execution environment attestation examples

Now, let us look at examples of how existing TEE hardware solutions support TEE attestation.

5.4.1 Intel SGX trusted execution environment attestation

Intel was the first to propose CPU-based attestation and sealing with SGX. It does not require a separate platform TPM; it provides RTR and RTS functionality directly through the CPU hardware. We will first introduce SGX local and remote attestation; sealing will be covered in later chapters.

5.4.1.1 SGX local attestation

SGX local attestation resembles Mode B.1, allowing one Enclave (the verifier) to attest another Enclave. The SGX Enclave REPORT is a data structure an Enclave uses to prove its identity to a local verifier. Important members include:

- CPUSVN: CPU hardware SVN.
- MISCSELECT: Bit field indicating which features are saved in the State Save Area upon AEX.
- ATTRIBUTES: Bit field representing Enclave attributes.
- MRENCLAVE: The Enclave's measurement value.
- MRSIGNER: The hash of the Enclave's signer's public key.
- CONFIGID: Software-provided ID representing the Enclave's configuration.
- ISVPRODID: Enclave's Product ID.
- ISVSVN: Enclave's SVN.
- CONFIGSVN: Software-provided ID representing the Enclave's configuration SVN.
- ISVFAMILYID: Enclave's software family ID.
- REPORTDATA: 64 bytes of arbitrary data provided by the verifier, typically containing a nonce to ensure freshness.
- KEYID: Report Key ID.
- MAC: MAC over the entire structure, ensuring integrity.

The SGX local attestation flow is shown in Fig. 5.17.

① The Enclave verifier randomly generates REPORTDATA.

② The Enclave verifier obtains its own MRENCLAVE, ATTRIBUTES, CONFIGSVN, MISCSELECT, and CONFIGID as Target Info for the target Enclave (the attester). This Target Info, along with the random REPORTDATA, is sent to the attester.

③ The Enclave attester, upon receiving the Target Info and REPORTDATA, calls the EREPORT instruction to request the generation of an Enclave REPORT.

④ The CPU uses the Root Seal Key, the report KEYID, and the Target Info to derive a Report Key, and generates the Enclave attester's REPORT.

⑤ The CPU returns the REPORT to the Enclave attester. This includes the report KEYID, indicating to the Enclave verifier which report KEYID to use when requesting the Report Key.

⑥ The Enclave attester returns the REPORT to the Enclave verifier.

⑦ The Enclave verifier extracts the report KEYID from the REPORT, creates a Key Request structure, and calls the EGETKEY instruction to retrieve the Report Key.

⑧ The CPU uses the Root Seal Key, the provided report KEYID, and the Enclave verifier's information to derive the Report Key. Because both Enclaves are on the same machine and share the same Root

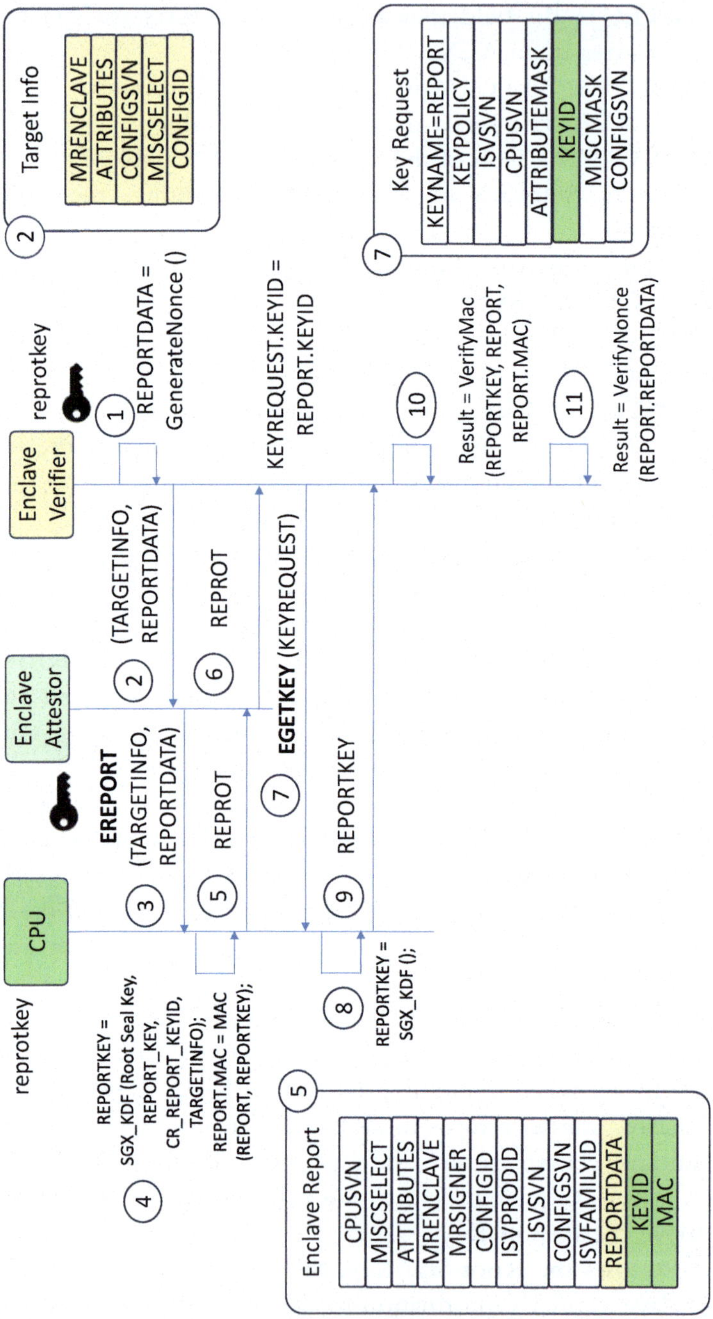

Figure 5.17 SGX local attestation flow. *MAC*, Message Authentication Code.

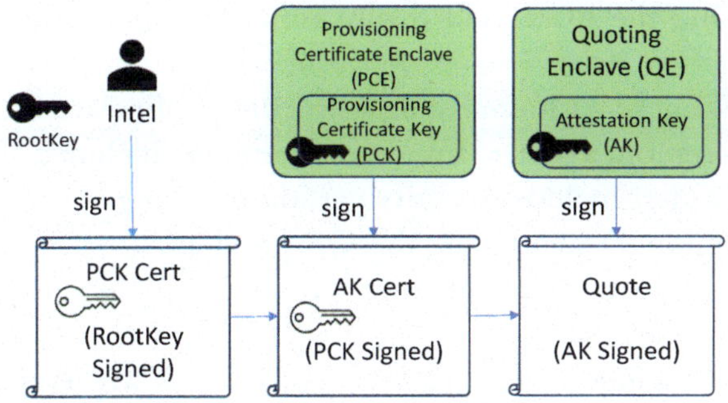

Figure 5.18 SGX remote attestation: modules and keys.

Seal Key, the derived Report Key will be the same as the one used by the CPU to generate the MAC in the REPORT.

⑨ The CPU returns the Report Key to the Enclave verifier.

⑩ The Enclave verifier uses the obtained Report Key to verify the MAC of the Enclave attester's REPORT, ensuring its integrity.

⑪ The Enclave verifier checks the REPORTDATA within the REPORT to ensure freshness.

5.4.1.2 SGX remote attestation

SGX supports two remote attestation methods: one based on Intel's Enhanced Privacy ID and one based on ECDSA. We will describe the ECDSA-based method, which resembles Mode C. Fig. 5.18 shows the modules and keys involved in SGX remote attestation.

- Enclave Quote: A data structure an Enclave uses to prove its identity to a remote verifier. It is signed by an AK.
- Quoting Enclave (QE): A special Enclave typically provided by Intel (but third parties can also provide one). It possesses the AK and is responsible for verifying the Enclave Report and then signing the Enclave Quote.
- AK Certificate: Certifies the identity of the AK, issued by the Provisioning Certificate Key (PCK).
- Provisioning Certificate Enclave (PCE): A special Enclave provided by Intel. It holds the PCK and issues the AK certificate.
- PCK Certificate: Certifies the identity of the PCK, issued by Intel's Root Key.

The public part of the Root Key is publicly known. Thus, a verifier can verify the PCK certificate using the Root Key, then verify the AK certificate using the PCK, and finally verify the Quote's signature using the AK.

The SGX Enclave Quote is a data structure an Enclave uses to prove its identity to a remote verifier. Important members include:

- Quote Header: Includes security version numbers of the QE and PCE, and a Vendor ID identifying the QE provider.
- Enclave Report: Contains the content of the original Enclave REPORT.
- Signature: Includes the signature over the Enclave Report, the AK's public key, the Enclave Report and signature of the QE itself, and the PCE certificate. The hash of the AK public key is contained within the Enclave Report. This information allows the verifier to validate a complete chain of trust from the Root Key down to the Enclave Report, including verifying the QE and PCE as additional TEE-TCB components.

The SGX remote attestation flow is shown in Fig. 5.19.

① The verifier randomly generates ReportData.

② The verifier sends a request to obtain an Enclave Quote.

③ The Enclave calls the EREPORT instruction to generate an Enclave REPORT.

④ The Enclave passes the Enclave REPORT to the QE.

⑤ The QE verifies the integrity of the Enclave REPORT.

⑥ Upon successful verification, the QE uses its AK to sign the corresponding Enclave Quote.

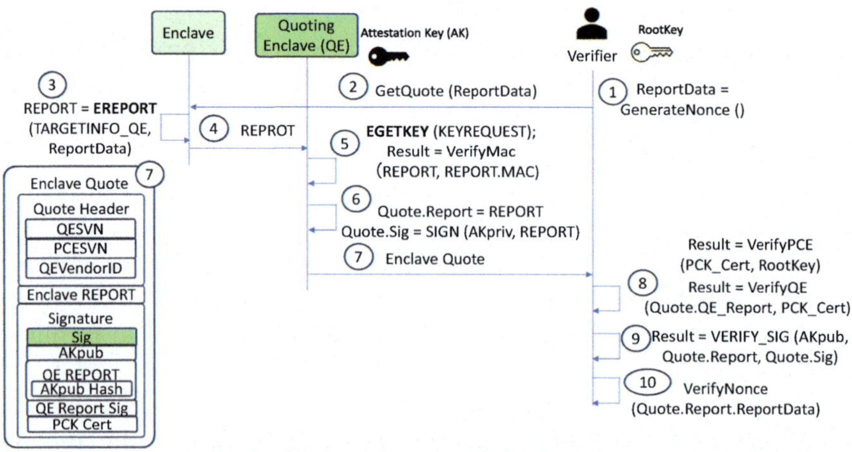

Figure 5.19 SGX remote attestation flow.

⑦ The QE returns the Enclave Quote to the verifier.
⑧ The verifier validates the PCE and QE information within the Quote to ensure these TEE-TCB components are trustworthy.
⑨ The verifier verifies the signature over the Enclave Report within the Quote, ensuring its integrity.
⑩ The verifier checks the ReportData within the Enclave Report to ensure freshness.

Complete documentation for Intel SGX and TDX remote attestation can be found at https://api.portal.trustedservices.intel.com.

5.4.2 Intel TDX trusted execution environment attestation

Intel TDX's attestation scheme is similar to SGX's. It does not require a separate platform TPM, providing RTR and RTS functionality directly through the CPU hardware and the TDX Module.

5.4.2.1 TDX local attestation

TDX local attestation resembles Mode B.2. It allows an SGX Enclave or another Trust Domain (TD) to act as a verifier for a TD. Unlike SGX, TDX has a separate software TEE-TCB module, the TDX Module, acting as the TSM managing all TDs. According to trusted boot rules, a non-RTM module cannot measure itself. Therefore, when establishing the chain of trust, a TD's MRs are managed (measured and extended) by the TDX Module, whereas the TDX Module's own MRs are managed by the CPU. Measurement registers in TDX are shown in Fig. 5.20.

The TD REPORT is a data structure a TD uses to prove its identity to a local verifier. Important members include:

- REPORTMAC: REPORT generated by the CPU, including an MAC. It contains the hardware CPUSVN, a hash of TCB_INFO (TCB_INFO_HASH), a hash of TD_INFO (TD_INFO_HASH), the verifier-provided random REPORTDATA, and the integrity-protecting MAC.

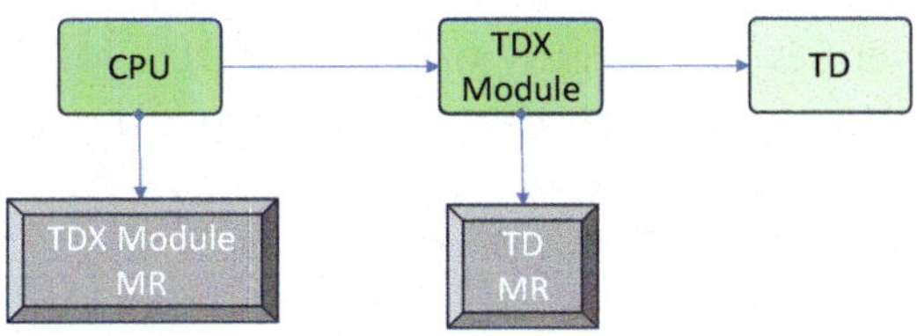

Figure 5.20 Measurement registers (MRs) in TDX.

- TCB_INFO: Information about the TDX Module, generated and maintained by the CPU. It includes the TDX Module's Security Version Number (TCB_SVN), its measurement (MRSEAM), the hash of its signer's public key (MRSIGNERSEAM), and its attributes (ATTRIBUTES).
- TD_INFO: Information about the TD, generated and maintained by the TDX Module. It includes the TD's attributes (ATTRIBUTES), its boot measurement (MRTD), its runtime measurement registers (RTMR), its configuration ID (MRCONFIGID), its owner ID (MROWNER), and its owner configuration (MROWNERCONFIG). Note that TD_INFO_HASH in the REPORTMAC is the hash of this TD_INFO structure.

The TDX local attestation flow is shown in Fig. 5.21.

① The TD verifier randomly generates REPORTDATA.
② The TD verifier sends the REPORTDATA to the TD attester along with the attestation request.
③ The TD attester calls the TDX Module command TDG.MR.REPORT to request generation of a TD REPORT.
④ The TDX Module calculates TD_INFO_HASH from its own TD_INFO for the requesting TD, and calls the CPU's SEAMREPORT instruction, passing TD_INFO_HASH and the REPORTDATA.
⑤ The CPU calculates TCB_INFO_HASH from its TCB_INFO, and generates the REPORTMAC using its MAC key.
⑥ The CPU returns the REPORTMAC and TCB_INFO to the TDX Module.
⑦ The TDX Module assembles the full TD REPORT by combining the REPORTMAC, TCB_INFO, and its own TD_INFO, and returns it to the TD attester.
⑧ The TD attester returns the TD REPORT to the TD verifier.
⑨ The TD verifier calls the TDX Module command TDG.MR.VERIFYREPORT to request verification of the REPORTMAC's integrity.
⑩ The TDX Module calls the CPU's VERIFYREPORT instruction.
⑪ The CPU verifies the integrity of the REPORTMAC.
⑫ The CPU returns the result to the TDX Module.
⑬ The TDX Module returns the result to the TD verifier.
⑭ The TD verifier further verifies that the TCB_INFO and TD_INFO in the report are consistent with TCB_INFO_HASH and TD_INFO_HASH from the REPORTMAC, ensuring their integrity.

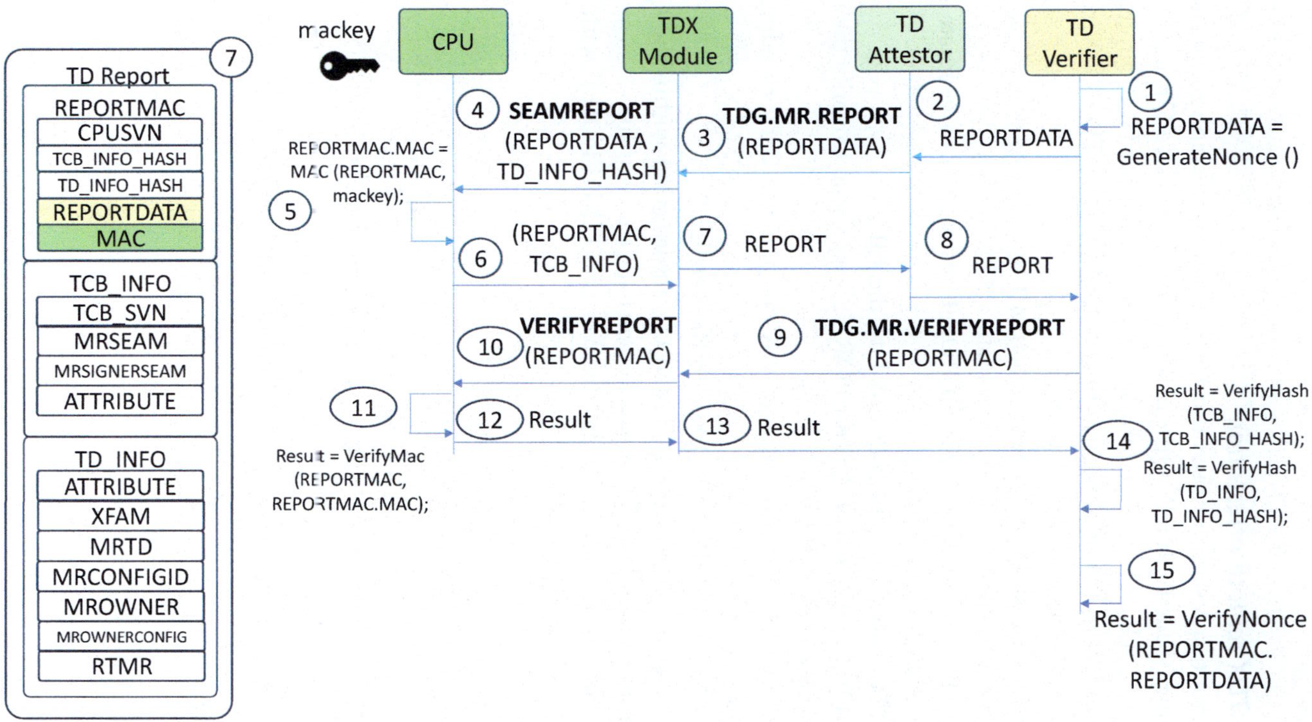

Figure 5.21 TDX local attestation flow. *MAC*, Message Authentication Code.

⑮ The TD verifier checks the REPORTDATA in the report to ensure freshness.

5.4.2.2 TDX remote attestation

TDX remote attestation reuses the SGX remote attestation infrastructure, resembling Mode C. Intel's QE can sign not only Enclave Quotes but also TD Quotes. The TD Quote format is similar to the Enclave Quote, with the TD REPORT replacing the Enclave REPORT. The TDX remote attestation flow is shown in Fig. 5.22.

① The verifier randomly generates ReportData.

② The verifier sends a request to obtain a TD Quote.

③ The TD calls the TDG.MR.REPORT instruction to generate a TD REPORT.

④ The TD passes the TD REPORT to the QE.

⑤ The QE uses the EVERIFYREPORT2 instruction to verify the integrity of the TD REPORT.

⑥ Upon success, the QE uses its AK to sign the corresponding TD Quote.

⑦ The QE returns the TD Quote to the verifier.

⑧ The verifier validates the PCE and QE information within the Quote to ensure these TEE-TCB components are trustworthy.

⑨ The verifier verifies the signature over the TD REPORT within the Quote, ensuring its integrity.

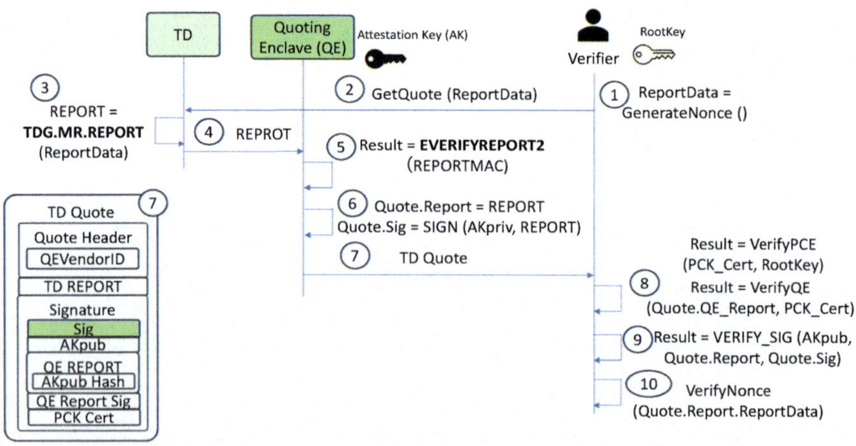

Figure 5.22 TDX remote attestation flow. *PCK*, Provisioning Certificate Key.

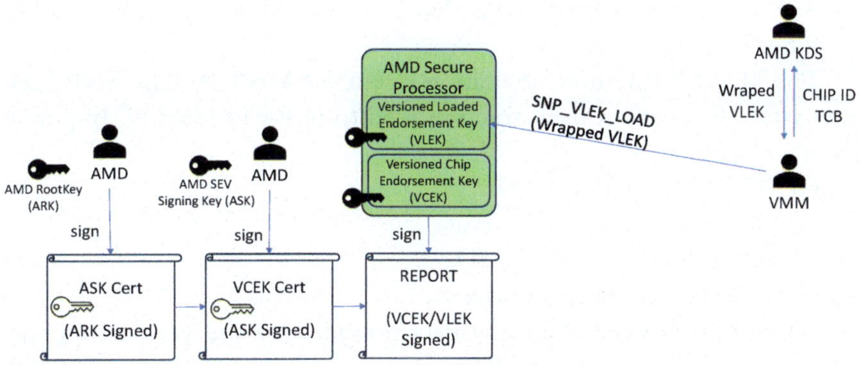

Figure 5.23 SEV-SNP remote attestation: modules and keys. *KDS*, Key Derivation Service.

⑩ The verifier checks the ReportData within the TD REPORT to ensure freshness.

5.4.3 AMD SEV-SNP trusted execution environment attestation

AMD Secure Encrypted Virtualization Secure Nested Paging uses the AMD Secure Processor (AMD-SP) as the RTR. The AMD-SP uses either the Versioned Chip EK (VCEK) or the Versioned Loaded EK (VLEK) to sign attestation reports. The difference is that VCEK is derived from a seed unique to the AMD-SP chip, whereas VLEK is derived from a seed maintained by the AMD Key Derivation Service (KDS). Using VCEK as an example, Fig. 5.23 shows the modules and keys involved in SEV-SNP remote attestation.

- SEV-SNP Attestation Report (REPORT): A data structure an SNP VM uses to prove its identity to a third-party verifier. It can be signed by VCEK or VLEK.
- VCEK: A signing key unique to each AMD SP chip.
- VLEK: A key maintained by the AMD KDS. VLEK can be used when a use case prefers a common key for signing rather than chip-specific keys.
- AMD KDS: AMD's service for maintaining VLEK keys. A VMM can send the Chip ID and TCB version to the AMD KDS to obtain a wrapped VLEK, and then load it using the SNP_VLEK_LOAD command.
- VCEK Certificate: Certifies the identity of the VCEK, issued by the AMD SEV Signing Key (ASK).

- ASK Certificate: Certifies the identity of the ASK, issued by the AMD Root Key.

The SEV-SNP remote attestation resembles Mode A. The SNP VM's Attestation Report is a data structure used to prove its identity. Important members include:

- GUEST_SVN: Guest SVN.
- POLICY: Guest policy structure.
- FAMILY_ID: Guest family ID.
- IMAGE_ID: Guest image ID.
- REPORT_DATA: Arbitrary data provided by the verifier, typically containing a nonce for freshness.
- MEASUREMENT: Boot-time measurement value.
- HOST_DATA: Data provided by the VMM at launch time.
- ID_KEY_DIGEST: Digest of the ID Key used to sign the ID Block.
- AUTHOR_KEY_DIGEST: Digest of the Author Key used to sign the ID Key.
- REPORT_ID: Guest report ID.
- REPORTED_TCB: TCB version used to derive the VCEK signing key.
- CHIP_ID: AMD-SP chip ID.
- SIGNATURE: Digital signature over the entire structure, ensuring integrity.

The SEV-SNP remote attestation flow is shown in Fig. 5.24.

① The verifier randomly generates REPORT_DATA.

② The verifier requests an attestation report from the attester (SNP VM).

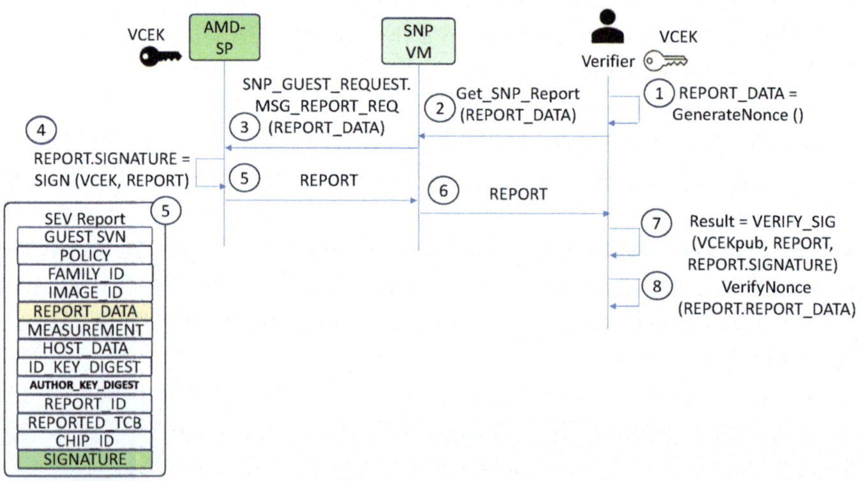

Figure 5.24 SEV-SNP remote attestation flow. *AMD-SP*, AMD Secure Processor; *VCEK*, Versioned Chip EK.

③ The attester calls the MSG_REPORT_REQ command to request the generation of an attestation report.
④ The AMD-SP signs the attestation report using VCEK or VLEK as appropriate.
⑤ The AMD-SP returns the signed attestation report to the attester.
⑥ The attester returns the signed attestation report to the verifier.
⑦ The verifier verifies the digital signature on the report, ensuring integrity.
⑧ The verifier checks the REPORT_DATA in the report, ensuring freshness.

5.4.4 ARM Realm Management Extension (RME) trusted execution environment attestation

The ARM Confidential Computing Architecture (CCA) documentation (DEN0127) briefly introduces the Realm attestation report, which includes:

- Realm measurements, including the Realm Initial Measurement (RIM) and runtime Extensible Measurements.
- TSM information: Information about the Realm Management Monitor (RMM) in the Realm Management Security Domain.
- Platform Firmware information: Information about the monitor in the Monitor Security Domain.
- Platform Hardware Identity: Information about the hardware in the CCA System Security Domain.

The Realm's attestation report is cryptographically bound to the physical hardware platform and generated/returned by the RMM (acting as TSM). This allows the Realm owner to verify and decide whether to trust the Realm.

The ARM CCA security model (DEN0096) introduces a general CCA attestation model. The core idea is to split the attestation report into two parts: a Realm token and a CCA platform token. The RMM specification (DEN0137) defines the attestation-related data structures in detail. The attestation report (CCA attestation token) is composed of:

- **Realm token**: Contains the Realm's initial and extended measurements, the challenge Nonce, and the public key of the Realm Attestation Key (RAK). This information is signed by the RMM using the RAK.
- **CCA platform token**: Contains the platform's hardware identity, platform lifecycle state, measurements of platform firmware/software

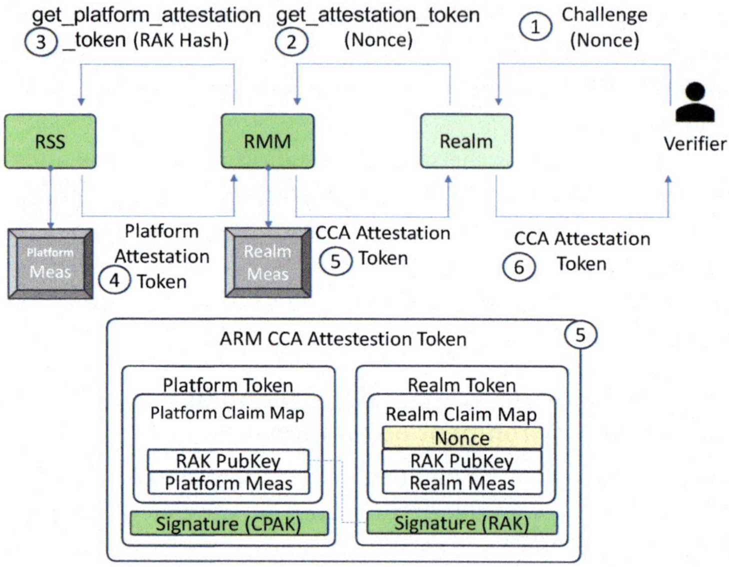

Figure 5.25 ARM RME attestation flow CPAK, CCA Platform Attestation Key; *RAK*, Realm Attestation Key; *RMM*, Realm Management; Monitor; *RSS*, Runtime Security Subsystem.

modules, and the hash of the RAK public key. This information is signed by the Root of Trust, typically the Runtime Security Subsystem (RSS), using its CCA Platform Attestation Key (CPAK).

Fig. 5.25 illustrates the ARM RME attestation process.

① The verifier randomly generates a Nonce and requests attestation from the Realm.

② The Realm requests a CCA attestation token from the RMM, passing the Nonce as a parameter.

③ The RMM requests a CCA platform token from the RSS, passing the hash of the RAK public key as a parameter.

④ The RSS generates the CCA platform token containing the RAK public key hash and returns it to the RMM.

⑤ The RMM generates the Realm token containing the Nonce, concatenates it with the CCA platform token to form the complete CCA attestation token, and returns it to the Realm.

⑥ The Realm returns the complete CCA attestation token to the verifier.

5.4.5 RISC-V CoVE TEE attestation

RISC-V CoVE adopts a trusted boot and attestation approach similar to DICE. The attestation report includes:

- TEE Virtual Machine (TVM) measurements: Includes initial measurements and runtime measurements.
- TSM information: Information about the Domain Security Manager and related modules.
- Platform Firmware information: Information about the M-mode firmware acting as the Root Security Manager, including the TSM driver.
- Platform Hardware Identity: Information from the hardware Root of Trust (RoT).

Because DICE is well-suited for smaller devices, we will provide more details in Chapter 11. Here, we only introduce some basic concepts.

Fig. 5.26 shows the CoVE boot and attestation process. On the left is the boot process. The RISC-V hardware RoT is responsible for extending measurements of M-Mode firmware, TSM driver, and TSM into platform TCB measurement registers. It also passes DICE attestation certificates and Compound Device Identifiers (CDIs) down to the next level module, eventually reaching the TSM. Finally, the TSM passes the CDI to the TVM but does not generate DICE attestation certificates for it. The right side shows the process initiated by a verifier:

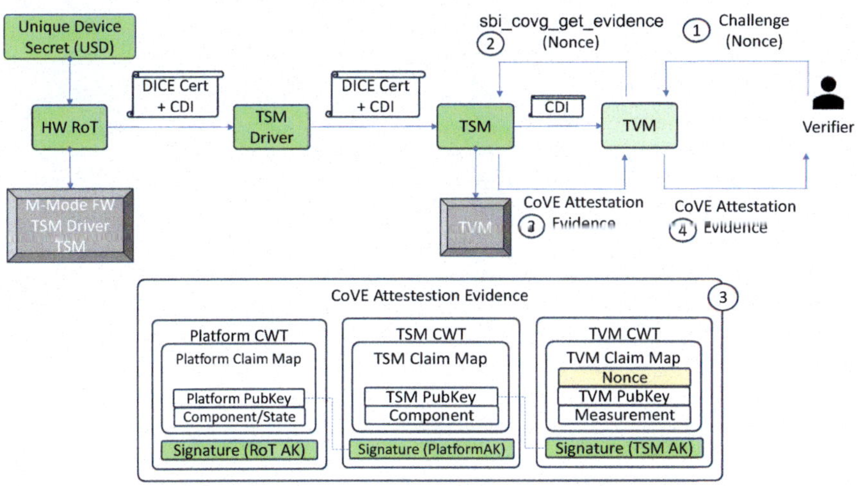

Figure 5.26 RISC-V CoVE attestation flow and data structures. *AK*, Attestation Key; *CDI*, Compound Device Identifier; *CWT*, CBOR Web Token; *DICE*, Device Identifier Composition Engine; *HW*, Hardware.

① The verifier randomly generates a Nonce and requests attestation from the TVM.
② The TVM calls the sbi_covg_get_evidence( ) command to request CoVE attestation evidence from the TSM.
③ The TSM generates the complete CoVE attestation evidence, including the Nonce, and returns it to the TVM.
④ The TVM returns the CoVE attestation evidence to the verifier.

A complete CoVE attestation evidence package contains these CBOR Web Tokens (CWTs):

- Platform CWT: Contains the platform's public key, platform manufacturer ID, platform state, and platform module information (e.g., SVN, measurements). This information is signed by the RoT's AK.
- TSM CWT: Contains the TSM's public key and TSM software module information. This is signed by the platform's AK.
- TVM CWT: Contains the challenge Nonce, the TVM's public key, and various TVM measurement values. This is signed by the TSM's AK.

The verifier can sequentially verify the integrity and freshness of the Platform CWT, TSM CWT, and TVM CWT, and then verify that the various measurement values in the TVM CWT match expectations.

CHAPTER 6

TEE special function

In Chapter 5, we introduced the attestation function of TEEs. In this chapter, we will introduce other optional features of TEEs.

6.1 Sealing

Sealing refers to protecting data using a Root of Trust for Storage (RTS), such that the data can be extracted/unsealed only when certain conditions are met. The sealing model is illustrated in Fig. 6.1.

The processes of sealing and unsealing data are:

- Sealing Data: The data owner inputs data and external configuration information into the RTS and specifies the RTS's internal state as sealing conditions. The RTS combines its own sealing seed and internal state,

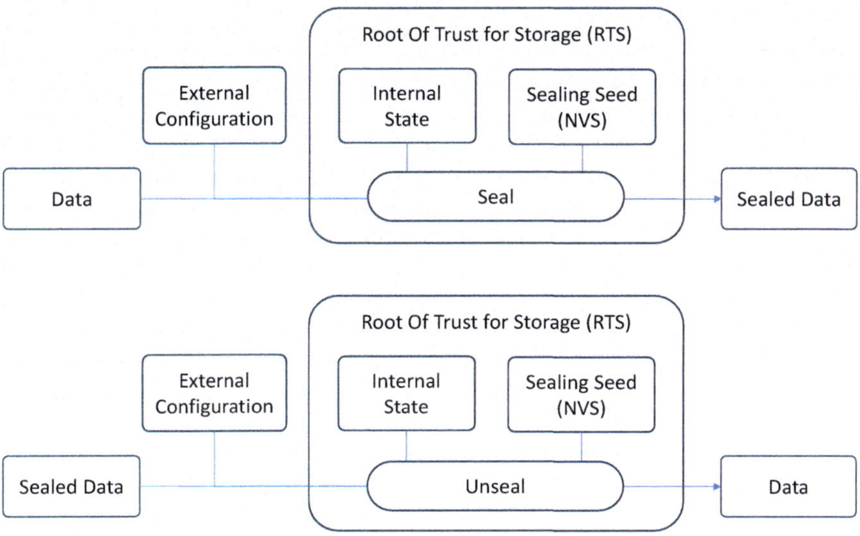

Figure 6.1 Sealing model.

Confidential Computing
ISBN 978-0-443-54067-7
https://doi.org/10.1016/B978-0-443-54067-7.00020-6

along with the input data and external configuration information, to generate sealed data.
- Unsealing Data: The data extractor inputs the sealed data and the same external configuration information into the RTS. The RTS checks its internal state and uses its sealing seed to unseal the data. Only when the external configuration, the RTS's internal state, and the RTS's sealing seed are consistent can the sealed data be correctly unsealed.

Sealing implies that the RTS must have nonvolatile storage (NVS) to store the seed, ensuring that data can be extracted even after a system reboot.

Generally, hardware RTS is relatively small and not suitable for directly sealing large amounts of data. Two more appropriate methods are:
- Seal a Key: In this case, the data being sealed are a cryptographic key.
- Generate a Sealed Key: The sealed data generated are a key. This key can then be used to encrypt/decrypt the actual data that need confidentiality.

However, the possibility of key loss must be considered: for example, if the RTS is damaged or its internal state is not met after a system update. Therefore, directly sealing or generating a data encryption key carries risks. A common practice is to seal a Key Encryption Key (KEK), use the KEK to encrypt a Data Encryption Key (DEK), and provide other backup mechanisms (such as user passwords or USB tokens) to recover the DEK. This process is illustrated in Fig. 6.2.

Now let us look at existing hardware that implements sealing.

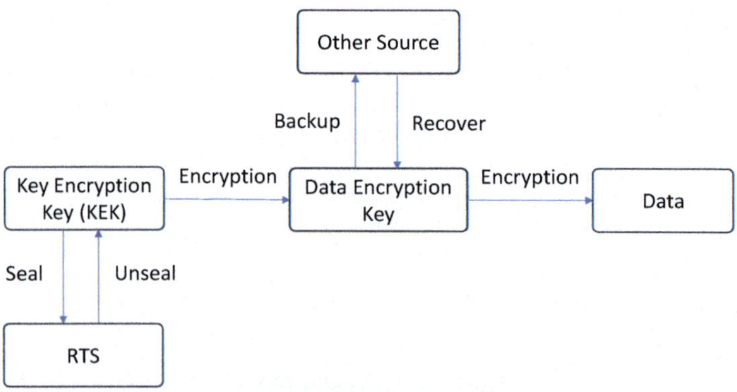

Figure 6.2 Key sealing process. *RTS*, Root of Trust for Storage.

6.1.1 TPM key sealing and Device Identifier Composition Engine key sealing

Both industry-standard Trusted Platform Module (TPM) and Device Identifier Composition Engine (DICE) support key sealing.

6.1.1.1 TPM key sealing

Like attestation, the TPM was the earliest implementation of key sealing. The TPM specification provides Seal and Unseal interfaces. Microsoft uses the TPM's sealing functionality to implement Windows BitLocker. The principle of TPM key sealing is shown in Fig. 6.3.

6.1.1.2 Device Identifier Composition Engine key sealing

The DICE architecture also supports key sealing. The DICE Protection Environment specification describes Seal and Unseal interfaces. Open-DICE implementations also describe methods for providing secret sealing using a Sealing Compound Device Identifier (CDI) (derived from the CDI). The principle of DICE key sealing is shown in Fig. 6.4. Details about the Unique Device Secret and CDI are covered in Chapter 11.

6.1.2 Trusted execution environment key sealing

TEEs themselves do not inherently require sealing functionality. However, TEE implementations can provide sealing capabilities, allowing TEEs to generate sealing keys as needed. Fig. 6.5 illustrates one method for generating a TEE sealing key.

1. The TEE specifies configuration information, such as a selector or a specific Security Version Number (SVN). The TEE sends this information to the TEE-Trusted Computing Base (TCB), requesting the generation of a sealing key.
2. The TEE-TCB ensures that the input SVN is less than or equal to the current TVM's SVN.

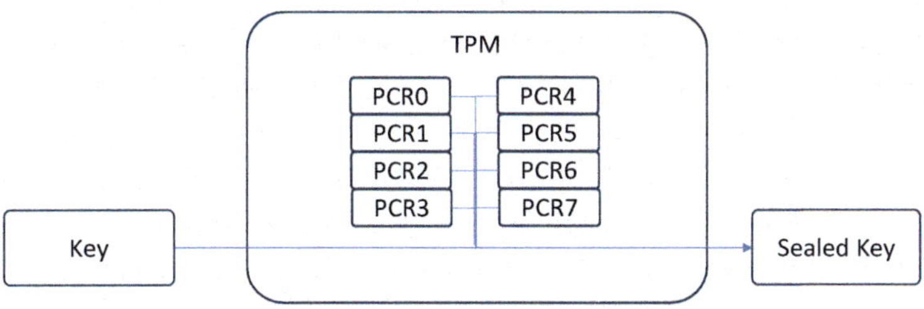

Figure 6.3 Principle of TPM key sealing.

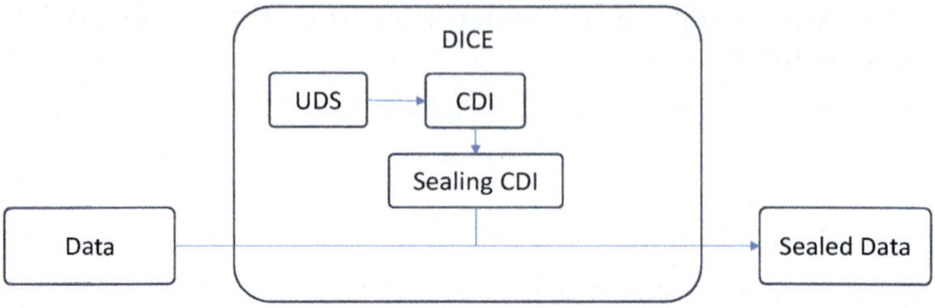

Figure 6.4 Principle of compound device identifier (DICE) key sealing. *CDI*, Compound Device Identifier; *UDS*, Unique Device Secret.

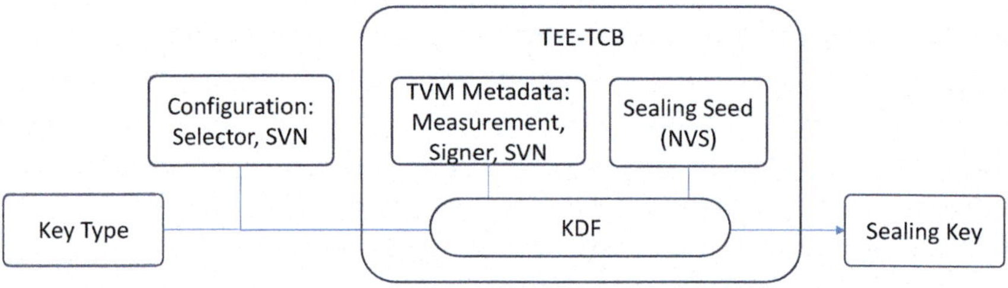

Figure 6.5 Trusted execution environment (TEE) key sealing model. *SVN*, Security Version Number; *TVM*, TEE Virtual Machine; *KDF*, Key Derivation Function.

3. The TEE-TCB uses the selector to determine which information from the TVM metadata should be included in the key generation parameters. This can include the TEE's measurement value, signer identity, or SVN.
4. The TEE-TCB generates the key based on its own sealing seed stored in NVS and the constructed key generation parameters.
5. The TEE-TCB returns the generated key to the TEE.

Selectors can be used to support flexible key generation policies. Sealing keys have two typical applications:

- Binding to TEE Identity: Binds the key to the TEE's measurement value. Only an identical TEE can unseal the data. The advantage is absolute security; the disadvantage is lack of flexibility. Once the TEE is updated, previously sealed data cannot be unsealed.
- Binding to Signer Identity: Binds the key to the TEE's signer identity and must be used in conjunction with SVN. As long as the signer is the same, any TEE with a higher security version can obtain sealing keys generated by all lower-version TEEs signed by the same key. This supports TEE upgrades but does not support TEE downgrades.

***Note**: Although a higher SVN TEE can obtain sealing keys generated by lower SVN TEEs, the higher SVN TEE needs to be aware of the security risks, because lower SVN TEEs may have been compromised. Conversely, lower SVN TEEs must not be allowed to obtain sealing keys generated by higher SVN TEEs; otherwise, a malicious attacker could use a downgrade attack to run a vulnerable TEE and gain access to current sealing keys.*

6.1.2.1 Intel SGX key sealing

Software Guard Extensions (SGX) hardware allows an Enclave to generate a sealing key deterministically using the EGETKEY instruction, as shown in Fig. 6.6. Dark gray boxes indicate mandatory key generation parameters; light gray boxes indicate optional parameters.

① The Enclave creates a KEYREQUEST data structure, setting KEYNAME to SEAL_KEY. The KEYPOLICY field can be used to select which items from the currently running SECS (SGX Enclave Control Structure) are added to the key generation parameters.

② The Enclave executes the EGETKEY instruction, passing the KEYREQUEST structure as a parameter to the CPU hardware to request generation of the sealing key.

③ Upon receiving the request, the CPU first applies MISCMASK and ATTRIBUTEMASK from the key request to filter out unnecessary attributes from the generation parameters. The purpose of using masks is to allow an upgraded Enclave, whose attributes might have changed, to still derive the sealing key from previous versions.

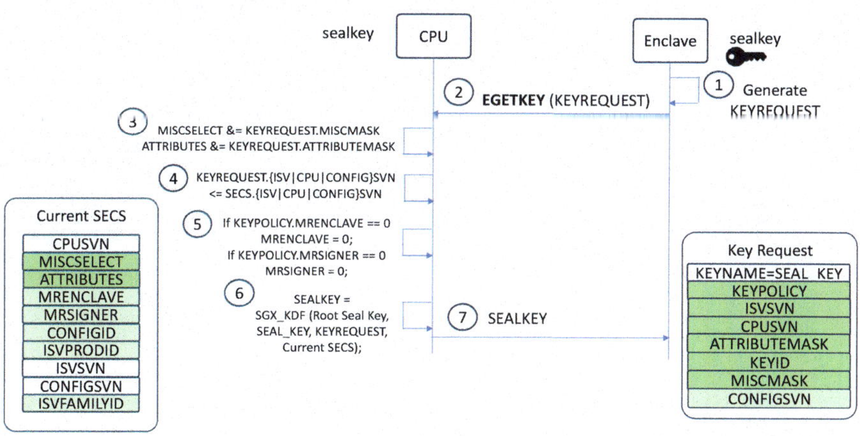

Figure 6.6 SGX key sealing. *SECS*, SGX Enclave Control Structure.

④ The CPU checks that the SVN values in the key request are less than or equal to the corresponding SVNs in the current SECS. If the check passes, the SVN values from the key request are included in the key generation parameters. The purpose of allowing SVN values less than the current SECS SVN is to enable an Enclave to retrieve sealing keys generated by its older versions after an SVN upgrade.

⑤ The CPU checks the KEYPOLICY to determine whether to include MRENCLAVE (the Enclave's measurement) and/or MRSIGNER (the signer's ID) in the key generation parameters. This allows the Enclave to bind the key flexibly to its identity or its signer.

⑥ The CPU derives the sealing key using the root sealing key (which never changes across boots) and the assembled key generation parameters. Because the root sealing key is persistent, the derived sealing key will also be consistent across boots.

⑦ The CPU returns the derived sealing key to the Enclave. The Enclave can use this key to encrypt data for storage in NVS outside the Enclave, or to decrypt data read from NVS.

6.1.2.2 AMD Secure Encrypted Virtualization (SEV) key sealing

AMD Secure Encrypted Virtualization - Secure Nested Paging supports requesting the generation of a subordinate key derived from a root key using the MSG_KEY_REQ command. This derived key can be used as a sealing key, as shown in Fig. 6.7. Dark gray parts are mandatory key generation parameters; light gray parts are optional.

① The SNP VM constructs a key request data structure (MSG_KEY_REQ), specifying the key to derive (typically from a

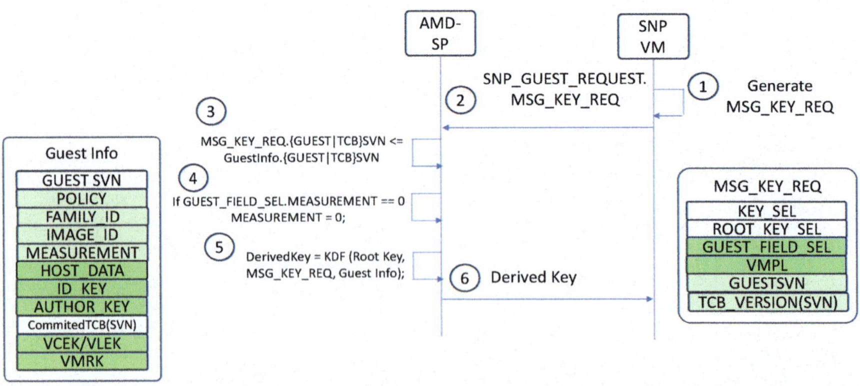

Figure 6.7 SEV-SNP key derivation (for sealing).

root key) and selecting which items from the guest information structure should be added to the key generation parameters.

② The SNP VM sends the request to the AMD Secure Processor (AMD-SP).

③ The AMD-SP checks that the SVN values in the key request are less than or equal to the corresponding SVNs in the current guest information.

④ The AMD-SP, according to the specified guest field selection policy, includes the chosen guest information (e.g., guest measurement) into the key generation parameters.

⑤ The AMD-SP derives the sealing key using the specified root key and the assembled key generation parameters. Because the root key does not change across boots, the derived key will also be consistent.

⑥ The AMD-SP returns the derived key to the SNP VM. The SNP VM can then use this key as a sealing key.

6.2 Nesting

Nested virtualization refers to running a Virtual Machine Manager (VMM) inside a virtual machine. For example, nested VMs involve launching a VM on an L0-VMM, and then launching an L1-VMM and corresponding L2-VMs inside that VM. Here, L0-VMM is called the bare-metal VMM, L1-VMM is called the guest VMM, and L2-VM is called the nested guest, as illustrated in Fig. 6.8. Mainstream hypervisors such as Windows Hyper-V and Linux KVM support nested virtualization.

TEEs also support nesting, for example, nested TEE VMs (TVMs), as shown in Fig. 6.9. An L1-VMM and several L2-VMs can be launched within a single TEE.

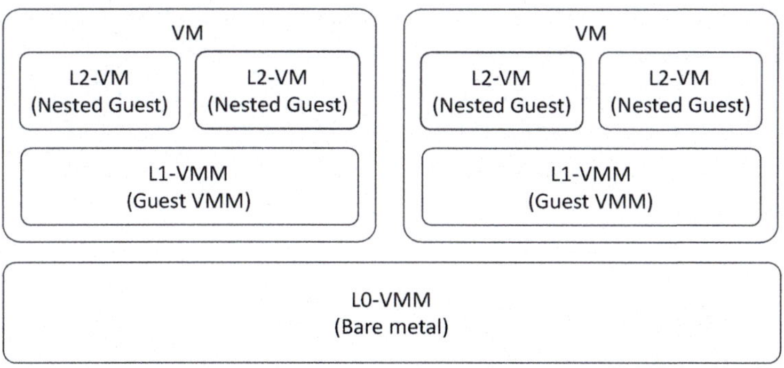

Figure 6.8 Nested virtualization. *VMM*, Virtual Machine Manager.

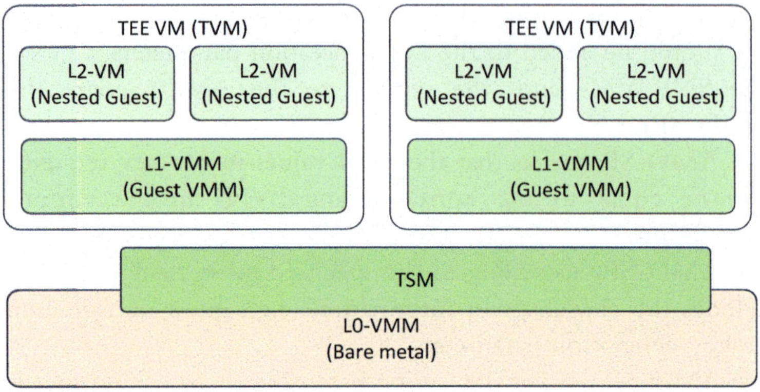

Figure 6.9 Nested TVM. *VMM*, Virtual Machine Manager.

Compared with a regular TVM, the security characteristics of a nested TVM change. The L1-VMM inside the TVM becomes part of the TCB for the L2-VMs. The L1-VMM is responsible for isolating the L2-VMs from each other, and L2-VMs cannot trust other L2-VMs. Security properties outside the TEE Virtual Machine (TVM) remain unchanged; for example, the TSM is still part of the TVM's TCB, and the L0-VMM remains untrusted.

The primary benefit of nested TVMs is enabling the use of minimal modified guest Operating Systems (OSes) as L2-VMs. Without nested TVMs, the guest OS would need to be modified to be aware of the TSM and use its interfaces for self-protection. However, with nested TVMs, the L1-VMM can be aware of the TSM and use its interfaces to protect the L2-VMs. This way, by adding a software layer (L1-VMM) within the TVM, compatibility for minimal modified guest OSes (L2-VMs) is maximized.

Another use case for nested TVMs is to launch a service L2-VM alongside user L2-VMs. This service VM can assist the L1-VMM in providing services to user L2-VMs, such as a virtual TPM (vTPM) service or a TVM migration service.

Nested TVMs introduce new challenges for attesting L2-VMs. Previous TEE reports contained information about the entire TEE. In architectures with only static measurement registers, typically only the boot-time modules of the L1-VMM are included in the TEE report, without information about L2-VMs. However, a user might provide only the image for the L2-VM and needs to know its measurement. One solution is to use a vTPM, which we will introduce later.

6.2.1 Intel TDX TD partitioning

Intel TDX 1.5 introduces Trust Domain (TD) Partitioning architecture to support partitioning within a TD. It allows launching one L1-VMM and up to three L2-VMs within a single TD. The TD Partitioning is shown in Fig. 6.10. Its primary purpose is to support Microsoft's Virtual Secure Mode (VSM) guest partitions, enabling virtualization-based security memory enclaves. VSM assigns different Virtual Trust Levels (VTLs) to partitions within a VM, with higher VTL numbers indicating greater security and trust. Typically, VTL0 runs the standard Windows OS and VTL1 runs Windows Defender System Guard (including the Secure Kernel and Isolated User Mode). An L1-VMM at VTL2 allows a Paravisor to provide isolation functions and services through a Service VM.

6.2.2 AMD SEV VM privilege levels

AMD SEV-SNP's VM Privilege Level (VMPL) is the mechanism supporting TVM nesting. An SEV-SNP TVM can support four privilege levels: VMPL0, VMPL1, VMPL2, and VMPL3. Typically, a Secure VM Service Module (SVSM) runs at VMPL0, providing services and security policies to the ordinary guest OS running at VMPL3. The SEV VMPL is shown in Fig. 6.11.

6.3 Virtual TPM

The concept of Virtual TPM (vTPM) was introduced by Berger et al. from IBM in their 2006 paper "vTPM: Virtualizing the Trusted Platform Module" to address the problem of using TPMs within virtual machines. Subsequently,

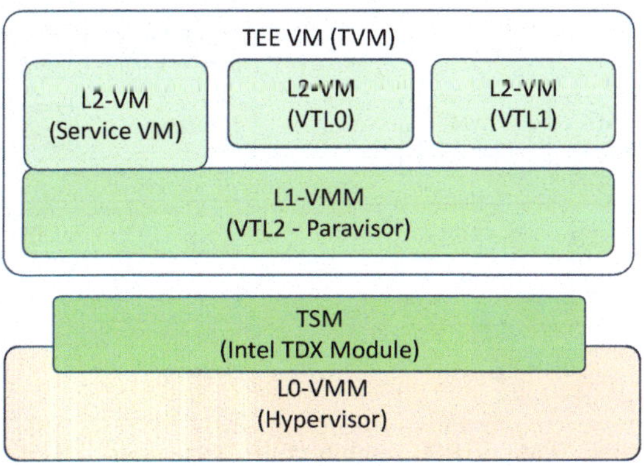

Figure 6.10 TD partitioning. *VMM*, Virtual Machine Manager.

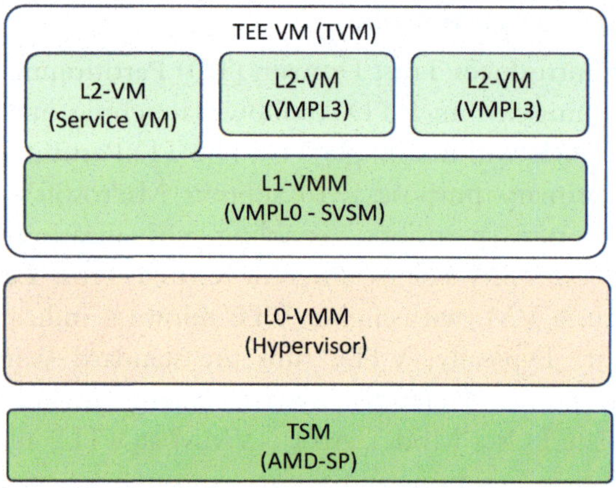

Figure 6.11 SEV VM Privilege Level (VMPL). *VMM*, Virtual Machine Manager.

the Trusted Computing Group (TCG) formed a working group and defined the Virtualized Trusted Platform Architecture specification.

There are various implementation methods for vTPM. Fig. 6.12 shows two examples. The left side depicts a typical three-layer VM architecture where the VMM provides vTPM services for each VM. The right side shows a typical four-layer nested VM architecture where the L1-VMM within a VM provides vTPM services for L2-VMs.

Because remote attestation for many existing industry platforms is based on TPMs, enabling TEEs to use vTPM for attestation is a viable approach. It allows existing TPM-based attestation services to be reused to prove the TEE's state. A practical challenge is that a physical TPM serves the entire

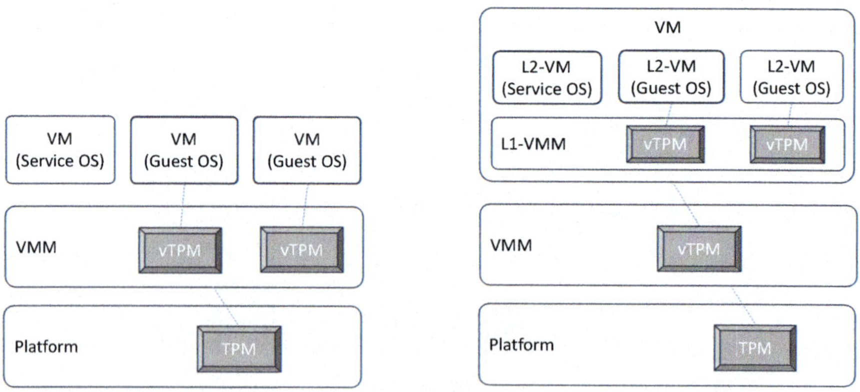

Figure 6.12 Virtual TPM (vTPM) architecture examples. *VMM*, Virtual Machine Manager.

host platform, which might be running multiple TEEs, but the TPM cannot be shared. vTPM technology addresses this need. However, vTPM in confidential computing TEEs has specific security requirements because the system platform and VMM are untrusted. Two typical TEE vTPM architectures are described next.

6.3.1 Trusted execution environment–based Virtual TPM

For a TEE, the vTPM is part of its TCB and therefore needs protection itself. Placing the vTPM implementation inside another TEE is one solution, as shown in Fig. 6.13. The vTPM TEE could be an SGX Enclave, a TD VM, or an SEV-SNP VM. In this mode, communication between the vTPM TEE and the user TEE must go through the untrusted VMM, requiring encryption using a secure protocol like TLS or SPDM.

Referencing Intel's "TD-based virtual TPM design guide," Fig. 6.13 illustrates a typical vTPM-based scheme composed of these modules:

- **vTPM service**: Provides the functionality defined in the TPM 2.0 specification to the TEE.
- **TPM driver**: The TPM hardware driver within the TEE.
- **TPM application**: Software modules within the TEE that use the TPM services, for example, to extend measurements of TEE dynamic modules into the vTPM's Platform Configuration Registers (PCRs) or to seal keys into the vTPM's nonvolatile storage.

In Chapter 5, we discussed TPM-based boot and attestation in detail. This process can also be applied to vTPM-based TEE boot and attestation. Here, the vTPM acts as the RTS and Root of Trust for Reporting (RTR), while the TSM continues to act as the RTM. Special attention is needed for the endorsement verification process of the TEE vTPM. Physical TPM endorsement certificates are issued and signed by the TPM manufacturer.

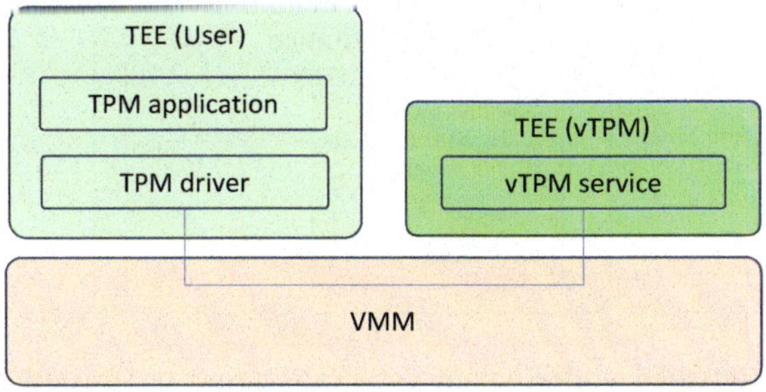

Figure 6.13 Trusted execution environment (TEE)-based Virtual TPM (vTPM). *VMM*, Virtual Machine Manager.

In contrast, endorsement certificates for non-TEE vTPMs are often issued by the VMM vendor. However, generating endorsement certificates for a TEE vTPM requires a specific process. Two possible methods are:

- **Self-Issued certificate based on TEE quote**: After the vTPM TEE starts, it generates an ephemeral Certificate Authority (CA) key pair. It then creates a TEE Quote based on the CA public key and uses this to generate a self-signed certificate, acting as the vTPM TEE's CA certificate. Next, the vTPM TEE creates a vTPM instance, generating an ephemeral Endorsement Key (EK) key pair and an EK certificate. Finally, the TEE uses the CA key to sign the vTPM instance's EK certificate. This process is illustrated in Fig. 6.14. Verifying the vTPM EK certificate chain essentially means verifying that the TEE Quote within the vTPM TEE's CA certificate matches the expected measurements. The advantage of this method is simplicity, requiring no external CA service. The disadvantage is that verifying the CA certificate is complex, requiring an additional TEE Quote verification step.
- **Endorsement certificate issued by vTPM CA service**: The vTPM TEE first creates a vTPM instance, generating an ephemeral EK key pair. It then creates a TEE Quote based on the EK public key and sends

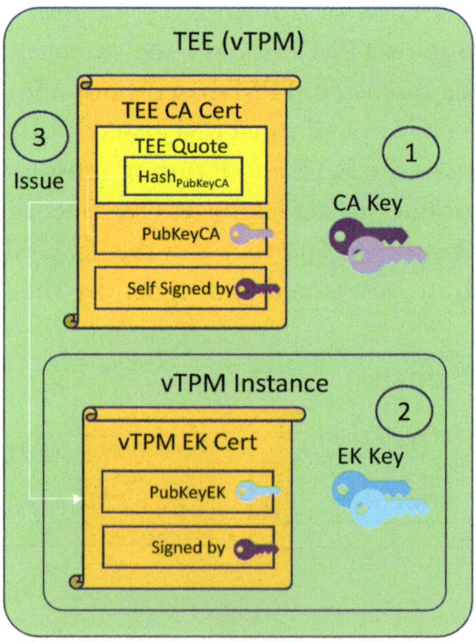

Figure 6.14 Self-issued endorsement certificate based on trusted execution environment (TEE) Quote. *CA*, Certificate Authority; *EK*, Endorsement Key; *vTPM*, Virtual TPM.

both to an external vTPM CA service. The vTPM CA service verifies the TEE Quote and, if successful, uses its own CA key to issue an EK certificate. Finally, the vTPM CA service returns the EK certificate to the vTPM TEE. This process is shown in Fig. 6.15. In this mode, verifying the vTPM EK certificate chain is the same as for a standard vTPM: directly verifying against the vTPM CA's certificate. Compared with the previous method, the advantage is reusability of existing vTPM EK verification schemes; the disadvantage is the necessity of a trusted vTPM CA service capable of verifying TEE Quotes.

6.3.2 Virtual TPM based on nested trusted execution environment virtual machines

Another method for implementing vTPM uses nested TEE virtualization, as shown in Fig. 6.16. The left diagram illustrates a vTPM residing in an L2 service VM communicating with an L2 user VM via the L1-VMM. The right diagram shows a vTPM integrated within the L1-VMM communicating directly with L2 user VMs. In this mode, communication between the vTPM and the user VM goes through the L1-VMM, which is part of the TCB for the L2 VM. Therefore, encryption via a secure protocol is not necessary, making this more convenient than the TEE-based vTPM scheme. Both Intel TDX TD Partitioning and AMD SEV-SNP VMPL support nested TEE VM schemes.

Referring to Intel's "TD Partitioning-based virtual TPM design guide," the attestation process in this mode is illustrated in Fig. 6.17. Because the L1-VMM is part of the L2-VM's TCB, it can provide vTPM services for the L2-VM. The L2-VM boot module within the L1-VMM acts as the

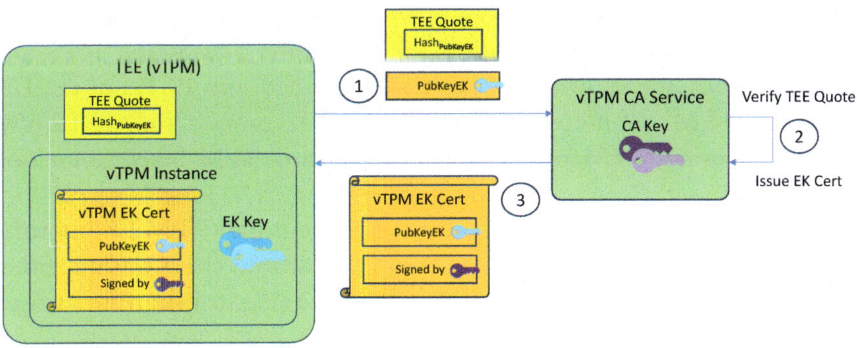

Figure 6.15 Endorsement certificate issued by Virtual TPM (vTPM) Certificate Authority (CA) service. *EK*, Endorsement Key; *TEE*, trusted execution environment.

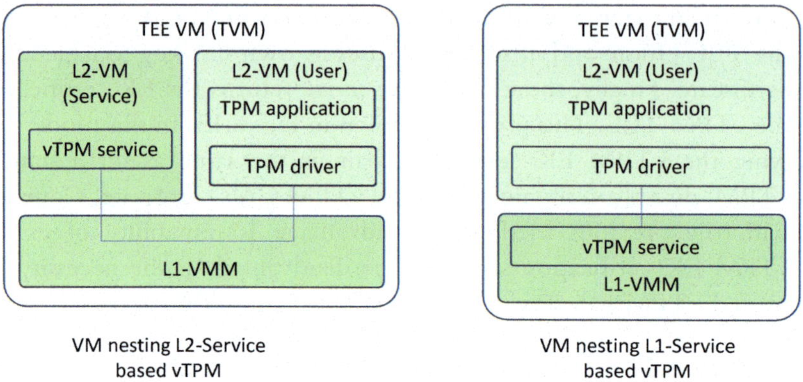

Figure 6.16 Virtual TPM (vTPM) based on nested virtualization. *TEE*, trusted execution environment; *VMM*, Virtual Machine Manager.

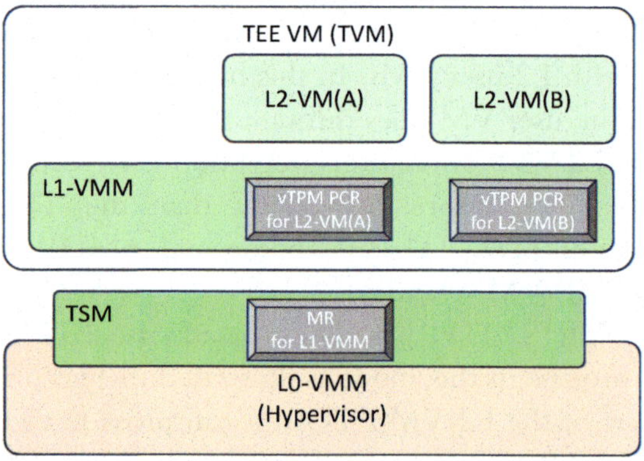

Figure 6.17 Attestation of nested TVM. *PCR*, Platform Configuration Register; *TEE*, trusted execution environment; *VMM*, Virtual Machine Manager.

RTM. The vTPM service within the L1-VMM acts as the RTS and RTR. Measurements of the L2-VM are extended into PCRs of the L1-VMM's vTPM. Consequently, the attestation process for an L2-VM within a nested TVM can follow the standard TPM-based attestation method:

1. **vTPM EK Verification**: The verifier requests the vTPM EK information from the L2-VM. The vTPM EK certificate chain can use either the self-issued method based on TEE Quote (Fig. 6.14) or the method using a vTPM CA service (Fig. 6.15).

2. **vTPM PCR Verification**: The verifier requests a vTPM PCR Quote from the L2-VM. The vTPM service signs the vTPM PCR values and returns the Quote to the verifier. The verifier validates the Quote's signature and the PCR values, ultimately trusting the L2-VM based on this.

6.4 Live migration

Migration refers to moving a program from a source platform to a target platform and continuing its execution there. A common example is VM migration in a VMM environment. When a VM is created by a VMM, the VMM can save its runtime state and move it from one machine to another. This is called offline migration or cold migration. Although simple, the disadvantage is that the service provided by the VM is interrupted during the migration, affecting availability. A more effective approach is live migration (also called online migration or hot migration), in which the migrating VM continues to provide services throughout the process, maintaining availability.

6.4.1 Overview of live migration

Live migration of virtual machines is a mature technology, supported by both Windows Hyper-V and Linux KVM. The live migration process is illustrated in Fig. 6.18.

① Preparation: The source and target platform VMMs prepare the migration environment. This includes checking network settings, enabling

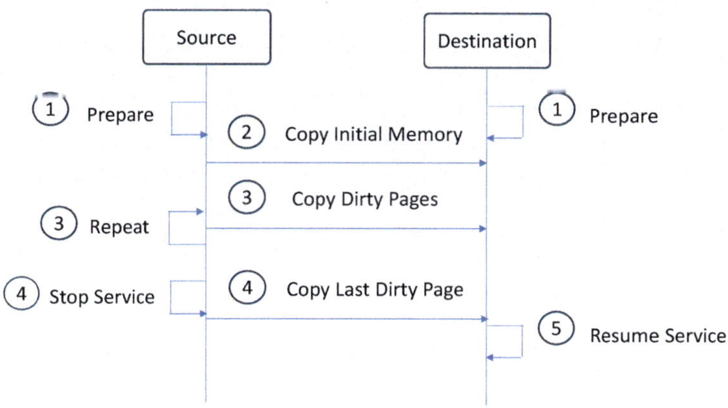

Figure 6.18 VM live migration process.

memory tracking on the source, and reserving resources for the VM on the target.

② Initial Memory Copy: The source VMM copies the source VM's memory to the target VMM. Simultaneously, it records any memory changes on the source VM after the copy started; pages that change are marked as dirty pages. During this step, the source VM continues to provide services.

③ Iterative Dirty Page Copy: The source VMM recopies the dirty pages from the source VM to the target VMM and continues tracking new dirty pages generated after this recopy. This step iterates. With each iteration, the copy speed typically increases and the number of dirty pages decreases until the difference between source and target memory falls below a certain threshold. The source VM continues to provide services throughout these iterations.

④ Final Dirty Page Copy: When the number of dirty pages reaches the threshold, the source VMM suspends the source VM's service. It performs one final copy of the remaining dirty pages to the target VMM. Service is paused during this step; the threshold determines the length of this pause.

⑤ New VM Online: After the final dirty page copy completes, the target VMM starts the target VM, which resumes providing services.

TEE live migration can reuse this basic process. However, in the confidential computing model, the resource manager (VMM) might be malicious and could attempt to attack the TEE using live migration. Therefore, TEE live migration has these additional security requirements:

- **Confidentiality and Integrity of TEE Private Memory**: During migration, the resource manager must not be able to read or modify the TEE's private memory. Shared memory used by the TEE does not require such protection, because TEE software should not trust content in shared memory.
- **Confidentiality and Integrity of TEE State and Metadata in TEE-TCB**: During migration, the resource manager must not be able to read or modify the TEE's state and metadata stored within the TEE-TCB. Migration typically involves only the TEE; the TEE-TCB itself is not migrated.
- **Target Platform's TEE-TCB Must Be Equally or More Secure Than Source's**: A common method is to ensure that the TEE-TCB SVN on the target platform is greater than or equal to the SVN on the source platform. Otherwise, a malicious resource manager could

perform a downgrade attack: launch a TEE on a platform with a vulnerable lower-version TEE-TCB, compromise it, and then migrate it to a higher-version platform to hide the evidence.

- **Postmigration TEE Attestation Must Include Information about the Least Secure TEE-TCB Encountered**: A TEE might be migrated multiple times (e.g., Platform 1 → Platform 2 → Platform 3). The TEE attestation report obtained on Platform 3 must include information (e.g., SVN) about the least secure TEE-TCB among all platforms on which it has resided. Otherwise, an attacker could compromise the TEE on a low-version platform, then migrate it to a high-version platform, and the final attestation report would hide that it ever ran on a vulnerable platform. If security levels between different platforms are incomparable, information about all distinct TEE-TCBs encountered must be recorded in the migration evidence.
- **If an Additional Migration TCB Module Assists Migration, Its Info Must Be in the Attestation Report**: A migration TCB refers to any extra module beyond the traditional TEE-TCB hardware and TSM that assists the migration process. Although it may not be possible to guarantee this module is entirely trustworthy, it must be ensured that it is bound to the TEE and its identity is verifiable by the attester.
- **If the Migration TCB Enforces Migration Policies, Those Policies Must Be Recorded in Its Attestation Evidence**: Migration policies are typically enforced by the migration TCB module.

Note: *Availability of the TEE service is not considered a security requirement. Because the resource manager may be malicious, it can stop the service at any time.*

To meet the first two security requirements, the source and target platforms need a TCB module to negotiate a Migration Key (MK). This MK is used to encrypt the TEE's memory, state, and metadata during transfer. From a security perspective, the MK should be exposed only to the TEE-TCB or the TEE itself.

To meet the third security requirement, the source and target platforms need a TCB module to verify the migration policy. If SVNs are comparable, relative comparison can be used. For example, migration might be allowed only if the target platform's TEE-TCB SVN is equal to the source's, or only if all measurements of the TEE-TCB match. Another scenario is when source and target platform SVNs are incomparable (e.g., completely different platform types). In this case, the migration policy might need to define absolute SVN requirements per platform type (e.g., for Platform X, SVN must be ≥ 5; for Platform Y, SVN must be ≥ 2).

To meet the fourth security requirement, the source and target platforms need a TCB module to record the lowest encountered TEE-TCB SVN among all platforms in the TEE's metadata, and include this information in the TEE's attestation report.

Note: *The emphasis here is on the lowest TEE-TCB SVN encountered, not the initial SVN. If the policy requires SVN > 3, a migration sequence such as 4 → 3 → 5 (from SVN4 to 3, then to 5) would be problematic because the lowest encountered SVN (3) does not meet the policy, even though the final platform (5) does. The report must reflect the lowest value (3).*

It is also not necessary to record all TEE-TCB SVNs; recording only the minimum suffices and avoids the complexity of maintaining a growing list. As long as the third requirement (no downgrade) is enforced during each migration step, the minimum SVN is the only one needed to assess the lowest security level experienced. Some might wonder about sequences such as 2 → 3 → 5 versus 2 → 4 → 5. If version 3 has a critical vulnerability fixed in version 4, is 2 → 4 → 5 safe? This is difficult to generalize. The safest approach is: if version 3 has a critical vulnerability, all lower versions (including 2) are considered to inherit the risk and are untrusted.

Finally, to support cross-platform migration, the minimum SVN for each distinct platform type needs to be recorded because SVNs are incomparable across platforms. For example, Platform X might be older and have a latest SVN of 5 after many updates, whereas Platform Y is newer and its latest SVN is only 2. At a given point in time, as long as both match their respective manufacturers' latest published SVNs, we might consider them equally secure in their own contexts, but their SVN numbers cannot be directly compared. The report needs to capture that the TEE ran on Platform X (with some minimum SVN) and Platform Y (with some minimum SVN).

Like vTPM, the live migration TCB module can be implemented in two ways: as a service TEE or as an L1-VMM component. To meet the fifth and sixth security requirements, the measurement of this migration TCB module, along with the migration policies it references, must be recorded and bound to the TEE's attestation evidence.

The live migration process for a TVM is illustrated in Fig. 6.19.

① Preparation: Source and target VMMs prepare the migration environment (e.g., initiating the migration TCB and binding it to the TEE).

② Notify Migration TCB: The VMMs on both sides notify their respective migration TCB modules.

③ Exchange MK: The migration TCBs on both sides exchange an MK. Typically, they establish an authenticated secure session (e.g., using Transport Layer Security (TLS) or Security Protocol and Data Model

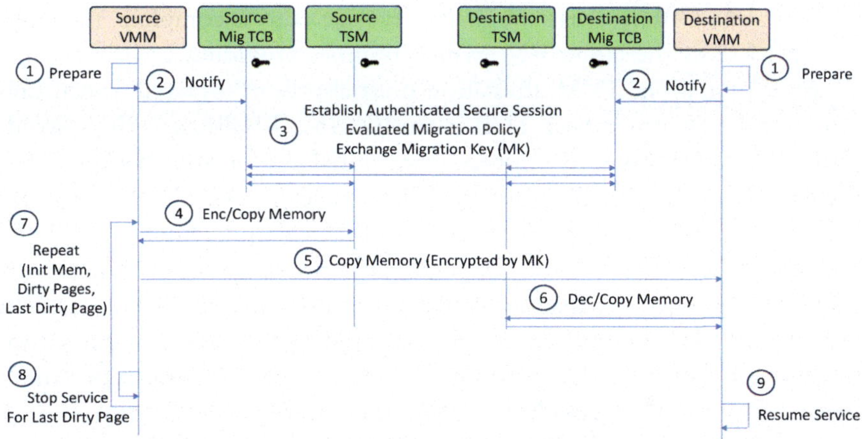

Figure 6.19 TVM live migration process. *VMM*, Virtual Secure Mode.

(SPDM)) and exchange information within it. The migration TCBs evaluate whether migration should proceed based on their migration policies, which may consider factors such as the peer platform's hardware, TEE-TCB SVN/measurements, the peer migration TCB's SVN/measurements, and attributes of the TEE being migrated. If the policies are satisfied, the migration TCBs can derive or exchange the MK. Finally, each migration TCB provides the MK to its local TSM. After this step, both TSMs possess the shared MK.

④ Migration Phase—Encrypt Memory: The source VMM requests the source TSM to copy TEE memory. The source TSM encrypts the TEE memory using the MK and returns the encrypted data to the source VMM.

⑤ Migration Phase—Copy Memory: The source VMM copies the encrypted TEE memory to the target VMM.

⑥ Migration Phase—Decrypt Memory: The target VMM requests the target TSM to copy TEE memory. The target TSM decrypts the received data using the MK and copies them into the TEE's private memory space on the target.

⑦ Migration Phase—Iterate: Steps 4 through 6 are repeated iteratively, migrating initial memory and then progressively smaller sets of dirty pages.

⑧ Service Suspension: When the dirty page threshold is reached, the source TVM service is suspended. Steps 4 through 6 are performed one last time to migrate the final set of dirty pages.

⑨ New VM Online: After the final dirty page copy is complete, the target VMM starts the target VM, which resumes providing services.

After migration, TVM attestation must also be considered, specifically whether the postmigration TCB is trustworthy. Ideally, a verifier would know the entire migration history (e.g., initial platform A1 SVN4, intermediate platform B SVN3, intermediate platform A2 SVN5, and final platform C2 SVN6). However, this is difficult to implement in practice and could be abused by an attacker performing excessive migrations, leading to resource exhaustion. A more practical approach is to record the minimum SVN encountered for each distinct platform type as part of the migration policy. For the previous example, the policy would be "minimum SVN for Platform A is 4, minimum SVN for Platform B is 3, minimum SVN for Platform C is 5." The migration TCB evaluates a potential target platform based on whether it meets the minimum SVN requirement for its platform type as defined in the policy.

Note: *Comparing absolute SVN values for known platform types is simple and effective. The main drawback is the need for continuous updates: new platform types must be added to the policy list, and SVN requirements must be updated as new versions are released.*

If migration is allowed only *between identical platform types, relative SVN comparison (target SVN ≥ source SVN) can be used. A prerequisite for this approach is that the final platform's TEE-TCB report must include the initial platform's SVN. If the report can reflect only the current platform's TEE-TCB, this method fails. Alternative strategies include requiring source and target SVNs to be equal, or using absolute SVN comparisons against a fixed threshold.*

6.4.2 Intel TDX VM migration

The Intel TDX 1.5 live migration architecture uses a special Migration TD (MigTD) to assist in negotiating the migration key, as shown in Fig. 6.20.

To support TVM attestation after migration, the measurement of the MigTD is recorded in the SERVTD_HASH field of the TD's TD_REPORT. Importantly, the TD's attestation report reflects the TCB_SVN of the platform where the TD is currently running, not the TCB_SVN of the initial platform where it was launched. Any TD_REPORT information from the initial platform is not carried over. The verifier must examine the migration policy associated with the MigTD to determine the minimum TCB_SVN encountered across all platforms during the migration process.

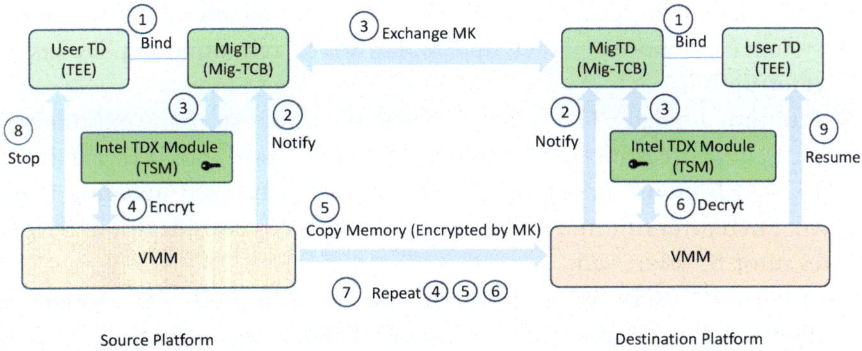

Figure 6.20 TDX live migration architecture based on migration TD. *MK*, Migration Key; *TEE*, trusted execution environment; *VMM*, Virtual Machine Manager.

6.4.3 AMD SEV VM migration

The AMD SEV-SNP white paper describes VMPL, in which the SVSM running at VMPL0 can provide migration services. This live migration architecture is illustrated in Fig. 6.21. The attestation report for the Guest VM should include a report from the SVSM.

6.5 Runtime update

During platform operation, software or firmware modules often need to be updated. Two main methods are employed:

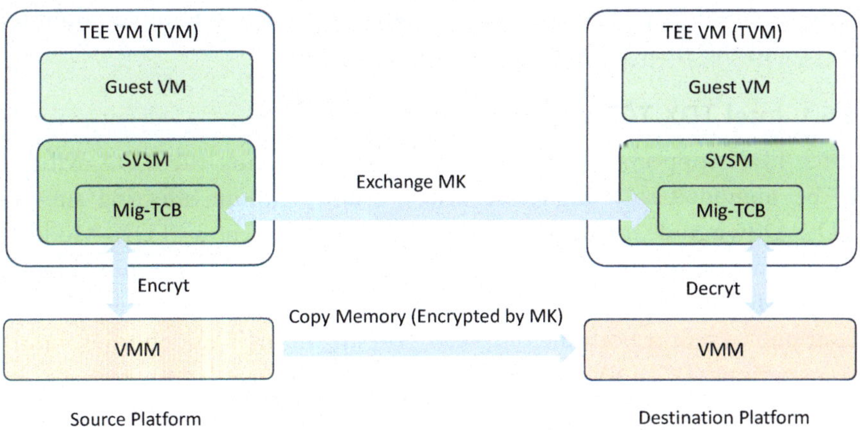

Figure 6.21 SEV-SNP live migration architecture based on Secure VM Service Module (SVSM). *TEE*, trusted execution environment; *VMM*, Virtual Machine Manager.

1. Reboot-based Update: Update can be performed after a reboot, or the system can reboot and then update. However, rebooting implies service interruption.
2. Runtime Update: The system is updated without stopping existing services. Examples include Windows Hotpatch and Linux LivePatch.

In a TEE environment, a key module that may need updating is the TSM. Therefore, runtime update of the TSM needs consideration. Several issues must be addressed:

- **Whether TCB_SVN Downgrade is Allowed**: A change in TCB_SVN typically indicates a new TSM version patching security vulnerabilities in the old version. Generally, downgrading TCB_SVN is not allowed. However, at the same TCB_SVN level, module versions might be downgraded if a newer version introduces functional defects and reverting to an older version is necessary.
- **How to Report TCB_SVN**: After a TSM upgrade, two pieces of information exist: the initial TCB_SVN (at TEE launch) and the current TCB_SVN (after upgrade). The TEE's attestation report could include both. Applying the wooden barrel principle from information security (a system's security is only as strong as its weakest link), if the report can only include one TCB_SVN, it should report the initial (lowest) TCB_SVN.

Broadly speaking, runtime update is a special form of live migration, so the issues regarding TCB_SVN reporting discussed in the previous section apply here as well. Similarly, TVM attestation after a TSM update can follow the principles of postmigration attestation. Ideally, the entire update history would be presented, but in practice, reporting the initial minimum SVN and the final SVN is often sufficient.

6.5.1 Intel TDX TCB runtime update

Intel TDX supports TD-preserving updates, allowing the TDX-Module to be upgraded to a higher security version without affecting running TDs. Downgrade updates are not permitted; the new TDX-Module's SVN must be greater than or equal to the SVN of the currently running TDX-Module. After a TDX-Module upgrade, already running TDs will continue to report both the old TCB_SVN from their launch time and the new current TCB_SVN (e.g., TCB_SVN2) in their attestation reports. Only newly launched TDs will report the new TCB_SVN.

6.5.2 AMD SEV TCB runtime update

AMD SEV-SNP supports online update of SNP firmware using the DOWNLOAD_FIRMWARE_EX command. SNP VM attestation reports provide both the launch TCB version (LAUNCH_TCB) and the current TCB version (CURRENT_TCB).

CHAPTER 7

Software development

In Chapters 3 through 6, we successively introduced various trusted execution environment (TEE) architectures, functions, and specifications. In this chapter, we will introduce the open-source software used to build TEE-based confidential computing solutions.

7.1 Application scenarios for trusted execution environment software

The software supporting TEE confidential computing is diverse. Let us first look at a typical practical scenario. Fig. 7.1 illustrates a background-check model and application scenario for a Confidential Virtual Machine (CVM).

The architecture of this model is as follows: The Virtual Machine Manager (VMM) is responsible for managing the entire system, launching the TEE security manager (TSM) and the CVM. The first module launched in the CVM is the virtual firmware, which is responsible for loading the operating system (OS). Subsequently, the OS runs applications. To ensure confidentiality, the application's data need to be transmitted to the CVM in the form of an encrypted disk image. Therefore, there must be a module that contacts an external key management system to obtain the disk decryption key. To ensure security, the key management system needs to verify the identity of the entity requesting the disk key to prevent leaking it to malicious attackers. This requires attesting the entity requesting the key, ensuring it is a known good CVM. The overall process is thus:

1. The VMM launches the TSM and the CVM.
2. The virtual firmware within the CVM loads the OS.
3. The Image Management Agent (IMA) and Attestation Agent (AA) within the OS start, beginning to process the encrypted disk image.
4. The AA connects to a remote Key Broker Service (KBS) and provides TEE attestation to prove its identity.

Confidential Computing
ISBN 978-0-443-54067-7
https://doi.org/10.1016/B978-0-443-54067-7.00017-6

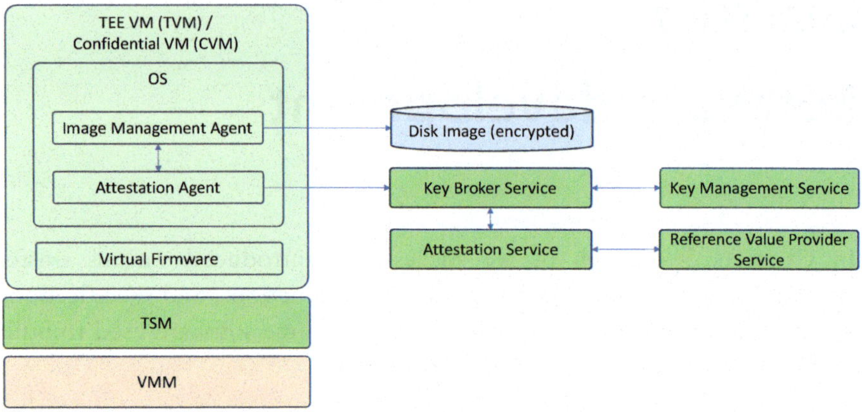

Figure 7.1 Background-check model and application scenario for confidential virtual machines. *OS*, operating system; *TEE*, trusted execution environment; *TSM*, TEE security manager; *VMM*, Virtual Machine Manager.

5. The KBS relies on a remote (AS) to perform remote attestation of the TEE entity.
6. The AS communicates with a Reference Value Provider Service to obtain the expected reference values for the TEE entity, compares them with the actual values from the TEE, and returns the result to the KBS.
7. If attestation is successful, the KBS obtains the disk key from a Key Management Service and returns it to the TEE.
8. The IMA within the TEE uses the key to decrypt the disk image.
9. The OS begins using the decrypted disk image data.

Fig. 7.2 illustrates an application scenario for the passport model of a CVM. The difference from the background-check model is that the AA is responsible only for performing attestation, obtaining an attestation result token, and presenting it to the IMA. The latter submits the attestation result token to the KBS to obtain the disk key and decrypt the disk image.

Fig. 7.3 shows an application scenario for a secure enclave.

The architecture of a secure enclave is as follows: The OS launches applications that need to run within an Enclave. To support unmodified applications and lower the development barrier for TEEs, the Enclave SDK provides standard libraries and a Library Operating System (LibOS). Unmodified applications can interact directly with the LibOS, and if

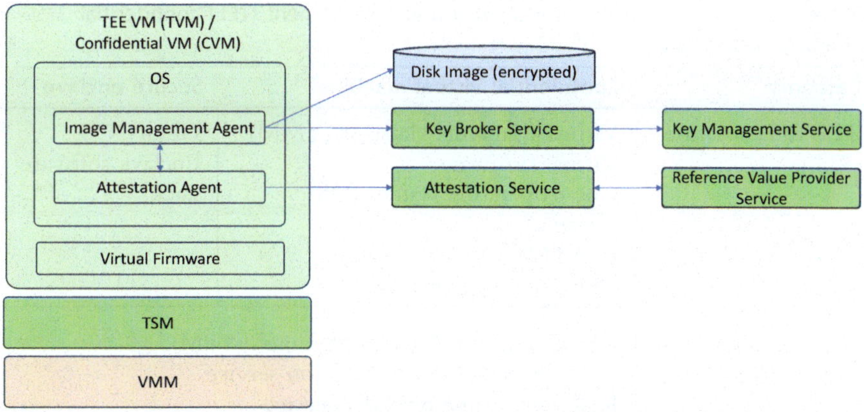

Figure 7.2 Passport model application scenario for confidential virtual machines (VMs). *OS*, operating system; *TEE*, trusted execution environment; *TSM*, TEE security manager; *VMM*, Virtual Machine Manager.

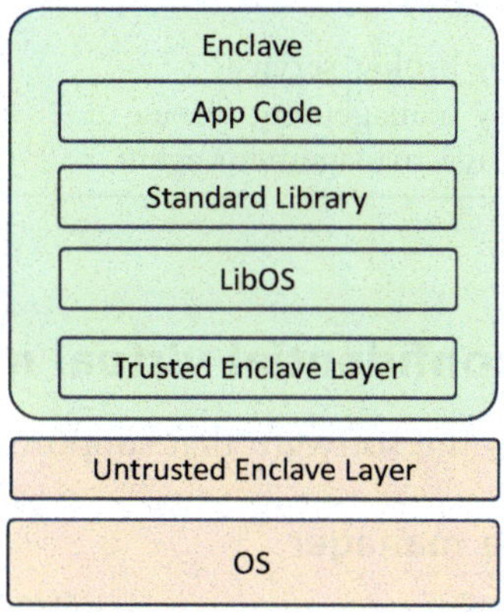

Figure 7.3 Secure enclave application scenario. *LibOS*, Library operating system.

necessary, the LibOS can also interact with the OS. Within the OS, the Enclave SDK provides an untrusted layer outside the Enclave and a trusted layer inside the Enclave to handle switching between the Enclave and the OS. Of course, the Enclave also needs to prove its authenticity through remote attestation services.

The book *Confidential Computing: AI Data Security and Privacy Protection*, by Yinwei Hu, Shoumeng Yan, and Yuan Wu provides a detailed description of SGX Enclave software and various usage scenarios, which can be referenced.

TEE confidential computing related software can be categorized into different types, as shown in Table 7.1.

Table 7.1 Classification of trusted execution environment (TEE) confidential computing software.

Category	Confidential virtual machine	Secure enclave
TEE infrastructure	Virtual Machine Manager (VMM) Virtual firmware Guest operating system (OS) kernel L1 VMM TEE security manager	Library OS Enclave software stack
TEE remote attestation	virtual Trusted Platform Module (vTPM) Attestation service, verification service Reference value provider service Policy engine	
TEE secure communication	Attestation-based Transport Layer Security (TLS) Attestation-based Security Protocol and Data Model (SPDM)	
TEE data security	Key broker service Key management service Image management agent	

7.2 Software in confidential virtual machines

This section introduces the software that supports TEEs within CVMs.

7.2.1 Virtual machine manager

The VMM acts as the resource manager in CVM solutions. Mainstream VMMs have begun supporting CVMs, such as Linux KVM and Microsoft Hyper-V. We will not elaborate further here.

In addition, some lightweight VMMs have also started supporting CVMs, including:

- Cloud Hypervisor: A project managed by the Linux Foundation, it is a lightweight VMM written in Rust. Its characteristics include a minimal set of emulated devices, fast startup, low memory footprint, support for Linux and Windows guests, and support for ×86 and Advanced RISC Machine (ARM) architectures.
- Dragonball Hypervisor: A lightweight VMM written in Rust, initially developed by Alibaba within the OpenAnolis community, and later contributed to the Kata Containers community.

7.2.2 Virtual firmware

In traditional virtual machine (VM) architectures, virtual firmware is the first module launched within the guest environment. CVM solutions adopt the same architecture; the virtual firmware is the boot module within the TEE, responsible for establishing a secure boot chain for the TEE. TEE virtual firmware options include Open Virtual Machine Firmware (OVMF) and TDX Shim Firmware.

- OVMF: An open-source firmware maintained by the Unified Extensible Firmware Interface (UEFI) EDK II open-source community, supporting UEFI interfaces. Its features include comprehensive support for various UEFI and Advanced Configuration and Power Interface (ACPI) interfaces, support for Intel TDX and AMD Secure Encrypted Virtualization–Secure Nested Paging (SEV–SNP), and dynamic switching between launching regular VMs, TDX VMs, and SEV-SNP VMs.
- TDX Shim Firmware (Td-Shim): A lightweight virtual firmware written in Rust, initially developed by Intel and later contributed to the Confidential Containers (CoCo) community. It primarily supports Intel TDX. Its characteristics include the removal of UEFI interface support, resulting in smaller and faster firmware capable of directly booting a kernel or TEE workload.

A comparison between OVMF and TDX Shim is shown in Table 7.2.

7.2.3 Guest operating system

For an OS to be used in a CVM solution, it needs to support the TEE architecture. For example, the Linux kernel has added support for Intel TDX and AMD SEV. Other open-source OSs are also considering adding TEE support such as Asterinas, a secure and fast general-purpose OS kernel written in Rust, unveiled by Ant Group in 2023, providing Linux ABI compatibility. Support for TEEs such as TDX and SEV is planned.

Additionally, the OS Loader needs to support the UEFI CC Measurement Protocol (EFI_CC_MEASUREMENT_PROTOCOL) to enable measurement of the kernel, initrd, and boot parameters for establishing a trusted boot chain. Examples include Grub2 and Shim.

CVM solutions can provide support for confidential container solutions. Related confidential container projects include:

- CoCo: A project created by the CoCo open-source community, dedicated to using TEE computing in the cloud to form Cloud Native

Table 7.2 Comparison of Open Virtual Machine Firmware (OVMF) and TDX Shim firmware.

Item	OVMF	TDX Shim firmware
Use case	Confidential Virtual Machines, complex services Trust Domain (TD)	Confidential containers, simple services
Development language	C	Rust
UEFI support	Yes, including UEFI network, UEFI file system	No
OS runtime services	UEFI runtime services	No
Device drivers	Virtio, Peripheral Component Interconnect (PCI) devices	No
ACPI tables	Full ACPI tables, including ACPI Source Language (ASI)	Static ACPI tables, e.g., Multi APIC Description Table (MADT)
IRQ information	Via ACPI Differentiated System Description Table (DSDT) table	Via boot parameters
Memory map info	UEFI memory map	ACPI E820 table
Trusted boot	Yes, Runtime Measurement Register (RTMR) + Event log	Yes, Runtime Measurement Register (RTMR) + Event log
Secure boot	Optional, UEFI secure boot	Optional, workload signature verification
Size	Default 4MiB	No secure boot: 140KiB, full features: 270KiB

Confidential Computing for protecting containers and their data. CoCo is a project under the Cloud Native Computing Foundation (CNCF) and hosts a series of subprojects supporting confidential computing.

- Constellation: A confidential Kubernetes project developed by Edgeless Systems, aiming to protect entire Kubernetes clusters using confidential computing technology. Constellation's security features include workload protection, control plane protection, and attestation/verification. Another approach for Kubernetes is to place only worker nodes within TEEs, leaving the control plane unprotected.

7.2.4 L1 Virtual Machine Manager

In nested VM solution, an L1 VMM runs inside the CVM to manage L2 VMs within the confidential VM, as shown in Fig. 7.4. One benefit of using an L1 VMM is the ability to support unmodified virtual firmware and OSs as L2 VMs, confining the TEE-specific support to the L1 VMM layer.

From a TEE architecture perspective, both Intel TDX TD Partitioning and AMD SEV-SNP VMPL support L1 VMM solution. Software support includes COCONUT-SVSM, a Rust-based Secure VM Service Module (SVSM) proposed by SUSE. The SVSM can also provide additional services for L2 VMs, such as VM migration and vTPM services.

7.2.5 Trusted execution environment security manager

The TSM is typically developed by the TEE architecture provider; TEE users generally do not need to perform secondary development on the TSM. Some typical TSM implementations are:

- Intel TDX-Module: The TSM software module developed by Intel supporting Intel TDX.
- AMD SEV Firmware: The TSM firmware module developed by AMD supporting the AMD SEV family.
- ARM Trusted Firmware Realm Management Monitor (RMM): Developed by the ARM Trusted Firmware community, it is the reference implementation of RMM in ARMv9 CCA and a key component of the ARM CCA TSM.

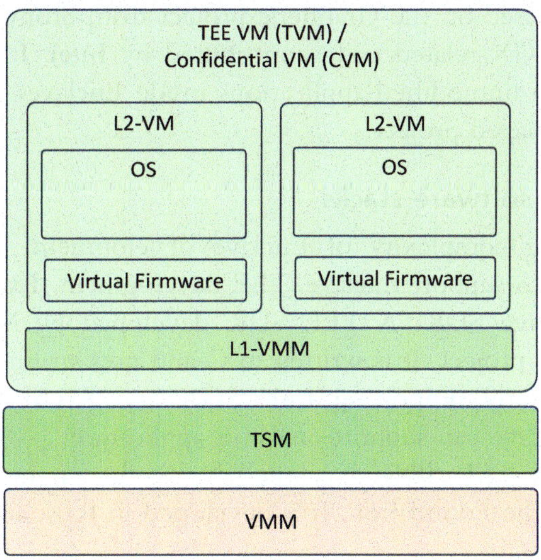

Figure 7.4 Nested virtual machine solution. *OS*, operating system; *TEE*, trusted execution environment; *TSM*, TEE security manager; *VM*, virtual machine; *VMM*, Virtual Machine Manager.

- RISC-V Salus: Developed by Rivos Inc., it is a reference implementation of the TSM for RISC-V CoVE.

The Intel whitepaper "Linux Stacks for Intel Trust Domain Extension 1.5" introduces the Linux software stack related to TDX.

7.3 Software support for secure enclaves

Compared with emerging CVMs, secure enclaves represented by Intel SGX are a more mature technology and thus have richer software support.

7.3.1 Library operating systems

The biggest challenge secure enclaves pose to existing applications is the need to partition the program into trusted and untrusted parts. Only the trusted part needs to reside inside the Enclave, whereas the untrusted part must operate outside the Enclave to support the application. The emergence of LibOS significantly reduces the burden on Enclave developers. With LibOS, developers can place the entire application inside the Enclave, eliminating the need for partitioning.

Notable LibOS projects for TEEs include:

- Occlum: A LibOS supporting Intel SGX, developed by Ant Group. It is written in Rust, supports multitasking, and provides a read-only hash-based filesystem, a read-write encrypted filesystem, and an untrusted host filesystem. It is one of the projects managed by the Confidential Computing Consortium (CCC).
- Gramine: Based on the Graphene project from Stony Brook University, with SGX-related code contributed by Intel. It is written in C and can run unmodified applications inside Enclaves. Gramine is also a CCC-managed project.

7.3.2 Enclave software stacks

Because of the complexity of Enclave development, various vendors provide SDKs to support Enclave/TEE development. Examples include:

Open Enclave SDK: A TEE SDK developed by Microsoft, and a CCC-managed project. It is written in C and uses an Enclave abstraction interface, currently supporting Intel SGX and ARM OP-TEE. Each application enclave can support one host application.

Teaclave: A TEE SDK developed by Baidu, an incubation project under the Apache Foundation. It is developed in Rust and supports Intel

SGX and ARM TrustZone. As such the application in Enclave can be written in Rust language.

Enclaves can also be provided to applications as part of a container. For example, Inclavare, a TEE container developed by Alibaba, is a sandbox project under the CNCF. It uses LibOSes such as Occlum or Gramine and supports Intel SGX.

Furthermore, Enclaves can also serve as a platform abstraction for TEEs. For example, Enarx, a WebAssembly-based TEE platform abstraction developed by Red Hat, is a CCC-managed project. It is written in Rust and supports Intel SGX and AMD SEV.

Additionally, developers at Ant Group have developed HyperEnclave. It is an open-source, cross-platform, process-based TEE that is not tied to any specific hardware CPU. HyperEnclave's TCB is a monitor written in Rust, and its Enclave SDK provides an abstract software interface similar to SGX, allowing existing SGX programs to run with minor modifications.

Amazon's AWS Nitro Enclaves represent another type of enclave, using Nitro VM technology to provide CPU and memory isolation for Amazon Elastic Compute Cloud (EC2) instances.

7.4 Trusted execution environment remote attestation related software

Remote attestation is an indispensable part of any TEE solution. This section introduces software related to supporting TEE remote attestation.

7.4.1 vTPM

Confidential computing TEE hardware designs are based on CPU architectures, with Intel, AMD, ARM, and RISC-V each launching their own solutions. This poses a challenge for TEE remote attestation software. From a user's perspective, having a single piece of software that can run on various TEE hardware is highly desirable. Therefore, vTPM-based TEE solutions have attracted significant attention.

Chapter 6 introduced vTPMs. Figs. 7.5 and 7.6 respectively show a vTPM solution based on a TEE and based on nested virtualization. Besides the vTPM service, TPM driver, and TPM application, these include a TPM remote attestation service. This service communicates with the TPM application within the TEE, for example, to obtain the TPM's Endorsement Key certificate to verify the vTPM's authenticity, or to obtain a TPM Quote to verify the TEE's measurements.

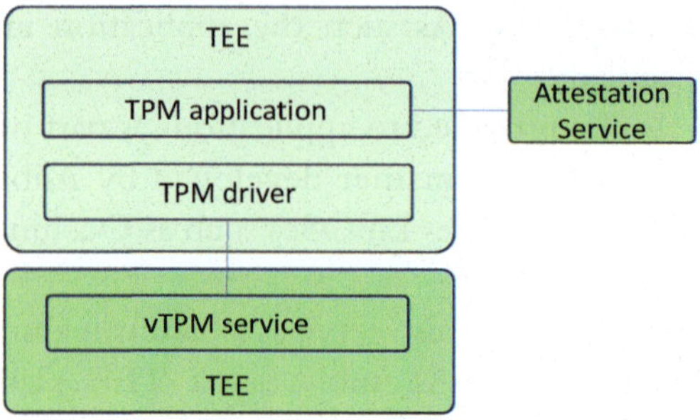

Figure 7.5 Trusted execution environment (TEE)-based vTPM.

There are many software stacks supporting TPM in the industry. Commonly used TPM service codebases include:

- TPM 2.0 Reference Code: Microsoft's C language reference implementation of the TPM 2.0 specification, forming the basis for software TPM implementations.
- Linux Software TPM: IBM's C language reference implementation of the TPM 2.0 specification, running on Linux systems.

Regarding vTPM solution for TEEs, several options exist:

- TD-based vTPM: Intel's vTPM solution based on TDX, with an architecture similar to Fig. 7.5.
- SVSM-based vTPM/Coconut-SVSM vTPM: vTPM solutions based on AMD SEV-SVSM or Intel TD Partitioning. Their architecture is similar to Fig. 7.6. Microsoft's vTPM in Azure Confidential VMs uses this approach.
- Inclavare Confidential vTPM: Alibaba's TEE-based vTPM solution.

On the application side, TPM support includes:

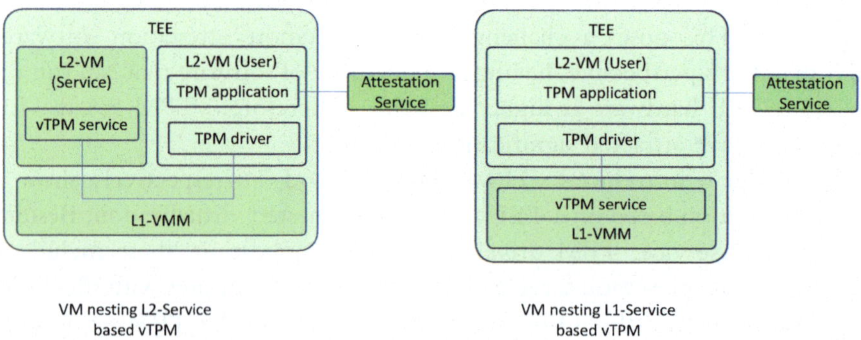

Figure 7.6 vTPM based on nested virtualization. *TEE*, trusted execution environment; *VM*, virtual machine.

- TPM Software Stack: A C language software stack provided by the TPM2 software community, including the TPM Command Transmission Interface, System Level Application Programming Interface (API), Enhanced System Level API, and Feature Level API. Fig. 7.7 shows the TPM2 software stack architecture. Additionally, the TPM2 software community provides a set of TPM2 command-line tools based on this stack.
- Linux Integrity Measurement Architecture (IMA): A subsystem within the Linux kernel responsible for integrity measurement. Linux IMA collects file hash measurements into TPM PCRs and supports local or remote verification of these measurements. It is a classic TPM application. Its architecture is shown in Fig. 7.8.
- Keylime: A CNCF project providing a remote attestation and integrity measurement solution based on TPM 2.0. Keylime is developed in Rust. The main modules include the Keylime Agent, Keylime Verifier, and Keylime Registrar. The Registrar maintains the public keys of all registered TPMs. At runtime, the Keylime Agent on the host collects TPM information, PCR values, and Trusted Computing Group (TCG) logs, and sends them to the remote Keylime Verifier for validation.
- go-tpm-tools: A TPM application layer library provided by Google, developed in Go. It supports attestation for TPMs as well as for confidential VMs such as TDX or SEV.

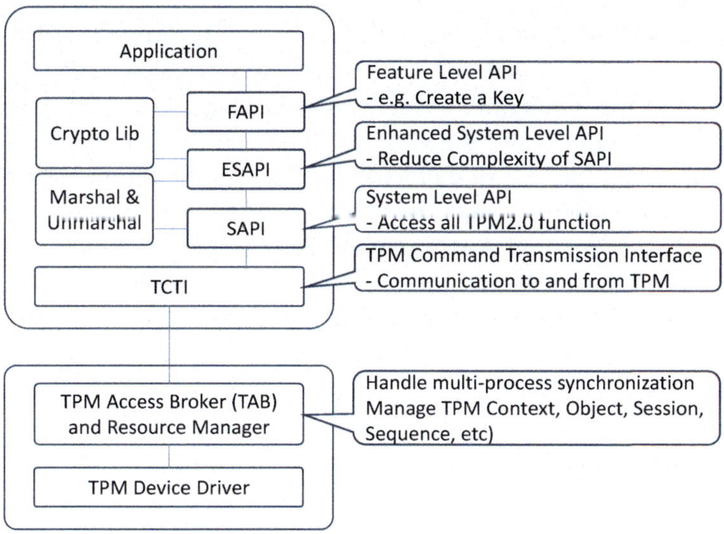

Figure 7.7 TPM2 software stack architecture.

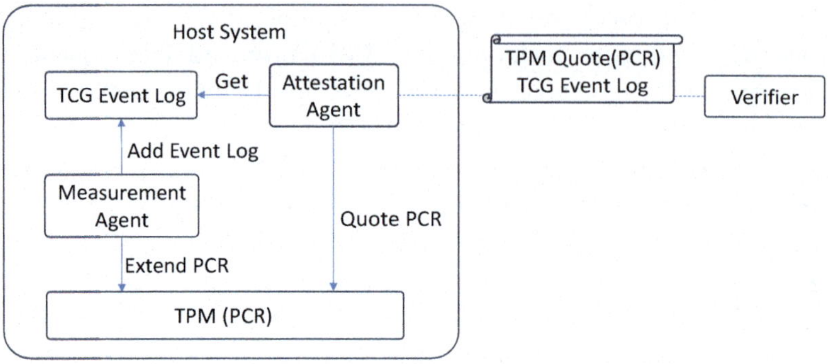

Figure 7.8 Linux IMA architecture.

7.4.2 Attestation and verification service software

For attestation and verification services, commonly used software includes:

- Intel Data Center Attestation Primitives: Provides library functions for attestation in Intel's confidential computing solutions (SGX and TDX), including generation and verification of SGX Quotes and TD Quotes. Additionally, Intel's Trusted Services (api.portal.trustedservices.intel.com) provides reference values for Intel TCB, including reference values or SVNs for CPU Microcode, TDX Module, and Quoting Enclave.
- Confidential Computing Trusted API: A project submitted to the CCC in late 2023, aiming to provide an abstraction for TPM-based attestation and CC-native measurement register-based attestation for confidential computing. Fig. 7.9 shows the CC Trusted API architecture, using vTPM and TDX as underlying examples.
- Constellation Container Project: Provides attestation for containers. Constellation uses the vTPM of the underlying CVM for remote attestation, where the use of vTPM PCRs follows the Linux UAPI definitions. Constellation supports CVMs on Microsoft Azure, Google Cloud Platform, and Amazon Web Services.
- Veraison Project: A collection of tools and libraries for remote attestation verification, managed under the CCC. The Veraison project's architecture resembles the one defined in IETF RFC 9334. It includes three parts: 1) Provisioning: Provides endorsements and trust anchors based on the CoRIM format. 2) Verification: Performs verification of evidence and provides attestation results based on the EAR format. 3) Policy: Uses policies written in the OPA Rego language for verification.

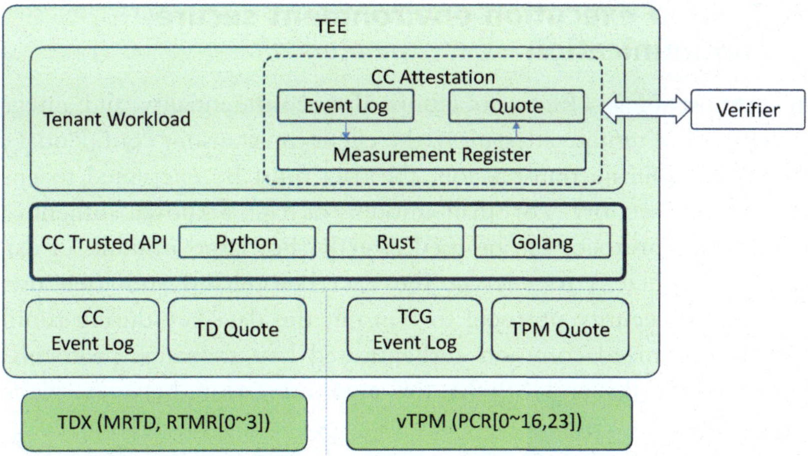

Figure 7.9 Confidential Computing (CC) trusted API. *TEE*, trusted execution environment.

- in-toto Project: Provides a software framework for general software supply chain integrity. The steps in software supply chain flow include write and package steps performed by personnel, and untar by the user. Each of the write, package and untar steps have an associated link. The link refers to metadata generated by those steps, which can be used to verify the functionality of those steps.

7.4.3 Policy engine-related software

After the verifier obtains runtime evidence data and the expected reference data, it needs to compare them. Using a policy engine offers the advantage of supporting policies beyond simple equality, such as greater than or equal to, within a range, and so on.

Software for policy engines includes:

- Open Policy Agent (OPA): An open-source, general-purpose policy engine that can be widely used in various cloud computing modules, such as microservices, Kubernetes, CI/CD pipelines, and API gateways. OPA is a CNCF graduated project. OPA itself is developed in Go. Users write policies using the Rego language and describe policy data using JSON format. The OPA engine accepts queries and returns decisions, both in JSON format.

7.5 Trusted execution environment secure communication

The purpose of a TEE is to ensure data confidentiality and integrity. Generally, after remote attestation, the client can transmit confidential data to the TEE. During transmission, the data must be encrypted to ensure data-in-transit security. For small amounts of data, a known authenticated key exchange protocol can be used directly. For large amounts of data, a common practice is to encrypt the data beforehand and then use an authenticated security protocol to transmit the data key during runtime. Industry-recognized common authenticated key exchange protocols are TLS for networks and SPDM for communication between platform components.

7.5.1 RA-TLS protocol

We introduced Remote Attestation (RA) TLS (RA-TLS) in Chapter 5. Many TEE projects support RA-TLS, such as Gramine, Open Enclave, and Inclavare.

7.5.2 RA-SPDM protocol

SPDM is a platform-to-platform communication protocol similar to TLS, generally used for communication between a TEE and a device. We will introduce it in Part Three. However, the SPDM protocol is relatively simple and can also be used for communication between TEEs. The TD-based vTPM project uses RA-SPDM to establish a secure connection directly between the vTPM and the TEE.

7.6 Trusted execution environment data security

On the TEE server side, after using an anthenticated key exchange protocol to establish a secure connection with the TEE and successfully verifying the TEE, the server can transmit keys to the TEE. This allows the TEE to decrypt encrypted disk data sent to it, as depicted in the scenario shown in Fig. 7.1.

7.6.1 Key broker service

In disk confidentiality scenarios, the TEE needs to invoke a KBS to obtain the decryption key.

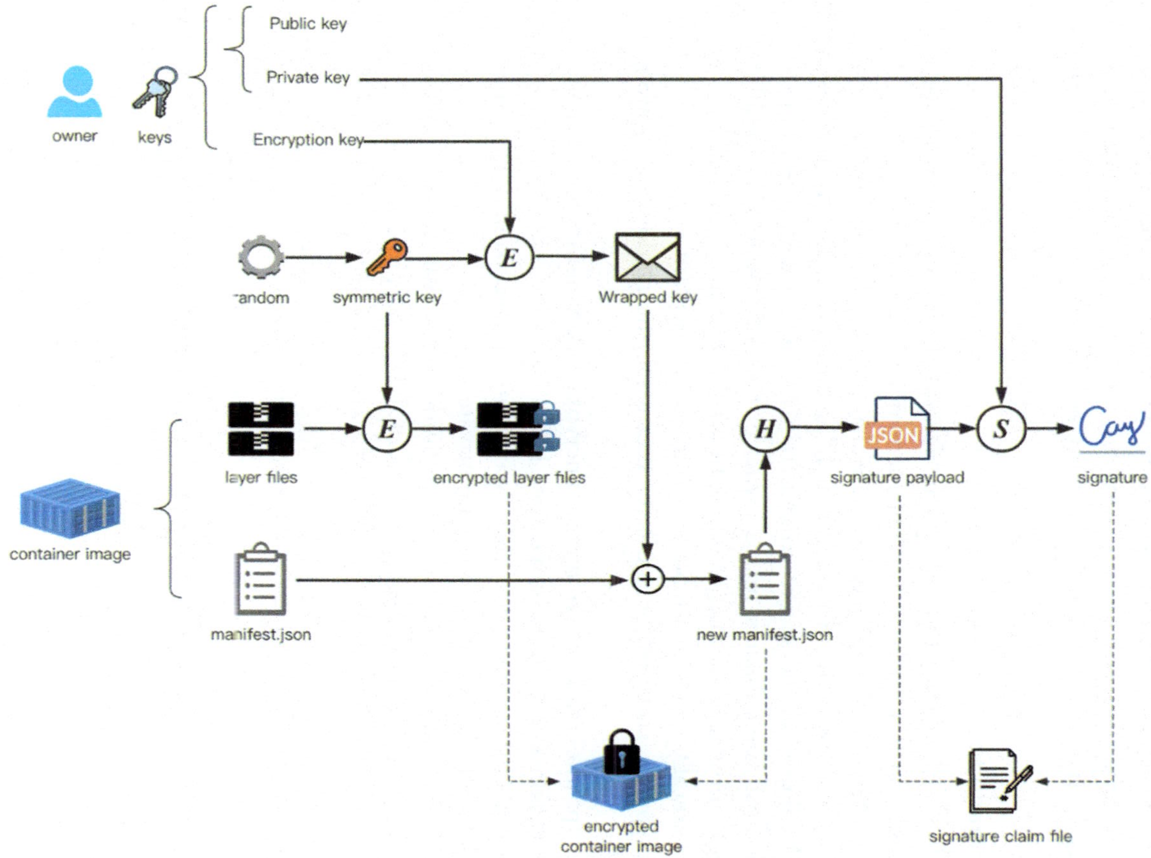

Figure 7.10 Confidential container image security design (Source: https://github.com/confidential-containers/guest-components/tree/main/image-rs).

The CoCo project provides an implementation of the CC KBS. It communicates with the AA via an AS, performs verification, and upon success, returns the registered key. Its architecture can be referenced in Fig. 7.1 or Fig. 7.2. Red Hat's confidential computing documentation series, "Confidential computing from root of trust to actual trust," also explains the interaction between attestation and key distribution services in detail.

7.6.2 Image management agent

Once the TEE obtains the key, it can decrypt the encrypted image file. The CoCo project provides an implementation of the CC IMA.

Encrypted image files require a mechanism to provide both confidentiality and integrity protection, such as dm-crypt and dm-integrity. Fig. 7.10 illustrates the secure container image design within the CoCo project. First, the container image owner possesses a private key, a public key, and an owner's symmetric encryption key. The steps are then:

1. Dynamically generate a random symmetric encryption key.
2. Encrypt the container image layer files using the random encryption key.
3. Encrypt the random symmetric encryption key using the owner's encryption key to create a wrapped key.
4. Combine the wrapped key with the container image manifest to form a new manifest, and sign it with the private key.

These steps, along with the corresponding verification and decryption work, can be accomplished using the CC OCI-Crypt project.

CHAPTER 8

TEE attack and mitigation

In Chapter 7, we introduced trusted execution environment (TEE) software SDKs. In this chapter, we will introduce attacks against TEEs and corresponding protections.

8.1 Attack methods

The security requirements of TEEs and TEE Security Managers (TSMs) differ from ordinary programs, primarily focusing on confidentiality and integrity. These are also the main targets of attacks. In Chapter 3, we introduced the security model and threat model for confidential computing. This section summarizes various attack methods.

8.1.1 Software attacks

If the TEE and TSM have software implementations, attackers may use common software attack methods to compromise them. A common attack method is exploiting buffer overflows to gain system access, then reading confidential information or tampering with code/data. For example, the Heartbleed attack exploited a buffer overflow owing to a missing bounds check. StringBleed involved Simple Network Management Protocol (SNMP) protocol authentication and access control issues. SMBleed exploited a memory leak vulnerability in the Windows SMB protocol decompression function. iLOBleed exploited a flaw by downgrading iLO firmware to a vulnerable version before attacking. Many books have introduced such attacks, including *Exploiting Software: How to Break Code*, by Hoglund and McGraw, *Hacking: The Art of Exploitation*, by Erickson, and *Encryption and Decryption*, by Gang Duan. We will not elaborate further here.

8.1.2 Attacks on cryptographic algorithms and protocols

TEEs and TSMs often need to select cryptographic algorithms for protection, such as digital signatures or encryption algorithms. TEEs and TSMs

Confidential Computing
ISBN 978-0-443-54067-7
https://doi.org/10.1016/B978-0-443-54067-7.00004-8

also need to implement cryptographic protocols to provide functions such as remote attestation or secure session establishment. Therefore, attackers often target cryptographic algorithms, protocols, and their implementations. The industry has well-documented the weaknesses in cryptographic application implementations; readers can refer to relevant literature (for example, "Top 10 developer crypto mistakes," "The many ways that cryptographic software can fail," and "Five encryption errors developers keep making").

8.1.2.1 Cryptographic algorithm and protocol standards

In this book, we will not delve into the theoretical flaws of cryptographic algorithms and protocols themselves; that work is left to cryptanalysts. We focus here on vulnerabilities in the application of cryptographic algorithms and protocols, which are frequent targets for attackers:

- **Using nonstandard algorithms and protocols.** Nonstandard algorithms and protocols often lack rigorous expert review and testing, and likely contain unknown security risks. Unless the designer is a cryptography expert, it is best to use standards defined by the National Institute of Standards and Technology (NIST) and recommended by National Security Agency (NSA), such as Rivest Shamir Adleman (RSA), Elliptic Curve Cryptography (ECC), Diffie-Hellman (DH), Advanced Encryption Standard (AES), Secure Hash Algorithm (SHA), and Postquantum Cryptography (PQC) algorithms, as well as internationally promoted standards such as China's SM3, SM2, and SM4.
- **Prematurely using algorithms and protocols under review or in draft status.** Algorithms and protocols under review or still in draft mean expert review and testing are not complete. Many security issues are discovered during this process, which can take several years. It is advisable to wait patiently for the review and testing to complete before using them.
- **Using outdated or known-vulnerable standard algorithms and protocols.** These include algorithms such as MD5, SHA1, DES, and protocols such as TLS 1.0/1.1. Such outdated or vulnerable algorithms and protocols pose security risks and should be disabled.
- **Supporting negotiation or use of outdated algorithms/protocols.** TLS can negotiate down to lower protocol versions. TPM 2.0 specification supports using the outdated SHA1 algorithm to meet transitional needs. These behaviors introduce security risks and should be disabled in project configurations. For example, the POODLE attack targets such vulnerabilities.

Table 8.1 Security strengths of modern cryptography.

Security strength (bits)	112	128	192	256
Collision resistance SHA	–	SHA-256	SHA-384	SHA-512
Preimage resistance Hash based Message Authentication Code (HMAC)	–	SHA1	–	SHA-256
Encryption AES	–	AES-128	–	AES-256
Finite field DH	DH-2048	DH-3072	DH-7680	DH-15360
Integer factorization RSA	RSA-2048	RSA-3072	RSA-7680	RSA-15360
Elliptic curve Elliptic Curve Diffie-Hellman (ECDH), Elliptic Curve Digital Signature Algorithm (ECDSA)	–	ECC-256	ECC-384	ECC-521

- **Incorrectly using modes of standard algorithms.** Encryption algorithms can have different modes, which can create risks. For example, using Electronic Codebook (ECB) mode might expose plaintext patterns in images; therefore, ECB mode should be disabled.
- **Using keys that are too short.** Cryptographic algorithms often support different key lengths to meet varying security strengths, such as 128-, 192-, or 256-bit security strength. The security strengths of common modern cryptographic algorithms are listed in Table 8.1. Using keys that are too short means insufficient security strength; if an attacker has enough computing resources, they might break the system. RSA-1024 is an example of this. Note: Cryptographic security strength can decrease with the discovery of new attack methods. For example, with the development of quantum computing, the security strength of commonly used asymmetric cryptography is effectively reduced to 0, and the security strength of symmetric cryptography is halved, as

Table 8.2 Security strengths of modern cryptography in the quantum computing era.

Security strength (bits)	0 (No. security)	64	128
Collision resistance SHA	–	SHA-256	SHA-512
Pre-image resistance HMAC	–	–	SHA-256
Encryption AES	–	AES-128	AES-256
Finite field DH	DH-*	–	–
Integer factorization RSA	RSA-*	–	–
Elliptic curve ECDH, ECDSA	ECC-*	–	–

shown in Table 8.2. NIST has begun defining PQC algorithms; their security strengths are listed in Table 8.3.

- **Using MAC tags that are too short.** AEAD algorithms are a class of encryption algorithms that simultaneously provide confidentiality and integrity. Some AEAD algorithms allow the caller to specify the length of the MAC tag, such as AES-GCM. Typically, a 128-bit tag is used; 96 bits might sometimes be acceptable, but lengths less than 64 bits are considered insecure.
- **Using initialization vectors (IVs) of incorrect length.** AES-GCM allows the caller to input IVs of various lengths. However, only 96-bit IVs are recommended; other lengths require additional operations and pose security risks.
- **Incorrectly assuming algorithm capabilities.** Users need to understand that ordinary encryption modes do not provide integrity; only AEAD provides both confidentiality and integrity. For example, AES-CBC and AES-XTS lack integrity protection, whereas AES-GCM and AES-CCM provide it. Using hashes or digital signatures does not provide confidentiality, because the processed message is still plaintext. Using a hash alone does not provide integrity because an attacker can recompute the hash. Message Authentication Codes (MACs) do not provide nonrepudiation because both parties share the MAC key.
- **Freely composing algorithms.** If a user needs both confidentiality and integrity, can they freely choose an encryption algorithm and an MAC algorithm and compose them? For example, Encrypt-and-MAC

Table 8.3 Security strengths of postquantum cryptography.

<table>
<tr><th>Security strength (bits)</th><th>128</th><th>192</th><th>256</th></tr>
<tr><td>Module lattice key encapsulation mechanism</td><td>ML-KEM-512</td><td>ML-KEM-768</td><td>ML-KEM-1024</td></tr>
<tr><td>Module lattice digital signature</td><td>ML-DSA-44</td><td>ML-DSA-65</td><td>ML-DSA-87</td></tr>
<tr><td>Stateless hash-based digital signature</td><td>SLH-DSA-[SHA2|SHAKE]-128[s|f]</td><td>SLH-DSA-[SHA2|SHAKE]-192[s|f]</td><td>SLH-DSA-[SHA2|SHAKE]-256[s|f]</td></tr>
<tr><td>Stateful hash-based digital signature (Leighton-Micali Signature (LMS))</td><td>–</td><td>LMS_[SHA256|SHAKE]_M24</td><td>LMS_[SHA256|SHAKE]_M32</td></tr>
<tr><td>Stateful hash-based digital signature (eXtended Merkle Signature Scheme (XMSS))</td><td>–</td><td>XMSS_[SHA2|SHAKE256]_192</td><td>XMSS_[SHA2|SHAKE256]_256</td></tr>
</table>

(E&M), MAC-then-Encrypt (MtE), or Encrypt-then-MAC (EtM). In E&M mode, encryption and MAC are applied independently to the plaintext, generating ciphertext and an MAC tag: Message → Enc(Message) || Mac(Message). However, the MAC tag does not provide confidentiality and might leak information about the message. In MtE mode, the message is first MACed, then both the message and the MAC tag are encrypted: Message → Enc(Message || Mac(Message)). However, the MAC tag might have special properties that give attackers opportunities for ciphertext attacks. MtE mode has potential risks; its security depends entirely on the specific encryption mode and MAC algorithm chosen. In EtM mode, the message is first encrypted, then an MAC is computed over the ciphertext: Message → Enc(Message) || Mac(Enc(Message)). This mode is considered safe. Therefore, users should generally not compose their own and instead use established AEAD algorithms.

Note: *Besides security strength, NIST also defines Security Categories, as shown in* Table 8.4. *FIPS 140-2, "Security Requirements for Cryptographic Modules," defines Security Levels describing different requirements for cryptographic module implementations, as shown in* Table 8.5.

8.1.2.2 Cryptographic implementation

Regarding vulnerabilities in cryptographic implementation, here is a summary:

- **Not using professional cryptographic libraries.** Unless the user is a cryptography expert, it is recommended to use established industry cryptographic libraries. Implementing a library that correctly performs

Table 8.4 National Institute of Standards and Technology security categories.

Security category	Attack type	Defended against example
1	Key search on 128-bit block cipher	AES-128
2	Collision search on 256-bit hash	SHA3-256
3	Key search on 192-bit block cipher	AES-192
4	Collision search on 384-bit hash	SHA3-384
5	Key search on 256-bit block cipher	AES-256

Table 8.5 Federal Information Processing Standard (FIPS) 140-2 security levels.

Cryptographic module security requirement	Level 1	Level 2	Level 3	Level 4
Production level module	√	√	√	√
Tamper detection	–	√	√	√
Tamper resistance	–	–	√	√
Key zeroization on tamper detection	–	–	–	√

encryption/decryption is not difficult; the challenge lies in understanding how to implement it securely to avoid typical software security vulnerabilities, including buffer overflows (such as Heartbleed) and various side-channel vulnerabilities such as Kocher attacks, Lenstra attacks, Bleichenbacher attacks, Manger attacks, Bellcore attacks, Bernstein attacks, Lucky 13 attacks, LadderLeak attacks, and Raccoon attacks. Well-known cryptographic libraries in the industry include OpenSSL, Mbed TLS, and Tongsuo. Using a cryptographic library does not guarantee safety; one must understand whether the library has third-party review records, security issue reporting mechanisms, and security advisory records—professional security handling processes.

- **Not promptly updating vulnerable cryptographic libraries.** Even professional cryptographic libraries can have security issues. Once a library has a security update, it is crucial to check immediately if the previous version's problems affect your application and ideally update to the latest version promptly. Vulnerable old versions of cryptographic libraries are treasures for hackers.
- **Not clearing keys and sensitive information after use.** Sensitive information such as symmetric keys, private keys of asymmetric cryptography, and passwords must be cleared from memory after use. This includes clearing global variables, heap, stack, and any copied

data. Otherwise, attackers exploiting buffer overflows could obtain this information.

- **Not using secure zeroing functions** (zero_mem). Clearing keys and sensitive information relies on zeroing functions. However, calling ordinary zeroing functions at the end of a function might be optimized away by the compiler. Therefore, known secure zeroing functions such as memset_s(a), SecureZeroMem(a), or explicit_bzero(a) must be used.
- **Hardcoding keys or passwords in code.** This is rare nowadays but still possible. Code might use other methods (such as obfuscation) to conceal them. From a cryptographic perspective, this is futile, as static or dynamic analysis could recover the secrets.
- **Incorrect password storage.** Usernames and passwords are often stored together as login credentials. Storing passwords in plaintext is insecure and easily obtained by attackers. Passwords should be hashed before storage. Moreover, simple hashing is insufficient owing to rainbow table attacks. Password storage needs to follow current best practices.
- **Insecure private key storage and use.** Private keys in public-key systems need confidentiality. Storing private keys in insecure locations risks exposure. Additionally, even if stored securely, access controls are needed when the key is used to provide services, to avoid confused deputy attacks (e.g., the entity requesting a signature must be verified). Private key use and storage must adhere to industry best practices.
- **Insecure symmetric key storage and use.** Key storage in symmetric key systems is critically important. For example, in the StarBleed attack on Field Programmable Gate Arrays (FPGAs), attackers could extract the MAC key because its plaintext was stored in the FPGA bitstream data. Once the bitstream was decrypted, the MAC key was exposed. This is a classic break once, run everywhere design flaw, extremely harmful, and must be avoided.
- **Key reuse.** Each key should serve one and only one purpose. For example, in message exchange, different keys should be used for sending and receiving; if both encryption and MAC are needed, the encryption key and MAC key should be different; in public-key systems, keys used for signing and encryption should be different.
- **Using noncryptographic random functions.** Noncryptographic random functions do not meet cryptographic standards and should be disabled in cryptographic applications. For example, the C standard

library's rand(a) function produces the same sequence each time; it is a noncryptographic random function.

- **Insufficient entropy for random numbers.** The security of encrypted ciphertext depends on key selection, which often requires uniform distribution. Because user password choices are limited and nonuniform, directly using a user password as a key drastically reduces the key space, making brute-force attacks much easier—a major mistake. If a user password must be used to derive a key, standard functions such as PBKDF2 should be used.
- **Nonrandom seed for random number generators.** Random number generation often requires a seed and a pseudorandom function to derive subsequent random values. The seed must be unpredictable. If the seed is within a predictable range, randomness is greatly reduced. For example, using the system boot timestamp or central processing unit (CPU) timestamp counter as a seed puts it within a predictable range.
- **Incorrect use of random numbers.** Misuse of random numbers is fatal for some algorithms. The classic example is the Sony PS3 Epic Fail incident. In that case, a function that should have returned a random number always returned the fixed value 4, ultimately leading to the ECDSA private key being compromised, allowing attackers to forge valid signatures freely. The LadderLeak attack also exploited ECDSA's reliance on random numbers. For each cryptographic algorithm, users need to understand the different requirements for randomness (seed, true random, pseudorandom, uniform random, nonce, counter, IV) and the requirements for confidentiality and integrity.

8.1.3 Side-channel and fault injection attacks

Side-channel attacks refer to obtaining information through unconventional means. There is a classic puzzle: In a sealed room with three light bulbs and three switches outside (one controlling each bulb), you can enter the room only once. How can you determine which switch controls which bulb? Relying solely on the bulb's on/off state makes it mathematically unsolvable. Based on life experience, the answer is: First, turn on the first switch for 5-10 minutes, then turn it off and turn on the second switch. Immediately enter the room and feel the bulbs that are off. If a bulb is warm, it was controlled by the first switch. The lit bulb is controlled by the second switch, and the remaining bulb by the third switch. In this example, the heat emitted by the bulb is side-channel information.

Scenes in movies where safecrackers use a stethoscope against a safe are also examples of side channels. In fact, researchers began exploring side channels as early as World War II. For example, the NSA document "Tempest, a Signal Problem" reveals that in 1943, Bell Labs records showed spikes on an oscilloscope when a system was active, a phenomenon that could be used to recover plaintext data. Wright, in his book *Spy Catcher*, described how in 1965, British intelligence deciphered information by listening to the sound of gear resets in a cipher machine to determine initial positions.

Side-channel attacks can be divided into passive and active attacks. Passive attacks mostly involve acquiring additional information from the physical system. Active attacks are mostly Fault Injection (i.e., physically interfering with the system to affect its behavior). Zhou and Feng's 2005 paper, "Side-channel attacks: 10 years after its publication and the impacts on cryptographic module security testing" and Boone's 2021 series, "An introduction to fault injection" provide good overviews. The side-channel attack model aims to obtain extra information such as code execution flow, memory data values, or specific bits of a key. Side-channel attacks can leverage electromagnetic radiation, visible light, heat, sound, power consumption, execution time, frequency, error message, and so on. In the fault injection attack model, flipping one or a few memory bits can achieve goals such as skipping instructions, causing data read errors, instruction prefetch/decode errors, or data write-back errors. Fault injection attacks can be realized through electromagnetic interference, voltage glitching, clock glitching, laser attack, row hammer, and such.

Side channels are a common method in TEE attacks. To build a secure TEE, architects and developers need to understand side-channel attack and defense processes thoroughly.

8.1.3.1 Traditional side-channel attacks

Common side-channel attack methods include:

- Error Message Side Channels: Obtaining extra information from software error response codes to launch attacks.
- Timing Side Channels: Obtaining extra information from software response times to launch attacks.
- Cache Side Channels: Using the time difference between cache hits and misses to obtain extra information and launch attacks. Examples include

classic Prime + Probe, Flush + Reload, and newer attacks such as Cachebleed, TLBled, and Spoiler.

Hardware side-channel attack methods include:

- Power Analysis: Obtaining extra information from the power consumption of hardware during computation.
- Electromagnetic Analysis: Obtaining extra information from electromagnetic radiation emitted by hardware during computation.
- Others: Using light, sound, heat, and so on as side channels; these are less common.

Hardware fault injection methods include:

- Voltage Glitching: Suddenly applying excessively high or low voltage to components.
- Clock Glitching: Sending faulty clock signals to a device.
- Electromagnetic Interference: Using electromagnetic radiation to cause interference.
- Laser Fault Injection: Using a laser beam to target specific areas.

Side-channel attacks have a long history, mostly targeting system-wide cryptography to recover keys. Books including *Cryptographic Side-Channel Analysis: Principles and Methods*, by Shize Guo, Tao Wang, and Xinjie Zhao, and *Fault Analysis in Cryptography*, by Marc Joye and Michael Tunstall provide detailed introductions to cryptography. Ge et al.'s 2016 paper, "A survey of microarchitectural timing attacks and countermeasures on contemporary hardware," surveys timing side-channel attacks and defenses on hardware microarchitecture.

To help understand CPU microarchitecture side channels, we introduce two classic cache side-channel attacks.

8.1.3.1.1 Prime + Probe

To improve performance, modern computer systems support internal caches. When the CPU needs to access memory (Dynamic Random Access Memory (DRAM)), it first checks if the relevant content is in the cache. If present (cache hit), it uses it directly. If not (cache miss), it accesses memory and places the content into the cache for future use.

Caches and memory have various mapping relationships. Fig. 8.1 shows the set-associative cache organization common in modern CPUs. Each memory line maps to a specific cache set. Each cache set contains several cache ways. A cache line is the content within one cache way. Cache replacement happens per cache line. Because memory is much larger than

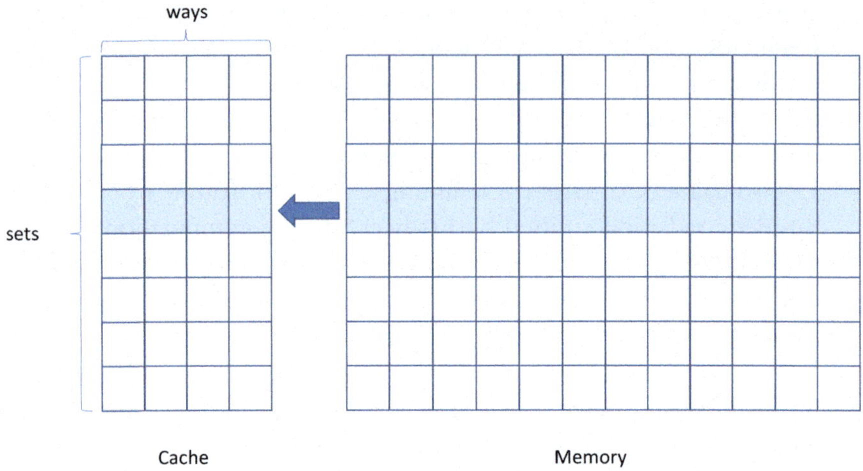

Figure 8.1 Set-associative cache organization.

cache, when a new cache line needs to be stored, the CPU must replace an existing one.

The Prime + Probe attack involves an attacker process and a victim process accessing the same cache set to gain information about which memory line the victim accessed. The attack proceeds as follows:

- Prime Phase: The attacker process fills all cache ways within the target cache set with its own data, as shown in Fig. 8.2.

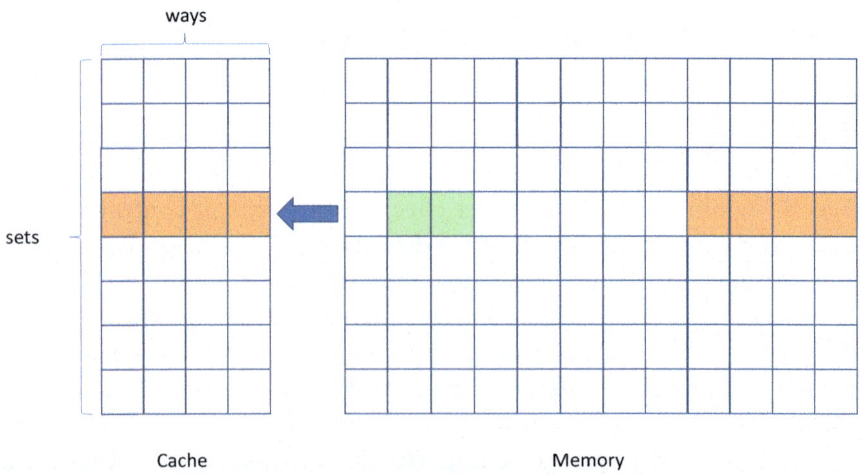

Figure 8.2 Prime + Probe attack: Prime phase.

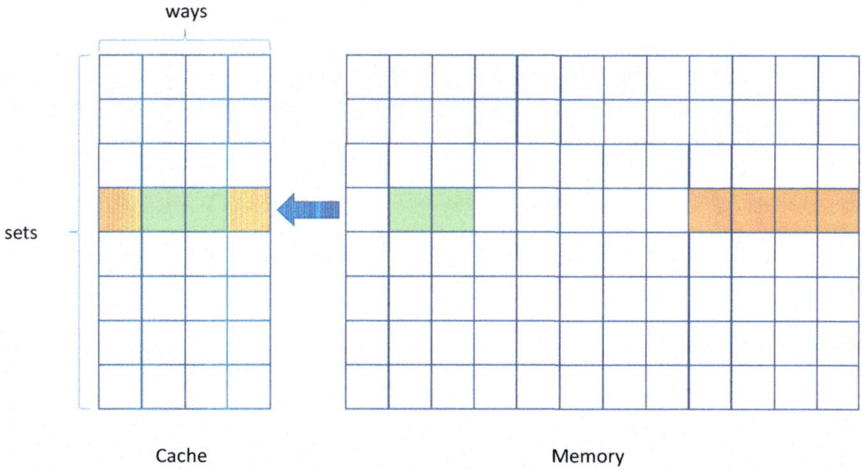

Figure 8.3 Prime + Probe attack: Probe phase. Prime + Probe can be used to detect accesses to global data structures such as lookup tables (e.g., AES S-box lookups), deducing key information.

- Idle Phase: The attacker process waits for the victim process to access memory, potentially replacing some of the attacker's cache lines.
- Probe Phase: The attacker process accesses all cache ways within the target cache set. By measuring the access time (cache hit vs. miss), the attacker can determine which cache way was evicted by the victim, inferring which memory line the victim accessed, as shown in Fig. 8.3.

8.1.3.1.2 Flush + Reload

Flush + Reload shares the same goal as Prime + Probe: to determine which memory line the victim accessed. However, it uses the opposite approach. Instead of priming the cache, it flushes the cache beforehand. It requires a shared page between the attacker and victim processes. The Flush + Reload attack proceeds as follows:

- Flush Phase: The attacker process flushes all cache lines associated with the target shared memory address from the cache (e.g., using the CLFLUSH instruction), as shown in Fig. 8.4.
- Idle Phase: The attacker process waits for the victim process to access the shared memory, which will bring the corresponding line into the cache.
- Reload Phase: The attacker process accesses the target shared memory address. If the victim accessed it, the access will be fast (cache hit);

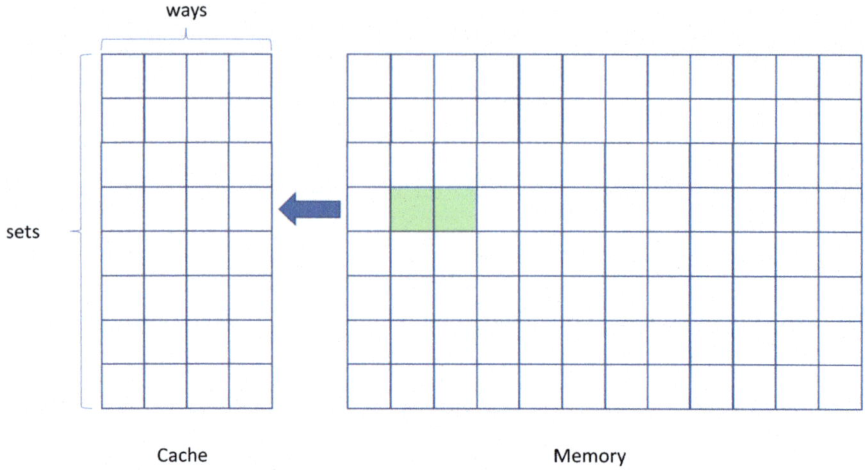

Figure 8.4 Flush + Reload attack: Flush phase.

otherwise, it will be slow (cache miss). By measuring access time, the attacker can determine whether the victim accessed that memory line, as shown in Fig. 8.5.

8.1.3.2 Central processing unit microarchitecture side channels

Since the discovery of Specter and Meltdown attacks, the industry has focused heavily on CPU microarchitecture side channels. CPU microarchitecture side-channel attacks include Microarchitectural Data Sampling (MDS) class attacks such as ZombieLoad, Rogue In-flight Data Load (RIDL), Fallout; Rage Against the Machine Clear attacks such as Floating Point Value Injection (FPVI), and Speculative Code Store Bypass (SCSB); microarchitectural speculative execution vulnerability class attacks such as Foreshadow, Load Value Injection (LVI), Crosstalk, Ret Bleed, Cacheout, SGXAxe, Downfall, Inception, and Phantom; fault injection attacks such as Cache Warp; and other attacks such as Platypus, Hertz Bleed, Collide Power, EPIC Leak, SEV-SNP Cipher Leaks, and GPU.zip.

To improve efficiency, modern processors introduce various optimizations such as Speculative Execution, Branch Prediction, and Out-of-Order Execution. These features are the root causes of CPU microarchitecture side-channel attacks. Canella et al. collectively term them Transient Execution and provide excellent summaries in "A systematic evaluation of transient execution attacks and defenses" and "The

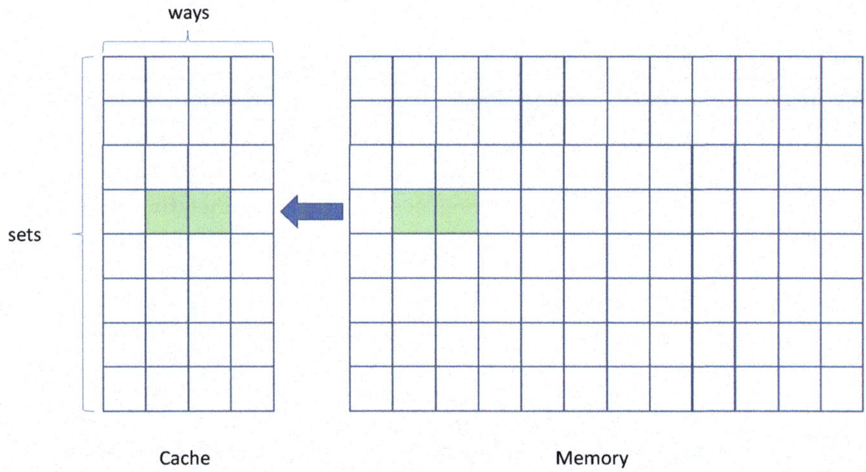

Figure 8.5 Flush + Reload attack: Reload phase. Flush + Reload can be used to detect accesses to shared code, such as the square-and-multiply steps in exponentiation functions, deducing key information.

evolution of transient execution attacks." Intel also summarizes transient execution attacks in "Refined speculative execution terminology." Transient execution attacks are diverse and can be classified by control-flow versus data-flow speculation, by data leakage versus data injection, by root cause, or by affected security domain. Table 8.6 shows a common classification method for transient execution attacks.

Canella et al., in "The evolution of transient-execution attacks," summarize a six-phase attack pattern for transient attacks:

① Setup Phase: The attacker prepares the microarchitecture to a state conducive to the transient attack and sets up a covert channel for transmitting secrets.

② Trigger Instruction Phase: The attacker triggers a transient execution instruction. Specter-class attacks use branch misprediction; Meltdown-class and LVI-class attacks can trigger exceptions.

③ Transient Secret Access Phase: Transient execution accesses a secret and places it into a microarchitectural covert channel such as a cache or various buffers.

④ Secret Transmission Phase: The attacker encodes the secret data and places them into the microarchitecture, most commonly the CPU

Table 8.6 Classification of transient execution attacks.

Method	Leakage	Injection
Control-flow speculation	BranchScope, bluethunder, Branch Shadowing	Specter class: Specter-Bounds Check Bypass, Specter-Branch Target Injection, Specter-RSB (ret bleed), Branch History Injection, Specter-Speculative Store Bypass, Speculative Code Store Bypass
Data-flow speculation	Meltdown class: Meltdown, foreshadow, Lazy Floating Point Microarchitectural Data Sampling subclasses: Fallout, ZombieLoad, Rogue In-flight Data Load	Load Value Injection (LVI) class: LVI, Floating Point Value Injection

cache. For example, the attacker uses the secret data as an index to access the cache, so the cache line accessed becomes the encoded data.

⑤ Recovery Phase: The CPU recognizes the misprediction or exception and begins architecturally visible recovery, flushing the pipeline and executing the correct path (e.g., the correct branch for Specter, the exception handler for Meltdown). However, the encoded secret data remain in the microarchitectural state (e.g., cache).

⑥ Secret Recovery Phase: The attacker retrieves the encoded data from the microarchitecture (e.g., using Flush + Reload on the cache) and decodes it to obtain the secret.

8.1.3.2.1 Specter-class attacks—Speculative execution misprediction

Specter-class attacks exploit mispredictions in speculative execution to **break isolation between different applications**. "Specter" alludes to

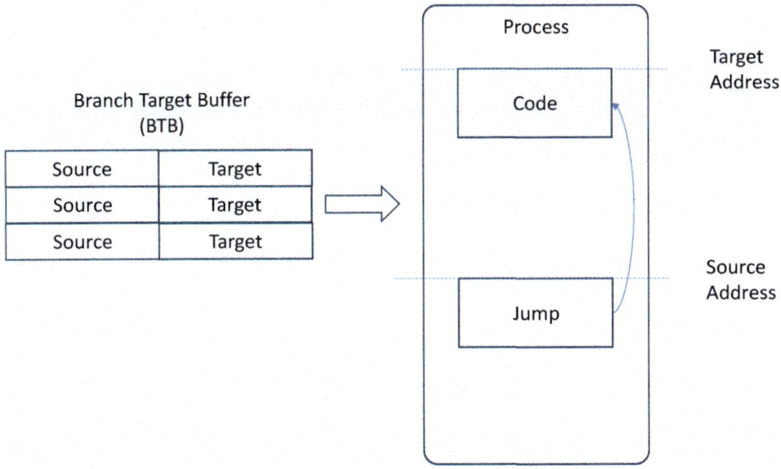

Figure 8.6 Branch prediction.

attackers being like a ghost to steal information from another process. Specter attacks include:

- **Conditional Branch Misprediction** (Specter Variant 1, or Bounds Check Bypass). This attack exploits the CPU frontend's branch predictor and its Branch Target Buffer (BTB), as shown in Fig. 8.6. The vulnerable code snippet below has an untrusted input x. If x is less than array1_size, it uses array1[x] as an index into array2. An attacker can train the branch predictor usually to predict the branch as taken. During speculative execution, the CPU may ignore the check's result and speculatively execute the body, reading array1[x] and then loading array2[array1[x] * 4096] into the cache. Architecturally, if the check fails, this result is discarded. Logically, this seems fine. But consider the attacker inputs x = &secret[0] - &array1. Then k = array1[x] = secret[0] becomes the first byte of the secret. The side effect of speculative execution is that array2[k * 4096] is brought into the cache. The attacker can use Flush + Reload to recover k, (e.g., by timing accesses to array2[n * 4096] for n = 0.255). The significantly faster access corresponds to k. By repeating with x = &secret[m] - &array1 for all m, the attacker can recover the entire secret.

```
uint8_t array1[ARRAY1_SIZE];
int array1_size = sizeof(array1);
uint8_t array2[ARRAY2_SIZE];
uint8_t secret[SECRET_SIZE];

data_process(int x) {
    if (x < array1_size) {
        k = array1[x]; // Speculatively executed
        y = array2[k * 4096];
    }
}
```

- **Indirect Branch Poisoning** (Specter Variant 2, or Branch Target Injection). This attack exploits the CPU frontend's indirect branch predictor, specifically the Branch History Buffer and Indirect BTB (IBTB), which store predicted target addresses for indirect branches. The attack method is shown in Fig. 8.7. First, find an indirect branch instruction in the victim process (e.g., CALL [EAX] or JUMP [EAX]); its address is the source address. Then, find a code gadget (a small code sequence) that leaks data via a cache side channel; its address is the target address. To trick the CPU, the attacker creates an attacker process with a similar code structure, including the same source address with an indirect branch. The attacker trains the CPU by making this indirect branch jump to the target gadget and return. This poisons the IBTB with this branch target information. When the victim process runs, the CPU may speculatively execute the gadget, leaking secret data into the cache, which the attacker then recovers via a cache side channel. The Specter gadget might be just two instructions:

```
adc edi, dword ptr [ebx+edx+13BE13BDh]
adc dl, byte ptr [edi] ; EDI register is set by the previous line
```

Specter Variant 2 can also target the Return Predictor and its Return Stack Buffer (RSB), which stores predicted return addresses for functions. This variant, sometimes called Specter-RSB or Ret Bleed,

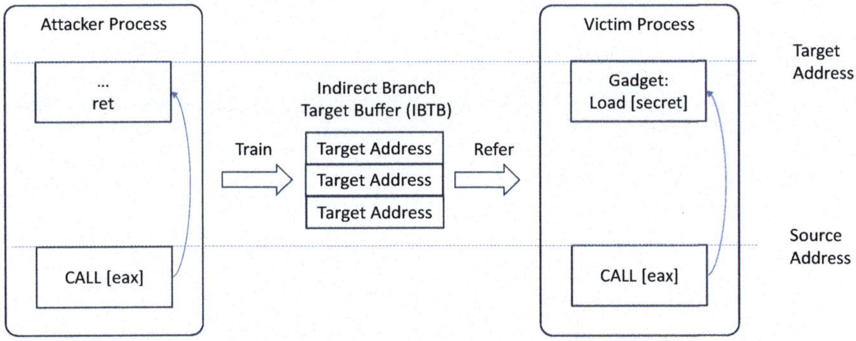

Figure 8.7 Indirect branch poisoning.

is shown in Fig. 8.8. In the following code, main(a) calls speculative(a), which calls pollute(a). pollute(a) manipulates the stack pointer such that it returns directly to main(a). Logically, the code in speculative(a) that accesses the secret should not execute. However, because the RSB is unbalanced, the CPU might speculatively execute the secret-accessing instructions, bringing the secret into the cache.

```
pollute() {
    add rsp, 8 * 3; // Unbalanced stack, skips the "secret = *secret_ptr"
    retq
}

speculative(char *secret_ptr) {
    pollute(); // Modifies the stack
    secret = *secret_ptr; // This may be speculatively executed
    temp &= Array[secret * 256]; // Access Array
}

main () {
    speculative (secret_address) ;
    for (i = 0; i < 256; i++) {
        junk = Array[i * 256]; // Check cache hit
    }
}
```

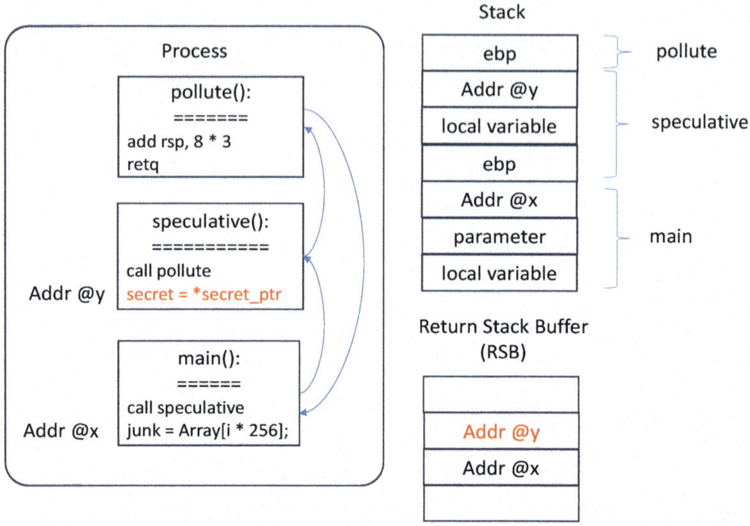

Figure 8.8 Return stack buffer prediction.

- **Speculative Store Bypass** (Specter Variant 4). Modern CPUs have a store buffer between the execution engine and the L1 data cache, holding data to be written. The CPU also looks into the store buffer when reading data, as shown in Fig. 8.9. To improve performance, CPUs may speculatively forward values from the store buffer to subsequent loads, which is a form of data-flow speculation. The next pseudocode illustrates the idea. The data pointer initially points to secret_area. Then it is set to point to public_area, and code reads data from public_area. During speculative execution, the CPU might use the old value of pointer (still pointing to secret_area) to perform the load, thus bringing the secret value into the cache. A subsequent cache side channel can recover it.

```
pointer = &secret_area; // Initialize

// Execute some operation

pointer = &public_area; // Write operation may be delayed

value = *pointer; // Read after write, speculatively execution

tmp = array[value]; // Search value in the cache
```

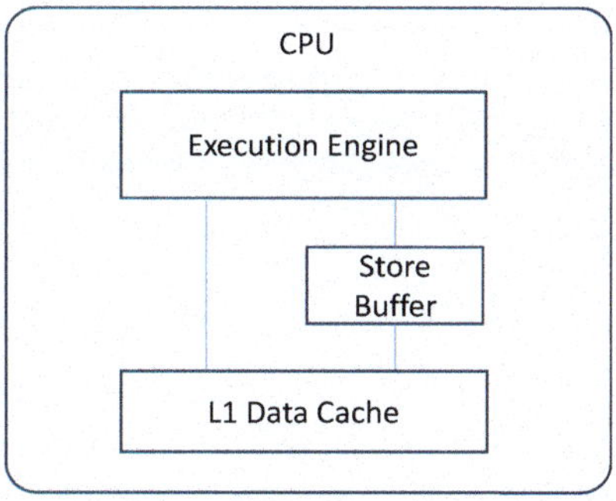

Figure 8.9 Speculative store bypass.

Specter-class attacks also include ret2spec, Branch History Injection, RSB underflow (also known as Retbleed), SgxPectre attacks, and the Speculative Store Bypass-related SCSB.

8.1.3.2.2 Meltdown-class attacks—Exception handling during speculation

Meltdown-class attacks exploit out-of-order execution to **break the isolation between applications and the kernel**. The name "Meltdown" metaphorically suggests that attackers melt down the isolation barrier between programs at different privilege levels.

Out-of-order execution attacks include these categories:

- **Rogue Data Cache Load**: Also known as Meltdown Variant 3. This code snippet illustrates Meltdown. Here, rcx points to a kernel address, and rbx points to the probe array. Logically, the instruction mov al, byte [rcx] will trigger an exception. However, because of out-of-order execution, the last instruction accessing the probe array may transiently execute before the exception is fully handled, loading the result into the cache. The information can then be retrieved within the exception handler. The attack process is shown in Fig. 8.10. Meltdown relies

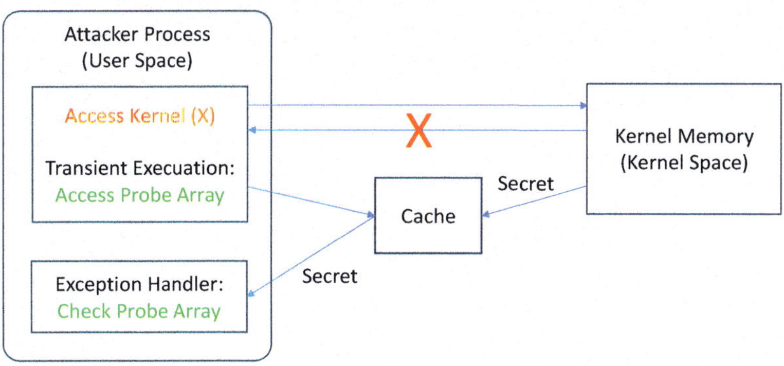

Figure 8.10 Meltdown-class attack example

on the kernel and user space sharing the same page table, allowing the speculatively executed kernel address access to be correctly resolved.

```
; rcx = kernel address
; rbx = probe array
retry:
    mov al, byte [rcx] ; Trigger exception; access secret
; Subsequent code begins transient execution
shl rax, 0xc
jz retry
mov rbx, qword [rbx + rax]; // Access probe array

; Exception handler; obtain secret
mov rbx, qword [rbx + rax] ; Check probe array
```

- **L1 Terminal Fault**: Also known as Foreshadow. The method of the Foreshadow attack is the same as Meltdown, with the following steps: 1) Accessing secret data triggers an exception; 2) Before the exception concludes, the secret data are read into the cache through transient execution; 3) The secret is probed from the cache within the exception handler. The difference from Meltdown is that the Foreshadow attack targets the L1 terminal fault. Modern processors typically map physical addresses to linear addresses through page tables. When the CPU accesses a linear address, it needs to look up information in the page tables. To speed access, the CPU builds a Translation Lookaside Buffer (TLB) for the page tables, a cache for page table entries. When the Present bit of the last-level page table entry is 0 or the Reserved bit is 1, the system triggers a terminal fault to abort the linear address translation. However, during transient execution, if the corresponding physical address is still present in the L1 data cache, the CPU will speculatively read the translated physical address and begin accessing it, recording the result in the cache.

Other Meltdown-class attacks include Store-to-Leak forwarding, Lazy Floating Point, Foreshadow-NG (Next Generation), and EFLAGS-based attacks (see "Timing the transient execution: a new side-channel attack on Intel CPUs").

8.1.3.2.3 Microarchitectural Data Sampling subclass attacks: Microarchitectural data sampling

MDS attacks also aim for data extraction but target other high-speed microarchitectural buffers besides the cache, including store buffers, line fill buffers (LFBs), load ports, and so forth. These are all located between the CPU execution engine and the cache; the data within these buffers are referred to as data in flight. The store buffer is an internal write buffer of the CPU, used to track pending stores and optimize data in flight, such as through Store-to-Load Forwarding. The LFB is an internal read buffer of the CPU, used to track outstanding memory requests and perform a series of optimizations, such as merging multiple in-flight stores.

Note: *MDS attacks can be considered a subclass of Meltdown-class attacks, as they both relate to data-flow speculation and are a form of use-after-free of micro-architectural structures.*

- **ZombieLoad Attack**: Here is an example of ZombieLoad Variant 1. First, a kernel virtual address K is needed, which the user cannot access, and K corresponds to a physical page P. Then, a user virtual address V is established, also mapped to the same physical page P. After this setup is complete, V is flushed, and then K is read. Subsequently, the Meltdown method can be used to read content from the LFB. Contrary to intuition, the content read here is not the content of P, but other data stored in the CPU. Hence, this attack is called ZombieLoad. For example, Variant 1 reads the content of an entire cache line.
- **RIDL Attack**: RIDL attacks also target LFBs. The code below illustrates the idea. Although logically correct, during speculative execution, the first line's load from a newly allocated page (new_page) might obtain data from the LFB that actually belong to other in-flight data. These secret data are then used to index a probe array, bringing the corresponding cache line into the cache. The attacker can then recover the secret using Flush + Reload.

```
char value = *(new_page); // Speculatively loads secret data

char *entry_ptr = buffer + (1024 * value); // Probe array based on secret

tmp = *(entry_ptr); // Loads probe array entry into cache


// Measure reload times for each probe array entry, to known the one cached

for (int k = 0; k < 256; ++k) {

    tmp = *(buffer + 1024 * k);

}
```

- **Fallout Attack**: Unlike ZombieLoad and RIDL, Fallout targets the store buffer using Store-to-Load forwarding. The following code snippet illustrates the basic idea. victim_page is a normally accessible page. attacker_address is an invalid address that will cause an exception. The code writes SECRET_VALUE to victim_page[offset]. Then it attempts to read from look_up_table indexed by attacker_address[offset], which will fault. However, because of Write Transient Forwarding, the CPU may speculatively forward the just-written SECRET_VALUE from the store buffer to the faulting load, executing memory_access (look_up_table + SECRET_VALUE * 4096). Although the result is ultimately discarded, the access pattern is left in the cache, allowing the attacker to recover SECRET_VALUE via Flush + Reload.

```
char* victim_page = mmap(..., PAGE_SIZE, PROT_READ|PROT_WRITE,
                                          MAP_POPULATE, ...);
char* attacker_address = 0x9876543214321000ull; // Invalid address
int offset = 7;
victim_page[offset] = SECRET_VALUE;

if (tsx_begin() == 0) {
    memory_access(look_up_table + 4096 * attacker_address[offset]); // Faults,
but speculatively uses SECRET_VALUE
    tss_end();
}

for (i = 0; i < 256; i++) {
    if (flush_reload(look_up_table + i * 4096)) {
        report(i);
    }
}
```

Other MDS-class attacks include Medusa Attack (targeting write-combining memory), Special Register Buffer Data Sampling, also known as the Crosstalk Attack, and Gather Data Sampling (GDS) also known as the Downfall Attack.

8.1.3.2.4 Load Value Injection–class attacks—Data injection

LVI attacks also target CPU microarchitectural buffers. Unlike leakage attacks, LVI allows the attacker to inject data.

Note: LVI can be considered a subclass of MDS attacks because they target similar buffers. Because it injects data, it is also called Reverse-Meltdown.

Here is the example of LVI attack process:

① The attacker prepares data A (which the attacker controls) to be injected into a microarchitectural buffer (such as a store buffer or LFB).

② The attacker invokes a gadget within the victim process that attempts to load trusted data B, but accessing B causes an exception (e.g., page fault).

③ During speculative execution, the CPU uses injected data A from the buffer instead of waiting for B. This speculative execution using A may cause the victim to access secret data based on A and bring them into the cache.

④ The CPU eventually rolls back the speculative execution, but the secret data remain in the cache and can be recovered via a cache side channel.

The code snippet below shows a potential gadget. The code stores untrusted_arg (attacker-controlled) into arg_copy. This store places untrusted_arg into the store buffer. If accessing *trusted_ptr causes an exception (as in Fallout), the CPU may speculatively use the value from the store buffer (untrusted_arg) for the subsequent access to the probe array, i.e., array[(*untrusted_arg) * 4096] instead of the intended array [(*trusted_ptr) * 4096]. The attacker can then recover (*untrusted_arg) via Flush + Reload.

LVI's power lies in injecting arbitrary addresses, but its limitation is the need to find such a specific gadget in the victim process.

```
void call_victim(size_t untrusted_arg) {

    *arg_copy = untrusted_arg;

    array[(*trusted_ptr) * 4096];

}
```

Other LVI-class attacks include FPVI and Gather Value Injection.

8.1.3.2.5 Branch information extraction

Specter-class attacks require training and injecting branch history information. Another class of attacks targets branch history information for extraction without needing injection.

- **Branch Shadowing Attack**: This attack aims to precisely determine the branch execution path of a program inside an enclave. The principle is illustrated by the code snippet on the left (victim) and the shadow code on the right (attacker), which mirrors the structure to probe branch history. The Branch Prediction Unit (BPU) and BTB are shared between enclave and nonenclave code, but can be noisy. Branch Shadowing leverages the Last Branch Record (LBR), which only records nonenclave branches. This is the attack flow:

  ① A branch executes inside the enclave, updating BPU/BTB but not the LBR.

② Enclave execution is interrupted (e.g., by an interrupt) and control passes to the untrusted operating system (OS).
③ The OS enables LBR and executes the shadow code.
④ The BPU correctly predicts the shadow branches (owing to training), but the BTB might mispredict because it contains enclave addresses.
⑤ The OS disables LBR and reads its contents. Successful predictions indicate which branches were likely taken in the enclave; mispredictions indicate branches not taken.

```
// Victim code in the Enclave        // Shadow code
if (a != 0) {                        if (c != c) {
    ++b;                                 nop; // never executed
    ...                                  ...
} else {                             } else {
    --b;                                 nop; // executed
    ...                                  ...
}                                    }
a = b;                               nop;
...                                  ...
```

Other branch information extraction attacks include BranchScope and Bluethunder.

- **Frontal Attack**: This is another branch information extraction method that exploits the CPU frontend's instruction prefetch window. The prefetch window is typically 16 bytes and 16-byte aligned. When a new instruction crosses a 16-byte alignment boundary, it cannot be prefetched together with the preceding instruction and can only be prefetched along with the following instructions. Consider the following program snippet: the code for the if and else branches is almost identical. The only difference is their starting addresses: the starting address of the if branch is 0×10, whereas the starting address of the else branch is $0 \times 2b$. This subtle difference causes the CPU frontend to behave differently during prefetch. For example, the first instruction

ADD of the if branch will prefetch ADD MOV ADD, and the second instruction MOV will execute the MOV within the prefetch window; however, for the else branch, the first instruction ADD is in the previous prefetch window, and the second instruction MOV will generate a prefetch of MOV ADD MOV RET. For a program inside an Enclave, SGX-Step can be used to execute instructions one by one, obtaining timing information. For instance, for the second MOV instruction, the if branch executes faster, whereas the else branch executes slower.

```
if (secret == 'a') { // 0x03:mov (var1), &rax
                     // 0x08:mov (var2), &rbx
                     // 0x0c:cmp (secret), 'a'
                     // 0x0e:jnz .else
    var1 = 1 + var1; // 0x10:add $1, &rax ; INT #1 ADD MOV ADD
                     // 0x14:mov &rax, (var1); INT #2 MOV ADD
    var2 = 1 + var2; // 0x19:add $1, &rbx ; INT #3 ADD
                     // 0x1d:mov &rbx, (var2); INT #4 MOV RET
                     // 0x22:ret
} else {             // .else
    var1 = 2 + var1; // 0x2b:add $2, &rax ; INT #1 ADD
                     // 0x2f:mov &rax, (var1); INT #2 MOV ADD MOV RET
    var2 = 2 + var2; // 0x34:add $2, &rbx ; INT #3 ADD MOV RET
                     // 0x38:mov &rbx, (var2); INT #4 MOV RET
                     // 0x3d:ret
}
```

8.1.3.2.6 Cache fault injection

As the name suggests, cache fault injection aims to modify data in the cache.

- CacheWarp Attack: This attack uses the INVD instruction (which invalidates the cache without writing back modified data) to target AMD SEV-SNP. The goal is to prevent modified cache lines from being written back to memory. Here is the example of CacheWarp attack process:

① The attacker (Virtual Machine Manager (VMM)) clears the Present (P) bit in the page table for a target page belonging to the victim TEE Virtual Machine (TVM).

② When the TVM accesses that page, a Nested Page Fault (NPF) occurs.

③ The VMM, in the NPF handler, sets up an Advanced Programmable Interrupt Controller (APIC) timer.

④ When the target instruction within the page executes, the APIC timer interrupt fires.

⑤ The VMM's interrupt handler is triggered. The attacker can selectively evict unrelated data from the cache and then use the INVD instruction to discard all modified cache lines, including the modifications made by the TVM.

⑥ The TVM resumes execution, but its modifications are lost.

For discarding arbitrary write operations, we introduce two exploitation techniques: The first is Dropforge, where discarding implicit or explicit function write operations leads to changes in the function's parameters and behavior. Consider the following program snippet. An attacker could discard the input parameters a or b of the victim function, the initial value of the local variable ret, or the return value ret. When the main function calls the victim function a second time, using this discard technique could make the second call return the result of the first call.

```
int main() {
    do {
        ret = victim(1, 1);
        reset = victim(2, 5);
    } while (ret == 11);
}
int victim(int a, int b) {
                            // push %rbp
                            // mov %rsp, %rbp
                            // mov %edi, -0x14 (%rbp) ; param:a
                            // mov %esi, -0x18 (%rbp) ; param:b
    int ret = 0;            // mov movl $0x0, -%0x4 (%rbp) ; local:ret
    ret += a * 10 + b;      // mov -0x14 (%rbp), %edx
                            // mov %edx, %eax
                            // shl $0x2, %eax
                            // add %edx, %eax
                            // add %eax, %eax
                            // mov %eax, %edx
                            // mov -0x18 (%rbp), %eax
                            // add %edx, %eax
                            // add %eax, -0x4 (%rbp) ; local: ret
    return ret;             // mov -0x4 (%rbp), %eax ; ret
                            // pop %rbp
                            // retq
}
```

The second technique is Timewarp. The implicit push of a function's return address onto the stack can be discarded, thereby redirecting the control flow to a previously called function. Consider the following program snippet. When the attacker calls the ret0 function, they discard the return address of ret0 on the stack. Consequently, the address remaining on the stack is the return address of the previously called ret1 function. This means that when the ret0 function returns, it jumps to the return location of the ret1 function. Ultimately, this could make ret1(a) == 0 true.

```
int ret1() { return 1; }
int ret0() { return 0; }
int main() {
                           // push &rbp
                           // mov &rsp, &rbp
    while(1) {
        if (ret1() == 0) { // mov $0x0, %eax
                           // call 1149<ret1> ; <- push rip
                           // <- old retaddr of ret1
                           // test %eax, %eax
                           // jne 118c
            puts("WIN");   // lea 0xe80(%rip), %rax
                           // mov %rax, %rdi
                           // call 1050<puts@plt>
        }
        ret0(); // victim // mov $0x0, %eax
                           // call 1158<ret0> ; <- victim
                           // <- retaddr of ret0
                           // jmp 116f<main+8>
    }
}
```

8.1.3.2.7 Other attacks

CPU side channels can leak information through other means.

- Platypus Attack: A power side-channel attack. Attackers can monitor and control CPU and DRAM power consumption via the Intel Running Average Power Limit (RAPL) interface to infer cryptographic key information.
- HertzBleed Attack: A frequency side-channel attack. Attackers can probe the CPU's dynamic frequency scaling to infer information about data being processed, such as keys.
- Collide Power Attack: A general power measurement side-channel attack independent of specific implementations. Attackers can use power variations to attack data in use (MDS power variant) or static data (Meltdown power variant).
- EPIC Leak Attack: Accessing the legacy APIC region can lead to undefined behavior, potentially leaking microarchitectural buffer information on some CPUs, creating a security risk.
- CipherLeak Attack: An attack against SEV-SNP that uses the encrypted VM Save Area as a side channel to obtain cryptographic information. Because SEV encryption is deterministic for a given physical address and plaintext within a VM's lifetime, repeated encryptions produce the same ciphertext, allowing correlation.
- ZenBleed Attack: An attack exploiting an execution vulnerability in AMD CPUs.

Examples of CPU fault injection include VoltJockey, Plundervolt, and VoltPillager attacks, which are voltage fault injection attacks against SGX.

Besides CPUs, other devices may also be susceptible to side-channel attacks, such as the GPU.zip compression side-channel attack, which will be further discussed in Chapter 14.

Finally, the CPU microarchitecture side-channel attacks listed here are just the tip of the iceberg, but they all can affect TEE software.

8.1.3.3 DRAM attack

The discovery of Rowhammer initiated research into DRAM fault injection attacks, such as Drammer, RAMBleed, TRRespass, Smash, and Half-Double. Rowhammer refers to accessing (hammering) specific memory rows repeatedly to cause bit flips in adjacent rows.

BatteringRam, WireTap.fail, and TEE.fail are a set of attacks targeting TEEs via DRAM. BatteringRam compromises memory integrity.

WireTap.fail intercepts data on the DDR4 bus, whereas TEE.fail does so on the DDR5 bus.

8.1.4 Simple physical attacks

Some simple physical attacks include:

- Cold Boot Attack (DRAM Offline Reading): The attacker cools the DRAM, removes it, and inserts it into another machine to read the memory contents. Cryptographic analysis can then be applied to recover secrets.
- Malicious Device DMA Access: The attacker inserts a malicious device (e.g., via PCIe, Thunderbolt) and attempts to issue Direct Memory Access (DMA) requests to read from or write to TEE memory.
- Device Bus Attack: The attacker taps into system buses (e.g., PCI, USB, memory bus) using an interposer to eavesdrop, intercept, tamper with, or forge bus data.
- Device Hot-Plug: The attacker performs hot-plugging of PCIe or USB devices, potentially causing exceptions or unexpected behavior in device drivers running inside the TVM.

8.2 Protection principles

This section focuses on protection methods against such attacks.

8.2.1 Secure software design

The software parts of TEEs and TSMs must adhere to secure software design principles. The presence of hardware security features does not excuse neglecting software security. Several excellent books are recommended: *Code Complete*, by Steve McConnell and *Writing Solid Code*, by Steve Maguire are both classics from Microsoft in the 1990s that guided a generation of programmers. *Building Secure Software*, by Viega and McGraw, and *Writing Secure Code*, by Howard and LeBlanc, published in the early 2000s, promoted security programming concepts that remain applicable today.

8.2.1.1 System security design principles

Saltzer and Schroeder, in their 1975 paper "The protection of information in computer systems," proposed fundamental computer security protection principles. Smith revisited these principles in his 2012 paper, "A contemporary look at Saltzer and Schroeder's 1975 design principles." They are still worth considering and following.

- **Economy of Mechanism**: Keep the design as simple and small as possible to facilitate testing and verification.

  Note: *Turing Award winner Hoare once said: "There are two ways of constructing a software design: one way is to make it so simple that there are obviously no deficiencies; the other way is to make it so complicated that there are no obvious deficiencies." TEE design should be as simple as possible. When you feel "this TEE is so complex," you should pause and consider if you are on the right track.*

- **Fail-Safe Defaults**: Access decisions should be based on permission rather than exclusion. The default state should be lack of access.

  Note: *This principle uses Fail-Safe, which differs slightly from Fail-Secure in focus. Using an access control system as an example: Fail-Safe might mean the door unlocks in a fire to ensure personnel safety. Fail-Secure might mean the door stays locked in a fire to protect documents inside. For system security, this principle is interpreted as Fail-Secure in the context of access control: default to no access.*

- **Complete Mediation**: Every access to every resource must be checked for authority. The system should not rely on cached permission information, because cache inconsistencies can lead to security bypasses. Although this may affect performance, it maximizes security.
- **Open Design**: According to Kerckhoffs's principle, the design of a security mechanism should be open; only the keys need to be secret. Kaspersky researchers demonstrated a complex iPhone attack named Operation Triangulation. One step involved sending a DMA address along with its hash, using an obscure custom hash algorithm—a classic example of security by obscurity, which is inherently insecure. If concerned about design theft, patenting is an effective defense.
- **Separation of Privilege**: Access to resources should be granted based on multiple attributes or conditions. For example, large withdrawals from a bank website might require a password, a mobile verification code, and facial recognition.
- **Least Privilege**: Every program should operate using the minimum privileges necessary to complete its task. If a task can be done with user privileges, it should not require administrator privileges.
- **Least Common Mechanism**: Mechanisms used to access resources should not be shared. Different users should not share files by default unless necessary.
- **Psychological Acceptability**: Security mechanisms should be easy to use so that users are not discouraged from using them correctly. If a

password policy is too complex, users may write it down, defeating its purpose.

- **Work Factor**: Designers need to consider the cost of defense versus the cost of attack. A user entering a wrong password once is normal; entering it five times consecutively is suspicious and warrants action (such as temporary lockout).
- **Compromise Recording**: Even if the system cannot prevent an attack, it should record the incident to alert administrators and facilitate analysis. This requires that the recording mechanism itself is reliable and cannot be easily altered by an attacker who compromises the system.

Additionally, the Open Web Application Security Project defines additional secure product design principles:

- **Separation of Duties**: No single individual should control an entire process. Although potentially less efficient, it helps defend against insider fraud and errors. For example, a purchase order might require approval from the finance department.
- **Defense in Depth**: Security checks should be layered to protect assets with different security requirements. For example, a building might have a perimeter guard, a lobby receptionist, and a lab door access system.
- **Zero Trust**: All users, devices, and networks are considered untrusted until verified and authenticated before granting access.
- **Security in Open Source**: Projects should be open source, adopt secure coding practices, secure testing practices, secure development tools, and encourage collaboration between developers and industry experts to ensure code security.

These security design principles are all considerations for TEE software designers.

8.2.1.2 Use of safe languages

In 2019, Microsoft reported in "A proactive approach to more secure code" that approximately 70% of software vulnerabilities are related to C/C++ memory safety, thus advocating for memory-safe programming languages. The NSA's "Software Memory Safety" report, the Cybersecurity and Infrastructure Security Agency's "Recommendation Memory Safety" report, and the NIST's Software Quality Working Group's "Safe Language List" all list safe languages. Among system programming languages, Rust stands out prominently.

Rust's three core tenets are performance, reliability, and productivity. While ensuring runtime performance, Rust provides memory safety, avoiding memory-related vulnerabilities, making it a natural alternative to C for systems programming. Companies such as Microsoft and Google use Rust for new projects, and both Windows and Linux OSs support Rust. Therefore, using Rust for TEE development is a good choice. (*The Rust Programming Language*, by Klabnik and Nichols and *Programming Rust*, by Blandy are excellent introductory books for the Rust language.)

8.2.2 Secure cryptographic application

Because security is paramount, code in TEEs and TSMs frequently uses cryptography. For ordinary developers, these rules of thumb are crucial:

1. Use existing standard algorithms and protocols; do not design your own.
2. Use existing well-vetted cryptographic libraries; do not implement your own.
3. Engage cryptography experts to review the cryptographic security design against requirements.
4. Engage cryptography experts to review the correct usage of cryptographic library Application Programmable Interfaces (APIs).

Several excellent applied cryptography books are also recommended:

- *Applied Cryptography*, by Bruce Schneier, a classic introducing various cryptographic use cases.
- *Cryptography Engineering: Design Principles and Practical Applications*, by Ferguson, Schneier, and Kohno, focusing on underlying principles in cryptographic application.
- *Serious Cryptography: A Practical Introduction to Modern Encryption*, by Jean-Philippe Aumasson, and *Real-World Cryptography*, by David Wong, emphasize practical, real-world cryptography use, helping beginners avoid common mistakes.

Jean-Philippe Aumasson maintains a cryptography programming guide with recommendations:

- Use constant-time comparison for cryptographic strings.
- Avoid code branches controlled by secret data.
- Avoid indexing lookup tables using secret data.
- Avoid loop bounds controlled by secret data.
- Prevent compiler interference with secret data operations.
- Avoid mixing secure and nonsecure APIs.

- Avoid exposing low-level cryptographic primitive APIs; provide high-level APIs instead.
- Use unsigned types for binary data.
- Clear memory containing secrets.
- Use strong random values.
- Use explicit casts for shift operations on potentially signed data.

8.2.2.1 Postquantum cryptography

Owing to the advent of quantum computing, PQC is actively developing. The United States, Europe, and China are researching and developing their own standards. Lattice-based cryptography is the most prominent. NIST's PQC selection results are Kyber (ML-KEM), Dilithium (ML-DSA), Falcon, and SPHINCS+ (SLH-DSA). The NSA's CNSA 2.0 recommends only Kyber and Dilithium. The United Kingdom's NCSC aligns with NIST. Germany's BSI chose FrodoKEM and McEliece. The Chinese Cryptography Society announced first prizes for Aigis-Sig, Aigis-Enc, and LAC-PKE in its 2020 PQC competition. The Internet Engineering Task Force also established a PQC working group to support PQC applications. A branch of PQC, Stateful Hash-Based Signatures, is specifically limited to firmware signing scenarios, with NIST and ETSI recommending LMS and XMSS.

TEE design and implementation need to consider PQC. Because PQC is emerging and in a transitional phase, a hybrid mode combining existing cryptography with PQC is generally recommended. This requires double verification, defending against both traditional and quantum attacks; compromising one is useless. Another view suggests using Key Encapsulation Mechanisms to replace digital signatures in some cases, addressing PQC signature length and efficiency issues.

Even with PQC algorithms, side-channel attack mitigation remains necessary. Ravi et al.'s 2023 paper, "Side-channel and fault-injection attacks over lattice-based post-quantum schemes (Kyber, Dilithium): survey and new results," summarizes side-channel attacks and protections for Kyber and Dilithium, the predecessors of ML-KEM and ML-DSA, providing valuable references.

Additionally, the NIST is conducting research on Lightweight Cryptography, seeking symmetric cryptography alternatives to AES and SHA for resource-constrained environments. The selection is ASCON, suitable for Authenticated Encryption with Associated Data (AEAD) and hashing.

8.2.2.2 Side-channel resistant coding

Intel's white paper, "Guidelines for mitigating timing side channels against cryptographic implementations," summarizes these timing side-channel protection principles for cryptographic implementations:

- **Secret Independent Runtime**: Defends against timing side channels.
- **Secret Independent Code Access**: Defends against timing and cache side channels.
- **Secret Independent Data Access**: Defends against cache side channels.

Protection needs to consider these sources of information leakage:

- **Conditional State Changes**: Consider the next code snippet. The if and else branches execute different instructions (assignment vs. increment). This difference in executed code leads to different execution times, leaking information about the branch condition.

```
int cond_stateInc(int estate, int maxState) {
    static int state = 0;
    if (state >= maxState) {
        state = estate; // Error state
    } else {
        state += 1;     // State transition
    }
    return state;
}
```

- **Variable-Length Operations**: The next classic memory comparison function must not be used in cryptographic contexts. The first if checks length and returns immediately on mismatch, leaking information about the length. The second if compares bytes and returns on first mismatch, leaking information about the position of the differing byte. An attacker can exploit this to guess secrets byte-by-byte.

```
bool equals(byte a[], size_t a_len, byte b[], size_t b_len) {
    if (a_len != b_len) { // data dependent!
        return false;
    }
    for (size_t i = 0; i < a_len; i++) {
        if (a[i] != b[i]) { // data dependent!
            return false;
        }
    }
    return true;
}
```

- **Computation Based on Secrets**: The following is a classic simple modular exponentiation pseudocode. The execution time of the if branch (calculating modular multiplication) differs significantly from the else branch (simple assignment). By observing the time taken for each round R[k], an attacker can precisely recover each bit of the exponent x. If used in RSA or DH exponentiation, this leaks the private key x.

```
naive_modular_exponentiation(y, x, n) // R = y^x mod n, where x is w bits.
{
    S[0] = 1;
    for (k = 0; k < w; k++) {
        if ((x & (1 << k)) != 0) {
            R[k] = (S[k] * y) mod n;
        } else {
            R[k] = S[k];
        }
        S[k+1] = (R[k] * R[k]) mod n
    }
    return R[w-1];
}
```

- **Lookup Table Access**: The AES cache-timing attack is a well-known example. AES defines a SubBytes(a) function using an S-box (a 256-byte constant table). The S-box itself is public, but the index used to look up a value is secret. On a CPU with 64-byte cache lines, the S-box spans 4 cache lines. By observing which cache line is accessed (via timing), an attacker can learn 2 bits of the round key. By observing many encryptions, the full key can be recovered.

8.2.3 Side-channel and fault injection protection

Side-channel protection involves both hardware and software aspects. *Introduction to Hardware Security and Trust*, by Tehranipoor and Wang, and *Hardware Security: From SoC Design to System-Level Defense*, by Bhunia and Tehranipoor provide excellent summaries from a hardware perspective. The white paper "Secure application programming in the presence of side channel attacks" categorizes software mitigation patterns.

8.2.3.1 Traditional side-channel protection

Against data leakage, these protection patterns can be used:

- **Key Access**: Programs should not directly access key material itself, but rather handles to keys. Keys should be protected by cryptographic libraries.

- **Key Integrity**: When comparing secret keys or data, use constant-time comparison that processes all bits regardless of whether a mismatch is found early.
- **Branches**: Avoid controlling if branches or for/while loop termination based on secret data.
- **Cryptography User**: Do not implement cryptographic functions at the application layer; applications should call established cryptographic libraries.
- **Access**: When copying secret data, consider starting the copy from a random offset within the memory region rather than always from the beginning.
- **Verification**: When comparing secrets, avoid functions such as memcmp, strcmp. Either start comparison from a random offset or compare all bits regardless.
- **Clear**: The best way to clear secrets is to overwrite with random data first, then clear.

Against fault injection, these protection patterns can be used:

- **Cryptographic Operation Verification**: After signing with a private key, reverify the signature. After encrypting data, decrypt it and verify.
- **Constant Usage**: Avoid simple constants such as 0 or 1 for security-critical flags, because they have a Hamming distance of 1 and are easier to flip. Use values with larger Hamming distance, such as 0xA5 and 0x5A (Hamming distance 8).
- **Detection**: Verify sensitive data using checksums before use.
- **Default Fail**: In switch or if-else if chains, ensure all possible cases are handled, and the default case performs error handling.
- **Code Flow**: Use counters to track the execution flow through critical code sections and verify that all expected steps were executed correctly.
- **Double-Check**: Recheck critical condition branches.
- **Loop Counter Check**: After a for loop, verify that the loop counter reached the expected value.
- **Branches**: Avoid using simple Boolean or 0/1 types in branch conditions, because these are easy targets for bit flips.
- **Error Response**: Log error occurrences and set a reasonable threshold. Consider disabling functionality after reaching the threshold.
- **Delay**: Introduce random delays in code to make timing side-channel attacks harder.
- **Bypass Prevention**: Call critical functions multiple times (e.g., verify signature twice) and compare results, ensuring both pass.

For software fault injection, Jeremy Boone's article series "An introduction to fault injection" summarizes these protection patterns:

1. **Failure Handling**: Many programs use infinite loops (e.g., while(1)) to handle fatal errors, but this might be bypassed by fault injection. A more robust approach is to cause an explicit crash by dereferencing a known-bad address, e.g., *(volatile uint32_t *)0.

```
void fatal() {
    *(volatile uint32_t *)0;
}
```

2. **Use Redundancy for Resiliency**: Redundancy forces an attacker to inject multiple faults, increasing attack difficulty.
   - **Redundant Memory Read**: Read the same address multiple times and compare.

```
#define READ_ADDR32(addr) (*(volatile uint32_t *)(addr))
void multi_read_addr32(void *addr, uint32_t *val) {
    *val = READ_ADDR32(addr);
    if (READ_ADDR32(addr) != *val || READ_ADDR32(addr) != *val) {
        fatal();
    }
}
```

   - **Redundant Memory Write**: After writing, read back and verify.

```
#define WRITE_ADDR32(addr, val) (*(volatile uint32_t *)(addr) = (val))
void multi_write_addr32(void *addr, uint32_t val) {
    WRITE_ADDR32(addr, val);
    if (READ_ADDR32(addr) != val || READ_ADDR32(addr) != val) {
        fatal();
    }
}
```

- **Redundant Condition Checking**: Repeat the condition within an if statement. For conditions guarding a fail-out (code that should run only if condition is true), use logical AND. For conditions guarding a fail-in (code that should run unless condition is true), use logical OR.

```
#define MULTI_IF_FAILOUT(cond) if ((cond) && (cond) && (cond))
#define MULTI_IF_FAILIN(cond) if ((cond) || (cond) || (cond))

uint16_t condition_test(void) {
    MULTI_IF_FAILOUT(READ_ADDR32(0x10002000) == 0xF00DBADD) {
        return 0x7EAF;
    }
    MULTI_IF_FAILIN(READ_ADDR32(0x10002000) < 3000) {
        return 0xB0A5;
    }
    return 0;
}
```

3. **Use Random Delays**: Fault injection often requires precise timing. Introducing random, unpredictable delays in the code flow makes it harder for an attacker to time the fault injection correctly.

4. **Code Restructuring for Fault Resistance**:
   - **Default to Safe State**: Ensure that before a critical if check, the system is already in a safe state. Faults often skip the check, so starting safe prevents unwanted access.

```
// Bad: If the check is skipped, an insecure open state default value is used
validate_signatuire = false;
if (status != STATE_INSECURE) {
    validate_signatuire = true;
}
// Good: If the check is skipped, a safe closed state default value is used
validate_signatuire = true;
MULTI_IF_FAILOUT(status == STATE_INSECURE) {
    validate_signatuire = false;
}
```

   - **Reset to Safe State**: If a variable is checked multiple times, reset it to a safe state before each check.

```
// Bad: A well-timed fault could skip the signature validation,
// preventing the 'success' variable from being updated.
int success = 0;
success = calculate_signature();
if (success < 0) {
    fatal();
}
success = validate_signature();
if (success < 0) {
    fatal();
}
// Good: Reset 'success' to a safe (-1) state between operations.
volatile int success = -1;
success = calculate_signature();
MULTI_IF_FAILIN(success < 0) {
    fatal();
}
success = -1; // Reset to safe state
success = validate_signature();
MULTI_IF_FAILIN(success < 0) {
    fatal();
}
```

- **Any Failure Leads to Safe State**: Structure conditions so that an attacker must successfully fault all checks to reach an insecure state. For entering an insecure state, use logical AND. For staying in a safe state, use logical OR.

```
Volatile uint32_t state;
// Bad: Faulting any single check leads to insecure open state.
MULTI_IF_FAILIN(state == STATE_INSECURE) {
    insecure_action();
} else {
    secure_action();
}
// Bad: Faulting any single check leads to insecure open state.
MULTI_IF_FAILOUT(state != STATE_INSECURE) {
    secure_action();
} else {
    insecure_action();
}

// Good: All checks must pass to enter insecure open state; otherwise, safe.
MULTI_IF_FAILOUT(state == STATE_INSECURE) {
    insecure_action();
} else {
    secure_action();
}

// Good: If any check indicates not insecure, go to secure close state.
MULTI_IF_FAILIN(state != STATE_INSECURE) {
    secure_action();
} else {
    insecure_action();
}
```

- **Representation of Safe/Insecure States**: Use constants with large Hamming distance (e.g., 0xA5, 0x5A) for state variables, not simple 0 or 1, to make bit flips harder.

  Note*: For loading constants, C provides no reliable way to add redundancy; a constant might be loaded once and kept in a register, making it potentially vulnerable.*

8.2.3.2 *Central processing unit microarchitecture side-channel protection*

Intel provides "Security best practices for side channel resistance" and offers mitigation schemes for various side-channel attacks in its Software Security Guidance. AMD's Product Security guidance also lists side-channel attack vectors and provides mitigation guidelines.

Looking at microarchitecture side-channel protection from another dimension:

8.2.3.2.1 Pure software mitigations

- Specter V1: Software can insert LFENCE instructions in potentially vulnerable code paths to prevent speculative execution.
- Specter V2: Software can use Return Trampoline (Retpoline) and RSB Stuffing.
- Meltdown: Software (OS kernels) can use Kernel Page Table Isolation to separate user and kernel page tables, and Kernel Address Space Layout Randomization.
- SCSB: Software needs to use serializing instructions (e.g., CPUID, INVLPG) or barriers (e.g., LFENCE, SYSRET, INVPCID) after self-modifying code to ensure modifications are visible.

8.2.3.2.2 Hardware-assisted software-enabled mitigations

- Specter V2: Hardware provides features such as Indirect Branch Restricted Speculation (IBRS) (prevents higher-privileged code from being influenced by lower-privileged predictions), Single Thread Indirect Branch Prediction (prevents prediction cross-talk between hyperthreads), and Indirect Branch Predictor Barrier (flushes predictor state). Software can use these interfaces for prediction isolation.
- Specter V4: Hardware provides Speculative Store Bypass Disable. Software can disable speculative store bypass.
- Foreshadow/LVI: Hardware provides IA32_FLUSH_CMD. Software needs to use it to flush L1 cache.
- MDS/LVI: Hardware provides MD_CLEAR functionality (including VERW and L1D_FLUSH commands). Software needs to use these to clear various microarchitectural buffers and L1 data cache.
- Transaction Asynchronous Abort: Hardware provides IA32_TSX_CTRL. Software can disable Intel TSX.
- Branch History Injection: Software uses Supervisor Mode Execution Protection and enhanced IBRS.

- RAPL Power Reporting: Hardware provides microcode updates for filtering; software can configure filtering based on scenarios.

8.2.3.2.3 Pure hardware mitigations

- L1DES, Crosstalk, GDS, EPIC Leak: Hardware provides direct microcode/firmware updates to patch the vulnerabilities.
- CacheWarp: Hardware provides microcode and firmware updates to patch the vulnerability.

8.2.3.2.4 No specific mitigations

- HertzBleed: Software uses traditional side-channel resistant cryptographic implementations.

As more and more side-channel attacks relate to CPU microarchitecture, developers should closely monitor the latest security guidance from CPU vendors, adopt software best practices, and apply hardware microcode patches.

8.2.3.3 DRAM Rowhammer protection

To date, Rowhammer-class attacks can be mitigated by memory encryption. For example, RAMBleed explicitly states that hardware encryption such as SGX and SEV can mitigate the attack.

8.2.4 Simple physical attack protection

TEE hardware is generally responsible for defending against these simple physical attacks:

- Cold Boot Attack (DRAM Offline Reading): The TEE's hardware Memory Encryption Engine (MEE) encrypts data written to DRAM. For confidential computing, the MEE must provide confidentiality. Whether it also provides integrity depends on the MEE design.
- Malicious Device DMA Access: TEE software can designate memory regions as private or shared. The TSM (or IOMMU) should block DMA access to private memory while allowing access to shared memory. This requires the TEE software to configure private/shared memory ranges correctly.
- Device Bus Attack: Confidential computing's default threat model considers devices untrusted. TEE software should not leak confidential information to devices. If the TEE software later verifies and decides to trust a device, it establishes a secure session (e.g., using encryption)

with that device. An attacker tapping the bus would see only encrypted data.
- Device Hot-Plug: Device hot-plug (physical or virtual) is managed by the untrusted system resource manager (e.g., VMM). TEE software must be robust and ready to handle device removal or errors gracefully.

8.3 Trusted execution environment–specific attacks and protections

8.3.1 Attacks and protections for SGX

The SGX introduction "Intel SGX: moving beyond encrypted data to confidential computing" mentions that SGX does not provide side-channel protection; it provides only an isolated execution environment. Wang et al. [462] and Fei et al. [463] summarized SGX security weaknesses and defenses. Bulck's "Tutorial: uncovering side-channels in Intel SGX enclaves" also provides detailed descriptions of SGX attacks and defenses. Attacks on SGX are summarized thus:
- Page Table/TLB-based Attacks: Pigeonhole, Stealthy Page Table, SGX-LEGO, CopyCat, Leaky Cauldron, Off-limits, and so on.
- Cache-based Attacks: SGX cache attacks, Cachezoom, Software Grand, CacheQuote, MemJam, Malware Guard, and so forth.
- CPU Microarchitecture Attacks: Branch Shadowing, SgxPectre, BranchScope, Bluethunder, RSB-based, SGX-Ax, Foreshadow, Nemesis, Frontal Attack, and such.
- Enclave Software Attacks: Return-Oriented Programming (ROP) based DarkROP, Enclave interface attacks, SGX-Bleed (uninitialized structures), and so on.
- Hardware Attacks: Rowhammer (SGX-Bomb), Voltage Fault Injection (Plundervolt), and so on.
- Tool-based Attacks: SGX-Step.

  Intel's various microarchitecture side-channel mitigation guides include sections relevant to SGX. Protection principles are described in Section 8.2, including secure TEE software design, secure TEE cryptographic application, and TEE software side-channel protection.

8.3.2 Attacks and protections for TDX

Known attacks against Trust Domain Extensions (TDX) include:
- Malicious Interrupt Injection: Heckler attack.
- Single-Stepping and Instruction Counting Attacks: TDXDown.

Intel provides TDX guest kernel hardening documentation and TDX side-channel guidance ("Trust domain security guidance for developers" and "MKTME side channel impact on Intel TDX") to help developers mitigate side-channel attacks. In addition to the "three essentials" (secure software design, secure crypto, and side-channel protection), several other aspects are crucial:

8.3.2.1 TVM guest virtual firmware

The TDX Virtual Firmware Design Guide lists security considerations, including general secure software practices and TEE-specific practices:

- Adhere to TCG trusted boot principles to establish a chain of trust. Measure all data that need measurement. Any configuration information input from the VMM must be measured, especially data in Configuration Firmware Volume, Hand-off Block, QEMU FW_CFG, and so forth.
- Use CPU instructions to obtain random numbers (e.g., RDSEED, RDRAND). Do not rely on VMM/QEMU provided sources such as virtio-rng.
- Use trusted time sources. The RTC provided by legacy CMOS is untrusted.

TDX-specific security practices:

- Do not accept already accepted memory. If memory is already accepted by the TD, it may contain active data. A second accept operation would zero the memory, allowing the VMM to inject zero data.
- MMIO handling in Virtualization Exception (VE) handlers. If an MMIO access causes a VE, the handler must check the SHARED bit of the MMIO address and request the VMM to emulate the MMIO access. Otherwise, the VMM could inject arbitrary data into private MMIO space.
- SEPT_VE_DISABLE. Setting this attribute in the TD can generate only EPT violations prevent on accesses to certain pages, instead VE exception.

8.3.2.2 TVM guest kernel

In the TDX architecture, the VMM is considered malicious. Therefore, the OS inside the TD needs to defend against any attacks from the VMM—this is a new security model. Threats and mitigations include:

- Unrobust Device Drivers: Use device driver filters. Disable certain ACPI tables.

- __init functions of drivers: Filters may not stop __init functions. Review their actions (e.g., restrict PCI space access, MMIO sharing, I/O port filtering, restrict hypercalls, restrict MSR accesses, restrict CPUID calls).
- Unrobust Core Kernel Code: Disable complex features to reduce attack surface.
- Specter Gadgets: Perform code reviews.
- Unrobust ACPI Machine Language (AML) Interpreter: Measure and filter ACPI tables.
- VMM-Controlled Randomness: Use RDRAND/RDSEED for random values.
- VMM-Controlled Time Source: Rely only on the Time Stamp Counter; other clocks are untrusted.
- VMM-Injected Interrupts: Do not allow injection of certain exception vectors (e.g., 0–30).
- Lost Interprocessor Interrupts (IPIs): Review and harden IPI loss handling.

For applications within the OS, the most important point remains: Transmit secrets only after TEE attestation. We detailed this process in Chapter 5; key points are reemphasized here:

- All modules in the TEE chain of trust need verification. For example, verifying the OS but not the virtual firmware is problematic.
- Trusted boot can transition to secure boot when appropriate. If many modules need loading, measure only the secure boot policy and verify modules using signatures. Attestation then proves the policy and the verified modules.
- Trusted boot can transition to disk encryption. An agent in the TVM can communicate with a remote KBS, perform TVM attestation, obtain a key, and decrypt the disk.

8.3.2.3 TDX single-stepping

Intel TDX-module prevents single-stepping (executing TD instructions step-by-step) or reexecuting TD instructions (zero-step). This is to prevent debugging tools such as TDX-Step.

8.3.3 Attacks and protections for SEV

Since its appearance, AMD SEV has been a target for attackers. Some SEV-specific attacks are:

- Integrity Check Attacks: Lack of integrity (see "Secure Encrypted Virtualization is Unsecure"), SEVered, Unprotected I/O (see "Exploiting Unprotected I/O Operations in AMD's Secure Encrypted Virtualization").
- Attacks on AMD-SP Hardware: CPU key leakage (see "Insecure Until Proven Updated: Analyzing AMD SEV's Remote Attestation"), AMD-SP fault injection (see "One Glitch to Rule Them All: Fault Injection Attacks Against AMD's Secure Encrypted Virtualization").
- Side-Channel Attacks: TLB Poisoning, CrossLine, CipherLeaks.
- Cache Fault Injection: CacheWarp.
- Malicious Interrupt Injection: Heckler attack, WeSee (VC) attack.
- Malicious Code Injection: AML Injection.
- Performance Counter Attacks: CounterSEVeillance.
- SEV Reverse Map Table Attacks: RMPocalypse.
- Others: Power leakage.
- Tools: SEV-Step.

Because first-generation SEV and SEV-ES have known vulnerabilities, developers should upgrade to SEV-SNP. The previously mentioned three essentials and TVM kernel threat mitigations also apply to SEV-SNP. For SEV-SNP, AMD released software guidance and hardware update guidance; developers should follow these to protect against attacks.

CHAPTER 9

Confidential computing TEE-IO model

In the previous chapters, we introduced host-side TEE-based confidential computing. Starting from this chapter, we will detail the general model of confidential computing TEE-IO, which incorporates confidential devices.

9.1 Confidential computing TEE-IO security model

The purpose of confidential computing is to protect data in use. In practical scenarios, this data not only needs processing by the CPU but may also be processed by hardware accelerators. A typical example is a GPU processing data related to AI large language models, which often contains personal privacy or commercial data and requires protection. Microsoft's research team published an article in 2022, "Powering the next-generation trustworthy AI in a confidential cloud using NVIDIA GPUs" stating, "Our vision is to extend this trust boundary to GPUs, allowing code running in the CPU TEE to securely offload computation and data to GPUs."

In existing TEE technologies, only the host-side hardware and TSM are part of the TEE-TCB. This leads to two types of limitations:

- **Device Untrusted**: This means the TEE cannot directly pass confidential data to the device for computation, as illustrated in Fig. 9.1a.
- **Connection Insecure**: This means the communication link (e.g., PCIe bus) between a trusted device and the CPU is at risk of information leakage. If a TEE wishes to exchange data with a trusted device, it must use a bounce buffer method. The TEE encrypts data from private memory, copies it to shared memory, and sends it to the device. After processing, the device encrypts the data, returns it to shared memory, and the TEE decrypts it and copies it back to private memory. This significantly reduces efficiency for I/O-intensive applications, as shown in Fig. 9.1b.

Confidential Computing
ISBN 978-0-443-54067-7
https://doi.org/10.1016/B978-0-443-54067-7.00007-3

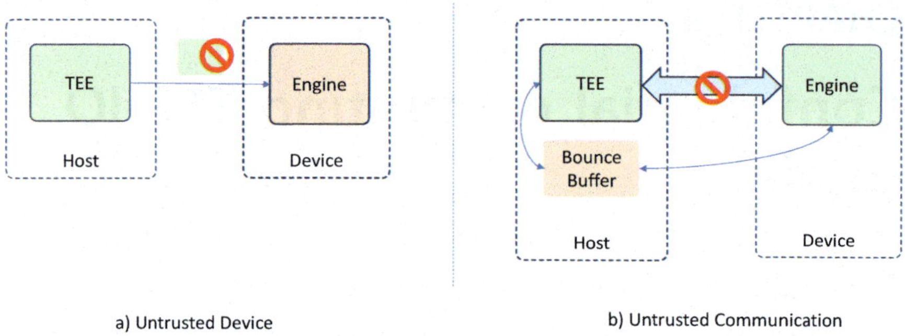

Figure 9.1 Limitations of existing confidential computing TEEs.

Industry standardization organizations have also released various specifications to support securely and efficiently offloading workloads from host-side TEEs to confidential devices. For example, DMTF's SPDM defines how two devices perform identity verification within a platform and establish a trusted secure channel. The PCI-SIG's PCIe Base Specification and the CXL Consortium's CXL Specification define Integrity and Data Encryption (IDE) functions for the PCIe and CXL link layers, using hardware encryption to protect data transmitted between the TEE and the device. The PCIe Base Specification also defines the TEE Device Interface Security Protocol (TDISP), which provides functionality for binding and managing a TEE and a TEE Device Interface (TDI).

Addressing the above limitations, there are several methods for using devices within a TEE:

- **Type 1: Continue using existing untrusted devices.** The TEE can use cryptographic techniques that allow the device to perform computations without understanding the result's meaning. For example, homomorphic encryption lets the device compute directly on ciphertext and return encrypted results. This method requires no hardware modification but has poor performance.
- **Type 2: Device trusted, but connection insecure.** The TEE can use SPDM to authenticate the device and simultaneously establish a secure software channel—an SPDM session. All data is transmitted within this SPDM session using the bounce buffer method. The benefit is that the device can directly access and process confidential data, improving efficiency. This is an intermediate transitional phase; the host-side TEE requires no modification, while the device needs to add SPDM functionality and provide security architecture protection.

- **Type 3: Device trusted and connection secure.** Building on SPDM authentication, a secure hardware channel—IDE—is established over PCIe between the host and device. Data can be transmitted directly over the PCIe or CXL bus, with IDE protecting the confidentiality and integrity of Transaction Layer Packets (TLPs); such TLPs are called IDE TLPs. The device can then access TEE private memory via DMA, greatly improving efficiency. This is the ultimate solution. The host-side hardware needs to add IDE support, software needs to manage the device using TDISP, and the device side must also add IDE and TDISP functionality.

Note*: We have not considered the option of "connection secure but device untrusted." From a cryptographic perspective, "connection secure" implies establishing a secure session, while "device trusted" implies successful authentication. Only an authenticated secure session can defend against active attacks; a plain secure session only prevents passive attacks.*

In this chapter, we will focus on the third type of solution—trusted devices and trusted connections.

9.1.1 General confidential computing TEE-IO security model

Fig. 9.2 shows a general architecture model for TEE-IO based confidential computing. The left side depicts the host system with TEE-IO capability, where the CPU resides, and we refer to the TEE Virtual Machine as TVM. The right side depicts the device side with TEE-IO capability.

On the device side, a Hardware Root of Trust (HRoT) is necessary to create the device's execution environment, loading other modules in conjunction with secure boot and trusted boot. The HRoT includes the Root of Trust for Measurement (RTM), Root of Trust for Storage

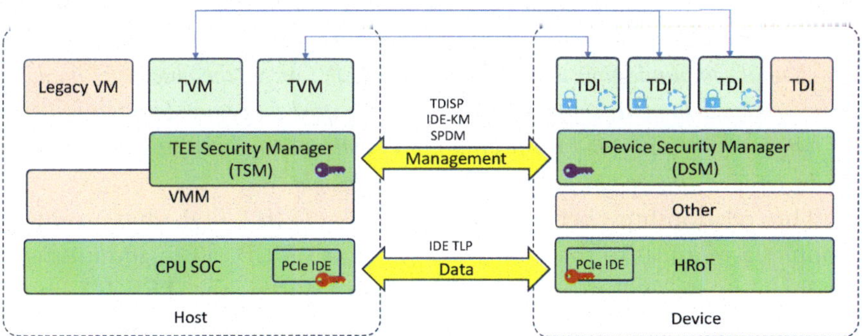

Figure 9.2 Confidential computing TEE-IO architecture model.

(RTS), and Root of Trust for Reporting (RTR) supporting remote attestation in trusted boot, as well as the Root of Trust for Detection (RTD), Root of Trust for Update (RTU), and Root of Trust for Recovery (RTRec) for secure boot and firmware-resiliency. All these belong to the device-side TCB.

On the device side, we define the smallest functional unit that can be allocated to a TEE as a TEE Device Interface (TDI). TDI is a logical concept. Physically, a TDI could be a virtual function (VF) of a PCI Single Root I/O Virtualization (SR-IOV) device, a non-IOV function, a physical function (PF) of a PCI device, or even the entire device. Each TDI must be isolated from other TDIs and non-TDI modules. A single TDI can be allocated to at most one TEE, but one TEE can own multiple TDIs.

To facilitate the management of multiple TDIs, the device side may have a Device Security Manager (DSM). The DSM is an extension of the hardware root of trust, responsible for the security assurance and isolation of all TDIs. The DSM is also part of the device-side TCB. The DSM must be isolated from all other modules, including the TDIs.

All other modules in the system are considered untrusted and cannot affect the security functions of the DSM and TDIs.

The connection between the device and the host can be logically divided into two types: the management channel and the data channel. The management channel is responsible for establishing authenticated secure channels, managing the state of TDIs, etc. It is not frequently used. The management channel can be a low-speed channel, such as DMTF-defined SPDM, as well as IDE Key Management (IDE-KM) and TDISP. The data channel is responsible for real-time data transmission and must be a high-speed channel, such as IDE defined by PCI-SIG and CXL.

Note: *This architecture assumes the presence of IDE and TDISP hardware modules as defined in the PCIe specification, requiring simultaneous support from both the host and device sides. In reality, hardware vendors can define proprietary confidential communication methods to replace IDE; or, in the absence of hardware trusted channel support, software methods can be used for secure data transmission. As long as the security and trustworthiness of both management and data channels can be ensured, the specific implementation is flexible.*

The relationships between the device's TCB, TDI, and untrusted modules are similar to those between the host's TCB, TEE, and untrusted modules, so we will not repeat them here. Within the TEE-IO framework, the device's TCB automatically extends to the host side and becomes part of the TEE-TCB. Remote attestation on the device side is also similar to that on the host side for TEEs. The device's DSM can return device certificates, hardware and firmware measurements, configuration measurements, etc., **for the entire device** via SPDM. It can also return TDI-specific interface reports via TDISP.

According to the TDISP section of the PCIe Base Specification, TEE-IO needs to ensure:

- **Confidentiality**: The code, data, and execution state of the TVM stored in the TDI cannot be read by any non-TCB module.
- **Integrity**: The code, data, and execution state of the TVM stored in the TDI cannot be tampered with by any non-TCB module.

The **availability of TVM data** is outside the scope of the security model, as the VMM, acting as the manager, can terminate the connection between the TDI and the TVM at any time. However, the **availability of the system** is within the scope. The system should not crash abruptly due to a vulnerable device or a malicious TVM; this is a responsibility of the VMM.

To ensure the above security properties, an architecture based on hardware I/O virtualization must achieve the following:

- **Host Authentication of Device Identity and Measurements**: The TVM must cryptographically verify the device's identity and measurements, including SVN, device debug status, etc. Based on this information, the TVM decides whether to accept or reject the allocated TDI. SPDM can fulfill this requirement. Essentially, this is device attestation and verification, conceptually similar to TEE attestation.
- **Host-Device Secure Channel Establishment**: The TSM and DSM must cryptographically ensure the confidentiality and integrity of transmitted data, including protection against replay attacks. SPDM can help establish a secure management channel, and IDE functionality can serve as a secure data channel. This is a fundamental secure communication requirement, conceptually similar to network TLS.
- **Host-Side TDI Management**: The host side needs to transition the TDI from the CONFIG_UNLOCK state to the CONFIG_LOCK state to instruct the DSM to lock the current configuration, enabling the TVM to obtain a locked device TDI report. The TSM must collaborate with the TVM to decide when to transition the TDI to the RUN state, allowing DMA and MMIO access. To ensure the security of DMA data transfer, the host-side TSM needs to manage a trusted I/O Memory Management Unit (IOMMU), allowing only encrypted DMA access to TVM private memory. Similarly, to ensure the security

of MMIO data transfer, the host-side TSM needs to manage trusted MMIO address translation page tables, allowing only encrypted MMIO access to the TDI's private memory. These are very specific requirements not typically considered by ordinary host applications; system software and device drivers generally need to be aware of them.

- **Internal Device Security Architecture**: The device's DSM must manage and isolate TDIs. TVM data should only be accessible by the TDI bound to it. For example, the DSM and TDI must ensure that when the TDI is in an ERROR state, no TVM confidential data is leaked. The TDI can only return to the CONFIG_UNLOCK state after scrubbing all TVM confidential data, allowing re-binding. Additionally, the device needs an internal root of trust to perform trusted boot, secure boot, secure updates, etc., ensuring the integrity of the DSM. This pertains to the device's own security design and implementation requirements and is not closely related to the host side.

9.1.2 Modules in TEE-IO

Let's discuss the roles and responsibilities of some important modules in the TEE-IO architecture.

- VMM (Virtual Machine Manager): As the **resource manager**, the VMM is not only the manager of TVMs but also the manager of device TDIs. It is responsible for allocating resources to device TDIs, locking their configurations, and then assigning the TDI to a TVM.
- TSM (TEE Security Manager): The TSM is the **enforcer of host-side TVM security policies.** It is responsible for providing security mechanisms such as trusted IOMMU and trusted MMIO page tables to protect TVM data from access by non-TCB modules. Other functions of the TSM include providing interfaces for the VMM to allocate TDIs to TVMs, managing the security state of TDIs using TDISP, and creating and managing IDE keys.
- TVM (TEE Virtual Machine): Inside the TVM, there is a **decision-maker.** It needs to obtain the device's identity, measurement information, and the device TDI report to decide whether to accept this device TDI.
- DSM (Device Security Manager): The DSM is the e**nforcer of device-side TVM data security policies.** It is responsible for isolating and protecting TVM data from access by non-TCB modules. Other functions of the DSM include reporting device identity and

measurements for authentication, configuring device IDE keys, managing TDI locked configurations, and reporting status.

9.1.3 Communication protocols in TEE-IO

Communication between the host and device can be divided into management channel protocols and data channel protocols. Several commonly used protocols are introduced below.

9.1.3.1 SPDM protocol

The management channel protocol is used for creating sessions and authentication. The TSM obtains the device identity and measurements through SPDM, enabling the TVM to verify and accept the device TDI. Simultaneously, the TSM and DSM establish a secure management channel between host and device, carrying the application layer IDE Key Management (IDE_KM) protocol and the TDISP protocol over SPDM. As shown in Fig. 9.3, the left part indicates the phases of the SPDM protocol, the middle part shows SPDM protocol commands, and the right part illustrates SPDM protocol functions.

The SPDM protocol includes the following phases:

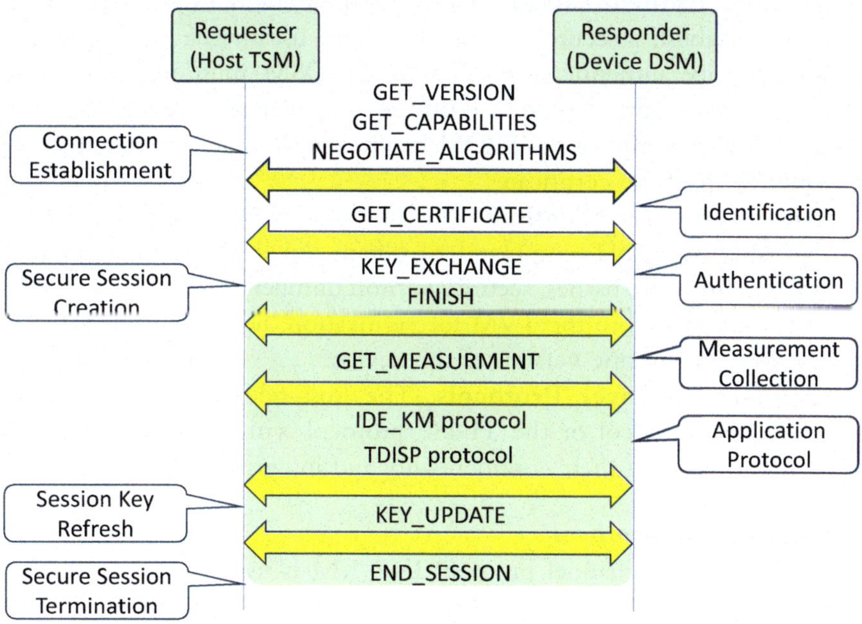

Figure 9.3 SPDM protocol.

- **Connection Establishment**: The host-side TSM sends GET_VERSION, GET_CAPABILITIES, and NEGOTIATE_ALGORITHMS commands to create an SPDM connection.
- **Secure Session Creation**: The host-side TSM sends KEY_EXCHANGE and FINISH commands to create an SPDM secure session. Any data within the SPDM session is encrypted using an AEAD algorithm, ensuring confidentiality and integrity.
- **Session Key Update**: During AEAD usage, each message corresponds to a unique message sequence number. When this counter approaches its theoretical limit, the SPDM secure session automatically terminates. Before reaching the limit, the host-side TSM uses the KEY_UPDATE command to update the AEAD encryption key.
- **Secure Session Termination**: When the secure session is no longer needed, the host-side TSM sends the END_SESSION command to terminate it.

  The SPDM protocol provides the following functions:
- **Identity Retrieval**: The host-side TSM sends the GET_CERTIFICATE command to obtain the device's certificate chain. This certificate chain is passed to the TVM for verification, helping decide whether to trust the device manufacturer.
- **Identity Authentication**: When the host-side TSM and the device DSM establish a secure session, they must use the device's certificate for identity authentication. The device DSM must use the private key corresponding to the certificate to generate a digital signature over the transcript of the SPDM handshake messages, thereby proving ownership of the certificate.
- **Measurement Collection**: The host-side TSM sends the GET_MEASUREMENT command to obtain the device's measurements, such as firmware hashes, security version numbers, etc. These measurements are passed to the TVM for verification, helping decide whether to trust this specific version of the device.
- **Application Layer Protocols**: The host-side TSM can send the IDE_KM protocol or the TDISP protocol within the SPDM secure session, ensuring their confidentiality and integrity.

9.1.3.2 IDE_KM protocol

The management channel protocol IDE_KM is used for key exchange. The TSM sends IDE keys to the DSM via the IDE_KM protocol, allowing the DSM to configure them on the device side. The IDE_KM protocol also manages the start and stop of IDE encryption, IDE key updates, etc. IDE_KM is an application layer protocol running over an SPDM secure session, ensuring the confidentiality and integrity of the IDE_KM protocol itself.

IDE has two main states: Insecure and Secure.

- **Insecure – Setup**: The initial IDE state. The host and device generate ephemeral keys and perform key exchange. The host can send IDE_KM QUERY commands to get information.
- **Insecure – Ready**: When all IDE keys have been programmed into the PCIe IDE hardware via the IDE_KM KEY_PROG command, IDE enters the Ready state.
- **Secure – Operating**: After the PCIe IDE hardware receives the IDE_KM K_SET_GO command, it enters the Secure state. PCIe IDE starts working, receiving and sending IDE TLPs. If any event occurs that compromises the security of the SPDM session or IDE connection, the IDE link automatically transitions back to the Insecure state.
- **Secure – Key Refresh**: IDE in operation uses AES-GCM-256 for encryption protection, with each message corresponding to a unique counter. When this counter approaches its theoretical limit, the IDE link automatically terminates. Before reaching the limit, the host can program another set of keys using IDE_KM KEY_PROG and then update the active keys for the secure IDE link using IDE_KM K_SET_GO.

Note: *In the PCIe specification, the theoretical upper limit for the IDE key counter is* 2^{64}. *However, recent IETF drafts on "Usage limits on AEAD algorithms" indicate that practical limits are lower. Users of AEAD algorithms need to set reasonable limits based on actual requirements. Evaluation factors include:*

1. *Attacker advantage* (e.g., 2^{-32}).
2. *AEAD algorithm* (e.g., *AES-GCM-256, AES-CCM-256, CHACHA20-POLY1305).*
3. *Number of AEAD encryption blocks per message* (e.g., *256 blocks for PCIe IDE, 32 blocks for CXL.cachemem IDE containment mode, 480 blocks for CXL.cachemem IDE skid mode).*
4. *Length of the AEAD message authentication code* (e.g., *128-bit MAC for SPDM, 96-bit MAC for IDE).*

9.1.3.3 PCIe IDE

The data channel protocol PCIe IDE is used to authenticate and encrypt TLP packets. The Root Port (RP) of the host-side PCIe Root Complex (RC) and the PCIe Port of the device Endpoint (EP) can use IDE to encrypt PCIe or CXL TLPs. IDE uses the AES-GCM-256 algorithm from the AEAD family. Only IDE TLPs guarantee the confidentiality and integrity of DMA or MMIO data exchanged between them.

PCIe IDE streams are divided into two types.

- **Selective IDE Stream**: Encrypts TLPs between any two ports, providing end-to-end encryption. IDE TLPs pass through PCIe switches directly, with the ciphertext remaining invisible to the switch. This is the mode supported by TEE-IO, offering the advantage of excluding the PCIe switch from the TCB.
- **Link IDE Stream**: Encrypts TLPs between two adjacent ports, providing point-to-point encryption. When passing through a PCIe switch, the TLP must be decrypted and re-encrypted, making the ciphertext visible to the switch. Using link IDE streams implies trusting the PCIe switch.

Ideally, IDE TLPs should be transmitted in order. Therefore, IDE TLP packets do not contain a counter for AEAD decryption; the sender and receiver each maintain an AEAD message counter and keep them synchronized. However, different TLP transactions have different flow control (FC) types. One type of message may be prioritized over another, potentially disrupting the reception order. To address flow control issues without introducing an explicit counter, PCIe uses the concept of IDE sub-streams. Each IDE stream is divided into three IDE sub-streams, corresponding to different classes of PCIe transactions. Each IDE sub-stream has its own IDE key, and only IDE TLPs within a single sub-stream need to be transmitted in order.

- **Posted Request (PR)** Sub-stream: Corresponds to PCIe PR transactions, which are TLPs that do not require a Completion (CPL) packet in response. Examples include Memory Write requests or Message requests.
- **Non-Posted Request (NPR)** Sub-stream: Corresponds to PCIe NPR transactions, which are TLPs that require a CPL packet in response. Examples include Read requests for Memory, I/O, or PCI Configuration space, or Write requests with data for I/O or PCI Configuration space.

- **Completion (CPL)** Sub-stream: Corresponds to PCIe CPL transactions, which are responses to NPR packets.

9.1.3.4 TDISP protocol

TDISP is a management channel protocol used to standardize the interface provided by the device to software. The VMM and TVM can manage device TDIs using the TDISP protocol, including switching between the four TDI states and binding IDE streams. TDISP is an application layer protocol running over an SPDM secure session; using the SPDM secure session ensures the confidentiality and integrity of the TDISP protocol.

There are four states of a TDI.

- **CONFIG_UNLOCK** (Configuration Unlocked): This is the initial state of a TDI. Non-TVM modules can use it directly. All resources of the TDI are open, and communication does not require IDE TLPs. The host can send TDISP GET_TDISP_VERSION, GET_TDISP_CAPABILITIES commands to obtain TDI information.
- **CONFIG_LOCK** (Configuration Locked): The host sends the TDISP LOCK_INTERFACE command to transition from CONFIG_UNLOCK to CONFIG_LOCK. At this point, all configurations that could affect the security of TVM data are locked. "Locked" means they either cannot be modified (remain in current state) or forced modification leads to the ERROR state. The TDI cannot yet send or receive IDE TLPs, as CONFIG_LOCK merely signifies that the TDI is allocated to a TVM. The TVM can now verify the device and TDI state; for example, the host can obtain TDI information for verification using the GET_INTERFACE_REPORT command. However, the TVM has not yet accepted the TDI.
- **RUN** (Running): The host sends the TDISP START_INTERFACE command to transition from CONFIG_LOCK to RUN. At this point, the TVM has accepted the TDI. The TDI can send DMA requests via IDE TLPs to access TVM private memory or receive MMIO requests via IDE TLPs to access TEE MMIO.
- **ERROR** (Error): When a TDI is in the CONFIG_LOCK or RUN state, any event that compromises the security of the SPDM session, IDE connection, or TDI security will cause the TDI to enter the ERROR state. A TDI in the ERROR state must not expose any TVM confidential information and cannot send or receive IDE TLPs. However, the TDI may use non-IDE TLPs to send error notifications to the TVM. For example, the TDI could use PCIe Message Signal Interrupt

(MSI) or MSI-X mechanisms, or the PCIe Advanced Error Reporting (AER) mechanism. There are two ways to exit the ERROR state. One method is for the TDI to receive a STOP_INTERFACE command, clear all TVM confidential data, and then return to the CONFIG_UNLOCK state. The other method is for the TDI to automatically clear all TVM confidential data and then return to the CONFIG_UNLOCK state.

9.1.4 Resource classification in TEE-IO

As shown in Fig. 9.4b, on the host side, TVM resources are divided into TEE Private Memory and TEE Shared Memory. As the names suggest, they respectively hold private data requiring encryption and shareable data. When a TDI uses DMA to access TVM private data, it must use IDE TLPs for protection. When accessing TVM shared data, it may or may not use IDE TLPs.

As shown in Fig. 9.4a, a device can provide MMIO interfaces for the host to store TVM private or shared data. This portion of MMIO is called TEE MMIO or device-side TEEMEM. Correspondingly, the device may have other MMIO interfaces that can only be used for accessing non-TVM private data, including TVM shared data or nonconfidential device data (e.g., configuration information). This portion is called Non-TEE MMIO or device-side Non-TEEMEM. Accesses to TEE MMIO must use IDE TLPs for protection. Accesses to Non-TEE MMIO may or may not use IDE TLPs for protection. The TDISP specification also allows the attributes of TEE MMIO and Non-TEE MMIO to change at runtime. The host can request a change by sending the TDISP SET_MMIO_ATTRIBUTE command, and the MMIO attribute change takes effect immediately.

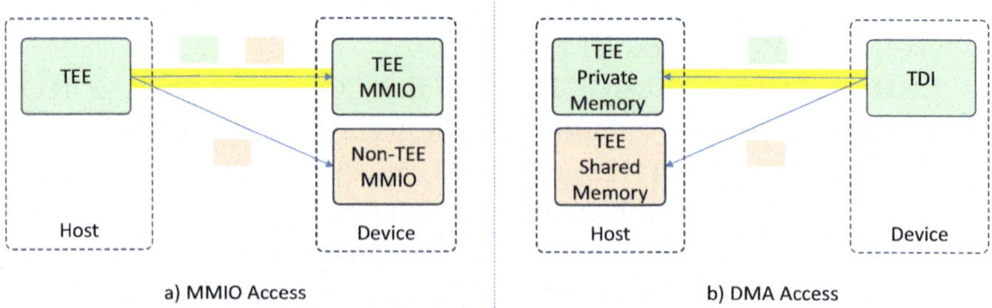

Figure 9.4 MMIO and DMA in the TEE-IO confidential computing.

Table 9.1 Keys in TEE-IO.

Key name	Specification	Function	Source	Sub-keys
SPDM session key	SPDM	AEAD key protecting SPDM session	Derived from SPDM session DHE key exchange	2 session phases: Handshake/ Application Each phase: Send/ Receive directions
IDE key	PCIe	AES-GCM key protecting PCIe IDE TLPs	Directly set via IDE-KM within SPDM session	3 IDE sub-streams: PR, NPR, CPL Each sub-stream: Send/ Receive directions
Memory encryption key	(Proprietary)	AES-XTS key protecting DRAM data	Generated internally by CPU SoC	–

***Note**: Let's clarify the concept of TEE MMIO here. A device, when manufactured, can pre-designate which parts of its MMIO space are TEE MMIO and which are Non-TEE MMIO. This is a device property. When we say that a TEE can only access TEE MMIO using IDE TLPs, the major premise is that the device's TDI has been allocated to the TEE and is in the RUN state. If the TDI is not yet allocated to a TEE, then that TDI functions as an ordinary device in the CONFIG_UNLOCK state. It only has regular MMIO; there is no distinction between TEE MMIO and Non-TEE MMIO. Since there is no confidential data in TEE MMIO at this point, ordinary non-confidential host programs can access it normally without needing IDE TLPs.*

The Intel TDX Connect TEE-IO Device Guide lists the access rules for MMIO and DMA based on the requestor and completer of the TLP.

9.1.5 Keys in TEE-IO

Based on the above protocols, the keys involved in TEE-IO can be summarized, as shown in Table 9.1.

9.2 Confidential computing TEE-IO threat model

This section summarizes the TEE-IO related threats mentioned in the PCIe Base Specification. These threats pertain to the external bus. For internal SoC buses, different vendors may have different considerations.

We assume here that the TEE-IO device is a standard PCIe device. Other types of devices may have specific threats and security requirements.

9.2.1 Threats to consider

Confidential computing TEE-IO expands the threat scope for TEEs. Additional considerations include:

- **Interconnect Security**: Attackers may use lab equipment such as interposers, malicious PCIe switches, route table modifications, debug hooks, etc., to eavesdrop, intercept, tamper, forge, or use combinations of these methods (e.g., replay or illegal reordering) to attack communication data between host and device. These threats can be mitigated by establishing a secure channel using SPDM and IDE. Fig. 9.5 shows four basic attack methods, and Fig. 9.6 shows some combined attack methods.

  Note: *Simple interception affects availability, which is considered a Denial of Service (DoS) attack and is outside the considered threat scope. However, interception combined with other methods can compromise integrity and confidentiality, thus falling within the considered threat scope.*
- **Identity and Measurement Reporting**: Attackers may use unknown or fake devices to impersonate legitimate devices, aiming to obtain

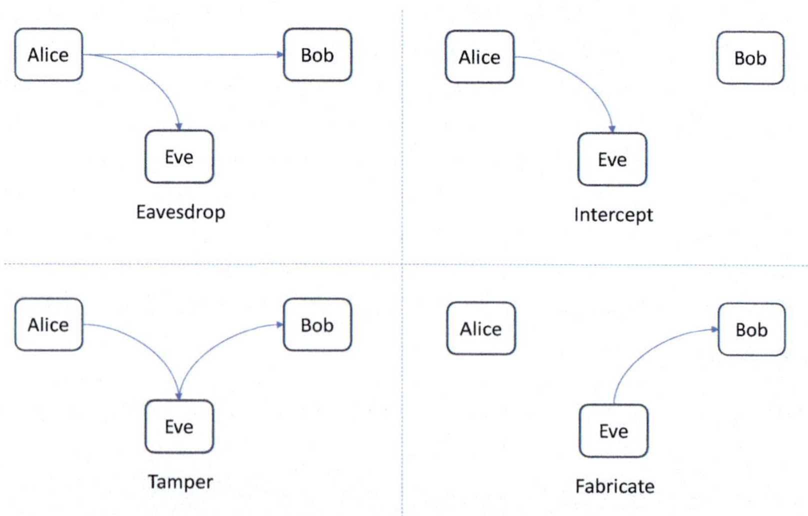

Figure 9.5 Basic attack methods on secure communication.

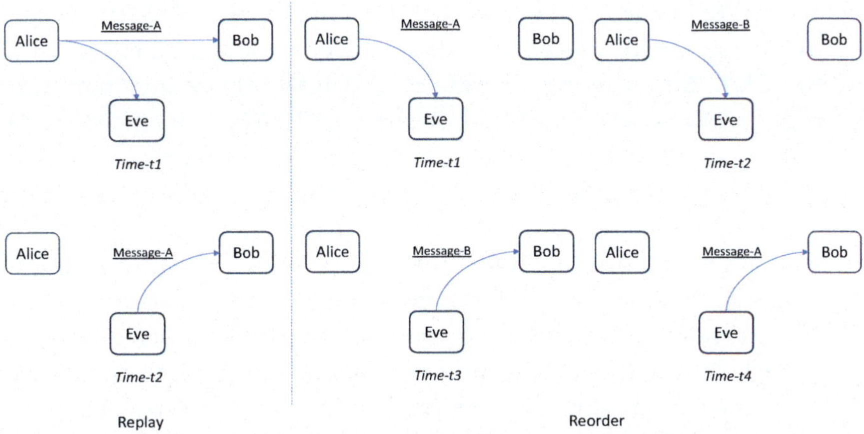

Figure 9.6 Combined attack methods on secure communication.

TVM private data. Attackers may downgrade the firmware of a legitimate device to a vulnerable version, turning it into a flawed device, and then exploit the flaw to obtain TVM private data. Attackers may also exploit debug interfaces on a legitimate device to obtain TVM private data. These threats can be defended against through SPDM identity authentication and measurement report verification. Various types of insecure devices and inspection methods are shown in Fig. 9.7.

- **TDI Allocation and Removal**: Attackers may obtain the contents of device private MMIO by maliciously modifying the device's MMIO

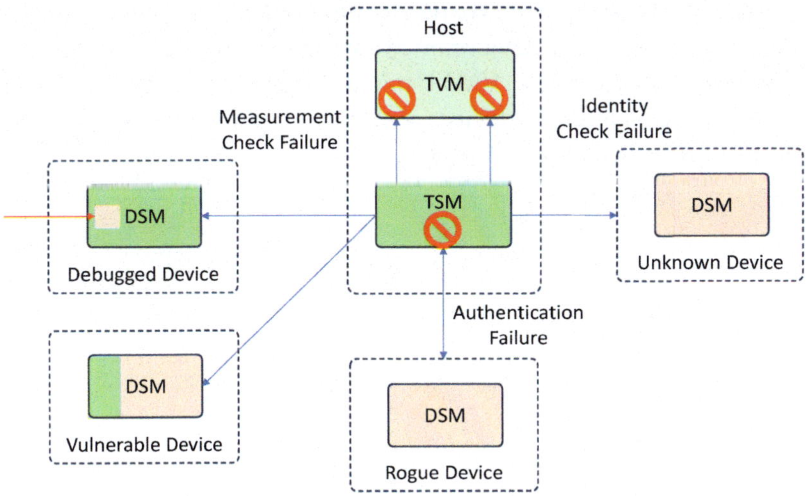

Figure 9.7 Various insecure devices and inspection methods.

address mapping, remapping MMIO, overlapping MMIO ranges, modifying MMIO address decoders, or even removing and reallocating the TDI. Attackers may modify trusted IOMMU address translation page tables to control DMA access and steal TVM private memory. Attackers may attempt to obtain device private memory contents by abruptly removing the device, resetting the device, or forcing the device TDI into an error state. Attackers may launch a malicious TVM to steal private memory contents from the TDI. These threats can be mitigated by using the TDISP protocol between host and device. Fig. 9.8 provides a simple summary: the TVM shares secrets with the trusted TDI, and the TDI must keep them secret. From the TVM's perspective, it must prevent non-TDI entities from accessing TVM private data via DMA. From the TDI's perspective, it must prevent non-TVM entities from accessing TVM private data via MMIO.

The TDX Connect architecture discusses various threats related to MMIO and DMA in detail. We describe them separately below.

9.2.1.1 Threats to trusted MMIO

Threats targeting trusted MMIO include the following, as illustrated in Fig. 9.9.

- **Malicious Interference**: Software other than the TVM to which the TDI is allocated (e.g., VMM, other TVMs, non-TEE VMs) might attempt to access the TDI's TEE MMIO.
- **Address Remapping Attack**: The VMM might map a contiguous MMIO HPA range to two non-contiguous GPA ranges, potentially mapping to different devices or swapping the order of mappings.
- **Overlap Attack**: The VMM might assign the same MMIO HPA range to two different devices, causing confusion during PCIe hardware address decoding.

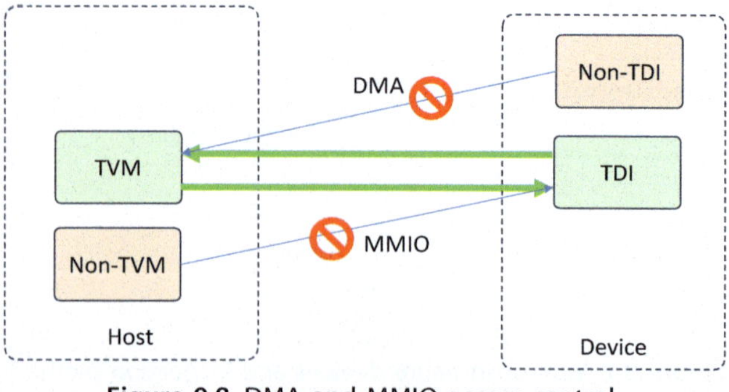

Figure 9.8 DMA and MMIO access control.

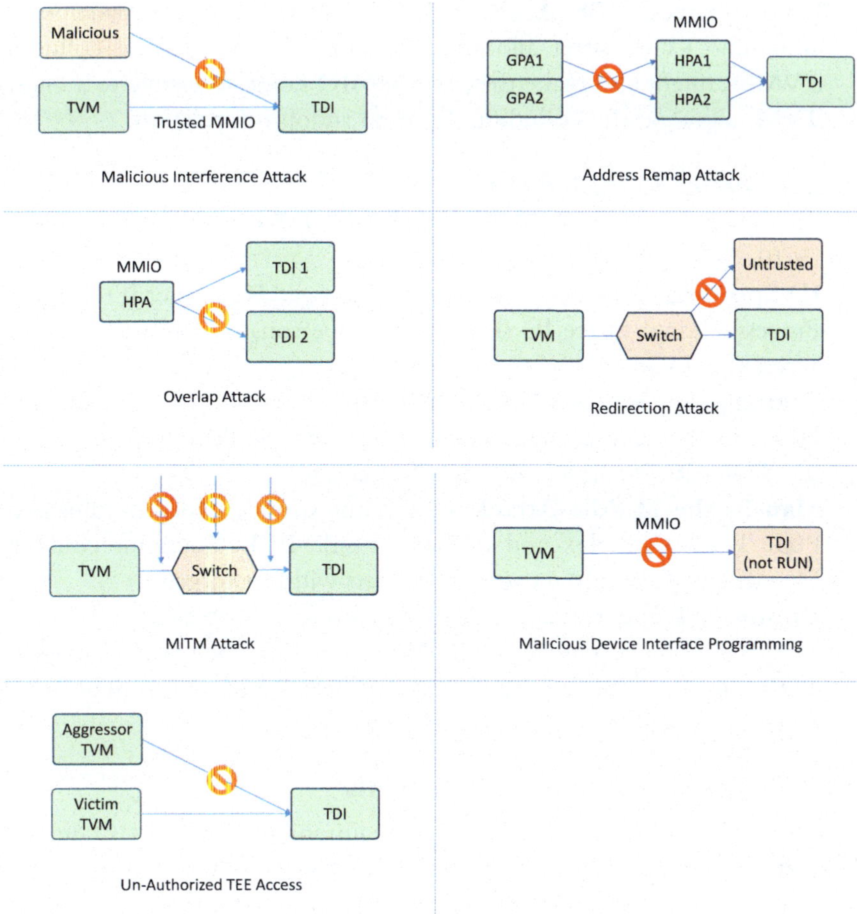

Figure 9.9 Threats to trusted MMIO.

- **Redirection Attack**: A PCIe switch might redirect MMIO access to another, untrusted device.
- **Man-in-the-Middle Attack**: Communication between the host-side PCIe Root Complex and the device-side PCIe Endpoint could be eavesdropped on, intercepted, tampered with, or forged.
- **Malicious Device Interface Configuration**: The VMM might allocate an unlocked TDI to a TVM. For example, immediately after a TDI is removed and reallocated, it might trick a TVM into issuing MMIO requests or accepting DMA requests intended for a different TDI.

- **Unauthorized TEE Access**: The VMM might start a malicious or colluding TVM. After allocating the TEE MMIO to the colluding TVM, it might also make the same MMIO range accessible to a victim TVM, allowing the colluding TVM to snoop information.

9.2.1.2 Threats to trusted DMA

Threats targeting trusted DMA include the following, as illustrated in Fig. 9.10.

- **ID Spoofing**: A malicious device uses a forged Requester ID (RID) or Process Address Space ID (PASID) to impersonate a genuine TDI and access the TVM.
- **Remapping Attack**: The VMM maps the same GPA to different HPAs in the secure page table and the trusted IOMMU, providing the TDI with incorrect address information.
- **Man-in-the-Middle Attack**: Communication between the host-side PCIe Root Complex and the device-side PCIe Endpoint could be eavesdropped on, intercepted, tampered with, or forged.
- **Confused Deputy Access Attack**: When a TVM accepts a TDI, it accepts the entire device TCB. However, this does not mean other TDIs on the same device can access this TVM. Even within the same device, TDIs not accepted by the TVM cannot access it.

9.2.2 Device-side security requirements

The following summarizes the security requirements for TEE-IO devices. For detailed descriptions, refer to the PCIe Base Specification.

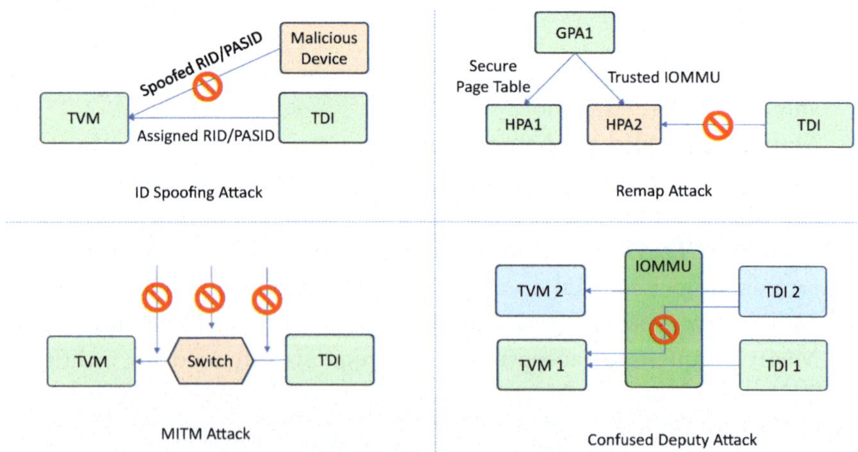

Figure 9.10 Threats to trusted DMA.

- **Device Identity and Authentication**: TEE-IO devices must support the SPDM protocol to convey identity information and perform identity authentication. Devices may use TPM-based trusted boot and identity authentication, or DICE-based trusted boot and identity authentication.
- **Firmware and Configuration Measurements**: TEE-IO devices must return device measurements via SPDM, which can be hash-based measurements or SVNs. If the device supports firmware updates, it is recommended to follow the firmware-resiliency functions defined in NIST SP 800-193. If the device supports runtime firmware updates without reboot, this capability must be indicated in the TDI report. The device must adhere to the host's NO_FW_UPDATE and SPDM secure session TerminationPolicy settings configured via TDISP. For example, if the host sets NO_FW_UPDATE to 1, the device must not support runtime firmware updates while the TDI is in the CONFIG_LOCK state. If the host sets TerminationPolicy to 0, then if a runtime firmware update occurs, the SPDM secure session must be terminated.
- **Secure Interconnect**: TEE-IO devices must use IDE to protect communication with the host Root Complex, as well as peer-to-peer (P2P) communication between devices. If an IDE stream transitions to the Insecure state, any TDI bound to that stream and in the CONFIG_LOCK or RUN state must transition to the ERROR state. If the device hardware, while a TDI is in CONFIG_LOCK or RUN, issues a TLP request and receives a completion with Unsupported Request (UR) status, Completer Abort (CA) status, or a completion timeout (indicating an uncorrectable error, such as an IOMMU translation error), the TDI must transition to the ERROR state.
- **Device-Attached Memory**: If the device has attached memory used to store TVM private data, the device must ensure that the plaintext of this private data is not leaked outside the device. Similar to the host side, the device may choose to use a memory encryption engine to encrypt the data and provide integrity protection.
- **TDI Security**: The device's DSM must use SPDM to establish a secure session with the TSM, supporting IDE key management and TDISP. The IDE stream bound to a TDI must be created within the same SPDM secure session; attempts to configure IDE from a different SPDM session must be rejected. If the SPDM secure session terminates, any IDE stream managed by this session must transition to the Insecure

state, and any TDIs managed by this session must transition to the ERROR state. The device must clear all TVM private data before transitioning back to the CONFIG_UNLOCK state. If the device's configuration changes in a way that could leak TVM private data, such as reconfiguring Base Address Registers (BARs) or remapping MMIO, any TDI in the CONFIG_LOCK or RUN state affected by the change must transition to the ERROR state. If the DSM encounters an unrecoverable error or loses track of a TDI's state, the TDI must transition to the ERROR state.

- **Data Integrity Errors**: If a TDI in the RUN state receives a poisoned TLP (indicating an uncorrectable error), unless the TDI has a recovery mechanism, the DSM must transition the TDI to the ERROR state. Upon any uncorrectable data integrity error, the DSM must transition any affected TDI in the CONFIG_LOCK or RUN state to the ERROR state.
- **Debug Mode**: If the device is in a debug mode that only collects information, it must not affect the device's security configuration or compromise the confidentiality and integrity of TVM data. If the debug mode affects security configurations (e.g., bypassing secure boot validation, influencing measurements), the device must not establish an SPDM secure session, or must terminate any existing SPDM secure session.
- **Conventional Reset**: Conventional resets (including cold and warm resets) must revert all states to initial conditions, including resetting TDIs to the CONFIG_UNLOCK state. Therefore, conventional resets require clearing all TVM private data.
- **Function Level Reset (FLR)**: An FLR of a VF or non-IOV function affects the associated TDI. An FLR of a Physical Function (PF) affects all subordinate VF TDIs. FLR must transition any affected TDI in the CONFIG_LOCK or RUN state to the ERROR state. For FLR on a function number other than 0, it does not affect the SPDM secure session or IDE streams.
- **DSM Tracking and Handling of Locked TDI Configurations**: If a device configuration change could affect a TDI in the CONFIG_LOCK or RUN state, the DSM must track these configurations. This could be PF configurations, non-IOV function configurations, or VF configurations. If a change occurs, the DSM must, depending on the impact, either transition the affected IDE stream to the Insecure state or transition the affected TDI's state to the ERROR state.

9.2.3 Host-side security requirements

The following summarizes the host-side security requirements. For detailed descriptions, please refer to the PCIe Base Specification.

- **MMIO Access Control**: The TSM must ensure the following: ① The TVM can access all MMIO resources listed in the TDI report allocated to it. ② The TVM can only access MMIO resources allocated to it. ③ Only the TVM and TCB entities can issue IDE TLPs for MMIO accesses to resources allocated to the TVM.
- **DMA Access Control**: The TSM must ensure that only after the TVM has accepted the TDI can it receive Untranslated Request or Translated Request TLPs from the device targeting TVM memory (which can be either private or shared). DMA accesses must be prohibited before the TDI is accepted. Note: Once the TVM accepts a TDI, it implicitly accepts the entire device TCB. The device must not issue spoofed packets (e.g., with fake source Requester IDs) to deceive the TVM.
- **Device Binding**: The TSM must have mechanisms to check whether the SPDM secure session established between the TSM and DSM is still alive and whether the TDI is using the IDE stream established by the TSM.
- **Secure Interconnect**: The TSM must ensure the security of secure channel keys, including ensuring that SPDM session keys and IDE keys are not leaked outside the TSM and TCB. The TSM must ensure that other unauthorized modules cannot modify the secure channel keys. The TSM must ensure that secure channel keys are not reused.
- **Data Integrity Errors**: The host side must use data containment mechanisms to ensure that poisoned TLPs are not used or propagated to the TVM. If an uncorrectable error is detected in a TLP, the host side must use data poisoning methods to prevent the propagation of corrupted data. If there are log registers recording error symptoms that could leak TVM information, the host side must clear the contents of these registers.
- **TSM Tracking and Handling of Locked Root Port Configurations**: If a Root Port configuration change could affect a TDI in the CONFIG_LOCK or RUN state, the TSM must track these Root Port configurations. If a change occurs, the TSM must, depending on the impact, either transition the affected IDE stream to the Insecure

state or transition the affected TDI's state to the ERROR state. Such configuration registers include the IDE Extended Capabilities registers.

9.3 Confidential computing TEE-IO host-side examples

In this section, we look at examples of host-side support for TEE-IO.

9.3.1 Intel TDX Connect

Intel's TDX Connect is Intel's TEE-IO solution based on TDX technology. Its architecture is shown in Fig. 9.11.

The TDX Connect host-side Intel SoC adds the following security features:

- **PCI IDE Functionality**: The Intel PCIe Root Complex includes IDE functionality, enabling encryption of PCIe TLPs to ensure confidentiality and integrity during transmission. After entering TDX Connect mode, only the TDX Module, acting as the TSM, can access the IDE-related registers for IDE key configuration and activation.
- **Trusted IOMMU Engine**: The Intel IOMMU (VT-d) engine is partitioned into untrusted and trusted parts, each comprising a set of registers and DMA remapping tables (DMARs) used for device address translation. The VMM can freely control the traditional untrusted part (DMAR tables). Only the TDX Module (TSM) can access the

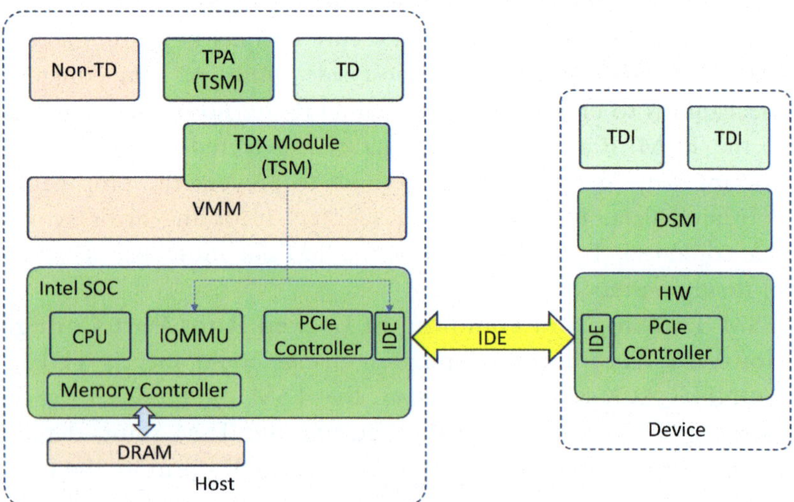

Figure 9.11 Intel TDX Connect architecture.

trusted part's registers, known as the trusted DMAR table. The VMM can submit requests to the TDX Module to update the DMAR table. After the update is completed and locked, the VMM cannot arbitrarily modify it.

- **Trusted DMA Access**: When a device accesses TD private memory, it must use IDE TLPs to protect the confidentiality and integrity of the private data. The IOMMU engine decides which DMAR table to consult based on whether the received TLP is an IDE TLP. IDE TLPs must reference the trusted DMAR table. The translation tables pointed to by the trusted DMAR table are Secure EPTs, ensuring a complete trusted address translation path.
- **Trusted MMIO Access**: When a TD accesses device TEE MMIO, it must use IDE TLPs to protect the confidentiality and integrity of the private data. If the device reports the existence of TEE MMIO, the addresses of this TEE MMIO must be included in the Secure EPT. When the TD accesses TEE MMIO, the Secure EPT translates the GPA to HPA, and after determining it is an MMIO access, passes it to the PCIe Root Port for encryption using IDE.

The host-side TSM in TDX Connect is also extended. The existing TDX Module now includes functionality for trusted IOMMU management and SoC IDE key management. The TEE-IO Provisioning Agent (TPA) is a new module added to assist the TDX Module in establishing SPDM secure sessions with the device DSM.

Fig. 9.12 illustrates the trusted DMA and trusted MMIO flows for Intel TDX Connect.

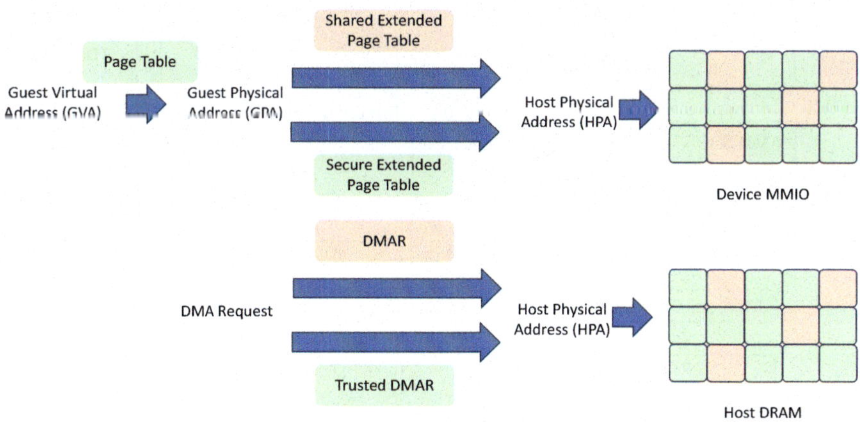

Figure 9.12 Trusted DMA and trusted MMIO in intel TDX Connect.

The trusted DMA flow: The device sends an encrypted DMA request (IDE TLP). The SoC's Root Port receives it, decrypts it, and forwards it to the IOMMU engine for address lookup. The IOMMU uses the trusted DMAR table for the first-level address translation, pointing to the CPU's Secure EPT. The Secure EPT performs the second-level address translation to obtain the physical address. After determining that this address is not MMIO, the MKTME engine points to the physical DRAM location for access.

Trusted MMIO flow: The TEE issues a private address MMIO request. The CPU checks the SHARED bit in the page table (which is 0) and looks up the Secure EPT for address translation. The Secure EPT finds the physical address of the MMIO region, adds a TDX tag, and passes it to the SoC's Root Port. The Root Port encrypts the request using IDE and sends it to the device.

9.3.2 AMD SEV-TIO

SEV Trusted IO (SEV-TIO) is AMD's TEE-IO solution. Its architecture is shown in Fig. 9.13.

The SEV-TIO host-side SoC adds the following security features:

- PCI IDE: The PCIe Root Complex adds IDE functionality to encrypt PCIe TLPs, ensuring data confidentiality and integrity.

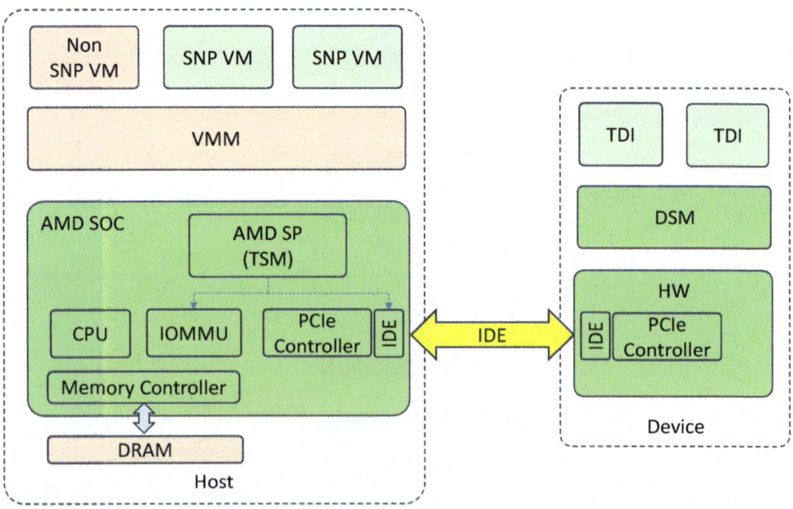

Figure 9.13 AMD SEV-TIO architecture.

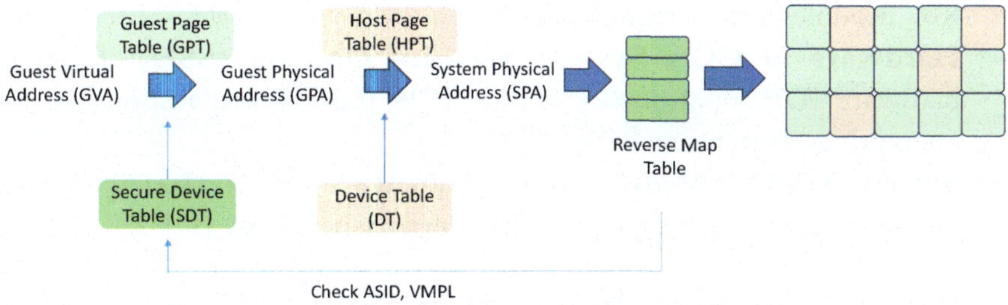

Figure 9.14 AMD SEV-TIO DMA management.

- IOMMU: The IOMMU is responsible for device address translation and access control. It uses the same Reverse Map Table (RMP) for DMA checks to ensure the confidentiality and integrity of SNP VMs. Each TDI is associated with a Secure Device Table (SDT) entry describing additional security attributes, such as ASID and VMPL, to determine whether access to the guest's private memory is permitted. The SDT must be stored in protected memory accessible only by the AMD-SP. See Fig. 9.14.

The host-side TSM in SEV-TIO is the AMD-SP. It is responsible for managing the trusted IOMMU and SoC IDE keys, and for establishing SPDM secure sessions with the device DSM.

9.3.3 ARM RME-DA

The ARM CCA DEN0129 RME specification introduces the RME Device Assignment (RME-DA) extension as its TEE-IO solution. The architecture of RME-DA is shown in Fig. 9.15.

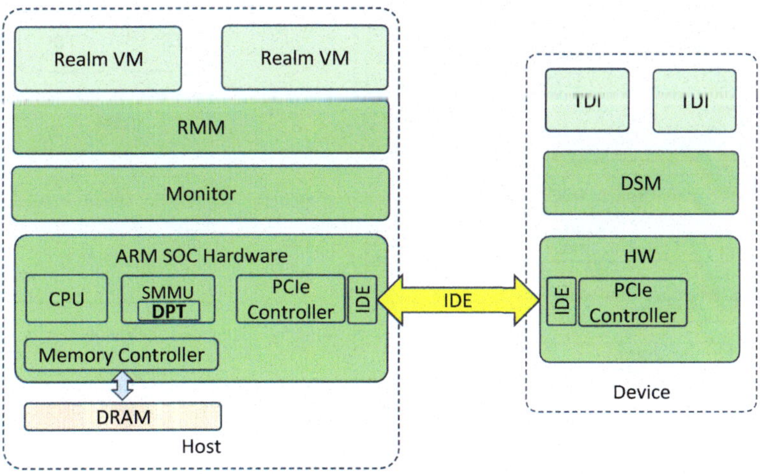

Figure 9.15 ARM RME-DA architecture.

Key modules added include:

- **Hardware in CCA System Security Domain (SSD)**: Provides hardware IDE functionality in the PCIe Root Ports, responsible for encrypting/decrypting PCIe TLPs.
- **System MMU (SMMU) in SoC Hardware**: The IH10070 SMMU introduces the concept of a **Device Permission Tree (DPT)**, responsible for precisely controlling access between device TDIs and Realms.
- **RMM Software in Realm Management Security Domain (RMSD)**: Acts as the TSM, implementing the SPDM protocol and providing the software functionality for TDISP and IDE_KM as specified in the PCIe specification. It is responsible for managing the TDI.

9.3.4 RISC-V CoVE-IO

The RISC-V AP-TEE-IO task group drafted the Confidential VM Extension IO (CoVE-IO) specification in 2023 to support TEE-IO solutions under the RISC-V architecture. The architecture of RISC-V CoVE-IO is shown in Fig. 9.16.

Key modules added include:

- **SoC Hardware**: Implements the IDE functionality required for PCIe Root Ports.
- **I/O Address Translation Agent (TA) in SoC Hardware**: Implements IOMMU extensions, such as the **I/O Memory Protection Table (IO-MPT)**, responsible for controlling device DMA access to TVM confidential memory. Its usage is similar to the MPT.

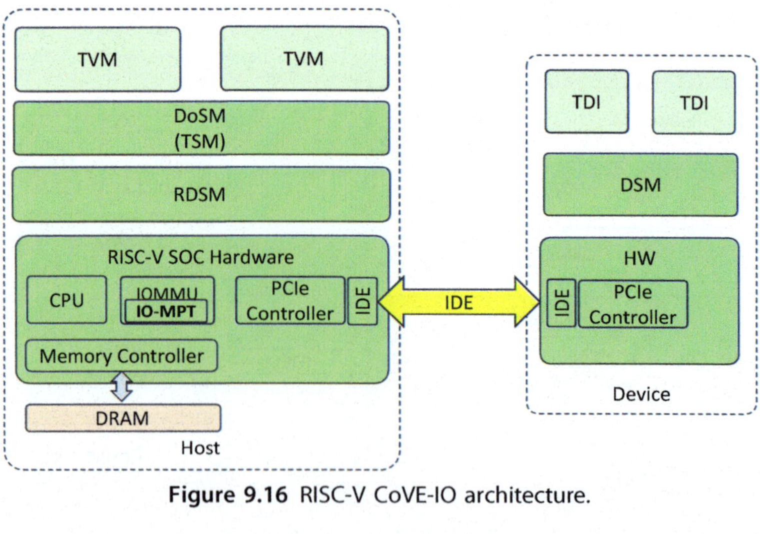

Figure 9.16 RISC-V CoVE-IO architecture.

- **TSM (Domain Security Manager - DoSM)**: Implements the SPDM protocol and is responsible for providing the software functionality for PCIe TDISP and IDE_KM, managing the TDI.

9.4 Confidential computing TEE-IO device-side examples

In this section, we look at an example of device-side support for TEE-IO.

9.4.1 NVIDIA GPU

NVIDIA, in its white papers "Confidential Compute on NVIDIA Hopper H100" and "NVIDIA H100 Tensor Core GPU Architecture," describes the Hopper H100 series GPUs supporting confidential computing.

***Note**: Hopper here refers to Grace Hopper, a highly respected legendary female programmer. Her life story is detailed in "Grace Hopper and the Invention of the Information Age" by Kurt Beyer. A well-known anecdote is that on September 9, 1945, a moth flew into the computer lab and died in a relay, causing a circuit failure. Hopper found the moth, removed it, and taped it in the logbook with the note: "Relay #70 Panel F. moth in relay. First actual case of a bug being found." Thus, the terms "bug" and "debugging" became synonymous with errors and fixing them. Hopper's greatest contribution to computing was the invention of the compiler. At that time, programmers wrote programs using machine code (0 and 1s) and punched them onto paper tape. Hopper envisioned writing instructions in a language closer to human language and using a special program to translate them into machine language. This special program became the compiler. She later developed the first compiler, A-0, which had versions in English, French, and German. One of her favorite sayings was, "A ship in port is safe, but that is not what ships are built for."*

The NVIDIA H100 is a device-side confidential computing solution that requires a host-side confidential VM (e.g., Intel TDX, AMD SEV-SNP, or ARM CCA) as an auxiliary.

The H100 supports three modes of GPU-to-TVM assignment, as shown in Fig. 9.17.

- **Single GPU Passthrough**: A single confidential GPU is assigned directly to one TVM. Suitable for AI inference, High-Performance Computing (HPC), light-weight AI training, etc.

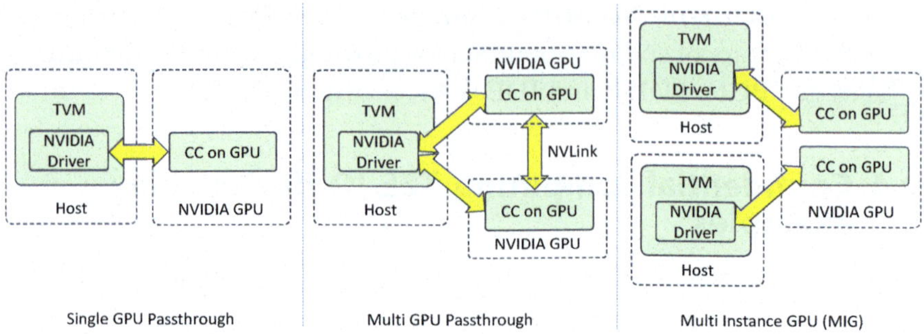

Figure 9.17 NVIDIA H100 GPU assignment modes.

- **Multi-GPU Passthrough**: Multiple confidential GPUs are assigned to a single TVM to work together, requiring NVLink support. Suitable for AI training workloads.
- **Multi-Instance GPU (MIG)**: A single GPU is partitioned into multiple instances, each assigned to a separate TVM. This requires PCIe SR-IOV support. Suitable for AI microservice inference, edge aggregation, and HPC.

The threat model defined in the NVIDIA H100 white paper "Confidential Compute on NVIDIA Hopper H100" is generally consistent with the CCC's definition. Threats considered include:

- Software attacks.
- Basic physical attacks.
- Software rollback attacks.
- Cryptographic attacks.
- Data replay attacks.

Threats out of the scope for NVIDIA H100 include:

- Complex physical attacks.
- Denial of Service (DoS) attacks.

Security features of the NVIDIA H100 confidential computing model:

- **Confidentiality**: H100 can prevent attackers from reading tenant data over PCIe or NVLink, prevent reading data via out-of-band management channels (e.g., SMBus, debug interfaces like JTAG), prevent reading data via memory remapping, prevent reading data via GPU cache side channels, prevent reading data via GPU TLB side channels, and prevent reading data via GPU performance counters. **H100 cannot prevent complex physical attacks** such as Differential Power Analysis (DPA), Electromagnetic (EM) attacks, or attacks involving interposers on High Bandwidth Memory (HBM).

- **Integrity**: H100 can prevent modification of customer data over PCIe or NVLink, prevent modification via out-of-band management channels (e.g., SMBus, debug interfaces like JTAG), and prevent replay attacks on memory or MMIO. **H100 cannot prevent complex physical attacks** such as advanced Fault Injection (FI) or attacks involving interposers on HBM.
- **Availability**: H100 can prevent a guest from performing a DoS attack against the VMM, prevent a guest from performing a DoS attack against other guests, and prevent a guest from causing permanent DoS damage to the GPU.
- **Other**: H100 can defend against nongenuine, nonauthentic, or known-defective TCB modules. It can defend against hardware side-channel extraction of permanent device keys (e.g., via DPA). H100 cannot defend against hardware side-channel extraction of ephemeral session keys (e.g., via DPA).

The NVIDIA H100 is a confidential computing GPU but does not yet have full TEE-IO functionality. Full TEE-IO support is expected to be refined in the NVIDIA Blackwell architecture.

CHAPTER 10

TEE-IO lifecycle

In Chapter 9, we introduced the security model and threat model of TEE-IO, where the VMM can allocate a device's TDI to a TEE as an extension of its TCB. In this chapter, we will introduce the lifecycle of a TEE-IO device, including TDI attachment and detachment.

10.1 Overview of the TEE-IO lifecycle

In the TEE-IO architecture, the lifecycle includes the following phases: System and Device Initialization, SPDM Secure Session Establishment, IDE Secure Link Establishment, TDI Locking and Allocation, TDI Acceptance and Running, IDE Key Update, SPDM Key Update, TDI Removal, IDE Secure Link Termination, and SPDM Secure Session Termination. We will introduce each of these steps one by one.

10.1.1 System and Device Initialization

System and device initialization follows a conventional process. The BIOS is responsible for PCI device enumeration, bus resource allocation, MMIO resource allocation, etc. The VMM can then reallocate resources for PCI devices.

The VMM needs to check the PCI device's Capability Registers. The device must have the following capabilities:

- SPDM capability: Presence of a Data Object Exchange (DOE) Extended Capability (DOEECAP) structure.
- IDE capability: Presence of an IDE Extended Capability (IDEECAP) structure.
- TDISP capability: In the PCIe Capability structure, the TEE-IO Supported bit in the Device Capability register must be set to 1.

Subsequently, the VMM can send a DOE Discovery command to query the DOE mailbox's capabilities, confirming that the DOE supports both SPDM normal messages and SPDM secure session messages.

Confidential Computing
ISBN 978-0-443-54067-7
https://doi.org/10.1016/B978-0-443-54067-7.00002-4

10.1.2 SPDM Secure Session Establishment

The VMM sends a request to the TSM, which then establishes an SPDM authenticated secure session with the device. The TSM needs to collect the device's identity certificate for later attestation. The process of establishing an SPDM secure session is shown in Fig. 10.1, with relevant modules and operations highlighted in bold. The key symbols within the TSM and DSM represent the SPDM session keys. The specific steps for establishing a secure session are as follows:

1. The VMM sends a request to the TSM to establish an SPDM secure session.
2. The TSM sequentially issues SPDM GET_VERSION, GET_CAPABILITIES, and NEGOTIATE_ALGORITHMS commands to establish an SPDM connection.
3. The TSM issues GET_CERTIFICATE to obtain the device's certificate information.
4. The TSM issues KEY_EXCHANGE and FINISH commands to establish an authenticated secure session.

10.1.3 IDE Secure Link Establishment

After establishing the SPDM secure session, the TSM and device use SPDM to establish an IDE secure link, specifically a Selective IDE Stream. The TSM creates six IDE keys, corresponding to the three IDE substreams (Posted Request – PR, Non-Posted Request – NPR, and Completion – CPL) for both the Transmit (Tx) and Receive (Rx) directions. This allows data for different directions and substreams to be encrypted with different keys. The TSM uses the IDE-KM protocol to convey these six keys to the

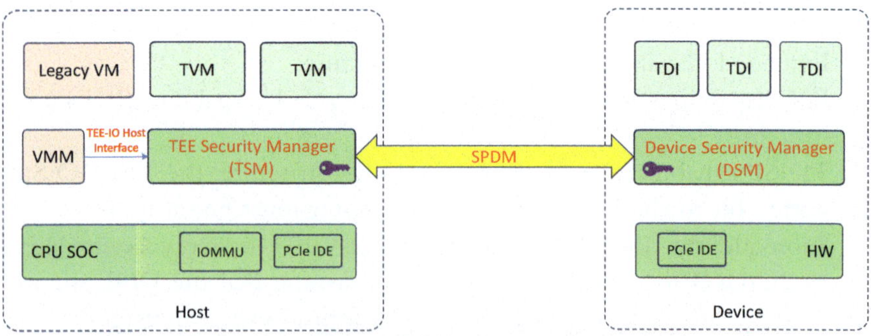

Figure 10.1 TEE-IO lifecycle: SPDM secure session establishment.

DSM over the SPDM secure session. The TSM and DSM then each write these six keys into their respective PCIe IDE registers. The process of establishing an IDE secure link is shown in Fig. 10.2, where the key icons in the host-side PCIe IDE and device-side PCIe IDE represent the IDE keys.

The specific steps for establishing an IDE secure link are as follows:

1. The TSM must ensure that the IDE Stream Enable bit in the IDE ECAP structures of both the Root Port and the device is 0.
2. The TSM issues IDE_KM KEY_PROG commands to configure the sixIDE keys into the Root Port and the device.
3. The TSM issues an IDE_KM K_SET_GO command to activate the six IDE keys in the Root Port and the device.
4. The TSM must ensure the device does not prematurely send IDE TLPs, for example, by disabling interrupts.
5. The TSM sets the IDE Stream Enable bit on the device side to 1.
6. The TSM sets the IDE Stream Enable bit on the Root Port side to 1.
7. The TSM reconfigures the device to allow it to send asynchronous IDE TLPs.

Note: Establishing an IDE secure link requires following a specific order. Step 4's purpose is to prevent the device from sending asynchronous IDE TLPs before the host is ready; otherwise, the host would reject them. Step 5 is performed before Step 6, considering the Link IDE scenario. If Step 6 were done first, the host might send PCI DOE commands using IDE TLPs before the device is ready, causing the device to reject them. After Step 5, the device can still receive non-IDE TLPs from the host until it receives its first IDE TLP.

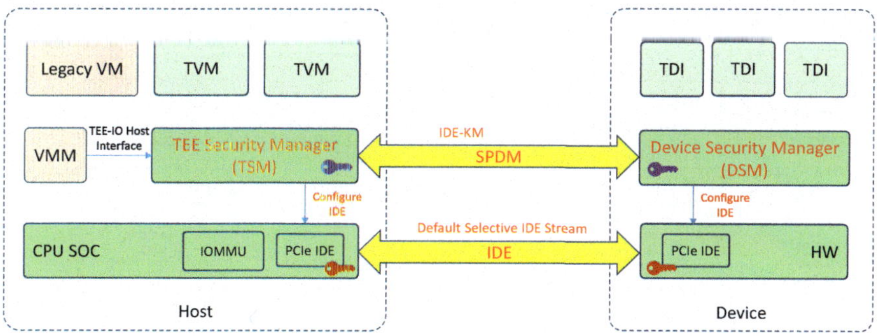

Figure 10.2 TEE-IO lifecycle: IDE secure link establishment.

10.1.4 TDI locking and allocation

The VMM instructs the TSM to use the TDISP protocol (running over the SPDM secure session) to transition the device TDI from the CONFIG_UNLOCK state to the CONFIG_LOCK state. The TSM also configures trusted MMIO and trusted DMA. Finally, the VMM allocates the TDI to the TVM. The process of TDI locking and allocation is shown in Fig. 10.3, where the lock icon on the TDI represents its locked state.

The specific steps for TDI locking and allocation are as follows:

1. The TSM issues TDISP GET_VERSION and GET_CAPABILITIES. At this point, the TDI is in the CONFIG_UNLOCK state.
2. The VMM requests the TSM to issue LOCK_INTERFACE, transitioning the TDI to the CONFIG_LOCK state.
3. The VMM configures the trusted IOMMU via the TSM, creating a trusted device DMA table (trusted I/O page tables) to allow the trusted device to access TEE private memory. The TSM must ensure that the Guest Physical Address (GPA) to Host Physical Address (HPA) mappings are identical in the CPU trusted page tables and the device trusted DMA page tables. To support the TEE accessing the device's trusted MMIO, the VMM needs to request the TSM to include the trusted MMIO addresses in the CPU trusted page tables.

10.1.5 TDI acceptance and running

The TVM must perform remote attestation and verification of the device to confirm it is a trusted device. This involves obtaining the device's identity certificate and measurements. The TVM also obtains the TDI report via TDISP and verifies the TDI's locking policy and the addresses of TEE-MMIO. This verification is crucial to prevent the VMM from maliciously configuring MMIO addresses in the PCI device's Base Address

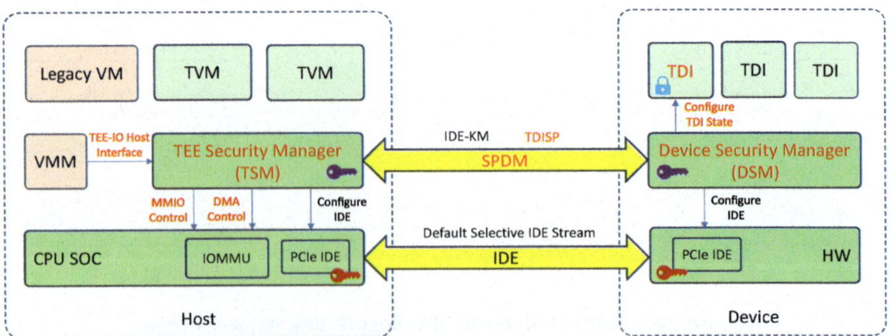

Figure 10.3 TEE-IO lifecycle: TDI locking and allocation.

Registers (BARs). After all checks pass, the TVM instructs the TSM to accept the TDI. Subsequently, the TVM and TDI can engage in trusted DMA and trusted MMIO operations. The process of TDI acceptance and running is shown in Fig. 10.4, where the circle icon on the TDI represents its running state.

The specific steps for TDI acceptance and running are as follows:

1. The TVM obtains the device's certificate via the TSM using SPDM GET_CERTIFICATE and the device's measurements via SPDM GET_MEASUREMENTS.
2. The TVM obtains the TDI report via the TSM using TDISP GET_DEVICE_INTERFACE_REPORT.
3. The TVM verifies the device's certificate and measurements. This device attestation process will be discussed in detail in Chapter 11.
4. The TVM verifies the device TDI report, including the TDI's locked configuration and the TEE-MMIO space.
5. After successful verification, the TVM instructs the TSM to send TDISP START_INTERFACE, transitioning the TDI to the RUN state.
6. The TVM notifies the TSM to accept the MMIO configuration.
7. The TVM notifies the TSM to accept DMA access. If the trusted DMA table only contains GPA to HPA mappings, the TVM does not need to take additional action. Some DMA tables allow configuration of Guest Virtual Address (GVA) to GPA mappings as first-level page tables, with GPA to HPA as second-level page tables. If the trusted DMA table supports first-level page table configuration, the TVM can provide its first-level page table to the TSM at this point.
8. The TSM finally allows DMA and MMIO accesses from the device.

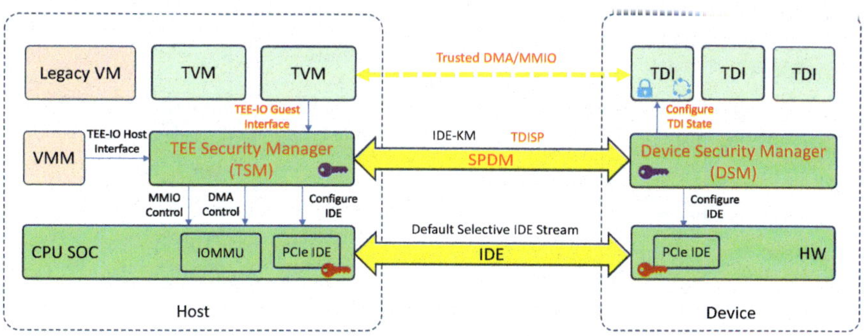

Figure 10.4 TEE-IO lifecycle: TDI acceptance and running.

10.1.6 IDE key update

The IDE secure link is protected using AES-GCM-256 encryption. Each message corresponds to a unique counter. When this counter approaches its theoretical limit, the secure session will automatically terminate. Before reaching the limit, the host side needs to perform an IDE key update using IDE_KM. The TSM and DSM also need to update the IDE registers in the PCIe IDE hardware. The process for IDE key update is shown in Fig. 10.5.

The specific steps for IDE key update are as follows:

1. The TSM must ensure that the IDE Stream Enable bit in the IDE ECAP structures of both the Root Port and the device is 1.
2. The TSM issues IDE_KM KEY_PROG commands to configure six new IDE keys into the Root Port and the device.
3. The TSM issues an IDE_KM K_SET_GO command to activate the three new Rx direction keys in the Root Port and the device. At this point, both ends continue communicating using the old IDE keys.
4. The TSM issues an IDE_KM K_SET_GO command to activate the three new Tx direction keys in the Root Port and the device. Now, both ends can start communicating using the new IDE keys.

10.1.7 SPDM key update

The SPDM secure session is also protected using an AEAD cipher (e.g., AES-GCM-256). Each message corresponds to a unique sequence number. When this sequence number approaches its theoretical limit, the secure session will automatically terminate. Before reaching the limit, the host side needs to trigger an SPDM key update. The process for SPDM key update is also shown in Fig. 10.5.

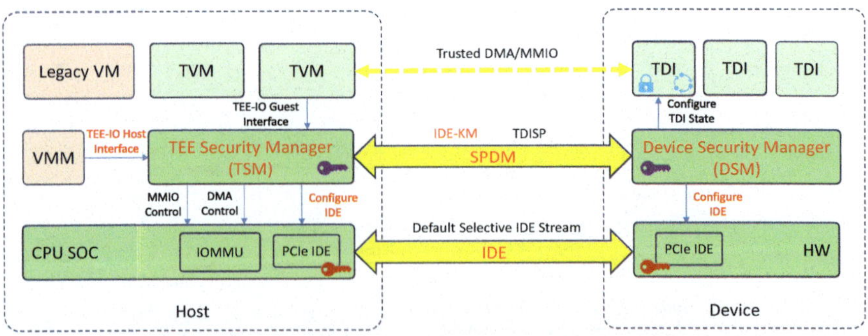

Figure 10.5 TEE-IO lifecycle: SPDM and IDE key updates.

The specific steps for SPDM key update are as follows:

1. The VMM instructs the TSM to send SPDM KEY_UPDATE (with UpdateAllKeys) to update the SPDM keys.
2. The TSM sends SPDM KEY_UPDATE (with VerifyNewKey) to confirm that the SPDM keys have been updated.

10.1.8 TDI removal

When the TVM no longer needs the TDI, or the VMM needs to reclaim it, the TSM must use the TDISP protocol to transition the TDI back to the CONFIG_UNLOCK state. Additionally, all TDI-related DMA and MMIO access permissions must be removed from the host-side TVM's access control lists. This allows the TDI to be reallocated in the future. The process for TDI removal is shown in Fig. 10.6.

The specific steps for TDI removal are as follows:

1. The TVM or VMM instructs the TSM to send TDISP STOP_INTERFACE, transitioning the TDI to the CONFIG_UNLOCK state.
2. The VMM reconfigures the TSM to remove the TDI-related MMIO and DMA regions from the trusted access lists.
3. The TVM confirms to the TSM that the TDI has indeed been removed and that no corresponding MMIO or DMA regions are still bound.

10.1.9 IDE secure link termination

Removing a TDI does not necessarily require terminating the IDE secure link. IDE is associated with the entire device. As long as at least one TDI is still assigned to a TVM, the IDE link is still needed. Only when all TDIs are unallocated should the host terminate the IDE secure link with the device.

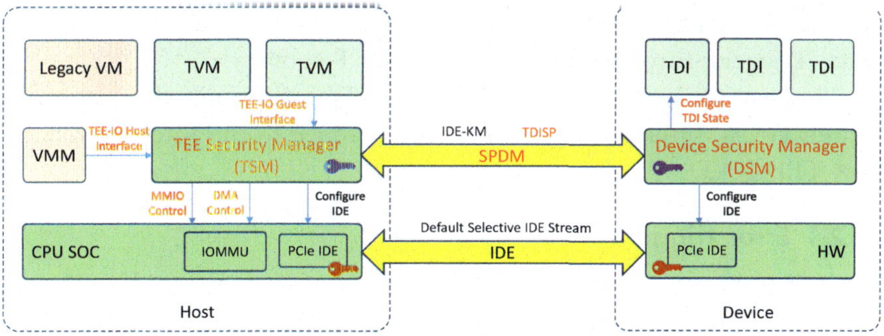

Figure 10.6 TEE-IO lifecycle: TDI removal.

The specific steps for IDE secure link termination are as follows:

1. The TSM first sets the IDE Stream Enable bit on the device side to 0. At this point, the device-side IDE is in the Insecure state, while the host-side IDE might still be Secure. Non-IDE TLPs (e.g., interrupts) that the device might send could be rejected by the host, but this should not have severe consequences.
2. The TSM sets the IDE Stream Enable bit on the Root Port side to 0. Now, both ends can communicate using non-IDE TLPs.
3. The TSM issues an IDE_KM K_SET_STOP command to deactivate the six established IDE keys.

Note: Considering the Link IDE scenario, step 1 must be performed before step 2. If step 2 were performed first, the host might send PCI DOE commands using non-IDE TLPs, which the device (with IDE still enabled) would reject, preventing the normal termination of the device-side IDE.

10.1.10 SPDM secure session termination

Removing a single TDI or terminating an IDE secure link may not require terminating the SPDM secure session. SPDM is associated with the entire device. The host should terminate the SPDM secure session only after all TDIs and IDE links associated with it have been stopped.

The specific steps for SPDM secure session termination are as follows:

1. The VMM sends a request to the TSM to terminate the SPDM secure session.
2. The TSM sends SPDM END_SESSION, terminating the SPDM secure session.

10.2 Error handling

This section discusses error handling in TEE-IO, divided into three parts: Error Triggers, Error Reporting, and Error Recovery.

This section references the PCIe Base Specification's descriptions of various errors, summarizing them with reference to the Intel TDX Connect TEE-IO Device Guide.

10.2.1 Error triggers

Error triggers can lead to SPDM session termination, an IDE Stream entering the Insecure state, or a TDI entering the ERROR state.

10.2.1.1 SPDM session termination

The following error conditions can trigger SPDM session termination:

- An unrecoverable error occurs in the PCIe DOE mailbox.
- SPDM session sequence number overflow.
- SPDM session heartbeat double timeout.
- Receiving a new GET_VERSION request on an established SPDM connection.
- Meeting device-specific SPDM session termination conditions, such as firmware updates, device resets, etc.

10.2.1.2 IDE stream entering insecure state

The following error conditions can trigger an IDE Stream to enter the Insecure state:

- The corresponding SPDM session terminates.
- Receiving an IDE_KM QUERY or KEY_PROG command within a different SPDM session.
- A device reset (conventional or function level reset) for a device with an IDE ECAP register.
- Access Control Service (ACS) termination when using Selective IDE.
- Detection of an inappropriate IDE reconfiguration.
- A debug configuration change that could expose secret data.
- An IDE TLP experiences an IDE Check Failed error, specifically including:
  - Receiving a disallowed TLP type.
  - Aggregation TLP errors, e.g., the K-bit is flipped in a TLP that is not the first TLP in an aggregation unit, or the M-bit is cleared when the device does not support aggregation.
  - Receiving a Completion (CPL) that does not match the Stream ID and T-bit of the corresponding Non-Posted Request (NPR).
  - Selective IDE TLP discard situations, e.g., MAC check failure, TLP counter underflow/overflow, unsupported fields detected.

Other IDE TLP errors, such as Misrouted IDE TLP or Plaintext Cyclic Redundancy Check (PCRC) check failure, do not cause the IDE stream to enter the Insecure state.

10.2.1.3 TDI entering error state

The following error conditions can trigger a TDI to enter the ERROR state:

- The corresponding IDE stream enters the Insecure state.
- The DSM detects a change in TDI configuration that could affect TDI security or trust.
- The Requester ID (RID) associated with the TDI changes.
- The TDI is reset using Function Level Reset (FLR).
- Receiving a poisoned TLP.
- While in the CONFIG_LOCK or RUN state, receiving a Completion (CPL) with Unsupported Request (UR) status or Completer Abort (CA) status, or a CPL timeout.
- An Address Translation Service (ATS) error, e.g., a Translation Completion or Page Request Group (PRG) response clears the T-bit for a request TLP that had it set.

10.2.2 Error reporting

10.2.2.1 Software protocol errors

Software protocols may report errors in the following ways:

- SPDM protocol: Can report errors via SPDM ERROR messages or by silently dropping SPDM requests.
- IDE_KM protocol: The KP_ACK response can return error reports via its status field.
- TDISP protocol: Can report errors via TDISP ERROR messages; TDISP GET_STATE can return the TDI's current state (which may indicate an error).

10.2.2.2 Hardware TLP errors

Hardware TLP errors can be reported in the following ways: TLPs can return completions with Unsupported Request (UR) status or Unexpected Completion (UC) status, Completer Abort (CA) status, or the TLP request may be silently dropped.

10.2.2.3 Hardware register errors

Hardware registers may report errors in the following ways:

- DOE mailbox can return an Error bit.
- IDE stream status registers can indicate integrity check failure information.
- PCIe Uncorrectable Error Status registers can log various errors, including IDE Check Failed, Misrouted IDE TLP, or PCRC check failure.

Note: *TDISP does not have a proactive error reporting mechanism because TLP transmission could be subject to DoS attacks, preventing errors from being reliably reported to the TEE.*

When a device is in an error state, reading from MMIO typically returns all ones (e.g., 0xFF for 8-bit, 0xFFFF for 16-bit, 0xFFFFFFFF for 32-bit). Therefore, device drivers are often designed to interpret such all-ones reads as an indication of an error state, allowing them to initiate recovery procedures.

10.2.3 Error Recovery

10.2.3.1 DOE recovery

The host needs to set the DOE Abort bit in the control register to clear the error.

10.2.3.2 SPDM recovery

If an SPDM session terminates, the host can send a new KEY_-EXCHANGE request to re-establish the session, or send GET_VERSION to re-establish the connection.

10.2.3.3 IDE recovery

For Link IDE errors, the host cannot communicate with the device to reconfigure it, so a device reset is required.

For Selective IDE errors, if PCI configuration requests are encrypted (and thus cannot be used for reconfiguration), the situation is similar to Link IDE errors, requiring a device reset. If PCI configuration requests are not encrypted (or if a secure but operational path exists), the host may be able to disable and then re-enable the corresponding Selective IDE stream, recover the IDE stream, and then restart the TDI.

10.2.3.4 TDISP recovery

When a TDI error occurs, the host can send a STOP_INTERFACE request. This instructs the device to clear the secrets associated with that TDI and then transition it back to the CONFIG_UNLOCK state.

The device side may also choose to proactively clear secrets and transition the TDI to the CONFIG_UNLOCK state upon detecting an internal error.

CHAPTER 11

TEE-IO attestation model

In Chapter 10, we introduced the Trusted Execution Environment Input/Output (TEE-IO) life cycle. During the startup process, a TVM needs to verify a TDI before accepting it. This is because once a TDI is accepted, it can access trusted execution environment (TEE) private memory via DMA, potentially obtaining private data. In this chapter, we will detail the TEE-IO attestation model, which is mainly divided into two parts: TVM attestation of the device TDI, and third-party attestation of a TVM bound to a device TDI.

11.1 TVM attestation of the device

We described the attestation model for TEEs in Chapter 5. The Internet Engineering Task Force (IETF) RFC 9334 Remote Attestation Procedures architecture provides an excellent reference, as shown in Fig. 11.1. We will use the same architecture to introduce TEE-IO device attestation, including Evidence Generation and Conveyance, Verification, and Attestation Result Conveyance.

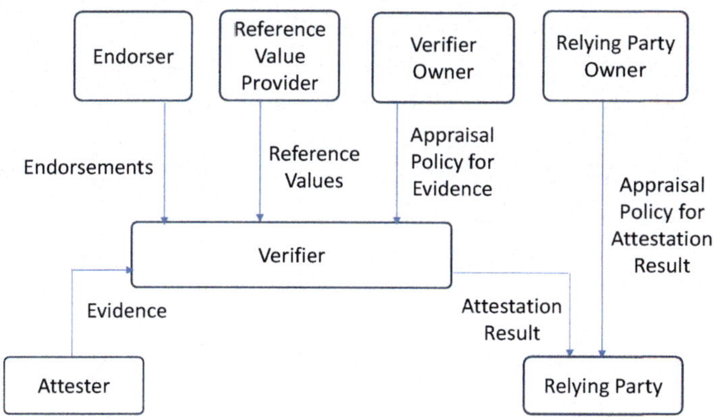

Figure 11.1 Remote attestation procedures architecture.

Confidential Computing
ISBN 978-0-443-54067-7
https://doi.org/10.1016/B978-0-443-54067-7.00010-3

11.1.1 Evidence generation and conveyance

In Chapter 5, we introduced the TPM-based trusted boot scheme. This is a classic method, and TEE-IO devices can potentially use a Trusted Platform Module (TPM). The only limitation is cost, because the device would need to include a TPM chip, increasing hardware expenses. Therefore, the Trusted Computing Group (TCG) introduced the DICE architecture as an alternative trusted boot option when a TPM is not present.

11.1.1.1 Device identifier composition engine trusted boot

DICE originated from Microsoft's Robust Internet-of-Things (RIoT) architecture. Microsoft later contributed this solution to the TCG, which established the DICE working group. The DICE architecture can provide trusted services, including device identity, key sealing, and remote attestation, with a small Trusted Computing Base (TCB).

The DICE architecture is a layered boot architecture. When the system boots, it goes through stages: Platform RoT, Firmware/BIOS, OS Loader, OS Kernel, and finally OS Applications. Each layer in the DICE architecture must define the TCB modules for that layer, which can access the following resources:

- **TCB component identifier (TCI)**: An identifier that can represent a TCB module. Any change to the TCB module necessarily results in a different TCI. Examples of TCIs include a hash of the code, a hash of the code plus version number or Security Version Number (SVN), an Field-Programmable Gate Array (FPGA) bitstream, and so on.
- **Compound device identifier (CDI)**: The CDI value for each layer is confidential information for that layer and must not be leaked. The CDI value received by layer in must be based on at least two inputs: the CDI from layer n-1 and the TCI of layer n. These inputs are bound together by a one-way function in layer n-1 to output the CDI for layer n. A layer cannot generate its own CDI.
- **One-Way function (OWF)**: A cryptographic pseudorandom function conforming to National Institute of Standards and Technology SP 800-56C. The most common one-way function is a hash function. The relationship between TCI, CDI, and OWF is:

$$CDI_{Ln+1} = f\_owf(CDI_{Ln}, TCI_{Ln+1})$$

The DICE Layering Architecture specification describes the boot process for DICE devices. Fig. 11.2 illustrates the DICE layered

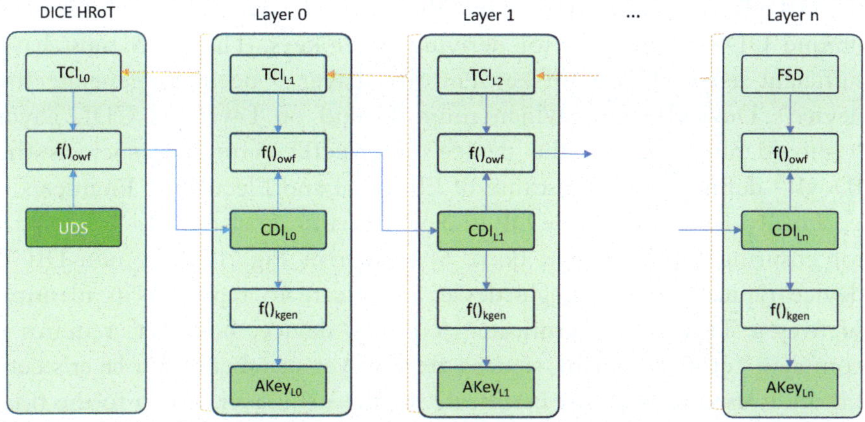

Figure 11.2 Device Identifier Composition Engine (DICE) layered architecture. *HRoT*, Hardware Root of Trust.

architecture, including the Hardware Root of Trust (HRoT) layer, Layer 0, Layer 1, up to Layer n.

From the DICE boot process, it can be seen that any change to the TCB at any layer changes its TCI, which is then reflected in that layer's CDI and all subsequent CDIs. Because the DICE HRoT has no upper layer, the HRoT layer uses a Unique Device Secret (UDS) to represent its CDI. Except for the HRoT, the CDI for layer n cannot be generated by layer n itself; it is generated by layer n-1 using its CDI and layer n's TCI through layer n-1's OWF. When generated, the CDI for layer n resides in layer n-1 and is then passed down to layer n. The final layer has no next layer's TCI; instead, the input to the one-way function at that position is a Firmware Security Descriptor. Software at each layer cannot modify its own CDI without being detected. If layer n could modify its CDI, it would effectively be able to modify its own TCI, violating the chain of trust. The CDI for each layer can be used to derive other keys needed by that layer. To ensure the confidentiality of the CDI and its derived keys, the software at layer n needs to protect its CDI and derived keys from being accessed by layer n+1. The simplest method is to destroy its CDI and derived keys before launching layer n+1.

CDI can be used to derive various keys at each layer. Besides keys similar to TPM's **Identity Key** and **Attestation Key**, DICE requires an **Embedded Certificate Authority (ECA) key**. The ECA key's purpose is to issue certificates for the next layer. DICE has special considerations for the HRoT layer and Layer 0. The DICE HRoT layer must have a device-unique UDS as the basis for deriving other keys. The UDS must have sufficient length to ensure key entropy. Layer 0 needs to generate the device's DeviceID key, which must depend on Layer 0's CDI. Layer 0 should also generate the device's DeviceID certificate, such as the IDevID defined by the Institute of Electrical and Electronics Engineers.

Finally, let us look at the DICE device certificate chain, which is crucial for ensuring DICE trusted boot, as shown in Fig. 11.3. A non-DICE device typically uses a single device certificate to represent its identity, such as a TPM's EK certificate. A DICE device, however, requires a complete certificate chain, starting from Layer 0, where each layer's certificate is used to issue the certificate for the next layer, down to the final layer. DICE certificates are typically ASN.1 DER encoded X.509 certificates, but IETF also supports Concise Binary Object Representation (CBOR) encoded C509 certificates (CBOR Encoded X.509 Certificate).

The DICE ECA can issue certificates directly. The process is shown in Fig. 11.4, with these specific steps:

① Layer n TCB obtains the firmware information for layer n+1 and generates TCI_{Ln+1}.

② Layer n TCB generates $CDI_{Ln+1} = f\_owf(CDI_{Ln}, TCI_{Ln+1})$.

③ Layer n TCB generates the asymmetric certificate key for layer n+1, $AKey_{Ln+1} = f\_kgen(CDI_{Ln+1})$.

④ Layer n ECA generates the certificate for layer n+1, $Cert_{Ln+1} = f\_gen\_cert(AKey_{Ln+1}, TCI_{Ln+1}, AKey_{Ln})$.

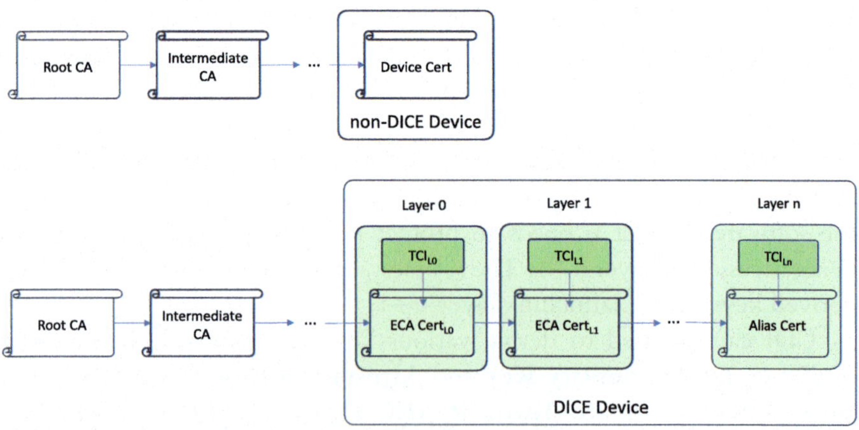

Figure 11.3 Device Identifier Composition Engine (DICE) device certificate chain. *CA*, Certificate Authority; *ECA*, Embedded Certificate Authority

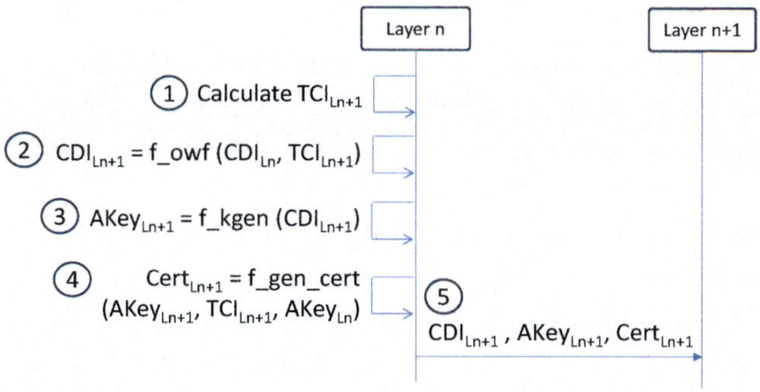

Figure 11.4 Device Identifier Composition Engine device certificate issuance: direct issuance flow. *TCI*, TCB Component Identifier.

⑤ Layer n TCB deploys CDI_{Ln+1}, $AKey_{Ln+1}$, and $Cert_{Ln+1}$ to layer n+1.

The DICE ECA can also issue certificates using a Certificate Signing Request (CSR) approach. The process is shown in Fig. 11.5, with these specific steps:

① Layer n TCB obtains the firmware information for layer n+1 and generates TCI_{Ln+1}.

② Layer n TCB generates $CDI_{Ln+1} = f\_owf(CDI_{Ln}, TCI_{Ln+1})$.

③ Layer n TCB deploys CDI_{Ln+1} to layer n+1.

④ Layer n+1 TCB generates the asymmetric certificate key for layer n+1, $AKey_{Ln+1} = f\_kgen(CDI_{Ln+1})$.

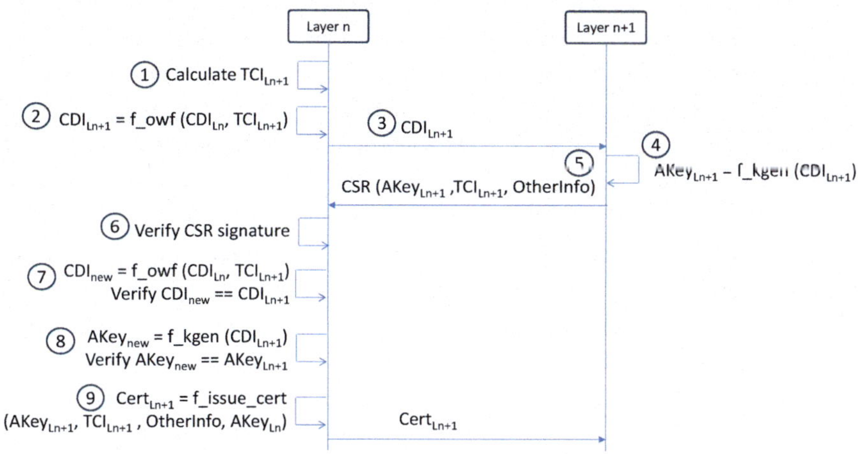

Figure 11.5 DICE device certificate issuance: Certificate Signing Request (CSR) issuance flow. *TCI*, TCB Component Identifier.

⑤ Layer n+1 TCB sends a CSR to layer n. The CSR includes the $AKey_{Ln+1}$ public key, TCI_{Ln+1}, and any other information layer n+1 wishes to include in the certificate. The CSR can be signed using the $AKey_{Ln+1}$ private key.
⑥ Layer n ECA verifies the CSR signature.
⑦ Layer n ECA generates a new $CDI_{new} = f\_owf(CDI_{Ln}, TCI_{Lnew})$ based on the TCI from the CSR, and compares it with the originally generated CDI. This helps determine if the TCI_{Lnew} in the CSR is trustworthy.
⑧ Layer n ECA generates a new asymmetric certificate key $AKey_{new} = f\_kgen(CDI_{Lnew})$ based on the new CDI, and compares it with the $AKey_{Lnew}$ from the CSR.
⑨ Layer n ECA issues the certificate for layer n+1, $Cert_{Lnew} = f\_issue\_cert(AKey_{Lnew}, TCI_{Lnew}, OtherInfo, AKey_{Ln})$, and deploys $Cert_{Ln+1}$ to layer n+1.

The TCI for each layer in the DICE certificate chain is reflected in that layer's certificate. Within the certificate, the TCI is contained in a structure called DiceTcbInfo, which includes the firmware measurement, security version number, and other data. Because the certificate for layer n is issued by layer n-1, each layer cannot forge its own certificate. This means the measurement TCI for each layer is faithfully recorded in its certificate by the previous layer. A verifier, after obtaining the DICE certificate chain, can extract the DiceTcbInfo structures and verify each layer of the DICE device.

Layer 0 of DICE has no internal upper-level module. Therefore, the certificate for Layer 0 is typically issued by an external Certificate Authority (CA) of the manufacturer. The process is similar to the ECA issuance described earlier, using either direct issuance or CSR, with the manufacturer acting as Layer-1. However, the manufacturer needs to know the value of TCI_{L0} in advance, rather than having it calculated during the boot process. The Layer 0 certificate is also called the Device Certificate, used to identify the device itself. Other certificates are called Alias Certificates, used to identify each firmware layer of the device.

Both methods for issuing DICE certificates are viable. The direct issuance method has the advantage of being simple and not requiring the next layer's participation. The CSR method is more flexible, allowing the next layer to define additional information within the certificate. In DICE's predecessor, RIoT, the initial intent was to use direct issuance. The RIoT white paper, "RIoT: A Foundation for Trust in the Internet of

Things," specifically mentions a key difference between DICE and TPMs: TPMs rely on a separate execution environment to protect keys, called spatial protection. DICE relies on the upper-level module destroying its own keys when loading the lower-level module, called temporal protection. The difference between TPM and DICE is illustrated in Fig. 11.6.

The DICE architecture specification does not define how to convey the DICE certificate chain. However, the DICE Concise Evidence Binding for Security Protocol and Data Model (SPDM) specification describes how to pass the DICE certificate chain to a verifier using the SPDM protocol.

11.1.1.2 TEE-IO device evidence generation and conveyance

TEE-IO devices can adopt TPM-based trusted boot, DICE-based trusted boot, or other proprietary methods. The key to ensuring evidence integrity lies in establishing a chain of trust, ensuring that a module cannot generate its own measurement values; this must be done by an upper-level module or a TCB module.

11.1.1.2.1 Types of TEE-IO device evidence

For DICE devices, the DiceTcbInfo within the DICE certificates is a crucial data structure describing the device. The DICE Attestation Architecture specification defines the DiceTcbInfo to include this information:

- Vendor: The entity that created the target TCB.
- Model: The product name of the target TCB.
- Version: The version of the target TCB.
- Security Version Number (SVN): The SVN of the target TCB.

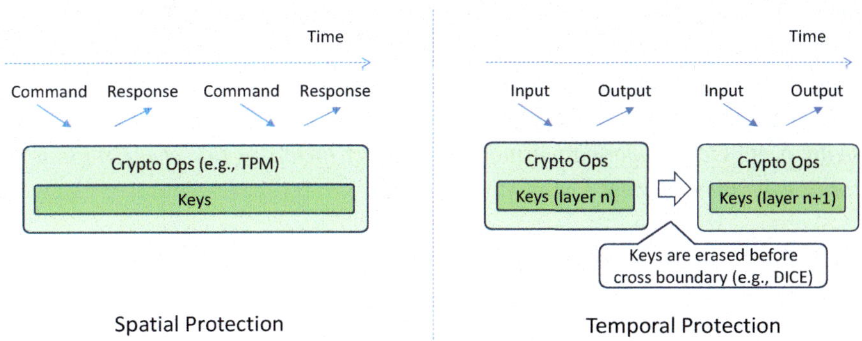

Figure 11.6 Difference between TPM and Device Identifier Composition Engine (DICE).

- Layer: The DICE layer where the target TCB resides.
- Index: Within a DICE layer that may have multiple firmware components, different indices identify them.
- Firmware ID: Information representing the target TCB firmware, including the firmware measurement value and the measurement algorithm used.
- Not-Configured: The target TCB requires additional information to operate.
- Nonsecure: The target TCB is in a nonsecure state.
- Recovery: The target TCB is in recovery mode.
- Debug: The target TCB is debuggable.

When a device uses the SPDM protocol to convey measurements, SPDM defines several measurement value types:

- Immutable ROM.
- Mutable firmware.
- Hardware configuration (e.g., strap pin information).
- Firmware configuration (e.g., configurable firmware policies).
- Debug status, including nonintrusive debug active, intrusive debug active, nonintrusive debug was active since last boot, intrusive debug was active since last boot, and intrusive debug was active since factory.
- Device life cycle state, including manufacturing mode, validation mode, normal operational mode, recovery mode, Return Merchandize Authorization mode, and decommissioned mode.
- Firmware version.
- Firmware SVN.

Note: *Among this information, the three most important categories are measurements, SVN, and debug information. Measurements faithfully reflect the version information of firmware modules, ensuring the device has not been altered after shipped from the manufacturer. SVN reflects security-related version information; often users care less about having the absolute latest version and more about using a version without known vulnerabilities. SVN is meaningful only when used with secure boot. Debug information indicates whether there is a risk of the runtime security environment being compromised.*

11.1.1.2.2 Security elements in TEE-IO evidence conveyance

Similar to TEE evidence conveyance, TEE-IO device evidence conveyance must consider these elements:

- **Integrity**: The TEE-IO device report must not be tampered with by anyone. The SPDM protocol ensures integrity through digital signatures.
- **Freshness**: The TEE-IO device report needs to be fresh. The SPDM protocol uses a challenge-response mechanism based on a Nonce to ensure freshness.
- **Atomicity**: The SPDM protocol supports retrieving single measurement blocks at a time, rather than the entire measurement record. However, to ensure the atomicity of the device's measurement record, the host must either retrieve the entire TEE-IO device measurement record in one operation or retrieve all measurement blocks across multiple operations and use a final digital signature to ensure none of the previous blocks have changed. For example, suppose a device has four firmware measurement blocks (1, 2, 3, 4). After the host retrieves blocks 1, 2, and 3, the device updates. When the host then retrieves block 4, the device reports that the measurement record has changed. The host must then discard the already retrieved blocks and refetch all four blocks (1, 2, 3, 4).
- **Completeness**: The TEE-IO device report must contain information about all modules; nothing can be omitted.
- **Binding**: The device providing the evidence must be the same device providing the TDI. This is a new requirement in TEE-IO. Typically, the TEE Security Manager (TSM) is responsible for this binding. The TSM creates a data structure containing the hash of the device evidence and the TDI management information, and provides this to the TVM.

11.1.1.2.3 TEE-IO device attestation example

After the TEE-IO device boots up to the Device Security Manager (DSM) layer, the DSM layer needs to implement the SPDM protocol and convey the device's information to the TEE via SPDM. The SPDM protocol defines a standard method for conveying device certificates, as shown in Fig. 11.7. The specific steps are:

① The host-side TSM sends an SPDM GET_CERTIFICATE command, requesting the device's certificate chain.

② The device-side DSM collects the certificates from each layer and concatenates them into a certificate chain. Starting from the Layer 0 device certificate down to the leaf certificate of the final DICE layer, each Alias Certificate contains DiceTcbInfo for that DICE layer (DiceTcbInfo$_{Ln}$) identifying the firmware of that layer. The DSM, as the final

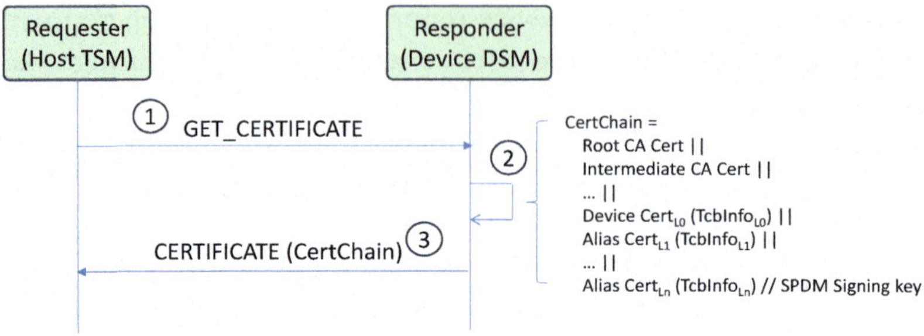

Figure 11.7 TEE-IO device certificate conveyance. *DSM*, Device Security Manager; *TSM*, Trusted Execution Environment Security Manager.

layer, possesses the private key corresponding to the leaf certificate, which serves as the SPDM signing key.

③ The device-side DSM returns the device certificate chain in a CERTIFICATE response, completing device identity retrieval. The public key from the leaf certificate will be used to verify subsequent SPDM signatures.

The SPDM protocol defines a standard method for conveying device measurements. Fig. 11.8 shows a method for retrieving all measurement records in one request. The specific steps are:

① The host-side TSM sends an SPDM GET_MEASUREMENT command requesting all device measurements. The request includes a requester-generated nonce (ReqNonce) to prevent replay attacks.

② The device-side DSM collects the measurement information from the DiceTcbInfo$_{Ln}$ of each layer, assembles them into SPDM-formatted measurement blocks (MeasurementBlock$_{Ln}$), and concatenates them

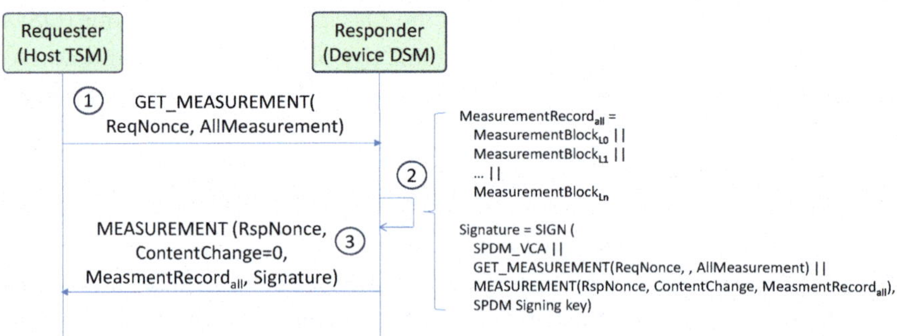

Figure 11.8 TEE-IO device measurement conveyance: single request for all records. *DSM*, Device Security Manager; *TSM*, Trusted Execution Environment Security Manager.

into a MeasurementRecord. The DSM also generates its own responder nonce (RspNonce). Finally, the DSM uses its SPDM signing key to generate a digital signature over the measurement request and response data.

③ The device-side DSM returns the device MeasurementRecord in a MEASUREMENT response. The response includes a digital signature covering ReqNonce, RspNonce, and the MeasurementRecord, ensuring integrity and freshness. Retrieving all records at once also ensures atomicity and completeness.

If the device's measurement record is large and exceeds the maximum transmission size, the host can retrieve all measurement blocks across multiple requests, as shown in Fig. 11.9. The specific steps are:

① The host-side TSM sends an SPDM GET_MEASUREMENT command, requesting the total number of measurement blocks.

② The device-side DSM calculates the number of measurement blocks based on all DiceTcbInfo layers.

③ The device-side DSM returns the number of measurement blocks n+1 in a MEASUREMENT response.

④ The host-side TSM sends an SPDM GET_MEASUREMENT command, requesting the first measurement block, including the index (1).

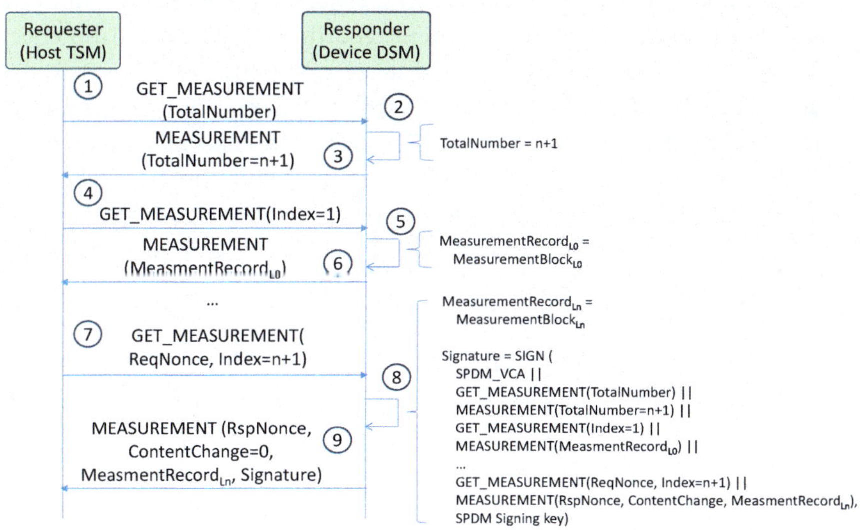

Figure 11.9 TEE-IO device measurement conveyance: Multi-request for all records. *DSM*, Device Security Manager; *TSM*, Trusted Execution Environment Security Manager.

⑤ The device-side DSM finds the corresponding DiceTcbInfo_{L0} for measurement block index 1, uses its measurement information to form an SPDM measurement block, and returns it as a measurement record.
⑥ The device-side DSM returns the single measurement record for the device in a MEASUREMENT response.
⑦ The process continues. The host-side TSM sends SPDM GET_MEASUREMENT commands for the second block, third block, and so on. When the host requests the final block n+1, the host-side TSM includes a Nonce (ReqNonce) and requests a digital signature.
⑧ The device-side DSM finds the corresponding DiceTcbInfo_{Ln} for measurement block index n+1, uses its measurement information to form an SPDM measurement block, and creates a measurement record. At this point, the DSM generates its own responder nonce (RspNonce) and checks whether any of the previously returned measurement blocks have been updated, recording this in a ContentChange field. Finally, the DSM uses its SPDM signing key to generate a digital signature over all previous measurement requests and responses (from measurement block index 1 up to index n+1).
⑨ The device-side DSM returns the single measurement record for the device in a MEASUREMENT response. This final response includes a digital signature covering ReqNonce, RspNonce, ContentChange, and all previous measurement records, ensuring the integrity and freshness of the entire set of measurement records. The host must also check the returned ContentChange field to ensure atomicity and verify that all measurement blocks have been retrieved to ensure completeness.

Finally, the TSM provides the device certificates and measurements to the TVM for verification. If the TVM needs to obtain the complete device certificate chain and measurements collected by the TSM through the untrusted Virtual Machine Manager (VMM), the TVM needs a simple method to ensure the VMM has not tampered with them. For example, the TSM can store a hash of the device certificates and measurements. The TVM obtains this hash from the TSM (via a secure channel) and compares it with the hash of the complete data received from the VMM. This process is shown in Fig. 11.10, with the following specific steps:
① The host-side TSM obtains the certificate chain and measurements from the device DSM.
② The device-side DSM returns the certificate chain and measurements.

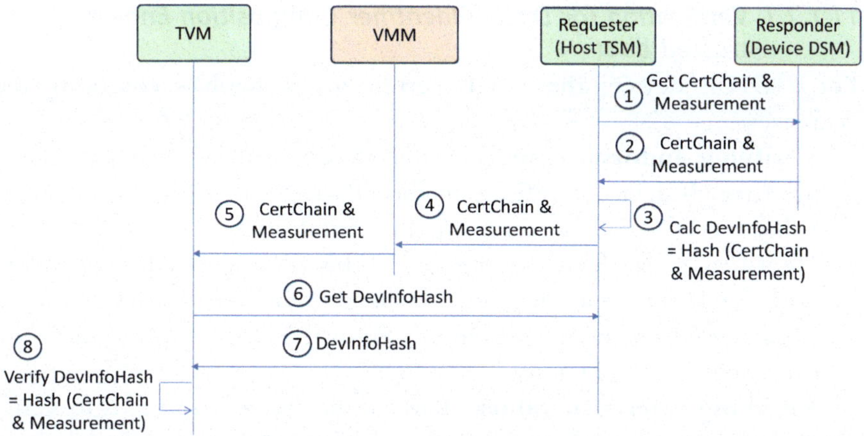

Figure 11.10 Trusted Execution Environment Security Manager (TSM) returning evidence to TVM. *DSM*, Device Security Manager; *TSM*, Trusted Execution Environment Security Manager.

③ The host-side TSM calculates a device information hash (DevInfoHash) for later use. This could be a single hash of all information, or multiple hashes for the certificate chain and measurements separately.

④ The host-side TSM provides the certificate chain and measurements to the VMM.

⑤ The VMM sends the certificate chain and measurements to the TVM.

⑥ The TVM requests the DevInfoHash from the TSM. This step does not involve the VMM and is therefore secure.

⑦ The TSM returns the DevInfoHash.

⑧ The TVM verifies that the DevInfoHash matches the hash of the certificate chain and measurements received from the VMM, detecting any tampering by the VMM.

11.1.2 Verification

Verifying a TEE-IO device can also follow the IETF RFC 9334 Remote Attestation Procedures architecture, as shown in Fig. 11.1. The verifier needs to consult three types of resources: Endorsements, Reference Values, and Appraisal Policies.

11.1.2.1 Verification for Device Identifier Composition Engine trusted boot

For a DICE device, the DICE certificates themselves constitute the evidence:

- **Verifying endorsements**: This means verifying the entity that issued the Layer 0 device certificate in the DICE certificate chain. This involves verifying all issuers from the manufacturer's Root CA up to the issuer of the device certificate. In this respect, DICE devices and non-DICE devices are the same. If the verifier trusts the device manufacturer, it trusts the manufacturer's Root CA certificate and therefore trusts the device's identity.
- **Verifying reference values**: This means the verifier needs to verify that the DiceTcbInfo in each layer of the DICE certificate chain matches the expected values. It is expected that the device manufacturer provides reference values for the DiceTcbInfo in the DICE certificate chain. If the verifier chooses to trust the device manufacturer, it can compare the manufacturer-provided DiceTcbInfo reference values with the actual DiceTcbInfo from each layer of the obtained certificate chain. The manufacturer might also define other extensions in the DICE certificate chain for comparison, such as the Universal Entity ID (UEID) described in DICE specifications.

Note: *Similar to the TPM case, we omit the step of verifying the digital signature on the DICE leaf certificate here, because integrity is a fundamental cryptographic requirement during secure transmission. We also omit freshness checks, because they are essential security requirements for transmission and not directly related to trust in the manufacturer.*

The DICE Endorsement Architecture for Devices describes a reference value provisioning method based on the Concise Reference Integrity Manifest (CoRIM). The specification is lengthy, but the core concept revolves around claims existing in subject-predicate-object triples. We use the Reference Value Triple as an example:

- **Subject**: The Target Environment (TE), which includes a Class Name and an Instance Name. For example, in DiceTcbInfo, the vendor, model, layer, and index constitute the Class Name, whereas the UEID constitutes the Instance Name.
- **Object**: The Measurement Value (MV), which includes class-specific measurements and instance-specific measurements. For example, in DiceTcbInfo, the version, SVN, and firmware ID are class-specific

measurements, whereas the UEID and device serial number are instance-specific measurements.

- **Predicate**: Existence, used in the statement "Target Environment (TE) has Measurement Value (MV)." For example, for a DICE device, a complete claim would be: "For a DICE environment TE with vendor w, model x, layer y, and index z, there should exist a measurement MV with version a, SVN b, and firmware ID c." The verification method is to first obtain the DICE certificate chain, parse the DiceTcbInfo structures, then locate the environment TE that matches the target layer and find the corresponding DiceTcbInfo, and finally verify that the measurement values match. Ideally, each $\text{DiceTcbInfo}_{\text{Ln}}$ should have a corresponding $\text{Environment}_{\text{Ln}}$ and $\text{Measurement}_{\text{Ln}}$ triple.

Fig. 11.11 illustrates the DICE CoRIM-based attestation method. The specific steps are:

① Layer n-1 of DICE issues the certificate for layer n. Layer n, as the final layer, is responsible for responding to attestation requests.

② The verifier, using a challenge-response method, obtains the DICE certificate chain, ensuring both integrity and freshness.

③ After obtaining the certificate chain, the verifier compares the content of its DiceTcbInfo structures with the reference value triples in the CoRIM and reaches a conclusion.

11.1.2.2 Verification of TEE-IO device evidence

Verification of TEE-IO device evidence also requires considering both endorsement verification and reference value verification, applying specific appraisal policies.

11.1.2.2.1 Verification of TEE-IO device endorsements

Generally, the endorser for a TEE-IO device is the device manufacturer. The manufacturer can issue a certificate for the hardware signed by its own CA during manufacturing. The manufacturer should also maintain a Certificate Revocation List (CRL) to record any problematic certificates, such as those for devices whose private keys have been compromised.

11.1.2.2.2 Security elements in TEE-IO device evidence verification

TEE-IO device evidence is transmitted via the SPDM protocol and should conform to the SPDM specification. Beyond that, TEE-IO device evidence can be generated in various ways: TPM-based, DICE-based, or

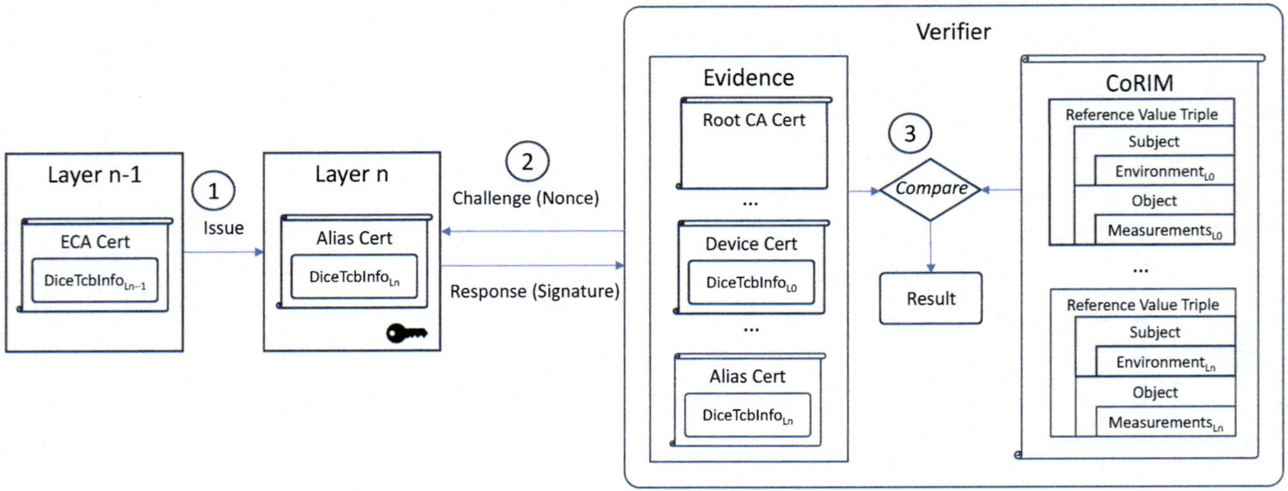

Figure 11.11 Device Identifier Composition Engine (Dice) Concise Reference Integrity Manifest (CoRIM)-based attestation. *CA*, Certificate Authority; *ECA*, Embedded Certificate Authority.

proprietary solutions based on specific hardware RoTs. Combining these, we need to consider these aspects:

- **Completeness of tcb set verification**: All TCB modules of the device hardware must be verified; none can be omitted. For example, with a TPM, the verifier needs to verify that the TEE-IO device's TPM hardware itself is trustworthy, and then verify the Platform Configuration Register (PCR) values reported by the TPM.
- **Completeness of boot chain verification**: The key to verifying a module's trustworthiness is verifying that all modules loaded before it are also trustworthy. For example, when using DICE, before verifying the DiceTcbInfo for layer n, one needs to verify that the DiceTcbInfo for layers 0 through n-1 are trustworthy.
- **Device time-of-check/time-of-use (toctou) binding**: The TVM needs to ensure that the device it verified is the same device it is using. This means preventing a TOCTOU attack, a type of race condition attack. Here, the TSM is responsible for locking the device allocation, ensuring the device verified by the TVM is the one being used. If the VMM reallocates the device, the TVM must reverify it.
- **Cross-Checking spdm evidence**: After obtaining the SPDM evidence, the verifier cannot just verify the signature within the SPDM message. It must also cross-check the evidence content against the underlying boot mechanism to prevent the SPDM implementation from forging measurements. For example, if the device uses a TPM, the TPM hardware signs its internal PCRs to generate a TPM Quote, and also signs externally provided SPDM measurement records. If the device firmware is malicious, it could create a fake SPDM measurement record and get it signed. Therefore, the verifier needs to verify that the SPDM measurement record content matches the TPM's PCR values, ensuring the SPDM record has not been maliciously altered. Similarly, if the device uses DICE, layer n, acting as the SPDM responder, signs the SPDM measurement record. If layer n is malicious, it could forge the SPDM measurement record and sign it. The verifier must check that the SPDM measurement record content matches the DiceTcbInfo from the DICE certificate chain, ensuring the SPDM record has not been maliciously altered.

Note: *This does not consider the SPDM implementation forging the digital signature itself, because that is a fundamental requirement of the SPDM protocol. The SPDM implementation requires the device TCB to protect the device private key from being obtained by other entities.*

SPDM can be implemented in a way that avoids the need for such cross-checking. If the RoT module responsible for SPDM signing is also the Root of Trust for Storage (RTS) and Root of Trust for Reporting (RTR), it can be responsible for signing all measurement request and response messages while guaranteeing the correctness of the measurement values. Fig. 11.12 provides an example of an SPDM RoT implementation. The specific steps are:

① The SPDM implementation software requests the SPDM RoT to sign all measurement request and response messages digitally.

② The SPDM RoT verifies that each measurement value in the MeasurementRecord matches its locally stored measurements. If any inconsistency is found (possibly indicating the SPDM software is forging measurements), it rejects the request. This is a critical step; it means the cross-checking of SPDM evidence is performed by the device's own RTS and RTR.

③ Only when all verifications pass does the SPDM RoT compute the correct digital signature.

④ The SPDM RoT returns the digital signature.

11.1.2.2.3 Examples of TEE-IO device reference value provisioning

Reference values for TEE-IO devices are typically provided by the device manufacturer. Common industry specifications include Software Identification Tags defined in ISO/IEC 19770-2:2015 Part 2, Concise Software Identification Tags defined in IETF RFC 9393, and the IETF draft on CoRIM. The DICE Endorsement Architecture uses CoRIM.

When providing reference values, device manufacturers need to provide integrity protection, typically using digital signatures.

11.1.2.2.4 Examples of TEE-IO device appraisal policies

Appraisal policies for TEE-IO devices vary. Common policies include matching all measurement values, matching all TCB measurements plus partial non-TCB measurements, matching all SVNs, and so forth.

11.1.3 Conveyance of attestation results

The conveyance of TEE-IO device attestation results involves the verifier and the relying party. This may occur entirely within the operating system, where both the verifier and relying party are kernel drivers, as shown in Fig. 11.13. It could also occur between modules potentially involving the

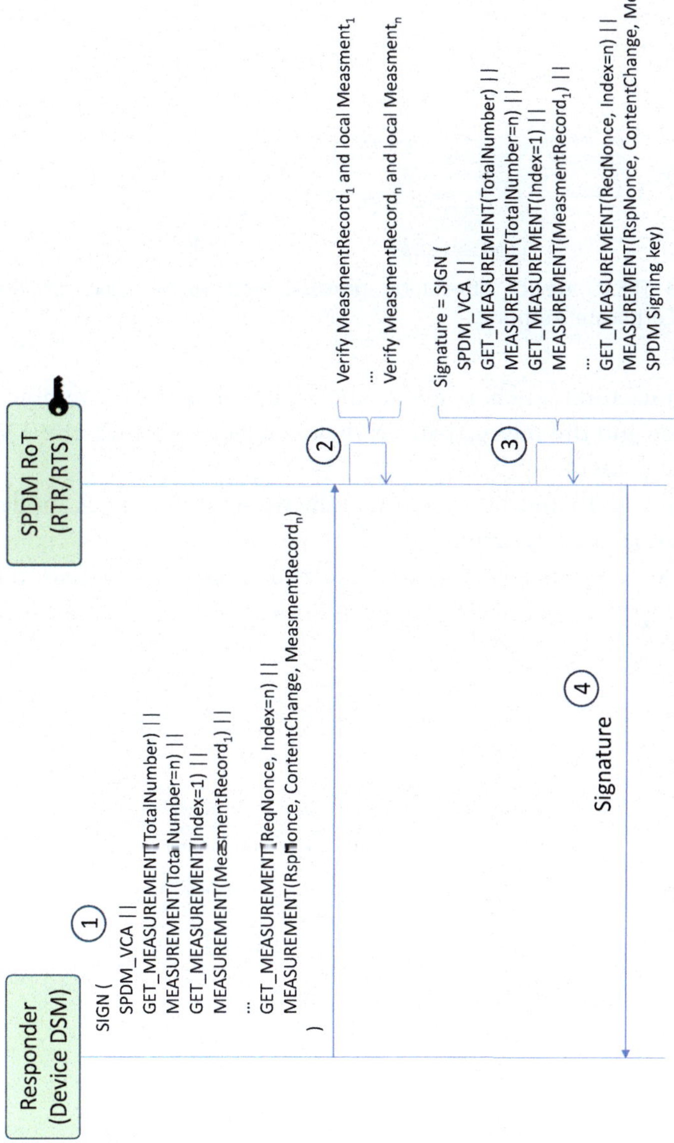

Figure 11.12 SPDM RoT implementation example. *DSM*, Device Security Manager; *RTR*, Root of Trust for Reporting; *RTS*, Root of Trust for Storage.

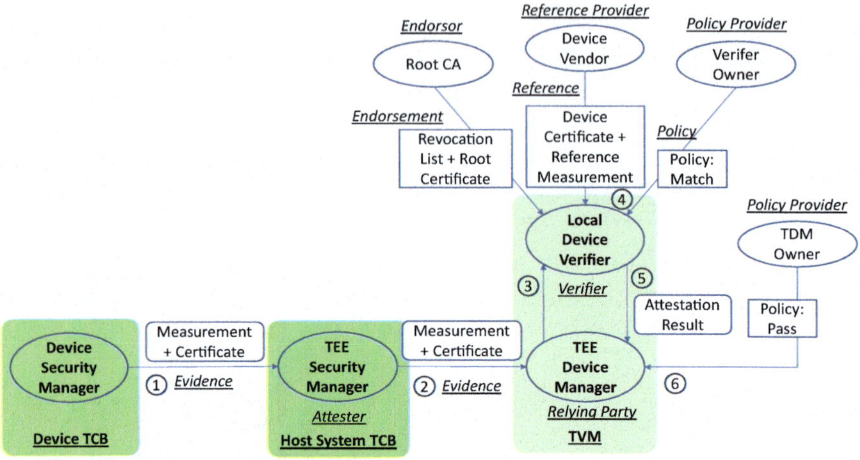

Figure 11.13 TEE-IO device attestation process: local verifier (background-check model). *CA*, Certificate Authority.

device manufacturer, such as where the verifier is a device remote attestation service and the relying party is the device driver inside the TVM, as shown in Fig. 11.14.

Both Figs. 11.13 and 11.14 illustrate the background-check model flow for TEE-IO device attestation.

Note: *The background-check model is used as an example here because it is more suitable for TEE use cases. If the passport model were adopted, it would require the*

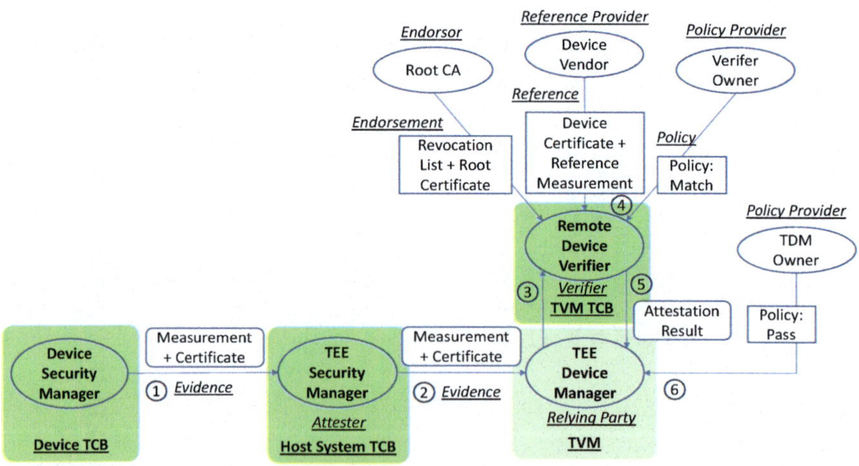

Figure 11.14 TEE-IO device attestation process: remote verifier (background-check model).

TSM to communicate with the verifier, obtain the attestation result, and pass it to the TVM. From a security perspective, this adds unnecessary functionality to the TSM, violating the principle of TCB minimization. From a compatibility perspective, it forces the TSM, which could otherwise remain neutral, to decide whether to use a local or remote verifier, and if remote, to know the address, making the TSM dependent on the specific use case. The background-check model places the decision with the TVM, allowing the tenant user to choose the most suitable approach based on their needs.

① The TSM and DSM establish an SPDM connection and obtain device certificates and measurements as evidence.

② The TSM passes the collected evidence to the TEE Device Manager (TDM) inside the TVM.

③ The TDM forwards the evidence to the verifier. This could be a local verifier (as in Fig. 11.13) or a remote verifier (as in Fig. 11.14). In the remote verifier mode, the remote verifier is part of the TVM's TCB.

④ The verifier performs verification based on endorsements, reference values, and appraisal policies, producing an attestation result.

⑤ The verifier returns the attestation result to the TDM.

⑥ The TDM decides whether to trust the device based on the attestation result and its own policies.

Note: *As seen in the figures, there are two distinct policies: one used by the verifier and another used by the TDM. They are different. Using a detective novel analogy: the verifier acts like a private investigator conducting an inquiry and then producing an investigation report (the attestation result) based on their own judgment. The TDM is like the client who makes a decision based on the report, deciding whether to accept the situation or take further action.*

Another example illustrates their difference:

Verifier's policy could be:

1. Endorsement: The certificate must be valid (within validity period, issued by a known Root CA, and not revoked in the CRL).
2. Reference Value: Compare only the latest SVN; do not compare measurements.
3. Attestation Result: Indicates whether the certificate is valid and up-to-date, and if the SVN is not the latest, provides a list of Common Vulnerabilities and Exposures (CVEs) associated with the running module version.

TDM's policy could be:

1. Endorsement: The certificate must be valid and its validity period must be less than 1 year.

2. Reference Value: The SVN must be the latest, or if not the latest, there must be no high or medium severity CVEs associated with the version (low-severity CVEs might be acceptable). In this scenario, a valid certificate from 3 years ago might be accepted by the verifier but rejected by the TDM. A module with a non–latest SVN but only low-severity CVEs would be flagged by the verifier but potentially accepted by the TDM.

A comparison between the local verifier mode (Fig. 11.13) and the remote verifier mode (Fig. 11.14) is shown in Table 11.1.

11.2 Third-party attestation of a TVM bound to a device

Third-party attestation of a TVM bound to a device is similar to third-party attestation of a TVM without a device. The difference lies in how the third party verifies the device TDI bound to the TVM. In the TEE-IO architecture, because the DSM is at the device level, not the TDI level, accepting a TDI means accepting the entire device. Therefore, attestation of the device TDI often implies attestation of the device itself (i.e., verifying the SPDM device certificate and device measurements).

Performing additional, TDI-specific attestation is also possible, depending on the device's capabilities. For example, a feature-rich device

Table 11.1 Comparison between local verifier mode and remote verifier mode.

Device attestation by TVM	Local verifier mode	Remote verifier mode
Verifier location	Inside TVM	Inside TVM or remote service
Endorsements (root certificate authorities, certificate revocation lists)	Deployed inside TVM	Managed by remote service
Reference values	Deployed inside TVM	Managed by remote service
Appraisal policies	Deployed inside TVM	Managed by remote service
Attestation data updates	No updates or scheduled updates	Service maintains latest versions

might have different execution engines for different TDIs. The TVM's device driver might desire more detailed information, such as TDI engine-specific information or data loaded into the TDI engine. This information could be returned in the opaque data field of an SPDM MEASUREMENTS response, or reflected as vendor-specific data in the TDI report.

11.2.1 Evidence generation and conveyance

In trusted boot with secure boot policies, there are three types of evidence: Policy Manifest, Authority, and Instance. The Policy Manifest is the set of public keys allowed to sign code for secure boot. The Authority is the specific key used to verify a module. The Instance is the hash of the module itself.

Similarly, evidence about a device TDI within a TVM can be categorized into Policy Manifest, Authority, and Entity:

- **Policy manifest**: The attestation data needed by the verifier for evaluation includes: device endorsements (root certificates and CRLs), device reference measurement values (firmware hashes, SVNs, etc.), and appraisal policies. Policy data can be updated securely (e.g., using digital signatures for verification). The policy manifest must be included in the TVM report.
- **Authority**: This is the specific policy from the manifest that was used to verify the device. For example, the manifest might contain root certificates for three different vendors: Vendor A, Vendor B, and Vendor C. During runtime, a device from Vendor B is bound to the TVM and verified. In this case, the authority is Vendor B's root certificate—the specific policy that was actually effective in verifying the device. The TVM report may or may not include the authority, depending on security requirements. Reporting the authority allows knowing which class of devices was allowed, but the downside is that it makes the TVM report vary dynamically.
- **Entity**: This is the actual evidence describing the device. It can be divided into Class Evidence, Instance Evidence, and Dynamic Evidence. Class evidence includes firmware measurements, SVNs, configuration information, debug information, and so on, conveyed via SPDM. Instance evidence includes the device certificate chain conveyed via SPDM. Dynamic evidence includes runtime operational

data such as voltage and temperature. The TVM report may or may not include the entity, depending on security requirements. If included, it might be practical to include only class evidence, omitting instance and dynamic evidence, because the latter two would make each TVM report unique and difficult to manage for deployment. The process of binding a device TDI to a TVM can be dynamic. The TVM might bind, unbind, rebind, and so forth, frequently. If the report were to include the entity or authority, every device ever bound would need to be recorded.

Depending on where the device verification takes place (local vs. remote verifier), the resulting TVM report containing device-related evidence will differ, as shown in Fig. 11.15.

- **TVM device local verifier**: The TVM needs to have the endorsements and reference values required for verification, including the set of root certificates and CRLs. These can be statically deployed in the TVM, dynamically input by the VMM when launching the TVM, or even dynamically updated by the cloud service provider. Typically, this collection of endorsements and reference values is measured into the TVM's attestation report as policy evidence. At runtime, the local

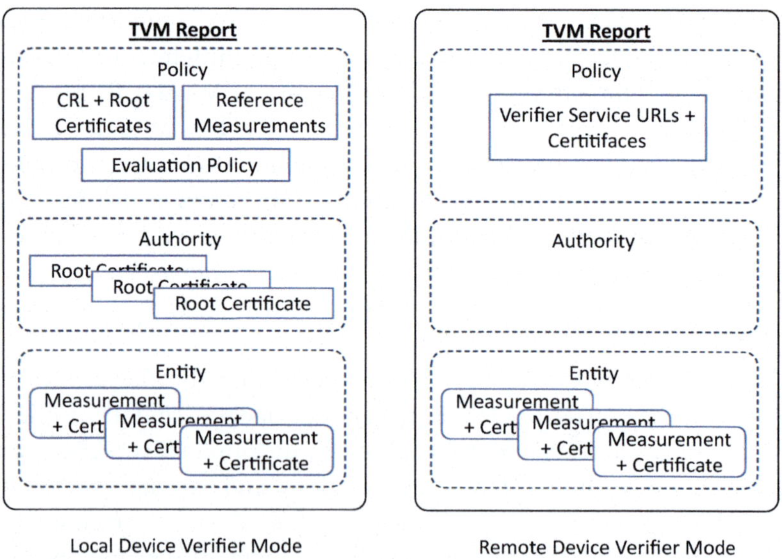

Figure 11.15 Third-party attestation of a TVM with a bound device TCB Component Identifier. *CRL*, Certificate Revocation List.

verifier uses this collection to verify the obtained device certificates and measurements. The specific verification path used (e.g., which root certificate) is recorded as authority evidence and measured into the TVM's attestation report. Simultaneously, the device's certificates and measurements are measured into the TVM's attestation report as entity evidence. Similar to TEE attestation, the class, instance, and dynamic components of the entity evidence need to be placed into separate TVM measurement registers (e.g., Runtime Measurement Registers (RTMRs)).

- **TVM device remote verifier**: The TVM only needs the address of the remote verifier service. This address can be measured into the TVM's attestation report as policy evidence. Since verification happens remotely, no authority evidence is needed. Finally, the TVM measures the device's certificates and measurements into its attestation report as entity evidence.

11.2.2 Third-party verification of the TVM

Third-party verification of the TVM must account for the two scenarios described earlier:

- **TVM device local verifier**: The third party must first verify the device verification program itself within the TVM. Then, based on actual needs, it verifies all or part of the policy evidence, authority evidence, and instance evidence present in the TVM report.
- **TVM device remote verifier**: The third party needs to trust the device verification service provided by the device manufacturer, which is part of the TVM-TCB. Then, based on actual needs, it verifies all or part of the policy evidence (including the remote attestation service address) and entity evidence in the TVM report.

The advantage of using a remote device verifier is that the online verification service actively fetches the latest endorsements and reference values published by the manufacturer, ensuring the **timeliness** of the attestation result. However, looking back at an attestation result, one can only know it was the latest at that time, but it is hard to know exactly which version that was. Device local attestation has the opposite characteristic. All policy information is deployed inside the TVM and reflected in the attestation result. This allows for precise historical knowledge of the state at the time of attestation. The disadvantage is that the endorsements and reference values deployed by the Cloud Service Provider (CSP) might lag behind the manufacturer's latest releases.

Table 11.2 Comparison between local and remote device verification.

TVM attestation from third-party	Device local verification mode	Device remote verification mode
Device verifier in TVM report	TVM verifier code	TVM verifier code or code communicating with verification service
Device policy in TVM report	TVM's endorsements, reference values, and appraisal policies	Verification service URL and service certificate
Device policy updates in TVM report	Code for policy updates and its signer	N/A
Device authority in TVM report	Device root certificate	N/A
Device entity in TVM report	Device certificates and measurements	Device certificates and measurements

The conveyance of the attestation result is not closely tied to TEE-IO and should be consistent with standard TVM attestation result conveyance. Readers can refer to the relevant introduction in Chapter 5.

In third-party attestation of a TVM bound to a device, there are also differences between local and remote device verification modes, as compared in Table 11.2.

11.3 Bidirectional attestation between device and host

In some use cases, not only can the host attest the device, but the device may also need to attest the host. SPDM is an authentication key exchange protocol designed for communication between two devices, supporting both certificate-based and preshared key modes. If used within a TEE environment, a Remote Attestation SPDM (RA-SPDM) scheme, similar to RA-TLS, can be adopted, as described in the Intel white paper "Intel device attestation model in confidential computing environment." This scheme uses TEE Quote-based certificates instead of ordinary X.509 certificates for the host. The RA-SPDM flow is illustrated in Fig. 11.16.

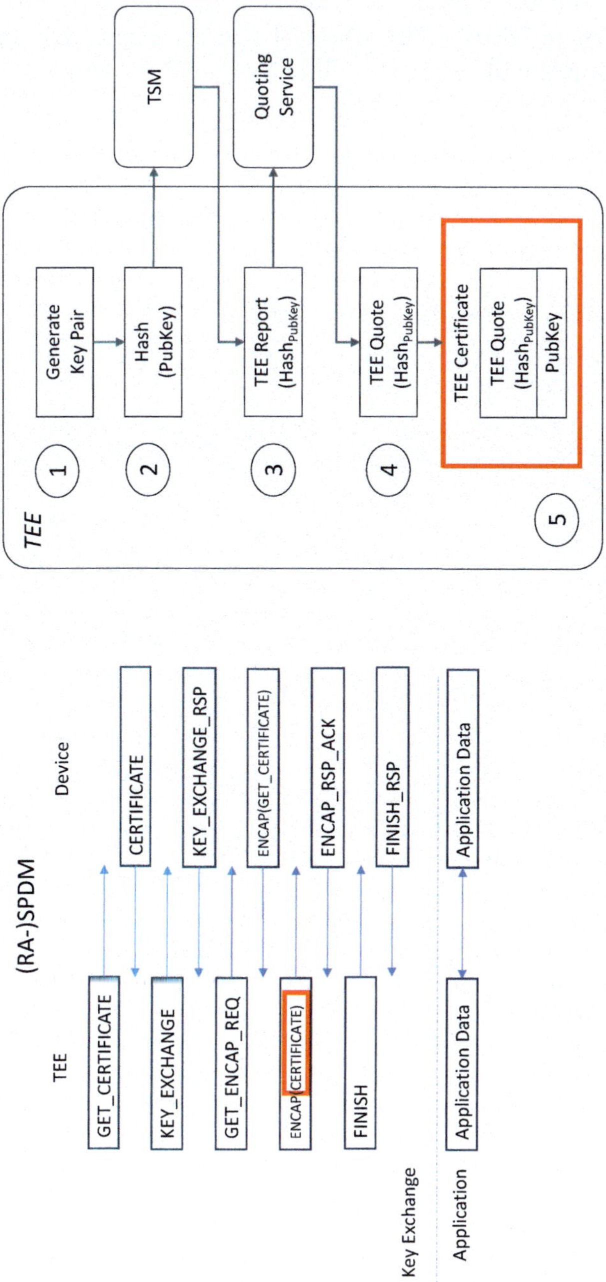

Figure 11.16 Remote Attestation SPDM (RA-SPDM) flow.

In a bidirectional attestation scenario using RA-SPDM between device and host, the device typically provides a standard X.509 certificate. The host, however, provides a TEE Quote-based certificate. The device must be preprovisioned with reference values for the TEE and the TEE platform to verify the TEE Quote, deciding whether to provide its services to that specific TEE.

CHAPTER 12

TEE-IO Special function

In Chapter 11, we introduced the attestation function of Trusted Execution Environment Input/Output (TEE-IO). In this chapter, we will continue to introduce other optional features.

12.1 Resiliency of TEE-IO devices

According to the TEE Device Interface Security Protocol (TDISP) section of the Peripheral Component Interconnect Express (PCIe) Base Specification, the Device Security Manager (DSM) in a TEE-IO device has a crucial role. It is responsible for providing device authentication, measurement information, establishing secure sessions with the host, managing TEE Device Interfaces (TDIs), implementing necessary security policies to maintain confidential computing requirements, monitoring all activities that could affect the security of TDI or TEE Virtual Machine (TVM) data, and so on. It is impractical for the DSM to be implemented entirely in hardware. Apart from the device Root of Trust (RoT), parts of the DSM should be implemented in firmware, such as Security Protocol and Data Model (SPDM) session establishment, Integrity and Data Encryption (IDE) key transport, and TDISP management. Therefore, securely implementing the DSM firmware is a necessary requirement for TEE-IO devices. These requirements can be divided into two categories:

- Trusted Boot Requirements: Involve defining the root of trust and the trusted boot chain, aiming to ensure that the provided device measurements have not been tampered with. Methods include Trusted Platform Module (TPM)-based secure boot and Device Identifier Composition Engine (DICE)-based secure boot. Related content was introduced in Chapter 11.
- Resiliency Requirements: Include secure boot, secure update, and secure recovery. The goal is to defend against malicious attacks targeting the device and maintain device availability.

Confidential Computing
ISBN 978-0-443-54067-7
https://doi.org/10.1016/B978-0-443-54067-7.00016-4

According to National Institute of Standards and Technology SP 800-193, the firmware resiliency requirements encompass three dimensions: Protection, Detection, and Recovery, as shown in Fig. 12.1.

12.1.1 Protection

Protection refers to the secure update function, used to maintain the integrity of static firmware. When the system is running, only authorized updates to the device firmware are permitted. Measures can include:

1. Locking the direct access permissions of the current device firmware to read-only.
2. Allowing updates only after a reboot, or within a secure environment.
3. Verifying the digital signature of the firmware update package during update.
4. Verifying the Security Version Number (SVN) of the firmware update package during update.
5. Not allowing bypass of digital signature or SVN checks, for example, using debug interfaces for updates.

The root of trust responsible for maintaining the secure update function is called the Root of Trust for Update. The content requiring protection typically includes firmware code and critical firmware data. The public key used for verifying digital signatures and the minimum SVN used for comparison also need protection.

12.1.2 Detection

Detection refers to the secure boot function, used to maintain the integrity of runtime firmware. When the system boots, as one module loads the next, it needs to verify the next module's digital signature and SVN value to prevent malicious tampering or downgrade. This way, even if the protection

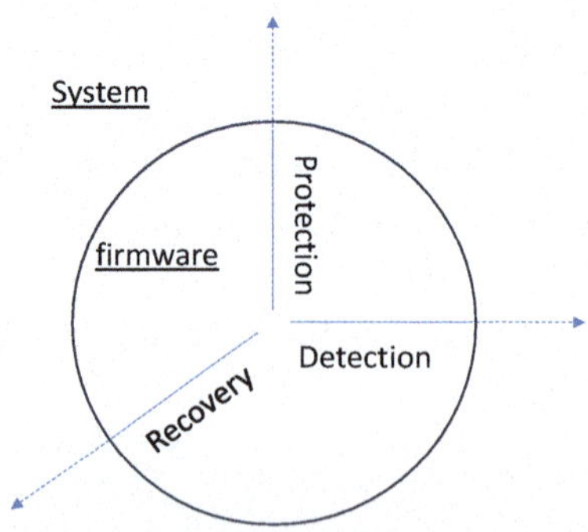

Figure 12.1 Firmware resiliency requirements.

function fails and the device firmware is maliciously updated, the system still has a mechanism to detect that the firmware has been tampered with.

The root of trust responsible for maintaining the secure boot function is also called the Root of Trust for Detection. The objects requiring detection typically correspond one-to-one with the objects requiring protection, usually including firmware code and critical firmware data.

12.1.3 Recovery

Recovery refers to the secure recovery function, used to maintain firmware availability. When the system is running, if it detects that the system firmware has been maliciously tampered with, the optimal solution is automatic recovery, rather than crashing or continuing to boot. The automatic recovery process could involve booting a known good backup firmware and then restoring the normal firmware code and critical firmware data.

The root of trust responsible for maintaining the secure recovery function is called the Root of Trust for Recovery. The known good backup firmware must also be subject to the same protection and detection functions. If the backup firmware is also tampered with owing to inadequate protection, recovery becomes ineffective.

12.2 Runtime update of TEE-IO devices

We previously mentioned that TEE-IO device firmware can be securely updated by updating after a reboot or within a secure environment. For the latter case (update within a secure environment), there are two further possibilities: one is that the device needs to be restarted after the update for the changes to take effect; the other is that the update takes effect immediately without requiring a restart, known as a runtime update.

Runtime updates have the unique advantage of not requiring reestablishment of connections with the TEE; the device can continue providing service to the TEE throughout the process. However, runtime updates also carry risks: they inherit the runtime environment from before the update. If the previous firmware had potential security vulnerabilities, these vulnerabilities might persist without being eliminated. Therefore, whether to support runtime updates depends on the security policy.

12.2.1 Runtime update policies

There are two policies for runtime updates of TEE-IO devices: the initiation policy for the update and the consequence policy after the update.

- **Initiation policy for the update**: In the PCIe TDISP protocol, the initiation policy for an update is controlled by the NO_FW_UPDATE bit in the flags of the LOCK_INTERFACE_REQUEST. When the TEE Security Manager (TSM), acting as the requester, sets this bit to 1, it indicates that the device, as the responder, is allowed to update while the TDI is in the CONFIG_LOCK or RUN state. When the requester sets it to 0, it indicates that the device is not allowed to update while the TDI is in the CONFIG_LOCK or RUN state.

  Note: *A few clarifications here:*

  1. NO_FW_UPDATE controls whether a firmware update can be performed at all, regardless of whether it is a runtime update or an update requiring a reboot.
  2. NO_FW_UPDATE controls whether an update is permissible specifically in the CONFIG_LOCK or RUN states. Updates in other states are always allowed.
  3. NO_FW_UPDATE applies to the entire device. As long as any TDI has NO_FW_UPDATE set and is in the CONFIG_LOCK or RUN state, the entire device cannot be updated.
- **Consequence policy after the update**: In SPDM protocol version 1.2, the consequence policy after an update is controlled by the Termination Policy bit in the Session Policy field of the KEY_EXCHANGE request. In the SPDM protocol, the TSM is the requester, and the device is the responder. When the TSM (requester) sets this bit to 0, it indicates that after the device (responder) completes an update, it must terminate the secure session. This implies runtime updates are not supported. When the requester sets it to 1, it indicates that after the update, the responder may retain the secure session, meaning runtime updates are supported.

  Note: *A few clarifications here:*

  1. When TerminationPolicy is 0, the secure session must be terminated after the update. When it is 1, the secure session may be terminated or retained. The responder can decide based on its current situation, so the final choice is made by the device. This is because only the device can accurately determine its capability to retain the secure session. In specific cases, such as a security-critical update or a major functional update, the device might be unable to retain the secure session after a runtime update. In such cases, the device should terminate the secure session regardless of whether TerminationPolicy is 0 or 1.

2. TerminationPolicy controls the decision after the update, not whether an update can occur.
3. TerminationPolicy applies individually to each secure session. After an update, some secure sessions might be terminated while others are retained.

Thus, NO_FW_UPDATE and TerminationPolicy are independent policy controls, resulting in four possible combinations. A TSM wishing to support runtime updates should choose NO_FW_UPDATE=0 and TerminationPolicy=1.

12.2.2 Verification of update policies

Both the SPDM session establishment and the TDISP interface lock commands are initiated by the TSM based on input from the VMM. Therefore, the TVM needs to verify whether these two update policies meet its requirements. The methods are as follows:

- Verification of the **Initiation policy for the update**: In the PCIe TDISP protocol, the interface report (DEVICE_INTERFACE_REPORT) contains interface information (INTERFACE_INFO). Bit 0 of this field reflects the current NO_FW_UPDATE setting. The TVM can directly obtain the device interface report (e.g., via the TSM) to verify this information.
- Verification of the **consequence policy after the update**: The TVM cannot directly obtain the SPDM protocol's TerminationPolicy from the device. Therefore, the TVM needs to request this information from the TSM.

12.2.3 Attestation of firmware updates

We discussed device attestation in detail in Chapter 11. When a TVM and device support runtime updates, the TVM may need additional steps to monitor the attestation of updated firmware. Broadly, this can be divided into two categories: Postupdate Attestation and Preupdate Attestation.

12.2.3.1 Postupdate attestation

A runtime update of a device can be triggered by the current TVM, another TVM, another Virtual Machine (VM), the TSM, the VMM, a cloud orchestrator, or even an out-of-band mechanism such as Baseboard Management Controller (BMC).

If the TSM has chosen NO_FW_UPDATE=0 and TerminationPolicy=1, and the TVM has accepted this choice, it means the TVM supports runtime updates for the device. The TVM can deploy policies for postupdate reattestation. For example, the TVM might perform periodic device attestation, on-demand device attestation based on cloud orchestrator requests, or reattestation triggered by SPDM 1.3 events such as MeasurementChange or CertificateChange. The reattestation process is shown in Fig. 12.2, with these specific steps:

① The host-side TVM sends a device evidence recollection request (Recollection) along with a ReqNonce to the TSM.

② The host-side TSM sends an SPDM GET_CERTIFICATE command, requesting the device's certificate chain.

③ The device-side DSM collects the current certificate chain.

④ The device-side DSM returns the device certificate chain in a CERTIFICATE response. The public key from the leaf certificate in the chain will be used to verify subsequent SPDM signatures.

⑤ The host-side TSM sends an SPDM GET_MEASUREMENT command, requesting all device measurements. The request includes the requester-generated nonce (ReqNonce) to prevent replay attacks.

⑥ The device-side DSM collects the current SPDM measurement record and generates its own responder nonce (RspNonce). Finally, the DSM uses its current SPDM signing key to generate a digital signature over the measurement request and response data.

⑦ The device-side DSM returns the device measurement record in a MEASUREMENT response. The response includes a digital signature covering ReqNonce, RspNonce, and the measurement record, ensuring integrity and freshness.

⑧ The TSM returns the device certificate chain and the signed measurement record to the TVM.

⑨ The TVM needs to verify the ReqNonce for freshness, verify the integrity of the certificate chain, and verify that the device certificate in the chain matches the one from before (ensuring device binding). It must also verify the digital signature on the measurement record to confirm the validity of the leaf certificate and the integrity of the measurements. Finally, the TVM needs to verify that the measurement values meet its requirements.

Note*: Postupdate attestation is almost identical to initial attestation. The key difference lies in verifying device binding. In an SPDM certificate chain, the device certificate (often the root or a specific immutable certificate) identifies the device's identity and typically does not change during runtime updates. The TVM can confirm the device has not changed by verifying that this device certificate remains the*

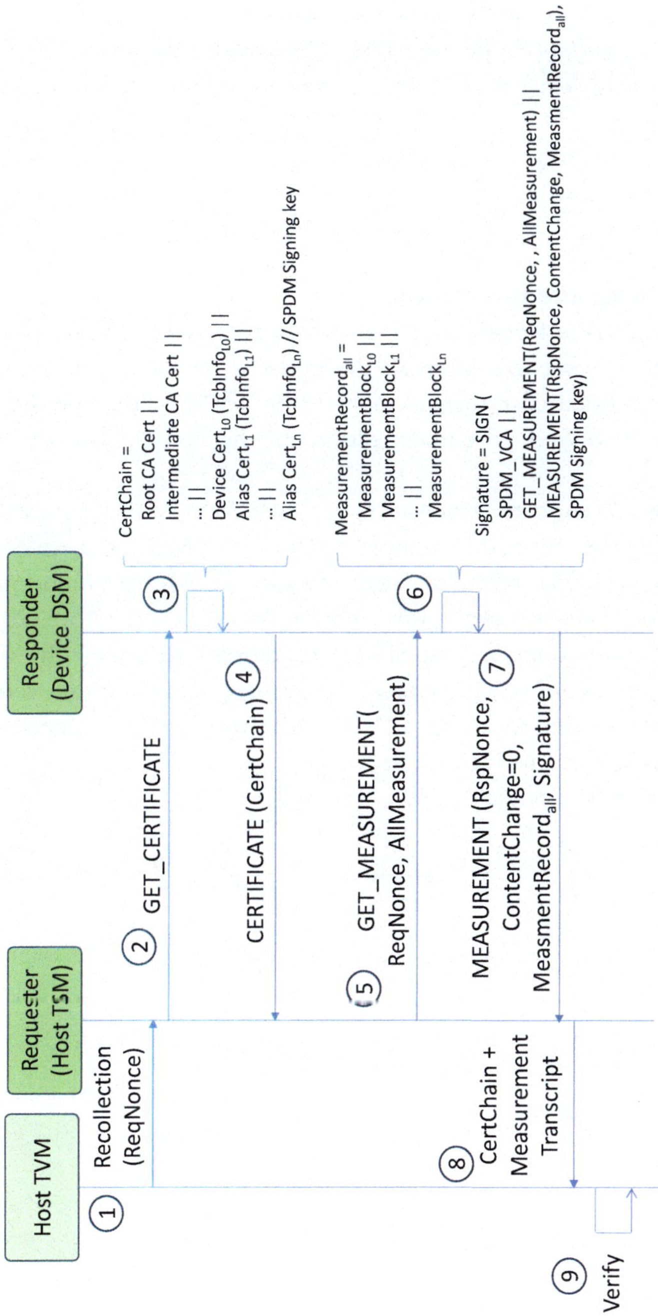

Figure 12.2 Postupdate attestation.

same. In non-DICE modes, the leaf certificate might be the device certificate and remain unchanged. In DICE modes, the device certificate (Layer 0) signs subordinate Alias Certificates. Because Alias Certificates contain measurement information, they may change during updates, and consequently, the leaf certificate might also change.

After completing reattestation, the TVM can choose to continue accepting the device or to reject it and immediately terminate the connection.

12.2.3.2 Preupdate attestation

Using postupdate attestation creates a window between the update and the verification. During this interval, the updated device would continue to exchange confidential information with the TVM before the TVM has a chance to verify and potentially terminate the connection, as shown in Fig. 12.3a.

To avoid this update/verification gap, SPDM version 1.3 introduced an in-session event mechanism and defined the MeasurementPreUpdate event. If an SPDM requester registers for the MeasurementPreUpdate event, the device must trigger this event to the requester before performing the update. Subsequently, the SPDM requester can obtain the measurements that are about to take effect (but are not yet active) for verification and decide whether to accept or terminate the device connection. This process is illustrated in Fig. 12.3b.

Note*: A few clarifications here:*

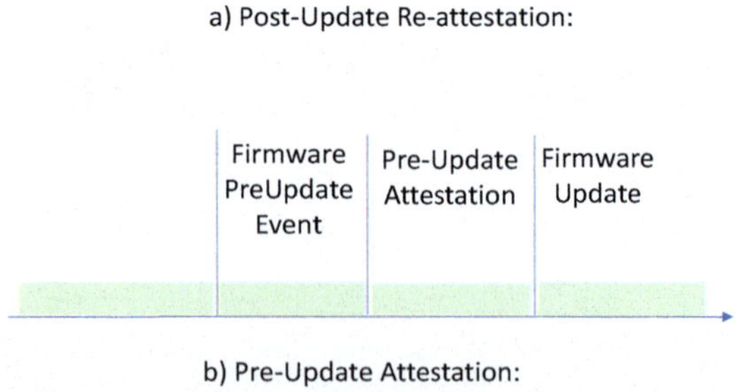

Figure 12.3 Postupdate versus preupdate attestation.

1. The recipient of the MeasurementPreUpdate event (the SPDM requester) cannot prevent the update from being carried out. If it cannot accept the update, the requester can choose not to acknowledge the event, allowing it to time out, and then terminate the session or device connection. However, the device will still proceed with the update. This prevents a malicious event recipient from blocking critical device firmware updates.
2. After sending the MeasurementPreUpdate event, the device waits for the event to be resolved, either by receiving an acknowledgment, session termination, or command timeout. The device will proceed only with the firmware update after the event is resolved.
3. The MeasurementPreUpdate event is session-based. The device waits for all MeasurementPreUpdate events within a session to be resolved before implementing the firmware update.

The preupdate attestation process is shown in Fig. 12.4, with these specific steps:

① The device-side DSM sends a MeasurementPreUpdate event.

② Upon receiving the event, the host-side TSM notifies the TVM.

③ The host-side TVM sends a request to the TSM to obtain the new device measurements, including a requester-generated nonce (ReqNonce) for freshness.

④ The host-side TSM sends an SPDM GET_MEASUREMENT command over the SPDM session.

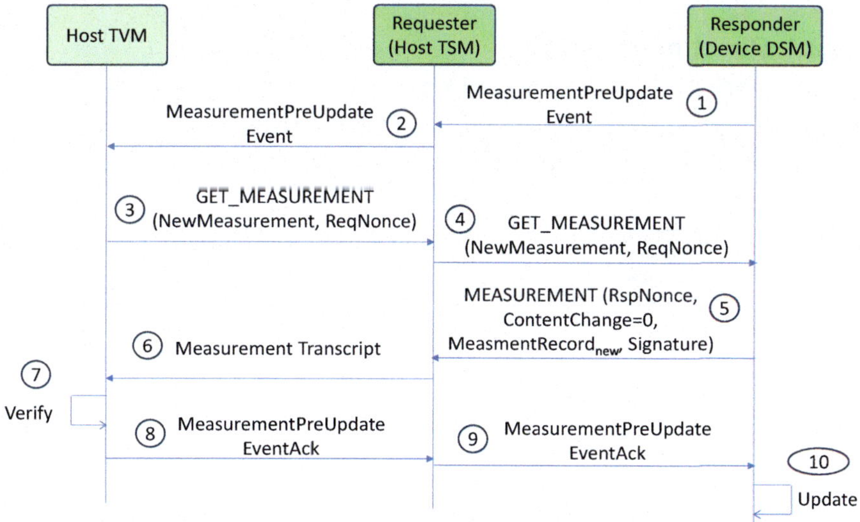

Figure 12.4 Preupdate attestation.

⑤ The device-side DSM returns the device measurement record in a MEASUREMENT response. The response includes a digital signature covering ReqNonce, RspNonce, and the measurement record, ensuring integrity and freshness.
⑥ The TSM returns the device certificate chain and the entire message sequence transcript (including the MEASUREMENT command and response) along with the digital signature to the TVM.
⑦ The TVM needs to verify the ReqNonce for freshness and verify the digital signature on the MEASUREMENT record to ensure the integrity of the measurements. Finally, the TVM needs to verify that the measurement values meet its requirements.
⑧ If the TVM accepts the new measurements, it sends an Event Acknowledgment (EventAck) to the TSM.
⑨ The TSM sends the EventAck to the DSM over the SPDM session.
⑩ The update is performed.

12.3 Peer-to-peer transmission between PCIe devices

Besides transmission between a device and the Root Port, PCIe TLP transmission can occur directly between devices, known as Peer-to-Peer (P2P). IDE TLPs are also applicable to P2P transmission. P2P itself is independent of TEE-IO; TEE-IO needs to configure IDE streams according to the specific form of P2P. According to the PCIe specification, there are two forms of P2P.

12.3.1 Direct peer-to-peer

Direct P2P is shown in Fig. 12.5a. Two endpoint devices establish an independent, directly connected P2P Selective IDE stream for communication. Communication can occur through a PCIe switch

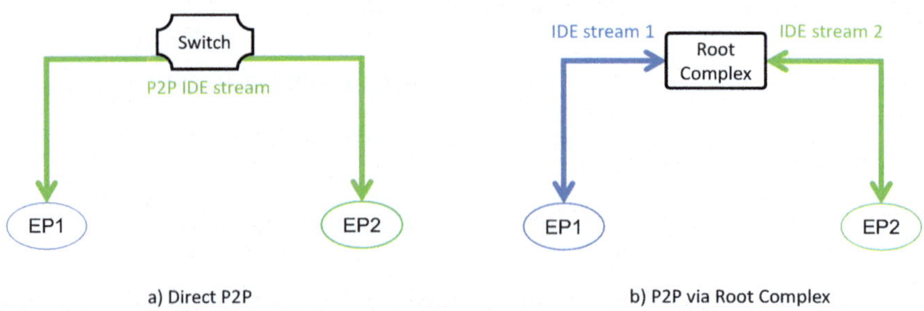

Figure 12.5 Two forms of peer-to-peer (P2P) transmission.

but does not need to go through the Root Complex. A P2P IDE stream requires the host to configure both endpoints separately using the TDISP BIND_P2P_STREAM message, setting up the same P2P IDE stream. This requires the devices to support Direct P2P.

12.3.2 Peer-to-peer via root complex

P2P via Root Complex is shown in Fig. 12.5b. Two endpoint devices each establish separate IDE streams with the Root Complex. The Root Complex is responsible for receiving on one IDE stream and reencrypting/transmitting on the other. In this case, the Root Complex becomes part of the TCB for the P2P transmission. The disadvantage is that it is less efficient than Direct P2P. The advantage is that it does not require the devices to provide additional support for Direct P2P.

CHAPTER 13

TEE-IO software development

In Chapters 9 through 12, we introduced various Trusted Execution Environment Input/Output (TEE-IO) architectures and specifications. In this chapter, we will introduce the open-source software used to build TEE-IO confidential computing solutions. Most TEE-IO related software is based on trusted execution environment (TEE) software, which was introduced in Chapter 7. This chapter will cover only the parts specific to TEE-IO.

13.1 TEE-IO software application scenarios

Fig. 13.1 shows a typical application scenario for TEE-IO.

The architecture of this application is as follows: The host-side virtual machine manager (VMM) is responsible for managing all devices, including

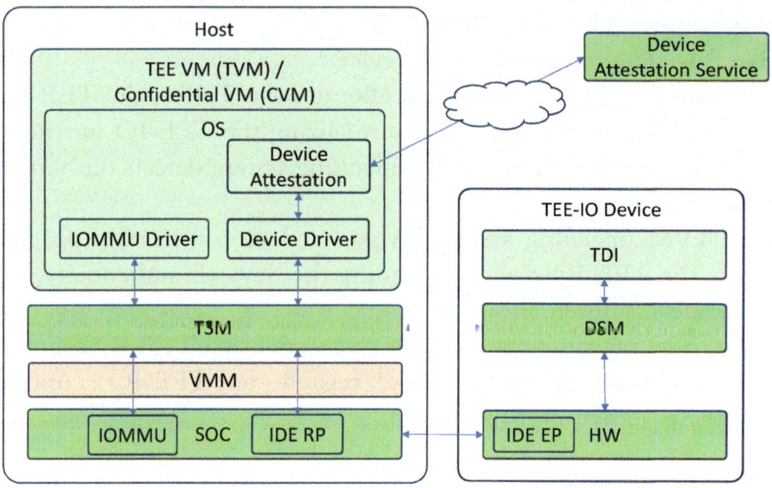

Figure 13.1 Typical application scenario for TEE-IO. *CVM*, Confidential virtual machine; *TEE*, trusted execution environment; *VM*, virtual machine; *VMM*, virtual machine manager; *DSM*, Device Security Manager; *EP*, Endpoint; *HW*, Hardware; *IDE*, Integrity and Data Encryption; *IOMMU*, Input/Output Memory Management Unit; *OS*, Operating System; *RP*, Root Port; *SOC*, System on Chip; *TDI*, TEE Device Interface; *TSM*, TEE Security Manager; *TVM*, TEE Virtual Machine; *VMM*, Virtual Machine Manager.

Confidential Computing
ISBN 978-0-443-54067-7
https://doi.org/10.1016/B978-0-443-54067-7.00013-9

Table 13.1 Classification of TEE-IO confidential computing software.

Type	Confidential virtual machine
TEE-IO infrastructure	VMM Guest OS kernel Device drivers
TEE-IO device attestation	Device attestation service, verification service Device reference integrity manifest service
TEE-IO secure communication	Security Protocol and Data Model (SPDM)

TEE-IO devices and non-TEE-IO devices. For systems supporting TEE-IO, the VMM selectively allocates TEE-IO device TDIs to TVMs. The device driver in the TVM's operating system detects this TEE-IO device but cannot fully trust it. Therefore, it needs to invoke a device attestation program to verify the authenticity of the TEE-IO device, confirm whether the device certificate is in the TVM operating system's trusted device list, and check if the device measurements are acceptable, and so on. Because a TEE-IO device can be shared simultaneously among multiple TVMs, the secure connection between the host and the TEE-IO device is managed by the TSM. If all verifications pass, the TVM operating system begins using the TDI of this TEE-IO device. The overall process is:

1. The VMM detects a TEE-IO device.
2. According to policy, the VMM allocates the TDI of the TEE-IO device to a TVM, also known as virtualizing the TEE-IO function.
3. The device driver in the TVM operating system detects this virtualized TEE-IO function.
4. The TVM operating system invokes a device attestation program to verify the TEE-IO device, including the device's authenticity, certificate, and measurements.
5. The TVM operating system uses this virtualized TEE-IO function.

The classification of software related to TEE-IO confidential computing is shown in Table 13.1.

13.2 Software supporting TEE-IO in confidential virtual machines

Architecturally, TEE-IO is only supported by confidential virtual machines (CVMs); secure enclaves do not support TEE-IO. This section focuses on software supporting TEE-IO within CVM.

13.2.1 Virtual machine manager

The VMM acts as the resource manager in CVM solutions. Mainstream VMMs have begun supporting TEE-IO enabled CVMs, such as Linux KVM and Microsoft Hyper-V.

13.2.2 Guest operating system

TEE-IO also requires support from the guest operating system. The Linux community has started discussions on TEE-IO support, aiming to unify support for Intel TDX Connect, AMD SEV-TIO, ARM RME-DA, RISC-V CoVE-IO, and so forth.

13.3 TEE-IO device attestation

Before the TVM operating system uses a TEE-IO device, it needs to attest and verify the device, including its authenticity, certificate, and measurements.

Software for device attestation and verification services includes:

- Trusted Device Manager (TDM) in Confidential Containers (CoCo) Project: An application written in Rust proposed by the CoCo community. It has device attestation capabilities and supports both local and remote attestation of devices. The architecture for TEE-IO device attestation and verification is shown in Fig. 13.2. After the OS kernel

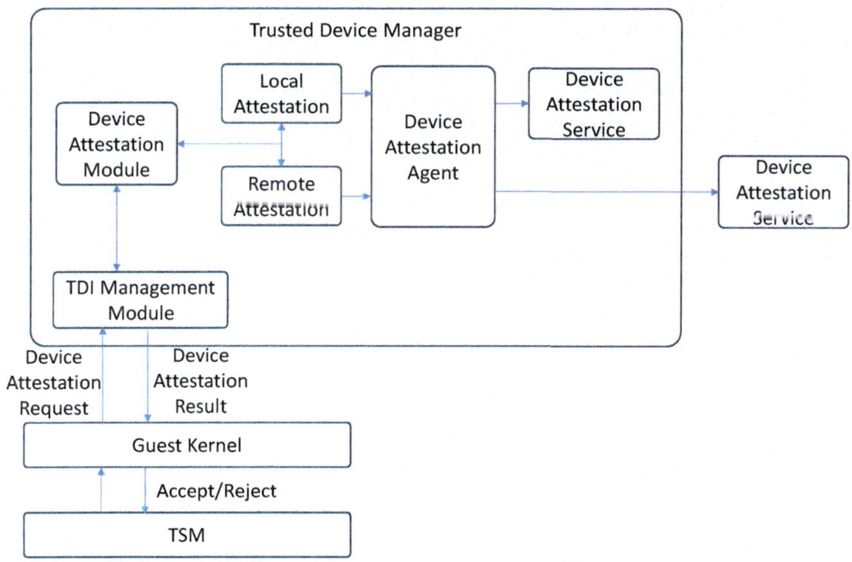

Figure 13.2 TEE-IO device attestation and verification architecture.

in the TVM obtains device evidence, it submits the evidence to the TDM, which issues a device attestation request. The TDM chooses either local or remote attestation to verify the device certificates and measurements. Finally, the TDM returns the device verification result to the OS kernel.

Device attestation within the TDM needs to be combined with TVM attestation. This means that the attestation report for a TVM supporting TEE-IO must include the device attestation information.

- nVTrust: A series of open-source tools and Software Development Kits (SDKs) developed by NVIDIA for H100 GPU confidential computing. It includes an NVIDIA Attestation SDK written in Python and a GPU local verifier.

13.4 TEE-IO secure communication

The host side of TEE-IO needs to use SPDM for secure communication with TEE-IO devices. The commonly used protocol in the industry is SPDM for communication between platform components.

Existing open-source SPDM protocol implementations include:

- libspdm: A series of SPDM-related code developed by DMTF in C. libspdm provides the foundation of the SPDM protocol stack. spdm-emu provides an SPDM emulator that can run in an operating system. spdm-dump can be used to parse SPDM commands. SPDM-

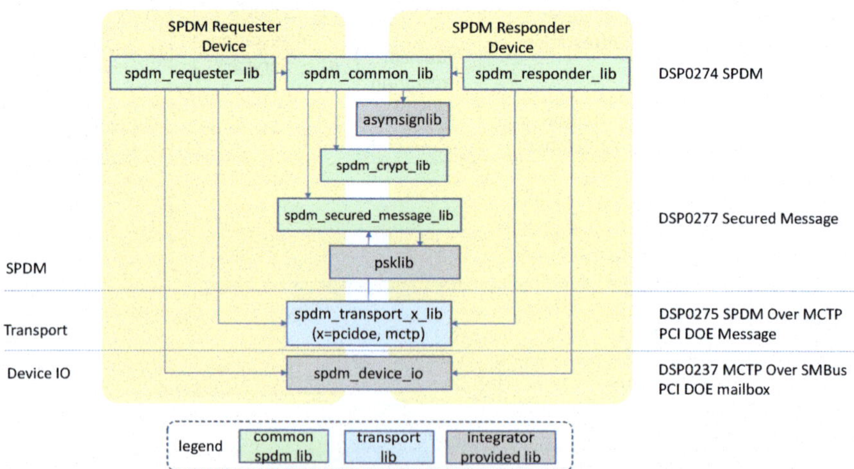

Figure 13.3 Libspdm architecture.

Responder-Validator is a test library for testing SPDM devices. Fig. 13.3 shows the various libraries within the libspdm architecture.

- spdm-rs: An SPDM protocol stack written in Rust, developed by Intel and contributed to the Confidential Computing Consortium (CCC) community. In addition to supporting SPDM, spdm-rs adds support for IDE and TDISP as defined in the PCIe specification for confidential computing.

TEE-IO interoperability testing tools include:

- SPDM-Responder-Validator: An open-source testing tool from DMTF used for testing SPDM devices. It includes test case documentation and a test library for the SPDM protocol.
- tee-io-validator: A test library from Intel used for testing TEE-IO devices. Besides the SPDM protocol, it includes test case documentation and a test library for PCIe specification IDE_KM and TDISP, as well as Compute Express Link (CXL) specification CXL_IDE_KM and TSP.

CHAPTER 14

TEE-IO attack and mitigation

In Chapter 13, we introduced software Software Development Kits (SDKs) related to TEE-IO. In this chapter, we will introduce attacks against TEE-IO and corresponding protections.

14.1 Attack methods

The TEE-IO architecture can be broadly divided into the host side, the device side, and the connection between the host and device. Attacks against the host-side trusted execution environment (TEE) discussed in Chapter 8 are still applicable in TEE-IO. Furthermore, TEE-IO exposes new attack surfaces, as shown in Fig. 14.1, including attacks on the TEE-IO device side and attacks on the host-device connection.

14.1.1 Attacking the TEE-IO host side

The TEE-IO architecture adds new functionality to the TEE host side, which also introduces potential attack points. Attacks related to the TEE part were described in Chapter 8 and will not be repeated here. This section introduces only new attack points related to TEE-IO.

14.1.1.1 Attacking the TEE-IO host-side TVM

The host-side TVM software needs to add device management functions. Attack points include these aspects.

- Attacking the device driver. For example, driver software vulnerabilities and ARM Mali GPU driver vulnerabilities.
- Attacking the device attestation process. For example, vulnerabilities in the attestation protocol flow and vulnerabilities in cryptographic implementations.
- Attacking host IOMMU management. For example, Funderbolt attacks, Thunderclap attacks and Thunderspy attacks.

Confidential Computing
ISBN 978-0-443-54067-7
https://doi.org/10.1016/B978-0-443-54067-7.00011-5

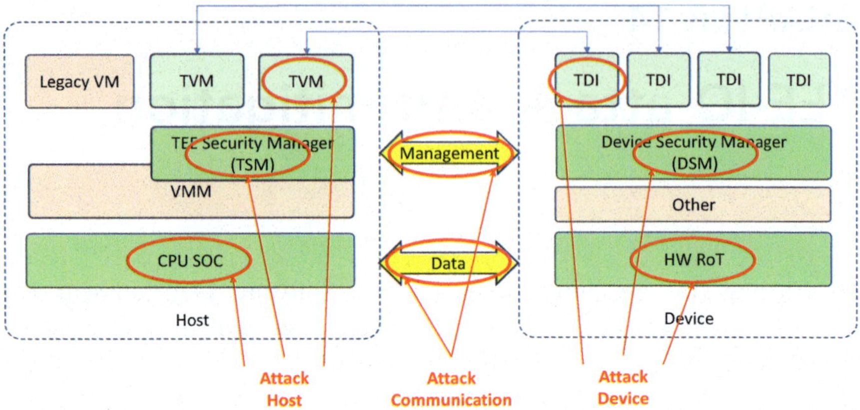

Figure 14.1 Attack surfaces in the TEE-IO architecture. *RoT*, Root of Trust; *HW*, Hardware; *SOC*, System on Chip; *TDI*, *TEE* Device Interface; *TVM*, TEE Virtual Machine; *VM*, Virtual Machine; *VMM*, Virtual Machine Manager.

14.1.1.2 Attacking the TEE-IO host-side trusted execution environment security manager

The host-side TEE Security Manager (TSM) and hardware need to provide mechanisms to securely manage device Memory Mapped Input/Output (MMIO), manage the Input/Output Memory Management Unit (IOMMU) to control Direct Memory Access (DMA) access, and control the encryption/decryption of IDE TLPs. Attack points include the following aspects:

- Attacking host MMIO access control hardware.
- Attacking host IOMMU and DMA access control hardware. For example, IOMMU occupancy side-channel attacks exploit the limited resources of the IOMMU (refer to "PCIe side-channel attack on I/O device via RDMA-enabled network card"). An attacker could use an Remote Direct Memory Access (RDMA) Network Interface Card (RNIC) to probe IOMMU work item allocation, thereby obtaining information about GPU execution.
- Attacking the host Integrity and Data Encryption (IDE) Transaction Layer Packet (TLP) encryption/decryption process.

The TEE Device Interface Security Protocol (TDISP) section of the Peripheral Component Interconnect Express (PCIe) specification defines a series of host-side security requirements, all of which can be considered attack points. We have already described them in detail in Chapter 9.

14.1.2 Attacking the TEE-IO device connection

The TEE-IO architecture requires a secure session connection to be established between the TEE and the device. Functionally, this can be divided into the management channel and the data channel. Regarding the implementation, it can involve software connections such as Transport Layer Security (TLS) or Security Protocol and Data Model (SPDM) protocols, as well as hardware connections. The IDE feature in the PCIe specification and CXL_IDE in the Compute Express Link (CXL) specification can serve as hardware-implemented secure data channels. Before these, devices could only rely on software for secure data channels.

14.1.2.1 Attacking the software connection of TEE-IO devices

Commonly used end-to-end secure session protocols in the industry include TLS and SPDM. TLS is a network transport layer security protocol published by the Internet Engineering Task Force (IETF), widely used for HTTP in browsers; a recent version is TLS 1.3. There are also various formal verifications of the TLS protocol to ensure the security of the protocol specification. There have been many attacks against TLS implementations, such as Heartbleed (exploiting buffer overflow owing to missing bounds check), POODLE (exploiting protocol version downgrade), and Raccoon (a side-channel vulnerability in TLS Diffie–Hellman (DH) key derivation). Open-source implementations of TLS such as OpenSSL, MbedTLS, and WolfSSL all have published implementation-related security advisories, with most common of which are buffer overflows and side-channel attacks. TLS can be an option, but in practice, device-side implementations often prefer the simpler and more practical SPDM protocol.

SPDM is a protocol published by DMTF for communication between platform components. SPDM 1.0 supports common Component Measurement and Authentication functions. SPDM 1.1 supports establishing secure sessions and mutual authentication. SPDM 1.2 adds device certificate deployment functionality, support for Device Identifier Composition Engine (DICE) devices, and Chinese cryptographic algorithms (Shang-Mi). SPDM 1.3 adds features such as asynchronous events, multikey support, end point information, Measurement Extension Log, and Hash Extended Measurement. Concurrently, security research on the SPDM protocol is evolving:

- SPDM 1.2 redesigned the digital signature transcript to include the Version-Capability-Algorithm (VCA) negotiation information, preventing attackers from using downgrade attacks. This addresses a

security issue in 1.0/1.1 where the signature form for MEASUREMENT messages did not include the VCA.
- In the SPDM 1.2 digital signature transcript, the signed message includes an spdm_prefix. This avoids the risk of signed message confusion.
- In SPDM 1.2, the calculation of the measurement summary hash uses the entire measurement block information, including Index and Type, not just the measurement value itself. This avoids the risk of measurement value length extension.
- SPDM 1.2 deprecated the CHALLENGE-based mutual authentication. Strictly speaking, the CHALLENGE mutual authentication was just two separate authentication steps without a mechanism to bind them. Therefore, SPDM 1.2 provides only mutual authentication based on secure sessions.
- SPDM 1.2 removed the InvalidSession error code to prevent information leakage.
- SPDM 1.3 strictly differentiates the session key derivation mechanisms for Ephemeral Diffie-Hellman (DHE) and Preshared Key (PSK), using different Salt_0 values, which aids formal proof.

Because SPDM is a relatively new secure session protocol, research and attacks on SPDM are limited. Cas Cremers, Dax, and Naska performed formal verification of SPDM and discovered vulnerabilities in the libspdm implementation. libspdm security advisory DMTF-2023-0001 describes a mutual authentication bypass attack. The SPDM specification defines two methods for mutual authentication: the first is certificate-based mutual authentication (Fig. 14.2a), in which the requester and responder initiate authentication with KEY_EXCHANGE, send certificates, and finally use FINISH to complete authentication. The second is PSK-based mutual authentication (Fig. 14.2b), in which the requester and responder initiate authentication with PSK_EXCHANGE and finally use PSK_FINISH. Either method alone achieves mutual authentication. However, if a device supports both methods simultaneously, an attacker could send KEY_EXCHANGE to complete the first part and then use PSK_FINISH to complete the second part. This mode switching can bypass the responder's authentication of the requester.

Secure session protocols generally use Authenticated Encryption with Associated Data (AEAD) algorithms for message encryption and MAC, because AEAD provides both confidentiality and integrity protection. Table 14.1 lists the AEAD parameters for SPDM and IDE, including

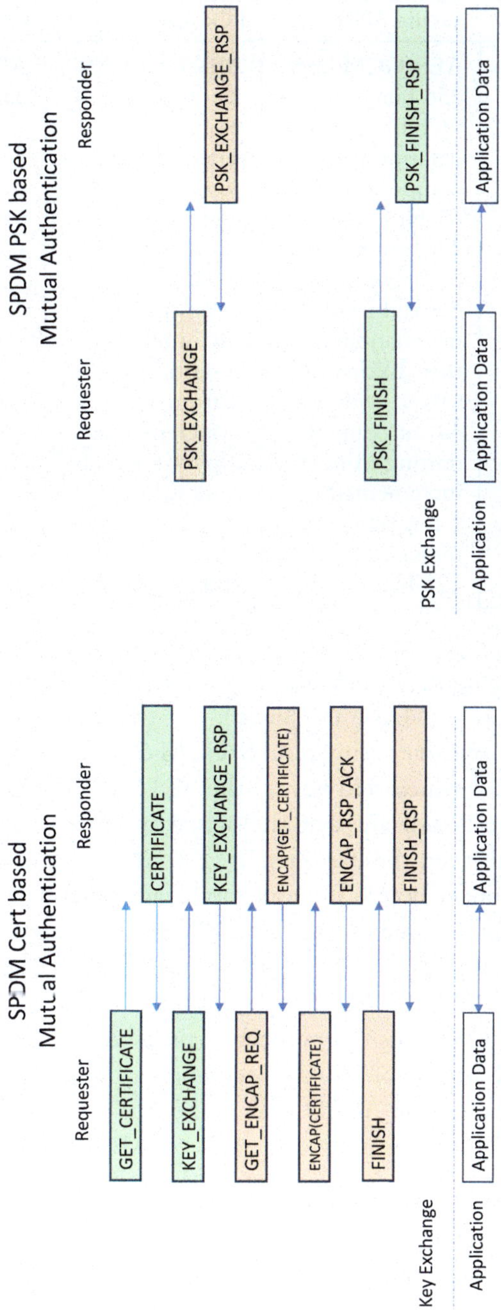

Figure 14.2 libspdm mutual authentication bypass attack. *PSK*, preshared key; *REQ*, Request; *RSP*, Response.

Table 14.1 AEAD parameters for SPDM and IDE.

Parameter	Secure SPDM	PCIe IDE	CXL IDE
Algorithm	AES-GCM-256	AES-GCM-256	AES-GCM-256
Key length	256 bits	256 bits	256 bits
Initialization Vector length	96 bits deterministic composition 64-bit counter The initial 96-bit value is derived from negotiation and then Exclusive ORed with a 64-bit counter starting from 0, incremented by 1 for each message.	96 bits deterministic composition 64-bit counter - Bits [95:64]: All 0 - Bits [63:0]: Counter starting from 1, incremented by 1 for each message.	96 bits deterministic composition 64-bit counter - Bits [95:92]: 1000b - Bits [91:64]: All 0 - Bits [63:0]: Counter starting from 1, incremented by 1 for each message.
MAC Tag length	128 bits	96 bits	96 bits

algorithm, key length, Initialization Vector (IV) length, and Message Authentication Code (MAC) tag length.

Table 14.1 shows that a single AES-GCM-256 key could theoretically be used up to 2^{64} times. However, the IETF drafts "Usage Limits on AEAD Algorithms" indicate that the actual number of IV uses may be significantly lower than the expected 2^{64}.

Assuming an upper bound on adversary attack probability p of 2^{-32}, according to the draft documents, the AEAD IV use limits shown in Table 14.2 can be derived. In the table, q represents the number of messages protected for confidentiality (number of AEAD encryptions), also known as the confidentiality limit. v represents the number of times an attacker can attempt to forge a message (number of AEAD decryption failures), also known as the integrity limit. The overall AEAD limit is the smaller of q and v.

An attacker could continuously collect AEAD messages until the AEAD limit is exceeded and then potentially achieve cryptanalysis.

14.1.2.2 Attacking the hardware connection of TEE-IO devices

According to the TDISP functionality defined in the PCIe specification, in the TEE-IO architecture, PCI TLP transmission between the device and

Table 14.2 AEAD IV use limits for SPDM and IDE (AES-GCM-256, $p = 2^{-32}$).

Parameter	Secure SPDM	PCIe IDE	CXL containment mode	CXL skid mode
L = Max AES blocks per message	4096	256	32	480
t = MAC length	128 bits	96 bits	96 bits	96 bits
q = Confidentiality limit	$2^{36.5}$	$2^{40.5}$	$2^{43.5}$	$2^{39.5}$
v = Integrity limit	2^{64}	2^{55}	2^{58}	2^{54}
AEAD limit	$2^{36.5}$	$2^{40.5}$	$2^{43.5}$	$2^{39.5}$

the host is protected by encryption using IDE. PCIe 5.0 IDE ECN added initial IDE support, which was integrated into the PCIe 6.0 specification. Regarding security, PCIe 6.0 additionally introduced Partial Header Encryption. Only the routing information part of the TLP header is transmitted in plaintext, whereas other parts of the header are encrypted as much as possible to reduce the risk of side-channel leakage. According to the paper "Controlled-channel attacks deterministic side channel for untrusted operating systems" by Xu, Cui, and Peinado, attackers can infer program flow by observing access patterns to different addresses.

TEE-IO requires the use of Selective IDE streams, so there is no security requirement for PCIe switches themselves. However, CXL IDE is a point-to-point secure link, so one must trust the CXL switches between the device and the host Root Port.

14.1.3 Attacking the TEE-IO device side

Because TEE-IO devices hold TEE confidential data, they are also potential attack points.

Side channels are a common method in TEE attacks. To build a secure TEE, architects and developers need to understand side-channel attack and defense principles thoroughly.

14.1.3.1 Attacking the TEE-IO device Root of Trust

The hardware Root of Trust (RoT) includes the measurement RoT, storage RoT, and reporting RoT for trusted boot, as well as the detection RoT, update RoT, and recovery RoT for resiliency. All of these can be the attack points.

In 2020, the Starbleed attack on Field-Programmable Gate Arrays (FPGAs) exploited register side-channel information leakage in Xilinx-7 FPGAs. Fig. 14.3 shows the design of a Xilinx-7 FPGA. The configuration bitstream contains the programming information for the FPGA. During the FPGA development phase, the bitstream is downloaded to the FPGA to turn

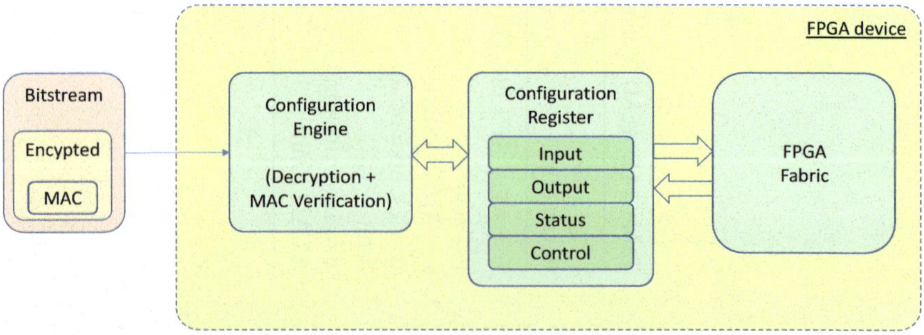

Figure 14.3 Xilinx-7 FPGA design.

the device into a functional device. To maintain the confidentiality and integrity of the hardware IP and the FPGA device, the bitstream is typically encrypted and protected with an MAC. Inside the FPGA, a configuration engine is responsible for decrypting the bitstream, verifying the MAC integrity, and then programming the FPGA fabric.

Fig. 14.4 illustrates the principle of the Starbleed attack. Ideally, any data should be verified before use. However, in Xilinx 7-series FPGAs, the FPGA configuration engine uses data from the bitstream before MAC verification. Simultaneously, Xilinx FPGAs have a nonvolatile register WBSTAR that is not cleared upon system reboot. In the Starbleed attack, the attacker modifies the bitstream data, causing the FPGA to write decrypted data into WBSTAR. After rebooting the FPGA, the malicious program can read the decrypted data from WBSTAR. Although only 4 bytes can be read per reboot, the attacker can repeat the process until all data are extracted. This is the first phase, aimed at breaking confidentiality. In the second phase, the attacker directly obtains the MAC key from the plaintext data—a cryptographic design flaw. As a result, the attacker can construct valid MACs, breaking authenticity.

Other forms of attack include using voltage glitching to attack the boot ROM of the NVIDIA Tegra X2 SoC (refer to "The Forgotten Threat of Voltage Glitching: A Case Study on Nvidia Tegra X2 SoCs"), and overwriting the EEPROM of PCIe switch devices (refer to "PCIe Device Attacks: Beyond DMA Exploiting PCIe Switches Messages and Errors").

14.1.3.2 Attacking the TEE-IO Device Security Manager

The Device Security Manager and hardware need to manage the device's identity and measurements, device and TEE Device Interface (TDI) configuration, TDI state, device resets, TDI memory isolation, and control the encryption/decryption of IDE TLPs. Attack points include these aspects:

- Attacking the device's identity or measurements: for example, malicious firmware updates or firmware SVN downgrade.

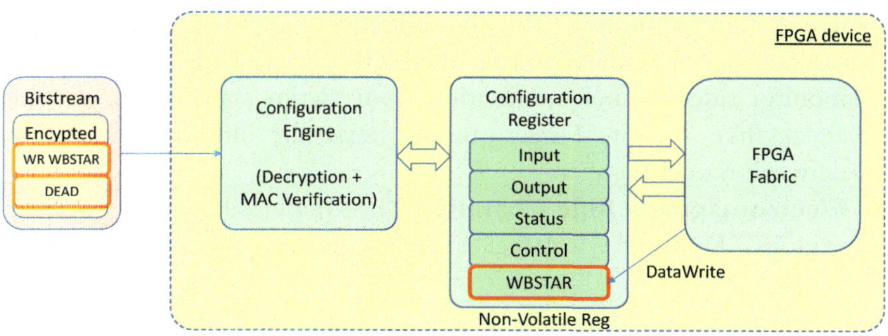

Figure 14.4 Principle of the Starbleed attack.

- Attacking the device's private MMIO space while the TDI is in CONFIG_LOCK or RUN state: for example, reading from or writing to private MMIO.
- Attacking the device's PCI configuration space while the TDI is in CONFIG_LOCK or RUN state: for example, reconfiguring MMIO BARs.
- Attacking the device's IDE TLP encryption/decryption process.
- Reading confidential data after IDE returns to the Insecure state.
- Reading confidential data after the device TDI returns to the ERROR or CONFIG_UNLOCK state.
- Reading confidential data or modifying security configurations after enabling device debug mode.

The TDISP section of the PCIe specification defines a series of device-side security requirements, all of which can become attack points. We have already described them in detail in Chapter 9.

14.1.3.3 Attacking the TEE-IO device TDI

The TDI is the functional module within the TEE-IO device. It receives input from the TEE, processes confidential data and may access confidential code and data. Therefore, protecting the TDI is crucial for the entire TEE-IO architecture.

TEE-IO devices are also susceptible to side-channel attacks. For example, side-channel attacks against GPUs include:

- **Instruction Information Leakage**: The CUDALeak attack exploits information leakage from Compute Unified Device Architecture (CUDA) instructions.
- **Cache Side Channels**: GPU key recovery timing attacks (refer to "A complete key recovery timing attack on a GPU"), GPU timing side channels (refer to "A timing side channel attack on a mobile GPU"), and the Trident attack exploit cache side channels on GPUs, leading to Advanced Encryption Standard (AES) key leakage.
- **GPU Software Side Channels**: The Rendered Insecure attack demonstrated the possibility of GPU side channels using methods like memory allocation APIs, performance counters, and timing measurements. "Side channel attacks on GPUs" used spy applications to monitor side-channel information from victim applications, enabling attacks like Website Fingerprinting, keystroke inference, and neural network model recovery.
- **Electromagnetic Side Channels**: The Graphics Peeping Unit attack exploits Dynamic Voltage and Frequency Scaling leading to

electromagnetic side-channel leakage: for example, for website fingerprinting and keystroke timing inference. The Clairvoyance attack uses GPU electromagnetic side channels to obtain information about Deep Neural Network (DNN) models.

- **Microarchitectural Side Channels**: The Spy in the GPU-box attack exploits shared L2 cache side channels in multi-GPU microarchitectures, allowing one GPU to obtain confidential information from a remote GPU.
- **GPU Algorithmic Side Channels**: The GPU.zip attack exploits data compression performed by GPUs, leading to pixel stealing from Scalable Vector Graphics filters.

Side-channel attacks exploiting the PCIe bus include:

- PCIe Bus Information: The Hermes Attack uses unencrypted PCIe packets to obtain information about DNN models.
- PCIe Traffic Congestion: The Invisible Probe attack exploits PCIe traffic congestion. When multiple devices are connected, an RNIC can attack a GPU for user input inference, webpage inference, or machine learning model inference. An Non-Volatile Memory Express (NVMe) device can attack a Network Interface Card for webpage inference. The LockedDown attack causes PCIe traffic congestion by locking page memory allocations via CUDA, enabling webpage inference. PCIe Bus Timing Attacks (refer to "Timing-based side channel attack and mitigation on PCIe connected distributed embedded systems"): When multiple devices (e.g., GPU/FPGA) share the PCIe bus simultaneously, a malicious device can probe the bus to learn about the data transmission timing and information of a victim device.

Fault injection must also be considered. There have been cases of using fault injection to attack Artificial Intelligence models:

- The Terminal Brain Damage attack and the DeepHammer attack use memory row hammer fault injection to attack DNN models.
- The Neural Machine Translation (NMT)-Stroke attack uses memory row hammer fault injection for bit flips, targeting NMT.

NVBitFI provides a fault injection tool for NVIDIA GPUs to test a program's error handling capabilities.

With the development of TEE-IO confidential computing, side-channel attacks targeting devices will become an effective attack vector and must be taken seriously, with protections implemented early on.

14.2 Protection principles

Addressing these attack methods, this section focuses on corresponding protection methods.

14.2.1 TEE-IO host-side protection

The software parts of the TEE and TSM should adhere to the secure software design principles discussed in Chapter 8, including cryptographic application security and side-channel protection. Special attention is needed for the security protection of new modules in the TEE-IO architecture.

14.2.1.1 TEE-IO host-side TVM

The host-side TVM is responsible for these tasks:

- Securely using device functions, handled by the device driver. Because the device may be attacked at any time, potentially transitioning to the TDI ERROR state or IDE Insecure state, the device driver cannot assume that the read private MMIO information is error-free. Before accessing MMIO data, the driver must check whether the device's error bits are set. Once an error bit is set, the driver needs to check the TDI state and perform necessary recovery.
- Securely managing device addition/removal, handled by the device management module. The VMM may add or remove devices at any time. The device management module needs to handle device state changes promptly.
- Verifying device identity and measurements, handled by the device attestation module. The device attestation module needs to update Certificate Revocation Lists (CRLs) and device reference values in a timely manner to prevent TVM from accepting outdated or vulnerable devices.

14.2.1.2 TEE-IO host-side trusted execution environment Security Manager

The host-side TSM is responsible for these tasks:

- Secure MMIO Management: The TSM needs to manage the list of private MMIO ranges. The VMM can only send MMIO modification requests to the TSM but cannot directly modify MMIO configurations.
- Secure DMA Management: The TSM needs to manage the trusted IOMMU, controlling DMA access to private memory. The VMM can only send IOMMU modification requests to the TSM but cannot directly access the trusted IOMMU configuration.
- Device Binding: The device used for establishing the SPDM secure protocol, identity authentication, measurement acquisition, establishing

IDE streams, and running trusted MMIO and DMA via the TDISP connection must be the same device.

- Controlling the host-side SoC PCIe Root Port's IDE configuration.

The TDISP section of the PCIe specification defines a series of host-side security requirements, all of which should be met. We have described them in detail in Chapter 9.

14.2.2 Protection for the TEE-IO device connection

The TEE-IO device connection typically involves a secure session protocol, which provides confidentiality and integrity.

14.2.2.1 Software connection for TEE-IO devices

The security of the software connection for TEE-IO devices is typically achieved using the SPDM protocol. For any secure protocol, these aspects generally need consideration:

- Security of the Protocol Specification: For example, performing formal verification of the SPDM protocol to prove that the protocol itself has no security vulnerabilities, including side-channel vulnerabilities via error messages.
- Security of the Protocol Cryptography: For example, when negotiating cryptographic algorithms, standardized algorithms should be used as much as possible, and algorithms with potential security threats should be filtered out, as detailed in Chapter 8.
- Security of the Protocol Implementation: For example, testing the SPDM protocol implementation, paying special attention to buffer overflows and side-channel security. When using third-party libraries, it is necessary to monitor security advisories and updates constantly.
- Security of the Protocol Application: For example, reviewing whether the method of using the SPDM protocol is secure, whether the input nonces are properly verified, whether SPDM session policies need to support device runtime updates, whether SPDM measurements are obtained inside or outside the secure session, whether measurements need periodic reacquisition, and so on.

According to IETF drafts "Usage Limits on AEAD Algorithms," the number of times an AEAD IV can be used may be significantly lower than the expected 2^{64}. Therefore, when using the SPDM protocol, timely SPDM key updates are necessary.

14.2.2.2 Hardware connection for TEE-IO devices

The security of the hardware connection for TEE-IO devices is typically achieved using the PCIe IDE protocol. Similar considerations apply:

- Security of the Protocol Specification: For example, performing formal verification of the IDE protocol to prove that the protocol itself has no security vulnerabilities, including side-channel risks.
- Security of the Protocol Implementation: For example, testing the IDE protocol implementation to ensure that requirements described in the PCIe specification for various scenarios are met. When using third-party IP libraries, it is necessary to monitor security advisories and updates constantly.
- Security of the Protocol Application: For example, deciding whether to use Selective IDE streams or Link IDE streams for PCIe IDE, and how to verify the security of CXL switches when using CXL IDE.

According to IETF drafts "Usage Limits on AEAD Algorithms," the number of times an AEAD IV can be used may be significantly lower than the expected 2^{64}. Therefore, when using IDE, timely key updates for the IDE streams are necessary.

14.2.3 TEE-IO device-side protection

TEE-IO devices need to follow general secure design principles. Several books can be referenced for guidance. *Introduction to FPGA Security*, by Huffmire et al. and *Embedded Systems Security: Practical Methods for Safe and Trustworthy Software and Systems Development*, by Kleidermacher summarize security design for FPGAs and embedded systems, respectively. *Building Secure Firmware*, by Yao and Zimmer summarizes methods for firmware security design, applicable to both system firmware and device firmware.

14.2.3.1 TEE-IO device Root of Trust

The hardware RoT needs to implement the measurement RoT, storage RoT, and reporting RoT securely for trusted boot. For example, existing TPM architectures or DICE architectures can be used. If choosing an independent RoT, a rigorous architecture review is necessary.

The hardware RoT needs to implement the detection RoT, update RoT, and recovery RoT securely for resiliency. More information can be found in NIST SP 800-193, "Platform Firmware Resiliency Guidelines."

14.2.3.2 TEE-IO Device Security Manager

The TDISP section of the PCIe specification defines a series of device-side security requirements. These security requirements should all be met. We have described them in detail in Chapter 9.

14.2.3.3 TEE-IO device TDI

The TDI is the functional unit. Protecting the TDI requires consideration of data confidentiality and integrity, with special attention needed to prevent side-channel attacks and fault injection attacks.

References

[1] BigData UN Global Working Group. UN handbook on privacy-preserving computation techniques. https://unstats.un.org/bigdata/task-teams/privacy/UN%20Handbook%20for%20Privacy-Preserving%20Techniques.pdf; 2023. https://arxiv.org/abs/2301.06167.

[2] Rivest R, Adleman L, Dertouzos M. On data banks and privacy homomorphisms. Foundations of Secure Computation; 1978. https://luca-giuzzi.unibs.it/corsi/Support/papers-cryptography/RAD78.pdf.

[3] Paillier P. Public-key cryptosystems based on composite degree residuosity classes. EUROCRYPT'99; 1999. https://link.springer.com/chapter/10.1007/3-540-48910-X_16.

[4] Craig G. Fully homomorphic encryption using ideal lattices. In: STOC'09: Proceedings of the Forty-First Annual ACM Symposium on Theory of Computing; 2009. https://dl.acm.org/doi/10.1145/1536414.1536440. https://www.cs.cmu.edu/~odonnell/hits09/gentry-homomorphic-encryption.pdf.

[5] Brakerski Z, Vaikuntanathan V. Efficient fully homomorphic encryption from (standard) LWE. In: 2011 IEEE 52nd Annual Symposium on Foundations of Computer Science; 2011. https://ieeexplore.ieee.org/document/6108154.

[6] Brakerski Z, Craig G, Vaikuntanathan V. (Leveled) fully homomorphic encryption without bootstrapping. In: ITCS '12: Proceedings of the 3rd Innovations in Theoretical Computer Science Conference; 2012. https://dl.acm.org/doi/10.1145/2090236.2090262. https://eprint.iacr.org/2011/277.

[7] Brakerski Z. Fully homomorphic encryption without modulus switching from classical GapSVP. In: Advances in cryptology—CRYPTO 2012; 2012. https://link.springer.com/chapter/10.1007/978-3-642-32009-5_50.

[8] Fan J, Vercauteren F. Somewhat practical fully homomorphic encryption. Cryptology ePrint Archive; 2012. https://eprint.iacr.org/2012/144.

[9] Craig G, Sahai A, Waters B. Homomorphic encryption from learning with errors: conceptually-simpler, asymptotically-faster, attribute-based. In: Advances in cryptology—CRYPTO 2013; 2013. https://link.springer.com/chapter/10.1007/978-3-642-40041-4_5.

[10] Jung HC, Kim A, Kim M, Song Y. Homomorphic encryption for arithmetic of approximate numbers. In: Advances in cryptology—ASIACRYPT 2017; 2017. https://link.springer.com/chapter/10.1007/978-3-319-70694-8_15.

[11] Zhong Y, Jiang L, Fang J. Cyberspace security technology—homomorphic encryption. China Machine Press, 2022.

[12] Cheng Z. Fully homomorphic encryption—from theory to practice. Tsinghua University Press; 2022.

[13] Yao AC. Protocols for secure computations. In: 23rd Annual Symposium on Foundations of Computer Science (SFCS 1982); 1982. https://ieeexplore.ieee.org/document/4568388.

[14] Rabin M. How to exchange secrets with oblivious transfer. In: Harvard University Technical Report, vol 81; 1981. https://eprint.iacr.org/2005/187.

[15] Evan S, Goldreich O, Lempel A. A randomized protocol for signing contract. Commun ACM 1985. https://dl.acm.org/doi/10.1145/3812.3818.

[16] Brassard G, Crepeau C, Robert J-M. Information theoretic reductions among disclosure problems. In: 27th Annual Symposium on Foundations of Computer Science (SFCS 1986); 1986. https://ieeexplore.ieee.org/document/4568208.

[17] Yao AC. How to generate and exchange secrets. In: 27th Annual Symposium on Foundations of Computer Science (SFCS 1986); 1986. https://ieeexplore.ieee.org/document/4568207.
[18] Goldreich O, Micali S, Wigderson A. How to play ANY mental game. In: STOC'87: Proceedings of the Nineteenth Annual ACM Symposium on Theory of Computing; 1987. https://dl.acm.org/doi/10.1145/28395.28420.
[19] Beaver D, Micali S, Rogaway P. The round complexity of secure protocols. In: STOC'90: Proceedings of the Twenty-Second Annual ACM Symposium on Theory of Computing; 1990. https://dl.acm.org/doi/10.1145/100216.100287.
[20] Shamir A. How to share a secret. Commun ACM 1979. https://dl.acm.org/doi/10.1145/359168.359176.
[21] Blakley GR. Safeguarding cryptographic keys. In: 1979 International Workshop on Managing Requirements Knowledge (MARK); 1979. https://ieeexplore.ieee.org/document/8817296.
[22] Ben-Or M, Goldwasser S, Wigderson A. Completeness theorems for non-cryptographic fault-tolerant distributed computation. In: STOC'88: Proceedings of the Twentieth Annual ACM Symposium on Theory of Computing; 1988. https://dl.acm.org/doi/10.1145/62212.62213.
[23] Chaum D, Crepeau C, Damgard I. Multiparty unconditionally secure protocols. In: STOC'88: Proceedings of the Twentieth annual ACM Symposium on Theory of Computing; 1988. https://dl.acm.org/doi/10.1145/62212.62214.
[24] Evans D, Kolesnikov V, Rosulek M. A Pragmatic introduction to secure multi-party computation. Now Publishers; 2019.
[25] Goldwasser S, Micali S, Rackoff C. The knowledge complexity of interactive proof-systems. In: STOC'85: Proceedings of the Seventeenth Annual ACM Symposium on Theory of Computing; 1985. https://dl.acm.org/doi/10.1145/22145.22178.
[26] Quisquater J-J, Quisquater M, Quisquater M, Quisquater M, Guillou L, Guillou MA, Guillou G, Guillou A, Guillou G, Guillou S. How to explain zero-knowledge protocols to your children. In: Advances in Cryptology—CRYPTO' 89 Proceedings; 1989. https://link.springer.com/chapter/10.1007/0-387-34805-0_60.
[27] Schnorr CP. Efficient signature generation by smart cards. J Cryptol 1991. https://link.springer.com/article/10.1007/BF00196725.
[28] Groth J. Short pairing-based non-interactive zero-knowledge arguments. In: Advances in cryptology—ASIACRYPT 2010; 2010. https://link.springer.com/chapter/10.1007/978-3-642-17373-8_19.
[29] Nir B, Ran C, Chiesa A, Tromer E. From extractable collision resistance tosuccinct non-interactive arguments of knowledge, and back again. In: Proceedings of the 3rd Innovations in Theoretical Computer Science Conference; 2012. https://dl.acm.org/doi/10.1145/2090236.2090263. https://eprint.iacr.org/2011/443.
[30] Ben-Sasson E, Bentov I, Horesh Y, Riabzev M. Scalable, transparent, and post-quantum secure computational integrity. IACR Cryptology ePrint Archive; 2018. https://eprint.iacr.org/2018/046.
[31] Dwork C, Kenthapadi K, McSherry F, Mironov I, Naor M. Our data, ourselves: privacy via distributed noise generation. In: Advances in cryptology—EUROCRYPT 2006; 2006. https://link.springer.com/chapter/10.1007/11761679_29.
[32] Stanley L. Warner. Randomized response: a survey technique for eliminating evasive answer bias. J Am Stat Assoc 1965;60(309). https://www.csc2.ncsu.edu/faculty/mpsingh/local/Social/f15/wrap/readings/Warner-Randomized-Response-2283137.pdf.

[33] Nissim K, Steinke T, Wood A, Altman M, Bembenek A, Bun M, Gaboardi M, O'Brien D, Vadhan S. Differential privacy: a primer for a non-technical audience. Vanderbilt J Entertain Technol Law 2018. https://scholarship.law.vanderbilt.edu/jetlaw/vol21/iss1/4/.
[34] McMahan B, Moore E, Ramage D, Hampson S, Arcas BAy. Communication-efficient learning of deep networks from decentralized data. In: Proceedings of the 20th International Conference on Artificial Intelligence and Statistics, PMLR 54; 2017. p. 1273–82. https://arxiv.org/abs/1602.05629.
[35] IEEE. IEEE3652.1-2020—IEEE guide for architectural framework and application of federated machine learning. https://standards.ieee.org/ieee/3652.1/7453/; 2020.
[36] Cheng K, Yang Q. Privacy preserving computing. Publishing House of Electronics Industry; 2022.
[37] Li W. Head first privacy preserving computation. China Machine Press; 2022.
[38] (China) Privacy preserving computing alliance. In: Research report on privacy computing communication applications; 2022. https://www.secrss.com/articles/50811.
[39] Confidential Computing Consortium. https://confidentialcomputing.io/; 2023.
[40] Confidential Computing Consortium. Common terminology for confidential computing. 2022. https://confidentialcomputing.io/wp-content/uploads/sites/10/2023/03/Common-Terminology-for-Confidential-Computing.pdf.
[41] Confidential Computing Consortium. A technical analysis of confidential computing v1.3. https://confidentialcomputing.io/wp-content/uploads/sites/10/2023/03/CCC-A-Technical-Analysis-of-Confidential-Computing-v1.3_unlocked.pdf; 2022.
[42] Confidential Computing Consortium. Confidential computing: hardware-based trusted execution for applications and data. https://confidentialcomputing.io/wp-content/uploads/sites/10/2023/03/CCC_outreach_whitepaper_updated_November_2022.pdf; 2022.
[43] NIST. NIST SP800-193 platform firmware resiliency guidelines. 2018. https://nvlpubs.nist.gov/nistpubs/SpecialPublications/NIST.SP.800-193.pdf.
[44] Schuster F. Welcome keynote and Introduction to confidential computing. OC3; 2023. https://www.oc3.dev/speakers-and-talks.
[45] Feng D. From trusted computing to confidential computing. In: Invited Report CNCC2021; 2021. https://mp.weixin.qq.com/s?__biz=MjM5MTY5ODE4OQ==&mid=2651514996&idx=1&sn=137088888feb23620cbb7c0ee8d49c05&chksm=bd4fd4168a385d00a7616aef7a8b379558bbb1558088742c9e50dfafc0f8b8a7968e5478ad11&scene=27.
[46] Intel. Software guard extensions. 2023. https://www.intel.com/content/www/us/en/developer/tools/software-guard-extensions/overview.html.
[47] Intel. Trust domain extensions. 2023. https://www.intel.com/content/www/us/en/developer/tools/trust-domain-extensions/overview.html.
[48] AMD. Secure encrypted virtualization. 2023. https://www.amd.com/en/developer/sev.html.
[49] ARM. Confidential compute architecture. 2023. https://www.arm.com/architecture/security-features/arm-confidential-compute-architecture.
[50] RISC-V. Confidential VM extension. 2023. https://github.com/riscv-non-isa/riscv-ap-tee. https://github.com/riscv-non-isa/riscv-ap-tee-io.
[51] NVIDIA. Confidential computing. 2023. https://docs.nvidia.com/confidential-computing/.
[52] ARM. TrustZone. 2023. https://www.arm.com/technologies/trustzone-for-cortex-a. https://www.arm.com/technologies/trustzone-for-cortex-m.
[53] Keystone. 2023. https://keystone-enclave.org/.
[54] Hex-Five. MultiZone. 2023. https://hex-five.com/multizone-security-tee-riscv/.

[55] SJTU. Penglai enclave. 2023. https://penglai-enclave.systems/.
[56] Apple. Apple T2 security chip overview. 2018. https://www.apple.com/mideast/mac/docs/Apple_T2_Security_Chip_Overview.pdf.
[57] Google. How does the Google Titan M2 and Tensor security core work?. 2021. https://www.androidcentral.com/how-does-google-titan-m2-and-tensor-security-core-work.
[58] Amazon. The security design of the AWS nitro system. 2024. https://docs.aws.amazon.com/pdfs/whitepapers/latest/security-design-of-aws-nitro-system/security-design-of-aws-nitro-system.pdf.
[59] TCG. TPM 2.0 library specification. 2024. https://trustedcomputinggroup.org/resource/tpm-library-specification/.
[60] Open container initiative (OCI). 2023. https://opencontainers.org/.
[61] Occlum. 2023. https://occlum.io/.
[62] Gramine. 2023. https://gramineproject.io/.
[63] Enarx. 2023. https://enarx.dev/.
[64] Open enclave. 2023. https://openenclave.io/.
[65] Mo F, Tarkhani Z, Haddadi H. Machine learning with confidential computing: a systematization of knowledge. ACM Comput Surv 2024;56(11). https://dl.acm.org/doi/10.1145/3670007. https://arxiv.org/abs/2208.10134.
[66] Mohan A, Ye M, Franke H, Srivatsa M, Liu Z, Gonzalez N. Securing AI inference in the cloud: is CPU-GPU confidential computing ready? IEEE Cloud 2024. https://research.ibm.com/publications/securing-ai-inference-in-the-cloud-is-cpu-gpu-confidential-computing-ready.
[67] Gueron S. A memory encryption engine suitable for general purpose processors. Cryptology ePrint Archive; 2016. https://eprint.iacr.org/2016/204.
[68] Goldreich O, Ostrovsky R. Software protection and simulation on oblivious RAMs. J ACM 1996;43(3). https://dl.acm.org/doi/10.1145/233551.233553.
[69] ARM. Building a secure system using TrustZone technology. 2009. https://developer.arm.com/documentation/PRD29-GENC-009492/latest/.
[70] Saltzer J, Schroeder M. The protection of information in computer systems. Proc IEEE 1975. https://www.cs.virginia.edu/~evans/cs551/saltzer/.
[71] Smith RE. A contemporary look at Saltzer and Schroeder's 1975 design principles. IEEE Secur Privacy 2012. https://ieeexplore.ieee.org/document/6226346.
[72] Lampson B, Abadi M, Burrows M, Wobber E. Authentication in distributed systems: theory and practice. In: ACM transactions on computer systems; 1992. https://dl.acm.org/doi/10.1145/138873.138874.
[73] Department of Defense (US). Trusted computer system evaluation criteria. In: DOD 5200.28—STD; 1985. https://csrc.nist.rip/publications/history/dod85.pdf.
[74] NIST. TCB definition. 2023. https://csrc.nist.gov/glossary/term/tcb.
[75] Tanenbaum-Torvalds dabate. 2023. https://www.cs.vu.nl/~ast/reliable-os/.
[76] TCG. TPM 2.0 library. 2019. https://trustedcomputinggroup.org/resource/tpm-library-specification/.
[77] TCG. PC client platform firmware profile specification. 2023. https://trustedcomputinggroup.org/resource/pc-client-specific-platform-firmware-profile-specification/.
[78] (China) State Cryptography Administration. GM/T0012-2020 Trusted computing interface specification of trusted cryptography module. 2020.
[79] TCG. D-RTM architecture specification. 2013. https://trustedcomputinggroup.org/resource/d-rtm-architecture-specification/.
[80] NIST. RoT definition. 2023. https://csrc.nist.gov/glossary/term/roots_of_trust.
[81] NIST. Post-Quantum cryptography. 2023. https://csrc.nist.gov/projects/post-quantum-cryptography.

[82] NIST. FIPS 203—Module-lattice-based key-encapsulation mechanism standard. 2023. https://csrc.nist.gov/pubs/fips/203/final.

[83] NIST. FIPS 204—Module-lattice-based digital signature standard. 2023. https://csrc.nist.gov/pubs/fips/204/final.

[84] NIST. FIPS 205—Stateless hash-based digital signature standard. 2023. https://csrc.nist.gov/pubs/fips/205/final.

[85] NIST. SP800-208—Recommendation for stateful hash-based signature schemes. 2020. https://csrc.nist.gov/pubs/sp/800/208/final.

[86] NIST. FIPS 197—Advanced encryption standard (AES). 2023. https://csrc.nist.gov/pubs/fips/197/final.

[87] NIST. FIPS 180-4—Secure hash standard (SHS). 2015. https://csrc.nist.gov/pubs/fips/180-4/upd1/final.

[88] NSA. Commercial national security algorithm suite 2.0. 2022. https://media.defense.gov/2022/Sep/07/2003071834/-1/-1/0/CSA_CNSA_2.0_ALGORITHMS_.PDF.

[89] Spectre and meltdown attack. 2023. https://spectreattack.com/. https://meltdownattack.com/.

[90] Intel. Understanding Intel software guard extensions. 2023. https://www.intel.com/content/www/us/en/architecture-and-technology/software-guard-extensions-enhanced-data-protection.html.

[91] McKeen F, Alexandrovich I, Berenzon A, Rozas C, Shafi H, Shanbhogue V, Savagaonkar U. Innovative instructions and software model for isolated execution. Hardware and Architectural Support for Security and Privacy (HASP); 2013. https://dl.acm.org/doi/10.1145/2487726.2488368. https://citeseerx.ist.psu.edu/document?repid=rep1&type=pdf&doi=ec79422e0bfdb61d8b6d2a6ec5b2dfbcab970852.

[92] Anati I, Gueron S, Johnson SP, Scarlata VR. Innovative technology for CPU based attestation and sealing. Intel Whitepaper; 2013. https://www.intel.com/content/www/us/en/developer/articles/technical/innovative-technology-for-cpu-based-attestation-and-sealing.html.

[93] Intel. Intel SGX introduction. 2015. https://www.intel.com/content/dam/develop/external/us/en/documents/332680-002-600685.pdf.

[94] Costan V, Devadas S. Intel SGX explained. Cryptology ePrint Archive; 2016. https://eprint.iacr.org/2016/086.

[95] Costan V, Lebedev I, Devadas S. Secure processors Part I: background, taxonomy for secure enclaves and intel SGX architecture. Now Foundations and Trends; 2017. https://ieeexplore.ieee.org/document/8186867.

[96] Costan V, Lebedev I, Devadas S. Secure processors Part II: intel SGX security analysis and MIT sanctum architecture. Now Foundations and Trends; 2017. https://ieeexplore.ieee.org/document/8187110.

[97] Kim Y, Daly R, Kim J, Fallin C, Lee JH, Lee D, Wilkerson C, Lai K, Mutlu O. Flipping bits in memory without accessing them: an experimental study of DRAM disturbance errors. In: 2014 ACM/IEEE 41st International Symposium on Computer Architecture (ISCA); 2014. https://ieeexplore.ieee.org/document/6853210.

[98] SSLab. Georgia institute of technology. SGX 101. 2023. https://sgx101.gitbook.io/sgx101/.

[99] Weichbrodt N, Kurmus A, Pietzuch P, Kapitza R. AsyncShock: exploiting synchronisation bugs in intel SGX enclaves. In: Computer security—ESORICS 2016; 2016. https://link.springer.com/chapter/10.1007/978-3-319-45744-4_22.

[100] Götzfried J, Eckert M, Schinzel S, Müller T. Cache attacks on intel SGX. In: EuroSec'17: Proceedings of the 10th European Workshop on Systems Security; 2017. https://dl.acm.org/doi/10.1145/3065913.3065915.

[101] Lee S, Shih M-W, Gera P, Kim T, Kim H, Peinado M. Inferring fine-grained control flow inside SGX enclaves with branch shadowing. In: SEC'17: Proceedings of the 26th USENIX Conference on Security Symposium; 2017. https://www.usenix.org/conference/usenixsecurity17/technical-sessions/presentation/lee-sangho.

[102] Van Bulck J, Piessens F, Strackx R. SGX-step: a practical attack framework for precise enclave execution control. In: SysTEX'17: Proceedings of the 2nd Workshop on System Software for Trusted Execution; 2017. https://dl.acm.org/doi/10.1145/3152701.3152706.

[103] Van Bulck J, Minkin M, Weisse O, Genkin D, Kasikci B, Piessens F, Silberstein M, Wenisch TF, Yarom Y, Strackx R. Foreshadow: extracting the keys to the intel SGX kingdom with transient out-of-order execution. In: SEC'18: Proceedings of the 27th USENIX Conference on Security Symposium; 2018. https://www.usenix.org/conference/usenixsecurity18/presentation/bulck.

[104] Van Bulck J, Piessens F, Strackx R. SGX-step: a practical attack framework for precise enclave execution control. In: SysTEX'17: Proceedings of the 2nd Workshop on System Software for Trusted Execution; 2017. https://dl.acm.org/doi/10.1145/3152701.3152706.

[105] Chen G, Chen S, Xiao Y, Zhang Y, Lin Z, Lai TH. SgxPectre: stealing intel secrets from SGX enclaves via speculative execution. In: 2019 IEEE European Symposium on Security and Privacy (EuroS&P); 2019. https://ieeexplore.ieee.org/abstract/document/8806740.

[106] Murdock K, Oswald D, Garcia FD, Bulck JVan, Gruss D, Pludervolt FP. Software-based fault injection attacks against intel SGX. In: 2020 IEEE Symposium on Security and Privacy (SP); 2020. https://ieeexplore.ieee.org/document/9152636.

[107] Puddu I, Schneider M, Haller M, Čapkun S. Frontal attack: leaking control-flow in SGX via the CPU frontend. In: SEC'21: Proceedings of the 30th USENIX Conference on Security Symposium; 2021. https://www.usenix.org/conference/usenixsecurity21/presentation/puddu.

[108] Wang J, Fan CY, Cheng YQ, Zhao B, Wei T, Yan F, Zhang HG, Ma J. Analysis and research on SGX technology. J Software 2018;29(9):2018. https://www.jos.org.cn/html/2018/9/5594.htm.

[109] Fei S, Yan Z, Ding W, Xie H. Security vulnerabilities of SGX and countermeasures: a survey. ACM Comput Surv 2021;54(6). https://dl.acm.org/doi/10.1145/3456631.

[110] Intel. Managed runtime speculative execution side channel mitigations. 2018. https://www.intel.com/content/www/us/en/developer/articles/technical/software-security-guidance/secure-coding/security-best-practices-side-channel-resistance.html.

[111] Intel. Security best practices for side channel resistance. 2019. https://www.intel.com/content/www/us/en/developer/articles/technical/software-security-guidance/secure-coding/security-best-practices-side-channel-resistance.html.

[112] Intel. Guidelines for mitigating timing side channels against cryptographic implementations. 2022. https://www.intel.com/content/www/us/en/developer/articles/technical/software-security-guidance/secure-coding/mitigate-timing-side-channel-crypto-implementation.html.

[113] Intel. Intel trust domain extensions (Intel TDX). 2023. https://cdrdv2.intel.com/v1/dl/getContent/690419.

[114] Intel. Runtime encryption of memory with Intel total memory encryption–multi-key (Intel TME-MK). 2023. https://www.intel.com/content/www/us/en/developer/articles/news/runtime-encryption-of-memory-with-intel-tme-mk.html.

[115] Intel. Intel TDX module 1.0 specification. 2023. https://cdrdv2.intel.com/v1/dl/getContent/733568.

[116] Aktas E, Cohen C, Eads J, Forshaw J, Wilhelm F. Intel trust domain extensions (TDX) security review. April 2023. https://services.google.com/fh/files/misc/intel_tdx_-_full_report_041423.pdf. https://cloud.google.com/blog/products/identity-security/rsa-google-intel-confidential-computing-more-secure/.

[117] Cheng P-C, Ozga W, Valdez E, Ahmed S, Gu Z, Jamjoom H, Franke H, Bottomley J. Intel TDX demystified: a top-down approach. In: Cryptography and security; March 2023. https://arxiv.org/abs/2303.15540.

[118] Intel. Trust domain security guidance for developers. 2023. https://www.intel.com/content/www/us/en/developer/articles/technical/software-security-guidance/best-practices/trusted-domain-security-guidance-for-developers.html.

[119] Intel. Intel trust domain extension guest kernel hardening documentation. 2023. https://intel.github.io/ccc-linux-guest-hardening-docs/index.html.

[120] Intel. MKTME side channel impact on intel TDX. 2023. https://www.intel.com/content/www/us/en/developer/articles/technical/software-security-guidance/best-practices/mktme-side-channel-impact-on-intel-tdx.html.

[121] Intel. Intel TDX connect architecture specification. 2023. https://cdrdv2.intel.com/v1/dl/getContent/773614.

[122] AMD. TLB poisoning attacks on AMD secure encrypted virtualization (SEV). 2023. https://www.amd.com/en/resources/product-security/bulletin/amd-sb-1023.html.

[123] AMD. AMD SEV-SNP: Strengthening VM isolation with integrity protection and more. 2020. https://www.amd.com/system/files/TechDocs/SEV-SNP-strengthening-vm-isolation-with-integrity-protection-and-more.pdf.

[124] Du Z-H, Ying Z, Ma Z, Mai Y, Wang P, Liu J, Fang J. Secure encrypted virtualization is unsecure. In: Cryptography and security; 2017. https://arxiv.org/abs/1712.05090.

[125] Morbitzer M, Huber M, Horsch J, Wessel S. SEVered: subverting AMD's virtual machine encryption. In: Proceedings of the 11th European Workshop on Systems Security; 2018. https://dl.acm.org/doi/10.1145/3193111.3193112.

[126] Buhren R, Werling C, Seifert J-P. Insecure until proven updated: analyzing AMD SEV's remote attestation. In: Proceedings of the 2019 ACM SIGSAC Conference on Computer and Communications Security; 2019. https://dl.acm.org/doi/10.1145/3319535.3354216.

[127] Buhren R, Jacob H-N, Krachenfels T, Seifert J-P. One Glitch to rule them all: fault injection attacks against AMD's secure encrypted virtualization. In: CCS'21: Proceedings of the 2021 ACM SIGSAC Conference on Computer and Communications Security; 2021. https://dl.acm.org/doi/abs/10.1145/3460120.3484779.

[128] Li M, Zhang Y, Lin Z, Solihin Y. Exploiting unprotected I/O operations in AMD's secure encrypted virtualization. In: Proceedings of the 28th USENIX Security Symposium; 2019. https://www.usenix.org/conference/usenixsecurity19/presentation/li-mengyuan.

[129] Li M, Zhang Y, Li K, Cheng Y. TLB poisoning attacks on AMD secure encrypted virtualization. In: ACSAC'21: Annual Computer Security Applications Conference; 2021. https://dl.acm.org/doi/10.1145/3485832.3485876.

[130] Li M, Zhang Y, Lin Z. CrossLine: breaking "Security-by-Crash" based memory isolation in AMD SEV. In: CCS'21: Proceedings of the 2021 ACM SIGSAC Conference on Computer and Communications Security; 2021. https://dl.acm.org/doi/abs/10.1145/3460120.3485253.

[131] Li M, Zhang Y, Wang H, Li K, Cheng Y. CIPHERLEAKS: breaking constant-time cryptography on AMD SEV via the ciphertext side channel. In: Proceedings of the 30th USENIX Security Symposium; 2021. https://www.usenix.org/conference/usenixsecurity21/presentation/li-mengyuan.

[132] Li M, Wilke L, Wichelmann J, Eisenbarth T, Teodorescu R, Zhang Y. A systematic look at ciphertext side channels on AMD SEV-SNP. In: 2022 IEEE Symposium on Security and Privacy (SP); 2022. https://ieeexplore.ieee.org/document/9833768.
[133] Cohen C, Forshaw J, Horn J, Brand M. AMD secure processor for confidential computing security review. 2022. https://storage.googleapis.com/gweb-uniblog-publish-prod/documents/AMD_GPZ-Technical_Report_FINAL_05_2022.pdf. https://cloud.google.com/blog/products/identity-security/google-amd-partner-to-build-a-more-secure-future-with-confidential-computing.
[134] AMD. Technical guidance for mitigating effects of ciphertext visibility under AMD SEV. https://www.amd.com/system/files/documents/221404394-a_security_wp_final.pdf; 2022.
[135] AMD. AMD SEV-TIO: trusted I/O for secure encrypted virtualization. https://www.amd.com/content/dam/amd/en/documents/developer/sev-tio-whitepaper.pdf; 2023.
[136] ARM. ARM confidential compute architecture. 2023. https://www.arm.com/architecture/security-features/arm-confidential-compute-architecture.
[137] ARM. DEN0125—Learn the architecture—Introducing arm confidential compute architecture. https://developer.arm.com/documentation/den0125/latest; 2023.
[138] ARM. DEN0129—Arm realm management extension (RME) system architecture. https://developer.arm.com/documentation/den0129/latest; 2023.
[139] ARM. DEN0096—ARM CCA security model 1.0. https://developer.arm.com/documentation/DEN0096/latest; 2021.
[140] ARM. Speculative processor vulnerability latest updates. https://developer.arm.com/Arm%20Security%20Center/Speculative%20Processor%20Vulnerability%20Latest%20Updates; 2023.
[141] RISC-V. CoVE specification. 2023. https://github.com/riscv-non-isa/riscv-ap-tee.
[142] RISC-V. RISC-V platform security model. 2023. https://github.com/riscv-non-isa/riscv-security-model.
[143] RISC-V. Memory tracking table for supervisor domain isolation specification. https://github.com/riscv/riscv-smmtt; 2023.
[144] RISC-V. Transient execution—Implementer's security guide (DRAFT). 2023. https://github.com/riscv-admin/uarch-side-channels/blob/main/docs/transient_implementer_guide.adoc.
[145] RISC-V. CoVE-IO specification. https://github.com/riscv-non-isa/riscv-ap-tee-io; 2023.
[146] Intel. Intel 64 and IA-32 architectures software developer's manuals. https://www.intel.com/content/www/us/en/developer/articles/technical/intel-sdm.html; 2023.
[147] Quarkslab. Overview of intel SGX—Part 1 SGX internals. https://blog.quarkslab.com/overview-of-intel-sgx-part-1-sgx-internals.html; 2018.
[148] Quarkslab. Overview of intel SGX—Part 2 SGX externals. https://blog.quarkslab.com/overview-of-intel-sgx-part-2-sgx-externals.html; 2018.
[149] Intel. Intel trust domain extensions. 2023. https://cdrdv2.intel.com/v1/dl/getContent/690419.
[150] Intel. Intel trusted execution technology (intel TXT)—Software development guide. https://www.intel.com/content/www/us/en/content-details/315168/intel-trusted-execution-technology-intel-txt-software-development-guide.html; 2023.
[151] Intel. Intel TDX loader interface specification. https://cdrdv2.intel.com/v1/dl/getContent/733584; 2022.
[152] Intel. Intel TDX virtual firmware design guide. 2022. https://cdrdv2.intel.com/v1/dl/getContent/733585.

[153] AMD. AMD SEV-SNP: strengthening VM isolation with integrity protection and more. https://www.amd.com/system/files/TechDocs/SEV-SNP-strengthening-vm-isolation-with-integrity-protection-and-more.pdf; 2020.
[154] AMD. SEV secure nested page firmware ABI specification. https://www.amd.com/system/files/TechDocs/56860.pdf; 2022.
[155] ARM. DEN0126—Learning the architecture—Realm management extension. https://developer.arm.com/documentation/den0126/latest; 2021.
[156] ARM. DEN0127—Learning the architecture—ARM confidential compute architecture software stack. https://developer.arm.com/documentation/den0127/latest; 2023.
[157] RISC-V. Confidential VM extension (CoVE) for confidential computing on RISC-V platforms. https://github.com/riscv-non-isa/riscv-ap-tee/blob/main/specification/riscv-cove.pdf; 2023.
[158] IETF. RFC9334—Remote attestation procedures architecture. 2023. https://datatracker.ietf.org/doc/rfc9334/.
[159] ARM. DEN0127—Learning the architecture—ARM confidential compute architecture software stack. https://developer.arm.com/documentation/den0127/latest; 2023.
[160] Prem Swami Y. Intel SGX remote Attestation is not sufficient. BlackHat USA; 2017. https://www.blackhat.com/us-17/briefings.html#intel-sgx-remote-attestation-is-not-sufficient.
[161] TCG. Trusted platform module library family 2.0. https://trustedcomputinggroup.org/resource/tpm-library-specification/; 2019.
[162] TCG. Platform firmware profile specification. 2023. https://trustedcomputinggroup.org/resource/pc-client-specific-platform-firmware-profile-specification/.
[163] Arthur W, Challener D. A practical guide to TPM 2.0. APress; 2015.
[164] TCG. TCG D-RTM architecture. https://trustedcomputinggroup.org/resource/d-rtm-architecture-specification/; 2013.
[165] Microsoft. ProtectKeyWithTPM method of the Win32_EncryptableVolume class. https://learn.microsoft.com/en-us/windows/win32/secprov/protectkeywithtpm-win32-encryptablevolume; 2021.
[166] Linux UAPI Group. Linux TPM PCR registry. https://uapi-group.org/specifications/specs/linux_tpm_pcr_registry/; 2023.
[167] TCG. TCG EK credential profile for TPM family 2.0. https://trustedcomputinggroup.org/resource/http-trustedcomputinggroup-org-wp-content-uploads-tcg-ek-credential-profile-v-2-5-r2_published-pdf/; 2023.
[168] tpm2-software. TPM remote attestation best known method. 2019. https://tpm2-software.github.io/tpm2-tss/getting-started/2019/12/18/Remote-Attestation.html.
[169] TCG. Platform firmware integrity measurement. https://trustedcomputinggroup.org/resource/tcg-pc-client-platform-firmware-integrity-measurement/; 2021.
[170] ISO/IEC 19770-2:2015 Part 2: software identification tag. 2015. https://www.iso.org/standard/65666.html.
[171] NIST. NISTID.8060 guidelines for the creation of interoperable SWID tags. 2016. https://csrc.nist.gov/publications/detail/nistir/8060/final.
[172] IETF. RFC9393—Concise software identification tags. 2023. https://datatracker.ietf.org/doc/rfc9393/.
[173] IETF. Concise reference integrity manifest. 2023. https://datatracker.ietf.org/doc/draft-ietf-rats-corim/.
[174] W3C. 2023. https://www.w3.org/TR/xml/.
[175] CBOR. 2023. https://cbor.io/. https://datatracker.ietf.org/doc/rfc8949/.

[176] TCG. Reference integrity manifest (RIM) information model. https://trustedcomputinggroup.org/resource/tcg-reference-integrity-manifest-rim-information-model/; 2020.
[177] TCG. PC client reference integrity measurement. https://trustedcomputinggroup.org/resource/tcg-pc-client-reference-integrity-manifest-specification/; 2020.
[178] OPA. 2023. https://www.openpolicyagent.org/.
[179] JSON. 2023. https://www.json.org/. https://datatracker.ietf.org/doc/rfc7159/.
[180] JWT. 2023. https://jwt.io/. https://datatracker.ietf.org/doc/rfc7519/.
[181] IETF. The entity attestation token (EAT). https://datatracker.ietf.org/doc/draft-ietf-rats-eat/; 2023.
[182] IETF. EAT attestation result. https://datatracker.ietf.org/doc/draft-fv-rats-ear/; 2023.
[183] Knauth T, Steiner M, Chakrabarti S, Lei L, Xing C, Vij M. Integrating intel SGX remote attestation with transport layer security. Cryptography and Security; 2018. https://arxiv.org/abs/1801.05863.
[184] CCC. interoperable-ra-tls. 2023. https://github.com/ccc-attestation/interoperable-ra-tls. https://confidentialcomputing.io/2023/03/06/unifying-remote-attestation-protocol-implementations/.
[185] IETF. Using attestation in transport layer security (TLS) and datagram transport layer security (DTLS). 2023. https://datatracker.ietf.org/doc/draft-fossati-tls-attestation/.
[186] IETF. EAT attestation result. https://datatracker.ietf.org/doc/draft-fv-rats-ear/; 2023.
[187] IETF. EAT attestation result. https://datatracker.ietf.org/doc/draft-fv-rats-ear/; 2023.
[188] Scarlata V, Johnson S, Beaney J, Zmijewski P. Supporting third party attestation for Intel SGX with Intel data center attestation primitives. Intel Whitepaper; 2023. https://www.intel.com/content/dam/develop/external/us/en/documents/intel-sgx-support-for-third-party-attestation-801017.pdf.
[189] Intel. SGX attestation services. 2023. https://www.intel.com/content/www/us/en/developer/tools/software-guard-extensions/attestation-services.html.
[190] Intel. Services for intel hardware-based trusted execution environments (TEEs). 2023. https://api.portal.trustedservices.intel.com/documentation.
[191] Intel. Intel CPU architecture extensions specification. https://cdrdv2.intel.com/v1/dl/getContent/733582; 2021.
[192] AMD. AMD SEV-SNP: strengthening VM isolation with integrity protection and more. https://www.amd.com/system/files/TechDocs/SEV-SNP-strengthening-vm-isolation-with-integrity-protection-and-more.pdf; 2020.
[193] AMD. Versioned chip endorsement key (VCEK) certificate and KDS interface specification. 2023. https://www.amd.com/system/files/TechDocs/57230.pdf.
[194] ARM. DEN0096—Arm CCA security model 1.0. https://developer.arm.com/documentation/DEN0096/latest; 2021.
[195] ARM. DEN0137—Realm management monitor specification. https://developer.arm.com/documentation/den0137/latest/; 2023.
[196] Microsoft. Bitlocker BitLocker drive encryption in windows 10 for OEMs. https://learn.microsoft.com/en-us/windows-hardware/design/device-experiences/oem-bitlocker; 2023.
[197] TCG. DICE attestation architecture. 2021. https://trustedcomputinggroup.org/resource/dice-attestation-architecture/.
[198] TCG. DICE layering architecture. https://trustedcomputinggroup.org/resource/dice-layering-architecture/; 2020.

[199] TCG. DICE Protection Environment specification (draft). 2023. https://trustedcomputinggroup.org/wp-content/uploads/TCG-DICE-Protection-Environment-Specification_14february2023-1.pdf.

[200] OpenDICE. 2023. https://pigweed.googlesource.com/open-dice/. https://pigweed.googlesource.com/open-dice/+/HEAD/docs/specification.md.

[201] AMD. AMD SEV-SNP: strengthening VM isolation with integrity protection and more. https://www.amd.com/system/files/TechDocs/SEV-SNP-strengthening-vm-isolation-with-integrity-protection-and-more.pdf; 2020.

[202] Microsoft. Nested virtualization. 2023. https://learn.microsoft.com/en-us/virtualization/hyper-v-on-windows/user-guide/nested-virtualization.

[203] Linux KVM nested guests. 2023. https://www.kernel.org/doc/html/v5.7/virt/kvm/running-nested-guests.html.

[204] Intel. Intel TDX module v1.5 TD partitioning specification. https://cdrdv2.intel.com/v1/dl/getContent/773039; 2023.

[205] Microsoft. Virtual secure mode. https://learn.microsoft.com/en-us/virtualization/hyper-v-on-windows/tlfs/vsm; 2023.

[206] Microsoft. Virtualization-based security (VBS) memory enclaves: data protection through isolation. 2023. https://www.microsoft.com/en-us/security/blog/2018/06/05/virtualization-based-security-vbs-memory-enclaves-data-protection-through-isolation/.

[207] Microsoft. Confidential VMs on Azure. https://techcommunity.microsoft.com/t5/windows-os-platform-blog/confidential-vms-on-azure/ba-p/3836282; 2023.

[208] AMD. SVSM specification. https://www.amd.com/system/files/TechDocs/58019-svsm-draft-specification.pdf; 2022.

[209] Berger S, Caceres R, Goldman KA, Perez R, Sailer R, van Doorn L. vTPM: Virtualizing the trusted platform module. In: Security'06: 15th USENIX Security Symposium; 2006. https://www.usenix.org/conference/15th-usenix-security-symposium/vtpm-virtualizing-trusted-platform-module.

[210] TCG. Virtualized trusted platform architecture. 2011. https://trustedcomputinggroup.org/resource/virtualized-trusted-platform-architecture-specification/.

[211] Clark C, Fraser K, Hand S, Hansen JG, Jul E, Limpach C, Pratt I, Warfield A. Live migration of virtual machines. USENIX NSDI; 2005. https://www.usenix.org/legacy/publications/library/proceedings/nsdi05/tech/clark.html.

[212] Microsoft. Virtual machine live migration overview. https://learn.microsoft.com/en-us/previous-versions/windows/it-pro/windows-server-2012-r2-and-2012/hh831435(v=ws.11; 2023.

[213] Linux KVM migration. 2023. https://www.linux-kvm.org/page/Migration.

[214] Intel. Intel TDX module v1.5 TD migration architecture specification. 2023. https://cdrdv2.intel.com/v1/dl/getContent/733578

[215] Microsoft. Hotpatch for virtual machine. 2023. https://learn.microsoft.com/en-us/windows-server/get-started/hotpatch.

[216] Microsoft. Hotpatch for windows. 2023. https://techcommunity.microsoft.com/t5/windows-os-platform-blog/hotpatching-on-windows/ba-p/2959541.

[217] Redhat. Linux kernel live patch. https://www.redhat.com/en/topics/linux/what-is-linux-kernel-live-patching; 2023.

[218] Oracel. QEMU live update. 2023. https://blogs.oracle.com/linux/post/qemu-live-update.

[219] Hu Y, Yan S, Wu Y. Confidential computing—Artificial intelligence data security and privacy protection. Publishing House of Electronics Industry; 2023.

[220] KVM. 2023. https://www.kernel.org/doc/html/latest/virt/kvm/index.html.

[221] Cloud hypervisor. 2023. https://www.cloudhypervisor.org/.

[222] Dragonball hypervisor. 2023. https://github.com/kata-containers/kata-containers/tree/main/src/dragonball.
[223] EDKII OVMF. 2023. https://github.com/tianocore/edk2/tree/master/OvmfPkg.
[224] UEFI. UEFI specification 2.10. https://uefi.org/specs/UEFI/2.10/; 2022.
[225] UEFI. ACPI specification 6.5. https://uefi.org/specs/ACPI/6.5/; 2022.
[226] TD-Shim. 2023. https://github.com/confidential-containers/td-shim.
[227] Asterinas. 2023. https://github.com/asterinas/asterinas.
[228] Grub2. 2023. https://github.com/rhboot/grub2.
[229] Shim. 2023. https://github.com/rhboot/shim.
[230] Confidential containers. 2023. https://github.com/confidential-containers.
[231] Edgeless. Constellation. 2023. https://github.com/edgelesssys/constellation. https://docs.edgeless.systems/constellation.
[232] Kubernetes. 2023. https://kubernetes.io/.
[233] Coconut-SVSM. 2023. https://github.com/coconut-svsm.
[234] Intel TDX module. 2023. https://www.intel.com/content/www/us/en/developer/tools/trust-domain-extensions/documentation.html.
[235] AMD SEV firmware. https://github.com/amd/AMD-ASPFW; 2023.
[236] ARM TF-RMM. https://www.trustedfirmware.org/projects/tf-rmm/; 2023.
[237] RISC-V Salus. https://github.com/rivosinc/salus; 2023.
[238] Intel. Linux* stacks for Intel trust domain extensions, vol 5; 2023. https://www.intel.com/content/www/us/en/content-details/790888/whitepaper-linux-stacks-for-intel-trust-domain-extensions-1-5.html.
[239] Open enclave. 2023. https://openenclave.io/.
[240] Teaclave. 2023. https://teaclave.apache.org/. https://github.com/apache/incubator-teaclave. https://arxiv.org/abs/2005.04367.
[241] Inclavare. 2023. https://github.com/inclavare-containers.
[242] Enarx. 2023. https://enarx.dev/. https://enarx.dev/docs/Technical/Trust-Architecture.
[243] HyperEnclave. 2023. https://github.com/HyperEnclave/hyperenclave.
[244] AWS nitro enclave. 2023. https://aws.amazon.com/ec2/nitro/nitro-enclaves/.
[245] TCG. TPM2.0 specification. https://trustedcomputinggroup.org/resource/tpm-library-specification/; 2019.
[246] Microsoft TPM2.0. 2023. https://github.com/microsoft/ms-tpm-20-ref.
[247] Linux swtpm. 2023. https://github.com/stefanberger/swtpm.
[248] Intel TD based vTPM. https://github.com/intel/vtpm-td; 2023.
[249] SVSM vTPM. https://github.com/svsm-vtpm; 2023.
[250] Coconut-SVSM vTPM. https://github.com/coconut-svsm/svsm/pull/135; 2023.
[251] Microsoft. Virtual TPMs in Azure confidential VMs. https://learn.microsoft.com/en-us/azure/confidential-computing/virtual-tpms-in-azure-confidential-vm; 2023.
[252] Microsoft. Azure confidential VMs attestation. https://github.com/Azure/confidential-computing-cvm-guest-attestation/blob/main/cvm-guest-attestation.md; 2023.
[253] Confidential vTPM. 2023. https://github.com/inclavare-containers/confidential-vtpm.
[254] Tpm2-tss. https://github.com/tpm2-software/tpm2-tss; 2023.
[255] Tpm2-tools. https://github.com/tpm2-software/tpm2-tools; 2023.
[256] TCG. TSS 2.0 overview and common structures specification. https://trustedcomputinggroup.org/resource/tss-overview-common-structures-specification/; 2021.
[257] Linux IMA. 2023. https://linux-ima.sourceforge.net/. https://sourceforge.net/p/linux-ima/wiki/Home/.
[258] Keylime. 2023. https://keylime.dev/.

[259] go-tpm-tools. https://github.com/google/go-tpm-tools/; 2023.
[260] Google. Confidential VM attestation. https://cloud.google.com/confidential-computing/confidential-vm/docs/attestation; 2023.
[261] Intel DCAP. 2023. https://github.com/intel/SGXDataCenterAttestationPrimitives.
[262] Intel attestation service. 2023. https://api.portal.trustedservices.intel.com/content/documentation.html.
[263] CC-trusted API. https://github.com/cc-api/cc-trusted-api; 2023.
[264] Edgeless. Constellation attestation. 2023. https://docs.edgeless.systems/constellation/architecture/attestation.
[265] Linux UAPI. Linux TPM PCR registry. https://uapi-group.org/specifications/specs/linux_tpm_pcr_registry/; 2023.
[266] Veraison. 2023. https://github.com/veraison.
[267] Rego policy language. 2023. https://www.openpolicyagent.org/docs/latest/policy-language/.
[268] In-toto. 2023. https://in-toto.io/. https://github.com/in-toto/docs/blob/master/in-toto-spec.md.
[269] Open policy agent. https://www.openpolicyagent.org/; 2023.
[270] DMTF. Security protocols and data models. https://www.dmtf.org/standards/spdm; 2023.
[271] CC key broker service. 2023. https://github.com/confidential-containers/kbs.
[272] CC attestation service. 2023. https://github.com/confidential-containers/kbs/tree/main/attestation-service.
[273] CC attestation agent. 2023. https://github.com/confidential-containers/guest-components/tree/main/attestation-agent.
[274] RedHat. Confidential computing: from root of trust to actual trust. https://www.redhat.com/en/blog/confidential-computing-root-trust-actual-trust; 2023.
[275] CC image management lib. 2023. https://github.com/confidential-containers/guest-components/tree/main/image-rs.
[276] CC OCI-Crypto. 2023. https://github.com/confidential-containers/guest-components/tree/main/ocicrypt-rs.
[277] Heartbleed. 2014. https://heartbleed.com/.
[278] Stringbleed. 2017. https://github.com/stringbleed/stringbleed.github.io.
[279] SMBleed. 2020. https://blog.zecops.com/research/smbleedingghost-writeup-chaining-smbleed-cve-2020-1206-with-smbghost/.
[280] Gazet A, Périgaud F, Czarny J. iLOBleed. BlackHat US. https://www.blackhat.com/us-21/briefings/schedule/#hpe-ilo-firmware-security—go-home-cryptoprocessor-youre-drunk-23398; 2021.
[281] Hoglund G, Gary MG. Exploiting software. Addison-Wesley Professional; 2004.
[282] Erickson J. Hacking: the art of exploitation (2nd). No Starch Press; 2008.
[283] Duan G. Encryption and decryption (4th). Publishing House of Electronics Industry; 2018.
[284] Top 10 developer crypto mistakes. 2017. https://littlemaninmyhead.wordpress.com/2017/04/22/top-10-developer-crypto-mistakes/.
[285] The many, many ways that cryptographic software can fail. https://www.freecodecamp.org/news/why-does-cryptographic-software-fail-often-d660d3cdfdc5/; 2023.
[286] 5 encryption errors developers keep making. https://www.infoworld.com/article/2923777/5-ways-developers-get-encryption-wrong.html; 2023.
[287] NSA. Commercial national security algorithm suite. https://media.defense.gov/2021/Sep/27/2002862527/-1/-1/0/CNSS%20WORKSHEET.PDF; 2021.

[288] NSA. Commercial national security algorithm suite 2.0. https://media.defense.gov/2022/Sep/07/2003071747/-1/-1/0/CSA_CNSA_2.0_ALGORITHMS.PDF; 2022.

[289] ISO/IEC 10118-3:2018 hash-functions—Part 3: dedicated hash-functions. 2018. https://www.iso.org/standard/67116.html.

[290] ISO/IEC 14888-3:2018 Digital signatures with appendix—Part 3: discrete logarithm based mechanisms. 2018. https://www.iso.org/standard/76382.html.

[291] IETF. RFC8998 ShangMi (SM) cipher suites for TLS 1.3. https://datatracker.ietf.org/doc/rfc8998/; 2021.

[292] ISO/IEC 18033-3:2010/Amd 1:2021 encryption algorithms—Part 3: block ciphers—amendment 1: SM4. 2021. https://www.iso.org/standard/81564.html.

[293] CISA. SSL 3.0 protocol vulnerability and POODLE attack. https://www.cisa.gov/news-events/alerts/2014/10/17/ssl-30-protocol-vulnerability-and-poodle-attack; 2014.

[294] NIST. SP 800-57 Part 1 Rev. 5, recommendation for key management: Part 1—general. 2020. https://csrc.nist.gov/pubs/sp/800/57/pt.1/r5/final.

[295] NIST. FIPS 203—Module-lattice-based key-encapsulation mechanism standard (DRAFT). 2023. https://csrc.nist.gov/pubs/fips/203/final.

[296] NIST. FIPS 204—Module-lattice-based digital signature standard (DRAFT). https://csrc.nist.gov/pubs/fips/204/final; 2023.

[297] NIST. FIPS 205—Stateless hash-based digital signature standard (DRAFT). 2023. https://csrc.nist.gov/pubs/fips/205/final.

[298] NIST. FIPS 140-2 security requirements for cryptographic modules. https://csrc.nist.gov/pubs/fips/140-2/upd2/final; 2001.

[299] Kocher PC. Timing attacks on implementations of diffie-hellman, RSA, DSS, and other systems. In: Advances in cryptology—CRYPTO'96; 1996. https://link.springer.com/chapter/10.1007/3-540-68697-5_9.

[300] Arjen K. Lenstra. Memo on RSA signature generation in the presence of faults. Technical Report; 1999. https://infoscience.epfl.ch/record/164524?ln=en.

[301] Bleichenbacher D. Chosen ciphertext attacks against protocols based on the RSA encryption standard PKCS #1. In: Advances in cryptology—CRYPTO '98; 1998. https://link.springer.com/chapter/10.1007/BFb0055716.

[302] Manger J. A chosen ciphertext attack on RSA optimal asymmetric encryption padding (OAEP) as standardized in PKCS #1 v2.0. In: Advances in cryptology—-CRYPTO 2001; 2001. https://link.springer.com/chapter/10.1007/3-540-44647-8_14.

[303] Aumüller C, Bier P, Fischer W, Hofreiter P, Seifert J-P. Fault attacks on RSA with CRT: concrete results and practical countermeasures. In: Cryptographic hardware and embedded systems—CHES 2002; 2002. https://link.springer.com/chapter/10.1007/3-540-36400-5_20.

[304] Bernstein DJ. Cache-timing attacks on AES. https://cr.yp.to/antiforgery/cachetiming-20050414.pdf; 2005.

[305] Al Fardan NJ, Paterson KG. Lucky thirteen: breaking the TLS and DTLS record protocols. In: 2013 IEEE Symposium on Security and Privacy; 2013. https://ieeexplore.ieee.org/document/6547131.

[306] Aranha DF, Rodrigues Novaes F, Takahashi A, Tibouchi M, Yarom Y. LadderLeak: breaking ECDSA with less than one bit of nonce leakage. In: CCS'20: Proceedings of the 2020 ACM SIGSAC Conference on Computer and Communications Security; 2020. https://dl.acm.org/doi/10.1145/3372297.3417268.

[307] Racoon attack. 2020. https://raccoon-attack.com/.

[308] OpenSSL. 2023. https://github.com/openssl.

[309] MbedTLS. 2023. https://github.com/Mbed-TLS/mbedtls.

[310] Tongsuo. 2023. https://github.com/Tongsuo-Project/Tongsuo.
[311] memset_s. https://en.cppreference.com/w/c/string/byte/memset; 2023.
[312] SecureZeroMem. 2023. https://learn.microsoft.com/en-us/previous-versions/windows/desktop/legacy/aa366877(v=vs.85.
[313] explicit_bzero. https://www.gnu.org/software/libc/manual/html_node/Erasing-Sensitive-Data.html; 2023.
[314] NIST. SP 800-63B digital identity guidelines: authentication and lifecycle management. 2020. https://csrc.nist.gov/pubs/sp/800/63/b/upd2/final.
[315] OWASP. Password storage cheat sheet. 2023. https://cheatsheetseries.owasp.org/cheatsheets/Password_Storage_Cheat_Sheet.html.
[316] NCSC. Design and build a privately hosted public key infrastructure. https://www.ncsc.gov.uk/collection/in-house-public-key-infrastructure; 2020.
[317] SSLDragon. Best practices to store the private key. https://www.ssldragon.com/blog/best-practices-to-store-the-private-key/; 2023.
[318] Ender M, Moradi A, Paar C. The unpatchable silicon: a full break of the bitstream encryption of Xilinx 7-series FPGAs. In: SEC'20: Proceedings of the 29th USENIX Conference on Security Symposium; 2020. https://www.usenix.org/conference/usenixsecurity20/presentation/ender.
[319] FailOverflow. Console hacking—PS3 epic fail. 27C3. www.cs.cmu.edu/~dst/GeoHot/1780_27c3_console_hacking_2010.pdf; 2010.
[320] 3 bulbs and 3 switches. https://www.geeksforgeeks.org/puzzle-7-3-bulbs-and-3-switches/; 2023.
[321] NSA. Tempest. A signal problem. https://www.nsa.gov/portals/75/documents/news-features/declassified-documents/cryptologic-spectrum/tempest.pdf; 1972.
[322] Wright P. Spy catcher. Viking Adult; 1987.
[323] Zhou YB, Feng DG. Side-Channel attacks: ten years after its publication and the impacts on cryptographic module security testing. NIST CSRC; 2005. https://csrc.nist.gov/csrc/media/events/physical-security-testing-workshop/documents/papers/physecpaper19.pdf.
[324] Jeremy Boone. An introduction to fault injection. https://research.nccgroup.com/2021/07/07/an-introduction-to-fault-injection-part-1-3/; 2021. https://research.nccgroup.com/2021/07/08/software-based-fault-injection-countermeasures-part-2-3/. https://research.nccgroup.com/2021/07/09/alternative-approaches-for-fault-injection-countermeasures-part-3-3/.
[325] Arne Osvik D, Shamir A, Tromer E. Cache attacks and countermeasures: the case of AES. In: CT-RSA'06: Proceedings of the 2006 The Cryptographers' Track at the RSA conference on Topics in Cryptology; 2006. https://dl.acm.org/doi/10.1007/11605805_1.
[326] Yarom Y, Falkner K. FLUSH+RELOAD: a high resolution, low noise, L3 cache side-channel attack. In: USENIX Security Symposium; 2014. https://www.usenix.org/conference/usenixsecurity14/technical-sessions/presentation/yarom.
[327] Yarom Y, Genkin D, Heninger N. CacheBleed: a timing attack on OpenSSL constant-time RSA. J Crypto Eng 2017. https://link.springer.com/article/10.1007/s13389-017-0152-y.
[328] Gras B, Razavi K, Bos H, Giuffrida C. Translation leak-aside buffer: defeating cache side-channel protections with TLB attacks. In: SEC'18: Proceedings of the 27th USENIX Conference on Security Symposium; 2018. https://www.usenix.org/conference/usenixsecurity18/presentation/gras.
[329] Islam S, Moghimi A, Bruhns I, Krebbel M, Gulmezoglu B, Eisenbarth T, Sunar B. Spoiler: speculative load hazards boost rowhammer and cache attacks. In: SEC'19:

Proceedings of the 28th USENIX Conference on Security Symposium; 2019. https://www.usenix.org/conference/usenixsecurity19/presentation/islam.
[330] Guo S, Wang T, Zhao X. Principles and methodologies of side-channel analysis in cryptography. China Science Publishing & Media Ltd.; 2014.
[331] Joye M, Tunstall M. Fault analysis in cryptography. Springer; 2012.
[332] Q. Ge, Y. Yarom, D. Cock, G. Heiser. A survey of microarchitectural timing attacks and countermeasures on contemporary hardware. J Crypto Eng 2016. 2016. https://link.springer.com/article/10.1007/s13389-016-0141-6.
[333] Spectre attack. 2017. https://spectreattack.com/.
[334] Meltdown attack. 2017. https://meltdownattack.com/.
[335] Zombieload. 2018. https://zombieloadattack.com/.
[336] van Schaik S, Milburn A, Österlund S, Frigo P, Maisuradze G, Razavi K, Bos H, Giuffrida C. RIDL: rogue in-flight data load. In: 2019 IEEE Symposium on Security and Privacy (SP); 2019. https://ieeexplore.ieee.org/document/8835281.
[337] Canella C, Genkin D, Giner L, Gruss D, Lipp M, Minkin M, Moghimi D, Piessens F, Schwarz M, Sunar B, Bulck JV, Yarom Y. Fallout: leaking data on meltdown-resistant CPUs. In: CCS'19: Proceedings of the 2019 ACM SIGSAC Conference on Computer and Communications Security; 2019. https://dl.acm.org/doi/10.1145/3319535.3363219.
[338] MDS attack. 2018. https://mdsattacks.com/.
[339] Page against the machine clear. 2021. https://www.vusec.net/projects/fpvi-scsb/.
[340] Foreshadow. 2018. https://foreshadowattack.eu/.
[341] LVI. 2018. https://lviattack.eu/.
[342] Crosstalk. 2020. https://www.vusec.net/projects/crosstalk/.
[343] Wikner J, Razavi K. RETBLEED: arbitrary speculative code execution with return instructions. In: SEC'22: Proceedings of the 31st USENIX Conference on Security Symposium; 2022. https://www.usenix.org/conference/usenixsecurity22/presentation/wikner.
[344] Cacheout. 2020. https://cacheoutattack.com/.
[345] SGAxe. 2020. https://sgaxe.com/.
[346] Downfall. 2023. https://downfall.page/.
[347] Inception and phantom. 2023. https://comsec.ethz.ch/research/microarch/inception/.
[348] Cache warp. 2023. https://cachewarpattack.com/.
[349] Platypus. 2021. https://platypusattack.com/.
[350] Hertzbleed. 2022. https://www.hertzbleed.com/.
[351] Collide power. 2023. https://collidepower.com/.
[352] ÆPIC leak. https://aepicleak.com/; 2022.
[353] CipherLeak. 2021. https://cipherleaks.com/.
[354] GPU.zip. https://www.hertzbleed.com/gpu.zip/; 2023.
[355] CPU fail. https://cpu.fail/; 2023.
[356] Claudio C, Jo Van B, Schwarz M, Lipp M, Berg Bvon, Ortner P, Piessens F, Evtyushkin D, Gruss D. A systematic evaluation of transient execution attacks and defenses. In: SEC'19: Proceedings of the 28th USENIX Conference on Security Symposium; 2019. https://www.usenix.org/conference/usenixsecurity19/presentation/canella.
[357] Canella C, Khasawneh KN, Gruss D. The evolution of transient-execution attacks. In: GLSVLSI'20: Proceedings of the 2020 on Great Lakes Symposium on VLSI; 2020. https://dl.acm.org/doi/abs/10.1145/3386263.3407583. https://graz.elsevierpure.com/en/publications/the-evolution-of-transient-execution-attacks.

[358] Intel. Refined speculative execution terminology. https://www.intel.com/content/www/us/en/developer/articles/technical/software-security-guidance/best-practices/refined-speculative-execution-terminology.html; 2022.
[359] Scott C. Software techniques to mitigate hardware transient execution attacks. IEEE SecDev; 2020. https://www.youtube.com/watch?v=Bus3P6Z3qZU&feature=youtu.be.
[360] Rage against the machine clear (FPVI and SCSB). 2021. https://www.vusec.net/projects/fpvi-scsb/.
[361] Mohammadian Koruyeh E, Khasawneh KN, Song C, Abu-Ghazaleh N. Spectre returns! Speculation attacks using the return stack buffer. In: USENIX Workshop on Offensive Technologies (USENIX WOOT 18); 2018. https://www.usenix.org/conference/woot18/presentation/koruyeh.
[362] Kiriansky V, Waldspurger C. Speculative buffer overflows: attacks and defenses. In: Cryptography and security; 2018. https://arxiv.org/abs/1807.03757.
[363] Maisuradze G, Rossow C. ret2spec: speculative execution using return stack buffers. In: CCS'18: Proceedings of the 2018 ACM SIGSAC Conference on Computer and Communications Security; 2018. https://dl.acm.org/doi/10.1145/3243734.3243761.
[364] BHI. https://www.vusec.net/projects/bhi-spectre-bhb/; 2022.
[365] Schwarz M, Canella C, Giner L, Gruss D. Store-to-Leak forwarding: leaking data on meltdown-resistant CPUs. In: Cryptography and security; 2019. https://arxiv.org/abs/1905.05725.
[366] Stecklina J, Prescher T. LazyPF: leaking FPU register state using microarchitectural side-channels. In: Cryptography and security; 2018. https://arxiv.org/abs/1806.07480.
[367] Jin Y, Qiu P, Wang C, Yang Y, Wang D, Qu G. Timing the transient execution: a new side-channel attack on intel CPUs. In: Cryptography and security; 2023. https://arxiv.org/abs/2304.10877.
[368] Moghimi D, Moritz L, Sunar B, Schwarz M. Medusa: microarchitectural data leakage via automated attack synthesis. In: SEC'20: Proceedings of the 29th USENIX Conference on Security Symposium; 2020. https://www.usenix.org/conference/usenixsecurity20/presentation/moghimi-medusa.
[369] Lee S, Shih M-W, Gera P, Kim T, Kim H, Peinado M. Inferring fine-grained control flow inside SGX enclaves with branch shadowing. In: SEC'17: Proceedings of the 26th USENIX Conference on Security Symposium; 2017. https://www.usenix.org/conference/usenixsecurity17/technical-sessions/presentation/lee-sangho.
[370] Evtyushkin D, Riley R, Abu-Ghazaleh ECE, Ponomarev D. Branchscope: a new side-channel attack on directional branch predictor. In: ASPLOS'18: Proceedings of the Twenty-Third International Conference on Architectural Support for Programming Languages and Operating Systems; 2018. https://dl.acm.org/doi/10.1145/3173162.3173204.
[371] Huo T, Meng X, Wang W, Chunliang H, Pei Z, Zhai J, Li M. Bluethunder: a 2-level directional predictor based side-channel attack against SGX. In: IACR transactions on cryptographic hardware and embedded systems; 2020. https://tches.iacr.org/index.php/TCHES/article/view/8401.
[372] Zenbleed. 2023. https://lock.cmpxchg8b.com/zenbleed.html.
[373] Qiu P, Wang D, Lyu Y, Tian R, Wang C, Qu G. VoltJockey. IEEE Trans Comput Aided Des Integrated Circ Syst 2020. https://ieeexplore.ieee.org/document/9200659.
[374] Plundervolt. 2020. https://plundervolt.com/.

[375] Chen Z, Murdock K, Dean E, Oswald D, Garcia FD. VoltPillager. In: SEC'21: Proceedings of the 30th USENIX Conference on Security Symposium; 2021. https://www.usenix.org/conference/usenixsecurity21/presentation/chen-zitai.
[376] Victor van der Veen, Fratantonio Y, Lindorfer M, Gruss D, Maurice C, Vigna G, Bos H, Razavi K, Giuffrida C. Drammer: deterministic rowhammer attacks on mobile platforms. In: CCS'16: Proceedings of the 2016 ACM SIGSAC Conference on Computer and Communications Security; 2016. https://dl.acm.org/doi/10.1145/2976749.2978406.
[377] RamBleed. 2020. https://rambleed.com/.
[378] Frigo P, Vannacc E, Hassan H, van der Veen V, Mutlu O, Giuffrida C, Bos H, TRRespass KR. Exploiting the many sides of target row refresh. In: 2020 IEEE Symposium on Security and Privacy (SP); 2020. https://ieeexplore.ieee.org/abstract/document/9152631.
[379] de Ridder F, Frigo P, Vannacci E, Bos H, Giuffrida C, Razavi K. SMASH: synchronized many-sided rowhammer attacks from JavaScript. In: SEC'21: Proceedings of the 30th USENIX Conference on Security Symposium; 2021. https://www.usenix.org/conference/usenixsecurity21/presentation/ridder.
[380] Kogler A, Juffinger J, Qazi S, Kim Y, Lipp M, Boichat N, Shiu E, Nissler M, Gruss D. Half-double: hammering from the next row over. In: SEC'22: Proceedings of the 31st USENIX Conference on Security Symposium; 2022. https://www.usenix.org/conference/usenixsecurity22/presentation/kogler-half-double.
[381] Battering RAM. 2026. https://batteringram.eu/.
[382] Wiretap.fail. https://wiretap.fail/; 2025.
[383] TEE.fail. https://tee.fail/; 2026.
[384] Steve McConnell. Code complete (2nd). Microsoft Press; 2004.
[385] Maguire S. Writing solid code. Microsoft Press; 1993.
[386] Viega J, McGraw G. Building secure software. Addison-Wesley Professional; 2001.
[387] Howard M, LeBlanc D. Write secure code. 2nd. Microsoft Press; 2003.
[388] Smith RE. A contemporary look at saltzer and schroeder's 1975 design principles. IEEE Secur Privacy 2012. https://ieeexplore.ieee.org/document/6226346.
[389] Hoare CAR. On design. 2008. https://cs.stanford.edu/people/eroberts/courses/soco/projects/2008-09/tony-hoare/index.html.
[390] A. Kerckhoffs. La cryptographie militaire. Journal des sciences militaires. vol. IX. 1883. www.petitcolas.net/kerckhoffs/index.html.
[391] Larin B, Bezvershenko L, Kucherin G. Operation triangulation: what you get when attack iPhones of researchers. In: 37th Chaos Communication Congress (37C3); 2023. https://securelist.com/operation-triangulation-the-last-hardware-mystery/111669/. https://www.youtube.com/watch?v=1f6YyH62jFE.
[392] OWASP. Secure product design cheat sheet. https://cheatsheetseries.owasp.org/cheatsheets/Secure_Product_Design_Cheat_Sheet.html; 2023.
[393] Microsoft. A proactive approach to more secure code. https://msrc.microsoft.com/blog/2019/07/a-proactive-approach-to-more-secure-code/; 2019.
[394] NSA. Software memory safety. 2022. https://media.defense.gov/2022/Nov/10/2003112742/-1/-1/0/CSI_SOFTWARE_MEMORY_SAFETY.PDF.
[395] CISA. CSAC TAC recommendations—memory safety. 2023. https://www.cisa.gov/sites/default/files/2023-12/CSAC_TAC_Recommendations-Memory-Safety_Final_20231205_508.pdf.
[396] NIST. Safer Language. 2023. https://www.nist.gov/itl/ssd/software-quality-group/safer-languages.
[397] Rust Language. 2023. https://www.rust-lang.org/.

[398] David Weston. Default security. BlueHat IL. https://github.com/dwizzzle/Presentations/blob/master/David%20Weston%20-%20Windows%2011%20Security%20by-default%20-%20Bluehat%20IL%202023.pdf; 2023.
[399] Linux rust support. 2023. https://github.com/torvalds/linux/tree/master/rust.
[400] Klabnik S, Nichols C. The rust programming language (2nd). No Starch Press; 2023.
[401] Blandy J. Programming rust (2nd). O'Reilly Media; 2021.
[402] Schneier B. Applied cryptography (20th anniversary). Wiley; 2015.
[403] Ferguson N, Schneier B. Practical cryptography. Wiley; 2003.
[404] Jean-Philippe Aumasson. Serious cryptography. No Starch Press; 2017.
[405] Wong D. Real world cryptography. Manning Publications; 2021.
[406] Cryptocoding. 2023. https://github.com/veorq/cryptocoding.
[407] NIST. PQC selected algorithm. 2022. https://csrc.nist.gov/Projects/post-quantum-cryptography/selected-algorithms-2022.
[408] NCSC. Next steps in preparing for post-quantum cryptography. https://www.ncsc.gov.uk/whitepaper/next-steps-preparing-for-post-quantum-cryptography; 2023.
[409] BSI. TR-02102-1. Cryptographic mechanisms: recommendations and key lengths, Version: 2023-1. 2023. https://www.bsi.bund.de/SharedDocs/Downloads/EN/BSI/Publications/TechGuidelines/TG02102/BSI-TR-02102-1.html.
[410] BSI. Quantum-safe cryptography—fundamentals, current developments and recommendations. 2022. https://www.bsi.bund.de/SharedDocs/Downloads/EN/BSI/Publications/Brochure/quantum-safe-cryptography.pdf.
[411] FrodoKEM. 2023. https://frodokem.org/.
[412] McEliece. 2023. https://classic.mceliece.org/.
[413] Chinese Association for Cryptologic Research. Announcement of the selection results of algorithms in the China cryptography algorithm design competition. https://www.cacrnet.org.cn/site/content/854.html; 2020.
[414] Zhang J, Yu Y, Fan S, Zhang Z, Yang K. Tweaking the asymmetry of asymmetric-key cryptography on lattices: KEMs and signatures of smaller sizes (Aigis). 2019. https://eprint.iacr.org/2019/510.
[415] Hu Y, Dong S, Dong X. Analysis on Aigis-Enc: asymmetrical and symmetrical. 2020. https://eprint.iacr.org/2020/036.
[416] Lu X, Liu Y, Zhang Z, Jia D, Xue H, He J, Li B, Wang K. LAC: practical ring-LWE based public-key encryption with byte-level modulus. 2018. https://eprint.iacr.org/2018/1009.
[417] IETF. PQC activity. 2023. https://wiki.ietf.org/group/sec/PQCAgility.
[418] IETF. Post-Quantum use in protocols (pquip). https://datatracker.ietf.org/wg/pquip/about/; 2023.
[419] NIST. SP800-208—Recommendation for stateful hash-based signature schemes. https://csrc.nist.gov/pubs/sp/800/208/final; 2020
[420] ESTI. TR 103 692 V1.1.1—State management for stateful authentication mechanisms. https://www.etsi.org/deliver/etsi_tr/103600_103699/103692/01.01.01_60/tr_103692v010101p.pdf; 2021.
[421] ITEF. RFC 8554—LMS. https://datatracker.ietf.org/doc/rfc8554; 2019.
[422] IETF. RFC 8391—XMSS. https://datatracker.ietf.org/doc/rfc8391; 2018.
[423] NIST. PQC FAC. https://csrc.nist.gov/Projects/post-quantum-cryptography/faqs; 2023.
[424] IETF. Terminology for post-quantum traditional hybrid schemes. 2023. https://datatracker.ietf.org/doc/draft-ietf-pquip-pqt-hybrid-terminology/.
[425] ENISA. Post-Quantum cryptography—Integration study. 2022. https://www.enisa.europa.eu/publications/post-quantum-cryptography-integration-study.
[426] Ravi P, Chattopadhyay A, D'Anvers JP, Baksi A. Side-channel and fault-injection attacks over lattice-based post-quantum schemes (kyber, dilithium): survey and new

results. ACM Trans Embed Comput Syst 2023. https://dl.acm.org/doi/10.1145/3603170.
[427] NIST. Lightweight cryptography. 2023. https://csrc.nist.gov/projects/lightweight-cryptography.
[428] NIST. Lightweight cryptography NIST select. 2023. https://csrc.nist.gov/news/2023/lightweight-cryptography-nist-selects-ascon.
[429] Tehranipoor M, Wang C. Introduction to hardware security and trust. Springer; 2011.
[430] Bhunia S, Tehranipoor M. Hardware security: A hands-on learning approach. Morgan Kaufmann; 2018.
[431] Witteman M. Secure application programming in the presence of side channel attack. Riscure Whitepaper; 2017. https://www.riscure.com/publication/secure-application-programming-presence-side-channel-attacks/.
[432] Intel. Software security guidance. https://www.intel.com/content/www/us/en/developer/topic-technology/software-security-guidance/advisory-guidance.html; 2023.
[433] AMD. Product security. https://www.amd.com/en/resources/product-security.html.
[434] AMD. Software techniques for managing speculation on AMD processors. 2023. https://www.amd.com/content/dam/amd/en/documents/epyc-technical-docs/tuning-guides/software-techniques-for-managing-speculation.pdf.
[435] AMD. Speculation behavior in AMD micro-architectures. 2019. https://www.amd.com/system/files/documents/security-whitepaper.pdf.
[436] AMD. Indirect branch control extension. 2018. https://developer.amd.com/wp-content/resources/Architecture_Guidelines_Update_Indirect_Branch_Control.pdf.
[437] AMD. Speculative store bypass disable. 2018. https://developer.amd.com/wp-content/resources/124441_AMD64_SpeculativeStoreBypassDisable_Whitepaper_final.pdf.
[438] Intel. Intel SGX: moving beyond encrypted data to confidential computing. https://www.intel.com/content/www/us/en/architecture-and-technology/software-guard-extensions-enhanced-data-protection.html; 2023.
[439] Fei S, Yan Z, Ding W, Xie H. Security vulnerabilities of sgx and countermeasures: a survey. ACM Comput Surv 2021;54(6). https://dl.acm.org/doi/10.1145/3456631.
[440] Jo Van Bulck. Tutorial: uncovering side-channels in intel SGX enclaves. https://jovanbulck.github.io/files/space18-tutorial-slides.pdf; 2018.
[441] Shinde S, Chua ZL, Narayanan V, Saxena P. Preventing page faults from telling your secrets. In: ASIA CCS'16: Proceedings of the 11th ACM on Asia Conference on Computer and Communications Security; 2016. https://dl.acm.org/doi/10.1145/2897845.2897885.
[442] Van Bulck J, Weichbrodt N, Kapitza R, Piessens F, Strackx R. Telling your secrets without page faults: stealthy page table-based attacks on enclaved execution. In: 26th USENIX Security Symposium (USENIX Security 17); 2017. https://www.usenix.org/conference/usenixsecurity17/technical-sessions/presentation/van-bulck.
[443] Kim D, Jang D, Park M, Jeong Y, Kim J, Choi S, Kang BB. SGX-LEGO: fine-grained SGX controlled-channel attack and its countermeasure. Comput Secur 2019;82. https://dl.acm.org/doi/abs/10.1016/j.cose.2018.12.001.
[444] Moghimi D, Jo Van B, Heninger N, Piessens F, Sunar B. CopyCat: controlled instruction-level attacks on enclaves. In: SEC'20: Proceedings of the 29th USENIX Conference on Security Symposium; 2020. https://www.usenix.org/conference/usenixsecurity20/presentation/moghimi-copycat.
[445] Wang W, Chen G, Pan X, Zhang Y, Wang XF, Vincent B, Tang H, Gunter CA. Leaky cauldron on the dark land: understanding memory side-channel hazards in

SGX. In: CCS'17: Proceedings of the 2017 ACM SIGSAC Conference on Computer and Communications Security; 2017. https://dl.acm.org/doi/10.1145/3133956.3134038.

[446] Gyselinck J, Van Bulck J, Piessens F, Strackx R. Off-limits: abusing legacy x86 memory segmentation to spy on enclaved execution. In: International Symposium on Engineering Secure Software and Systems; 2018. https://link.springer.com/chapter/10.1007/978-3-319-94496-8_4.

[447] Moghimi A, Irazoqui G, Eisenbarth T. Cachezoom: how SGX amplifies the power of cache attacks. Crypto Hardware Embedded Sys CHES 2017;2017. https://link.springer.com/chapter/10.1007/978-3-319-66787-4_4.

[448] Brasser F, Müller U, Dmitrienko A, Kostiainen K, Capkun S, Sadeghi A-R. Software grand exposure: SGX cache attacks are practical. In: 11th USENIX Workshop on Offensive Technologies (WOOT 2017); 2017. https://www.usenix.org/conference/woot17/workshop-program/presentation/brasser.

[449] Dall F, De Micheli G, Eisenbarth T, Genkin D, Heninger N, Moghimi A, Yarom Y. CacheQuote: efficiently recovering long-term secrets of SGX EPID via cache attacks. In: IACR Transactions on cryptographic hardware and embedded systems; 2018. https://tches.iacr.org/index.php/TCHES/article/view/879.

[450] Ahmad M, Eisenbarth T, MemJam BS. A false dependency attack against constant-time crypto implementations in SGX. In: Topics in cryptology—CT-RSA 2018; 2018. https://link.springer.com/chapter/10.1007/978-3-319-76953-0_2.

[451] Schwarz M, Weiser S, Gruss D, Maurice C, Mangard S. Malware guard extension: using SGX to conceal cache attacks. Cybersecurity 2020;3. Article number: 2, https://cybersecurity.springeropen.com/articles/10.1186/s42400-019-0042-y.

[452] Van Bulck J, Piessens F, Strackx R. Nemesis: studying microarchitectural timing leaks in rudimentary CPU interrupt logic. In: CCS'18: Proceedings of the 2018 ACM SIGSAC Conference on Computer and Communications Security; 2018. https://dl.acm.org/doi/10.1145/3243734.3243822.

[453] Lee J, Jang J, Jang Y, Kwak N, Choi Y, Choi C, Kim T, Peinado M, Kang BB. Hacking in darkness: return-oriented programming against secure enclaves. In: 26th USENIX Security Symposium; 2017. https://www.usenix.org/conference/usenixsecurity17/technical-sessions/presentation/lee-jaehyuk.

[454] Wang J, Cheng Y, Qi L, Jiang Y. Interface-based side channel attack against intel SGX. In: Cryptography and security; 2018. https://arxiv.org/abs/1811.05378.

[455] Lee S, Kim T. Leaking uninitialized secure enclave memory via structure padding. In: Cryptography and security; 2017. https://arxiv.org/abs/1710.09061.

[456] Jang Y, Lee J, Lee S, Kim T. SGX-Bomb: locking down the processor via Rowhammer attack. In: SysTEX'17: Proceedings of the 2nd Workshop on System Software for Trusted Execution; 2017. https://dl.acm.org/doi/10.1145/3152701.3152709.

[457] SGX-Step. https://github.com/jovanbulck/sgx-step; 2023.

[458] Heckler attack. 2024. https://ahoi-attacks.github.io/heckler/.

[459] Intel. TDX virtual firmware design guide. https://cdrdv2.intel.com/v1/dl/getContent/733585; 2022.

[460] Buhren R, Jacob H-N, Krachenfels T, Seifert J-P. One glitch to rule them all: fault injection attacks against AMD's secure encrypted virtualization. In: CCS'21: Proceedings of the 2021 ACM SIGSAC Conference on Computer and Communications Security; 2021. https://dl.acm.org/doi/abs/10.1145/3460120.3484779.

[461] Li M, Zhang Y, Lin Z. CrossLine: breaking "Security-by-Crash" based memory isolation in AMD SEV. In: CCS'21: Proceedings of the 2021 ACM SIGSAC Conference on Computer and Communications Security; 2021. https://dl.acm.org/doi/abs/10.1145/3460120.3485253.

[462] WeSee attack. 2024. https://ahoi-attacks.github.io/wesee/.
[463] Wang W, Li M, Zhang Y, Lin Z. PWRLEAK: exploiting power reporting interface for side-channel attacks on AMD SEV. In: DIMVA 2023: Detection of intrusions and malware, and vulnerability assessment; 2023. https://link.springer.com/chapter/10.1007/978-3-031-35504-2_3.
[464] RMPocalyps. 2025. https://rmpocalypse.github.io/.
[465] Wilke L, Wichelmann J, Rabich A, Eisenbarth T. SEV-step: a single-stepping framework for AMD-SEV. In: Cryptography and security; 2023. https://arxiv.org/abs/2307.14757.
[466] SEV-Step. 2023. https://github.com/sev-step/sev-step.
[467] AMD. AMD INVD instruction security vulnerability. https://www.amd.com/en/resources/product-security/bulletin/amd-sb-3005.html; 2023.
[468] Microsoft. Powering the next generation of trustworthy AI in a confidential cloud using NVIDIA GPUs. https://www.microsoft.com/en-us/research/blog/powering-the-next-generation-of-trustworthy-ai-in-a-confidential-cloud-using-nvidia-gpus/; 2022.
[469] Delignat-Lavaud A. Unlocking the potential of privacy-preserving AI with Azure confidential computing on NVIDIA H100. 2023. https://techcommunity.microsoft.com/t5/azure-confidential-computing/unlocking-the-potential-of-privacy-preserving-ai-with-azure/ba-p/3776838.
[470] DMTF. DSP0274—Security protocol and data model (SPDM) specification. https://www.dmtf.org/dsp/DSP0274; 2023.
[471] DMTF. DSP0277—Secured messages using SPDM specification. https://www.dmtf.org/dsp/DSP0277; 2022.
[472] PCI-SIG. PCI express base specification revision 6.1. https://members.pcisig.com/wg/PCI-SIG/document/19849; 2023.
[473] CXL. Compute express link (CXL) specification 3.1. https://www.computeexpresslink.org/download-the-specification; 2023.
[474] IETF. RFC8446—The transport layer security (TLS) protocol version 1.3. https://datatracker.ietf.org/doc/rfc8446/; 2018.
[475] IETF. RFC9147—The datagram transport layer security (DTLS) protocol version 1.3. https://datatracker.ietf.org/doc/rfc9147/; 2022.
[476] IETF. Usage limits on AEAD algorithms. 2023. https://datatracker.ietf.org/doc/html/draft-irtf-cfrg-aead-limits.
[477] Intel. Intel TDX connect TEE-IO device guide. https://cdrdv2.intel.com/v1/dl/getContent/772642; 2023.
[478] Intel. Root complex IDE key configuration unit—Software programming guide. https://www.intel.com/content/www/us/en/io/pci-express/pci-express-architecture-devnet-resources.html; 2022.
[479] Intel. Virtualization technology for directed I/O architecture specification. https://www.intel.com/content/www/us/en/develop/download/intel-virtualization-technology-for-directed-io-architecture-specification.html; 2022.
[480] ARM. DEN0129—Arm realm management extension (RME) system architecture. https://developer.arm.com/documentation/den0129/latest; 2023.
[481] ARM. IHI0070—Arm system memory management unit architecture specification. https://developer.arm.com/documentation/ihi0070/latest/; 2023.
[482] RISC-V. RISC-V AP-TEE IO specification. https://github.com/riscv-non-isa/riscv-ap-tee-io; 2023.
[483] RISC-V. RISC-V IOMMU specification. https://github.com/riscv-non-isa/riscv-iommu; 2023.
[484] NVIDIA. Confidential compute on NVIDIA hopper H100. 2023. https://images.nvidia.cn/aem-dam/en-zz/Solutions/data-center/HCC-Whitepaper-v1.0.pdf.

[485] NVIDIA. NVIDIA H100 tensor core GPU architecture. 2023. https://resources.nvidia.com/en-us-tensor-core/gtc22-whitepaper-hopper.
[486] Beyer KW. Grace hopper and the invention of the information age. MIT Press; 2012.
[487] NVIDIA. NVIDIA blackwell. 2024. https://www.nvidia.com/en-us/data-center/technologies/blackwell-architecture/.
[488] IETF. RFC9334—Remote attestation procedures architecture. 2023. https://datatracker.ietf.org/doc/rfc9334/.
[489] TCG. Trusted platform module library family 2.0 specification. https://trustedcomputinggroup.org/resource/tpm-library-specification/; 2019.
[490] Paul E, Marochko A, Mattoon D, Spiger R, Thom S, Wooten D. RIoT—A foundation for trust in the internet of things. In: MSR-TR-2016-18; 2016. https://www.microsoft.com/en-us/research/publication/riot-a-foundation-for-trust-in-the-internet-of-things/.
[491] IETF. Internet X.509 public key infrastructure certificate and certificate revocation list (CRL) profile. 2008. https://datatracker.ietf.org/doc/rfc5280/.
[492] IETF. CBOR encoded X.509 certificates. https://datatracker.ietf.org/doc/draft-ietf-cose-cbor-encoded-cert/; 2023.
[493] TCG. DICE concise evidence binding for SPDM. https://trustedcomputinggroup.org/wp-content/uploads/TCG-DICE-Concise-Evidence-Binding-for-SPDM-Version-1.0-Revision-53_1August2023.pdf; 2023.
[494] TCG. DICE endorsement architecture for devices. https://trustedcomputinggroup.org/resource/dice-endorsement-architecture-for-devices-v1-0-r0-38/; 2022.
[495] IETF. RFC9393—Concise software identification tags. 2023. https://datatracker.ietf.org/doc/rfc9393/.
[496] Intel. Device attestation model in confidential computing environment. 2023. https://cdrdv2.intel.com/v1/dl/getContent/742533.
[497] NVIDIA. NVIDIA hopper confidential computing attestation verifier. 2023. https://docs.nvidia.com/hopper-confidential-computing-attestation-verifier.pdf.
[498] OPA. 2023. https://www.openpolicyagent.org/.
[499] Open ID. 2023. https://openid.net/.
[500] NIST. SP800-193 platform firmware resiliency guidelines. 2018. https://csrc.nist.gov/pubs/sp/800/193/final.
[501] Yao J, Zimmer V. Building secure firmware: armoring the foundation of the platform. APress. 2020. https://link.springer.com/book/10.1007/978-1-4842-6106-4.
[502] Linux secure I/O. 2023. https://lpc.events/event/17/contributions/1633/.
[503] CC trusted device manager (TDM). 2023. https://github.com/confidential-containers/guest-components/pull/290.
[504] nvTrust. 2023. https://github.com/nvidia/nvtrust.
[505] DMTF. libspdm. 2023. https://github.com/DMTF/libspdm.
[506] DMTF. spdm-emu. 2023. https://github.com/DMTF/spdm-emu.
[507] DMTF. spdm-dump. 2023. https://github.com/DMTF/spdm-dump.
[508] PCI-SIG. PCI express base specification revision 6.1. https://members.pcisig.com/wg/PCI-SIG/document/19849; 2023.
[509] DMTF. SPDM-Responder-Validator. 2023. https://github.com/DMTF/SPDM-Responder-Validator/.
[510] CCC. spdm-rs. 2023. https://github.com/ccc-spdm-tools/spdm-rs.
[511] Intel. tee-io-validator. 2024. https://github.com/intel/tee-io-validator.
[512] ARM Mali GPU issue. 2022. https://bugs.chromium.org/p/project-zero/issues/detail?id=2325.
[513] Russ Sevinsky. Funderbolt. BlackHat US; 2013. https://media.blackhat.com/us-13/US-13-Sevinsky-Funderbolt-Adventures-in-Thunderbolt-DMA-Attacks-Slides.pdf.

[514] Thunderclap. 2019. https://thunderclap.io/. https://www.ndss-symposium.org/ndss-paper/thunderclap-exploring-vulnerabilities-in-operating-system-iommu-protection-via-dma-from-untrustworthy-peripherals/.
[515] Thunderspy. 2020. https://thunderspy.io/.
[516] Kim H, Hur J. PCIe side-channel attack on I/O device via RDMA-enabled network card. In: 2022 13th International Conference on Information and Communication Technology Convergence (ICTC); 2022. https://ieeexplore.ieee.org/document/9952853.
[517] IETF. RFC8446—TLS 1.3. https://datatracker.ietf.org/doc/rfc8446/; 2018.
[518] IETF. RFC9147—DTLS 1.3. https://datatracker.ietf.org/doc/rfc9147/; 2023.
[519] IETF usable formal methods proposed RG. https://wiki.ietf.org/group/ufm; 2023.
[520] OpenSSL advisory. 2023. https://www.openssl.org/news/vulnerabilities.html.
[521] MBedTLS advisory. 2023. https://mbed-tls.readthedocs.io/en/latest/security-advisories/.
[522] WolfSSL advisory. 2023. https://www.wolfssl.com/docs/security-vulnerabilities/.
[523] Cremers C, Dax A, Naska A. Formal analysis of SPDM: security protocol and data model version 1.2. https://eprint.iacr.org/2022/1724.pdf; 2022.
[524] Libspdm advisory. 2023. https://github.com/DMTF/libspdm/security/advisories.
[525] IETF. AEAD Limit (draft). https://datatracker.ietf.org/doc/draft-irtf-cfrg-aead-limits/; 2023.
[526] Xu Y, Cui W, Peinado M. Controlled-channel attacks: deterministic side channels for untrusted operating systems. In: 2015 IEEE Symposium on Security and Privacy; 2015. https://ieeexplore.ieee.org/document/7163052.
[527] Synopsys IDEIP. https://www.synopsys.com/designware-ip/technical-bulletin/security-ide-ip.html; 2023.
[528] Ender M, Moradi A, Paar C. The unpatchable silicon: a full break of the bitstream encryption of xilinx 7-series FPGAs. In: SEC'20: Proceedings of the 29th USENIX Conference on Security Symposium; 2020. https://www.usenix.org/conference/usenixsecurity20/presentation/ender.
[529] Bittner O, Krachenfels T, Galauner A, Seifert J-P. The forgotten threat of voltage glitching: a case study on Nvidia Tegra X2 SoCs. 2021. https://arxiv.org/abs/2108.06131.
[530] Khattri H, Kodalapura NN, Nguyen NN. PCIe device attacks: beyond DMA. In: Exploiting PCIe switches, messages and errors. Blackhat US; 2021. https://www.blackhat.com/us-21/briefings/schedule/#pcie-device-attacks-beyond-dma-exploiting-pcie-switches-messages-and-errors-23530.
[531] Di Pietro R, Lombardi F, Villani A. CUDA leaks: a detailed hack for CUDA and a (partial) fix. ACM Trans Embed Comput Syst 2016;15(Issue 1). https://dl.acm.org/doi/10.1145/2801153.
[532] Jiang ZH, Fei Y, Kaeli D. A complete key recovery timing attack on a GPU. In: 2016 IEEE International Symposium on High Performance Computer Architecture (HPCA); 2016. https://ieeexplore.ieee.org/document/7446081.
[533] Karimi E, Jiang ZH, Fei Y, Kaeli D. A timing side-channel attack on a mobile GPU. In: 2018 IEEE 36th International Conference on Computer Design (ICCD); 2018. https://ieeexplore.ieee.org/document/8615670.
[534] Ahn J, Jin C, Kim J, Rhu M, Fei Y, Kaeli D, Kim J. Trident: a hybrid correlation-collision gpu cache timing attack for aes key recovery. In: 2021 IEEE International Symposium on High-Performance Computer Architecture (HPCA); 2021. https://ieeexplore.ieee.org/document/9407157.
[535] Naghibijouybari H, Neupane A, Qian Z, Abu-Ghazaleh N. Rendered insecure: GPU side channel attacks are practical. In: CCS'18: Proceedings of the 2018 ACM

SIGSAC Conference on Computer and Communications Security; 2018. https://dl.acm.org/doi/10.1145/3243734.3243831.
[536] Naghibijouybari H, Neupane A, Qian Z, Abu-Ghazaleh N. Side Channel attacks on GPUs. IEEE Trans Dependable Secure Comput 2019. https://ieeexplore.ieee.org/document/8852671.
[537] Zhan Z, Zhang Z, Liang S, Fan Y, Koutsoukos X. Graphics peeping unit: exploiting EM side-channel information of GPUs to eavesdrop on your neighbors. In: 2022 IEEE Symposium on Security and Privacy (SP); 2022. https://ieeexplore.ieee.org/document/9833773.
[538] Liang S, Zhan Z, Fan Y, Cheng L, Zhang Z. Clairvoyance: exploiting far-field EM emanations of GPU to see your DNN models through obstacles at a distance. In: 2022 IEEE Security and Privacy Workshops (SPW); 2022. https://ieeexplore.ieee.org/document/9833894.
[539] Baran Dutta S, Naghibijouybari H, Gupta A, Abu-Ghazaleh N, Marquez A, Barker K. Spy in the GPU-box: covert and side channel attacks on multi-GPU systems. In: ISCA'23: Proceedings of the 50th Annual International Symposium on Computer Architecture; 2023. https://dl.acm.org/doi/abs/10.1145/3579371.3589080.
[540] Zhu Y, Cheng Y, Zhou H, Lu Y. Hermes attack: steal DNN models with lossless inference accuracy. In: 30th USENIX Security Symposium; 2021. https://www.usenix.org/conference/usenixsecurity21/presentation/zhu.
[541] Tan M, Wan J, Zhou Z, Zhou L. Invisible probe: timing attacks with PCIe congestion side-channel. In: 2021 IEEE Symposium on Security and Privacy (SP); 2021. https://ieeexplore.ieee.org/document/9519482.
[542] Side M, Yao F, Zhang Z. LockedDown: exploiting contention on host-GPU PCIe bus for fun and profit. In: 2022 IEEE 7th European Symposium on Security and Privacy (EuroS&P); 2022. https://ieeexplore.ieee.org/document/9797371.
[543] Abdul Khaliq S, Ali U, Khan O. Timing-based side-channel attack and mitigation on PCIe connected distributed embedded systems. In: 2021 IEEE High Performance Extreme Computing Conference (HPEC); 2021. https://ieeexplore.ieee.org/document/9622848.
[544] Hong S, Frigo P, Kaya Y, Giuffrida C, Dumitras T. Terminal brain damage: exposing the graceless degradation in deep neural networks under hardware fault attacks. In: 28th USENIX Security Symposium; 2019. https://www.usenix.org/conference/usenixsecurity19/presentation/hong.
[545] Yao F, Rakin AS, Fan D. Deephammer: depleting the intelligence of deep neural networks through targeted chain of bit flips. In: 29th USENIX Security Symposium; 2020. https://www.usenix.org/conference/usenixsecurity20/presentation/yao.
[546] Cai K, Chowdhuryy Md HI, Zhang Z, Yao F. Seeds of SEED: NMT-stroke: diverting neural machine translation through hardware-based faults. In: 2021 International Symposium on Secure and Private Execution Environment Design (SEED); 2021. https://ieeexplore.ieee.org/document/9604360.
[547] Tsai T, Hari SKS, Sullivan M, Villa O, Keckler SW. NVBitFI: dynamic fault injection for GPUs. In: 2021 51st Annual IEEE/IFIP International Conference on Dependable Systems and Networks (DSN); 2021. https://ieeexplore.ieee.org/abstract/document/9505068.
[548] NVBitFI. 2023. https://github.com/NVlabs/nvbitfi.
[549] Huffmire T, Irvine C, Nguyen TD, Levin T, Kastner R, Sherwood T. Handbook of FPGA design security. Springer; 2010.
[550] Kleidermacher D, Kleidermacher M. Embedded system security. Newnes; 2012.
[551] Yao J, Vincent Z. Building secure firmware: armoring the foundation of the platform. APress; 2020.

Index

'*Note:* Page numbers followed by "f" indicate figures and "t" indicate tables.'

D

O

P

R

S

T

U

V

Printed and bound by CPI Group (UK) Ltd, Croydon, CR0 4YY
14/09/2026
02216408-0004